Educational subnormality

International Library of Sociology

Founded by Karl Mannheim

Editor: John Rex, University of Aston in Birmingham

Arbor Scientiae
Arbor Vitae

A catalogue of the books available in the **International Library of Sociology** and other series of Social Science books published by Routledge & Kegan Paul will be found at the end of this volume.

Educational subnormality

A study in decision-making

Sally Tomlinson

Routledge & Kegan Paul

London, Boston and Henley

First published in 1981
by Routledge & Kegan Paul Ltd
39 Store Street, London WC1E 7DD,
9 Park Street, Boston, Mass. 02108, USA and
Broadway House, Newtown Road,
Henley-on-Thames, Oxon RG9 1EN
Printed in Great Britain by
Redwood Burn Ltd, Trowbridge & Esher

British Library Cataloguing in Publication Data

Tomlinson, Sally
Educational subnormality.
– (International library of sociology)
1. Slow learning children – England
2. Educational sociology – England
I. Title   II. Series
371.92'0942   LC4696.G7

ISBN 0–7100–0697–7

To Susan, Simon and Joanna

Contents

Figures

Tables

Acknowledgments

I would like to record my grateful thanks to the following people for their help and assistance during the period of research for, and writing up of this study: The Birmingham Local Education Authority, particulary Mr M. F. Brittain, Assistant Education Officer Special Services; Dr G. Herbert, Chief Psychologist, and the educational psychologists who participated in this study, particularly Paul Brindle and Martin Powell; Dr Johnson, until recently Senior Specialist in Community Medicine (Child Health) and the medical officers who participated in the study; The Heads and teachers of Birmingham primary, secondary and special schools who kindly gave up much time to talk to me, particularly Mr M. Duncan at Mayfield School; The children who formed the 'study population' and their parents; Andrew Sutton, at the Centre for Child Study, University of Birmingham; Dr M. S. Archer for her helpful supervision; Professor J. Rex for allowing me 'time off' to collect data while I was working for him; my friend Chris Heward, for her encouragement; Christine Nightingale for typing the study.

To preserve confidentiality all names and sometimes sex of respondents, have been changed in the text, and in case studies information has been juxtaposed to prevent possible indentification of individuals.

Introduction

'The first and most important thing to do with the backward child is to discover him', Cyril Burt, 'The Backward Child', 1961 edition, London University Press, p. 15.

This book is concerned with the decision-making processes by which children move from the normal education offered to the majority of children in England and Wales into special (ESN-M) education, and with the beliefs and judgments which inform these decisions.

The category of educational subnormality (1) was created as recently as 1945, one of eleven possible categories of handicap, and since that time has always encompassed the largest number of all designated 'handicapped' children. The criteria by which children are referred, assessed and admitted to ESN schools, a process known as ascertainment, are decided on a discretionary basis by a group of professional people using professional judgments. These judgments are constituted from the knowledge and the beliefs held by the professionals about what an educationally subnormal child actually is. The criteria, as this study seeks to demonstrate, are generally unformulated and unclarified, and the beliefs upon which the criteria and judgments are based, are themselves influenced by a series of social, legal and political processes concerning subnormality, developed over the past hundred years.

The professionals who refer and assess children, and in so doing create and perpetuate a category of 'educational subnormality', act as they do in the light of what Max Weber (1964, p. 124) described as 'a belief in the existence of a legitimate order'. That is: their action is oriented towards the assumption that the current legitimate moral order includes some people who are normal and

some who are subnormal.   They also believe in the existence of adequate measuring instruments within the social
world which make it possible to demonstrate who falls
within a category of subnormality and who does not.   If
the professionals do doubt their categorisation, they can
defend their actions on the very reasonable grounds that
they are involved in the day-to-day social transactions of
'doing a job'.

This study takes as its background the overall problem
of the way in which complex industrial societies deal with
that section of their population which has come to be
called mildly educationally subnormal - those who find
difficulty in coping with the educational, technological
and social demands made upon them, but unlike people
designated as severely subnormal are often able to function at an economic level that is beneficial to society.
An emphasis has always been placed upon helping mildly
subnormal young people to undertake productive work.
Collman's (1956) study of the employment success of ex-ESN
pupils concluded that: 'It would appear that at least
70% of ESN ex-pupils are employable and that this group is
a reliable source of labour.' (2)

ESN schools have by and large been concerned to prepare
their pupils for routine work, with an emphasis on punc-
tuality and docility (Knight and Walker, 1965; Jerrold
and Fox, 1968), and while ESN school-leavers had usually
been more dependent on the assistance of their schools in
finding work (Durajaia, 1969), it is by no means the case
that they are an unproductive group in industrial society.

In questioning the concept 'ESN', the study situates
itself within a continuing debate within the discipline of
sociology concerning the reality of 'a priori' categories.
The Kantian premise, that we come to have a belief in a
shared world of physical objects subject to law-like
regularities because we impose categories on the world in
the course of perceiving it, began the debate as to
whether, in the social world, there is in reality any set
of 'a priori' categories which command universal assent in
a similar manner.

Specifically, this study questions the epistemological
status of the concept 'educational subnormality' and
starts from the premise that the category is socially constructed by the judgments, and decisions made by professionals about children, rather than being an innate
quality within children, and that the category may have
less to do with education, than with other attributes
demonstrated by the children and their families.

The professionals (3) order their knowledge and beliefs
in such a way that they are able to recognise and

categorise educationally subnormal children.   The task of
the sociologist is to question the 'a priori' status of
the category 'ESN' and to question how, and on what basis,
some children come to be excluded from the important
institutions of 'normal education', and included instead
in a category which for historial reasons (commented upon
in chapter 1), carries a stigma of inferiority and
difference.

Thus, this study can be described as a study within the
sociology of special education.

Research, comment and opinion in the field of educational subnormality has to date mainly been undertaken
from a clinical, psychological, or a prescriptive educational viewpoint.   The ambiguity of the administrative
category ESN sometimes led to the subsuming of the
category within the broader pre-war notion of mental
deficiency. (4)   Those classed as ESN are sometimes
regarded as the upper end of a continuum of subnormality -
as 'high-grade' mental defectives, sometimes as merely a
limited type of normal person.

Tizard, writing in the introduction to Clarke and
Clarke's classic volume on 'Mental Deficiency' (1965, p.
11), encapsulated this dilemma:

> Great confusion exists in regard to high-grade defec-
> tives, since the term is applied to an administra-
> tively defined group....   The great majority of those
> who are merely grossly backward intellectually never
> come to notice, except in schools where they are con-
> sidered educationally subnormal....   Nor is there any
> reason why they should be regarded as anything other
> than ordinary, if somewhat limited, citizens.

In the literature on mental handicap the ESN tend to be
allocated a separate chapter (Hilliard and Kirman, 1965;
Mittler, 1970; see also Kirman, 1965; Williams, 1970).
Some writers have found the category problematic enough to
discuss the ascertainment of ESN children (Segal, 1960;
Williams, 1965; Presland, 1970).

Other work has been concerned with the response of the
ESN to special schooling (Williams and Gruber, 1967), with
their attainments (Ascher, 1970), with their possible
'maladjustment' (Chazan, 1964), and more particularly,
with curriculum and pedagogy for ESN children.   Literature in this latter area has consistently highlighted the
problematic nature of the category as an administrative
category which separated ESN children from slow-learning
'remedial' children in normal schools (Tansley and Gulliford, 1960; Gulliford, 1969, 1971; Cleugh, 1961; Bell,
1970; Brennan, 1974, 1979).

Sociology has made little or no contribution towards

understanding the particular ways in which children who
are ascertained as suitable for a different education than
that offered to the majority of children, come to be
classified and treated.   There is, in effect, no sociology of special education.   Yet there is scope for the
development of such an area of enquiry, using the variety
of theoretical perspectives and methodologies currently
available within the sociology of education.   A sociology
of special education could, as this book attempts to do,
question the nature of the categories of 'handicap' to
which children are assigned, and ask specific questions
about the beliefs and values which underpin decisions to
categorise children into types and degrees of handicap.
It could also examine what goes on in special schools in
terms of knowledge, controls, goals and achievements, and
could ask what are the social consequences of categorising
more and more children as in need of a 'special education'. (5)

On a broader sociological front, a sociology of special
education could ask what is the relationship between
supposed genetic endowment and the stratification systems
of advanced technological societies, and what sort of
power structures exist that allow some people to determine
the life chances of others who are deemed to be 'less
intelligent'.

The need for a sociology of special education has
recently been articulated by Booth (1978), who studied
another category of handicapped child - the severely subnormal.   He noted that: 'Few sociologists have tried to
make sense of mental handicap....   By and large they have
never attempted to step outside the meanings attributed to
subnormality by clinical definitions.'

Booth attempted to show how becoming a mentally handicapped person is an intricate social process leading
eventually to the acceptance of a social role that cannot
solely be defined in clinical terms.

Similarly, this study rejects the view that mildly
educationally subnormal children present a set of purely
educational characteristics and potentialities that can
readily be identified and assessed by 'objective' tools of
diagnosis and asks instead, on what basis do some children
come to be assessed as ESN-M and perhaps sent to special
schools?   The study starts from the premise that mild
educational subnormality is not a quality within a child,
but a status allocated by social and professional judgments.

This study then is intended as a contribution to the
sociology of special education.   It asks specific questions concerning the decisions by which children are

referred and assessed as ESN-M.   The initial impetus for asking these questions came from two observations concerning educational subnormality.   The first observation, gleaned from the literature, was that, while the other categories of 'handicap' contain a cross-section of children from all social classes, the category ESN predominantly contains children of manual working-class parentage (see, for example, Stein and Susser, 1960; Williams and Gruber, 1967).   The second observation was of a situation which developed during the 1960s when black immigrant parents began to question the procedures by which their children were being ascertained as ESN and sent to special schools.   Immigrants have been described as the 'barium meal' of a society (Patterson, 1963), that is, their presence throws into sharp relief the deficiencies of certain social provisions in a society.   The over-representation of West Indian children, in proportion to their numbers in the total school population, helped to draw attention during the 1960s, to the confusions surrounding the classificatory process for ESN education. Complaints from the West Indian community, in particular, helped to highlight the basic question, what is an ESN-M child and what are the procedures by which he or she becomes thus classified?

It is not possible to study how any particular group of children are referred to and assessed for special, ESN-M education without an understanding of how all children are thus categorised.   This study, therefore, concentrates on the processes affecting all children, but information on decision-making related to children of immigrant parentage is extracted and discussed in a separate chapter.

This introduction describes the apparently logical and rational accounts which can be found in the literature referring to ESN children, and which relate to the way in which academics and professionals recognise an ESN child. It then uses perspectives from the sociology of knowledge to suggest that implicit in the creation and perpetuation of the category, there are structural aspects which are not necessarily apparent in the actual accounts given by the professionals.   In particular the notions of the social construction of categories (Berger and Luckmann, 1966), the creation of social problems (Spectre and Kitsuse, 1978), and the relationship between cultural and social reproduction (Bourdieu and Passeron, 1977) are discussed in the light of selected phenomenological and structuralist perspectives.   The study in itself constitutes a critique of the limitations of phenomenological perspectives.

In chapter 1 an historical overview of the concept of

subnormality is presented as a background to understanding
current debates and problems.   This chapter also discusses the development of IQ testing and psychometric
models of assessment, as such 'objective' measures have
played a critical role in the development of the concept
of educational subnormality.   A final section documents
the development of the concern evinced by the West Indian
community over the classification of a disproportionate
number of their children as ESN, in order to demonstrate
the strong sense of grievance which the classification has
aroused in this particular group of people.

Chapter 2 outlines the methodology of the study.
Since the relative de-centralisation of the English education system allows local education authorities a wide
degree of autonomy in determining their own arrangements,
the processes by which children move into special education can vary between authorities.   The City of B has
been taken as a specific local authority, to examine and
discuss the processes within one authority.   There is no
claim that the processes of this authority are typical of
any other local authority arrangements.   The LEA gave
permission for a study population of forty children to be
followed - either in retrospect, the child having been
placed in a special school, or currently, the child being
in the process of ascertainment.   Interviews were conducted with all the professional people who had made a
decision on the children.   They included head teachers of
referring schools, educational psychologists, medical
officers, head teachers of special schools, and a variety
of 'other personnel', including psychiatrists, social
workers, remedial teachers and Guidance and Assessment
Centre staff.   The parents of the children were also
interviewed to discover what part they played in the
assessment process.   Chapter 2 also documents features of
the administrative practices concerning special education
and then goes on to describe briefly some of the characteristics of the study population children.   Case studies
of the children are presented throughout the study to give
qualitative insight into the way the professionals dealt
with the children.

Chapter 3 examines the schools which referred the study
population children as possibly being in need of special,
ESN-M education.   This part of the research attempted to
explore the important question, how do teachers and heads
recognise a potentially ESN child and how do they perceive the whole referral process and the involvement of
other professionals and the parents?   This part of the
research also explored the cultural beliefs which teachers
hold about West Indian and Asian children, that might lead

to a higher rate of referral of West Indian children, than indigenous or Asian children.

Chapter 4 describes how the educational psychologists perceived their own involvement and that of other professionals in the decision-making process and how they recognised a potentially ESN child.

Chapter 5 similarly analyses the involvement of the clinical medical officers in the ascertainment process, and how they decide that a child is 'ESN'.   These two chapters also note what problems the psychologists and medical officers consider that the children of immigrant parentage might present, which might lead to classification as ESN.   Chapter 5 also analyses and discusses the involvement of other personnel who saw and made decisions on some of the study population children.

Chapter 6 examines the special schools that received twenty-eight of the study population children.   This chapter specifically discusses some ways in which special ESN-M schools regard themselves as different from ordinary schools and what 'special' characteristics they appeared to have.   It also looks at how special school heads regard the involvement of other professional people, and parents, in the assessment process, considers what sort of children the schools expect to incorporate as ESN-M, and what sort of cultural belief they hold about the children of immigrant parentage.

Chapter 7 describes and assesses the extent of involvement of the parents of the forty study population children, in order to gain some understanding as to how far, and at what point, parents are consulted as their children pass through the often lengthy process of referral and assessment for special education.   The chapter particularly notes the lack of formal machinery for treating parents as equal and caring people with some 'rights' in a complex process that ultimately carries an element of legal compulsion.

Chapter 8 notes that the study so far has suggested that the category ESN-M might encompass 'dimensions' of social class and social control in addition to educational attributes, and that, since the arrival and settlement of black immigrants and their children, a racial dimension has been added to the attributes of the category. (6) Using data from the case histories of the children and the professionals, the chapter particularly explores the position of the children of West Indian parentage in English schools in terms of their achievements and their characteristics that might lead them to be over-referred as potentially ESN.   The chapter also discusses the decisions made about Asian children from the point of

view of the low rate of referral, assessment and placement
of Asian children in ESN schools.

In conclusion, the category ESN is shown to be created
by a series of decisions on the part of professional
personnel, which leads to a change in a child's educational status.   It is the judgments of professionals
which are crucial in creating the category.   However, it
can be demonstrated that different professionals base
their judgments on different accounts of 'what is' an ESN
child, and thus use different criteria to allocate
children to the category.   The conclusions question
whether the judgments of professionals are based solely on
'scientific', 'objective', 'educational' knowledge and
suggest that the beliefs which the professionals hold
about the behavioural, family and class characteristics of
the children help determine their judgments about the
educational characteristics and potential of the children.
It is also suggested that the beliefs held by the professionals are related to their own positions in the social
structure, and their perceptions about the inadequacies of
different social and racial groups.   The conclusions also
demonstrate that the process of ascertainment is not a
matter of smooth agreement between the professionals.
Professional ideologies manifest themselves in a variety
of ways - in particular personal and professional
'clashes' emerge between psychologists and medical
officers, between head teachers and psychologists, and
between other professionals and the administration.   The
manner in which categories are socially constructed and
social problems defined is a matter for personal conflict
rather than professional 'team-work'.   The category ESN
is also considered to possess social class, social control
and racial 'dimensions' in that there is a structural
relationship between the historical development of ESN
education and the way in which the category is currently
defined by professionals.   ESN education can be considered as a form of social control for troublesome working-
class children - and the proposals of the Warnock Report
('Special Educational Needs ...', 1978), to combine those
children now known as 'remedial' and 'disruptive' with the
ESN-M category are seen as a logical outcome of the
development of such a categorisation.   The wider category
suggested to combine and replace these - the child with
learning difficulty - will in fact encompass more working-
class (and black) children.

PROFESSIONAL ACCOUNTS OF EDUCATIONAL SUBNORMALITY

Those who make judgments about educational subnormality and profess to distinguish between normal and subnormal provide apparently logical, rational accounts of subnormality. Thus, from academic research, professional journals, prescriptive books written to assist practitioners, government acts, circulars, and other publications, it is possible to abstract a series of analytic categories which can be described as accounts of ESN children. Table I.1 attempts to encompass a series of analytic accounts that are used to decide 'what is' an ESN child. Scott and Lyman (1968) have pointed out that: 'Organisations systematically provide accounts for their members in a variety of situations. The rules of bureaucracy, for instance, make available accounts for actions taken towards clients.... The accounts "work" because of a set of background expectations.'

The accounts documented here probably 'work' largely because the professional status of those providing the accounts precludes questioning. Empirically, however, the categories are often not regarded as separate. In particular, certain categories are used to 'explain' other categories. Thus, in the literature it is commonplace for category 1, a functional category, to be explained in terms of category 2, a statistical category: 'Child X cannot read because his IQ is 55.' Categories 1, 2 and 3, functional, statistical and behavioural categories, tend to be explained in terms of 4, 5 and 6 - organic, social and psychological. Since there are no standard criteria for deciding who is ESN, the emphasis placed upon the various accounts as descriptions and explanations varies historically and varies as to who is providing the explanation. Thus, a doctor diagnosing a defective child in the early 1900s would be likely to produce different accounts of the child's subnormality than a psychologist assessing the same child in the 1970s.

Some writers maintain that the current ESN-M category is a 'descriptive' category only, to be contrasted with a pre-war diagnostic approach (Williams, 1965), but in practice accounts of ESN children are both descriptive and explanatory. The category ESN-M is often regarded as a 'handicap' comparable to blindness or deafness - the 'diagnosis' of ESN requiring attendance at ESN school. Medical officers, in particular, regard the administrative category in this manner.

The accounts easily become reified. Once an account has been given, the professionals come to believe in the reality of the account and act upon the assumption that, for example, a 'low IQ' accounts for an ESN child.

TABLE I.1 Accounts of educational subnormality

1 Functional		1 Child cannot do X (X may be social, educational, technological, but is usually connected to 'learning' or intellectual functioning)
		2 Child cannot communicate adequately
2 Statistical		1 Child has a 'low' IQ as measured on standardised tests
		2 Child falls into lowest 1 per cent (or 20 per cent) of school population in school achievement
3 Behavioural		1 Child is disruptive, troublesome, uncontrolled
		2 Child exhibits bizarre, odd, non-conformist behaviour
		3 Child unable to behave 'appropriately'
4 Organic	Child has:	1 Genetic disorder or 'innate incapacity'
		2 Pre-natal or birth 'damage'
		3 Organic or metabolic disorder
		4 Medically demonstrable 'illness' or 'condition'
5 Psychological		1 Child is 'emotionally disturbed'
6 Social	Child has:	1 Family with low socio-economic status; father semi- or unskilled
		2 Family 'disorganised' - poor maternal care, single parent, working mother, etc.
		3 Poor or different socialisation techniques
		4 Adverse material factors - poor housing, bad physical environment
		5 Cultural deficiency - poor cultural milieux; poor preparation for school
7 School		1 Unsatisfactory school conditions
		2 Normal school rejects child
		3 Child rejects school, i.e. truants
8 Statutory		Child may be 'certified' as in need of special education

9	Intuitive	Child has 'something wrong with him'
10	Tautological	Child is in need of special educational treatment

The most popular account of educational subnormality is in terms of function - a child is unable to perform certain tasks which it is implicitly understood that a 'normal' child of that age could do. The tasks may be educational - a child cannot read or write, or manipulative - a child cannot tie a shoe-lace or use a machine, or social - a child cannot eat using a knife and fork. The key concept behind functional accounts is that of attainment. It is understood that a child who cannot attain a given level of skill or competence may be subnormal. Children are compared to others of the same age, social class, siblings, etc. on both an explicit and an intuitive basis. Functional accounts may refer to a child's level of conceptual development, or to linguistic development, particularly communication. Functional definitions of ESN children predominate in the literature written for practitioners: 'The phrase ESN was used in the 1944 Education Act to categorise a certain group of children with low achievement in school work' (Williams, 1965).

In theory the term ESN could be applied to a large group of children who are very backward in school work ranging from those who are barely capable of responding to schooling to others, who apart from their backwardness in basic subjects, are capable of following much in the normal school curriculum. (Gulliford, 1966)

Functional accounts have always created confusion by their failure to stipulate clear distinctions between the 'official' Ministry of Education category created in 1945 and children variously described as backward, retarded, slow-learning, etc. Burt (1937) used the words 'backward' and 'retarded' synonymously, and accounted for a functional deficiency by a statistical account. Backward children had an educational 'ratio' falling below 85 per cent. Schonnell (1942) defined retardation in terms of innate potential - retardation was the discrepancy between a child's attainment and his intellectual ability. Gulliford (1969) explains that ESN children are in practice distinguished from slow learners by an innate account - they have lower intelligence. Brennan (1974) encapsulated the problem by pointing out that 'slow learners and ESN are general terms which label a condition without indicating its nature or causation'.

Functional accounts tend to be descriptive and, there-

fore, are usually accompanied by other accounts which
purport to be explanatory.   One of the most usual
accounts accompanying functional explanations are statistical accounts in terms of measured IQ - with the implicit
assumption that IQ tests are scientific measuring instruments which describe a child's position relative to other
children.   The notion of IQ is sometimes used as an
explanation of poor performance.   Teachers, in particular, often consider that an IQ score explains a child's
attainment.   Squibb (1977) has recently called attention
to this: 'Many teachers believe I.Q. and backwardness to
be objective facts, that test scores are perfectly
accurate indicators and that I.Q. is fixed for life within
very narrow margins.'   Statistical accounts of ESN
children have popularly followed Cyril Burt and the Wood
Committee (Board of Education and Board of Control, 1929)
recommendation that an IQ of 50-70 points 'is ESN'.
Statistical accounts of children falling within a category
that encompasses 1-2 per cent of the school population
such as that offered in a Ministry of Education pamphlet
in 1945, or comprise 20 per cent of the school population
as suggested by the Warnock Report in 1978, are relatively
meaningless without a functional description of the characteristics of the children in question.   It is worth
noting that functional accounts in 1978 are less specific
than functional accounts in the 1890s (see chapter 1 of
this study).   The Warnock Report refers briefly to
'children with learning difficulties' having 'learning
problems' and uses behavioural and social accounts as
explanatory factors, but by and large the Report neatly
escapes any requirement to consider the epistemological
status of the category, by concentrating purely on the
concept of educational 'need'.
   Behavioural accounts of ESN children are usually presented in conjunction with functional accounts, but there
is no consensus in the literature (or in this research) as
to which accounts should take precedence as referral
criteria.   One of the reasons for the creation of
special schools in the late nineteenth century was that
troublesome children who were difficult to teach interrupted the system of 'payment by results', and the subsequent history of ESN referral indicates a tendency for
schools to refer children who exhibit troublesome, odd or
nonconformist behaviour.   The 1945 Handicapped Children
Regulations attempted an artificial simplification - badly
behaved children with emotional and psychological problems
were to attend maladjusted schools;   backward children
were to attend ESN schools.   In practice, teachers have
preferred to give both functional and behavioural accounts

for children and it was the ESN category that expanded
rapidly post-war.   This situation gave rise to the belief
that there exists a 'true ESN child' often mentioned by
professionals.   By this they mean a child for whom a
purely descriptive functional account can be given, a
dull, conforming child.   This mythological figure is
sometimes used as a yardstick to judge children to be
excluded from ESN schools.   'Another distinction which is
often made in practice is that between the ordinary ESN
child and the backward maladjusted child.   The distinction is sometimes made in the context of suggesting that
maladjusted children should go to maladjusted schools -
not ESN schools' (Gulliford, 1966).   There has indeed
been a quantity of research indicating that a large proportion of the ESN school population are troublesome or
maladjusted (Burt, 1937; Chazan, 1964).   However, much
of this research would appear to be conceptually tautological.   If it is true that teachers refer children for
ESN schooling partly on behavioural criteria then teachers
in ESN schools are likely to record numbers of their
children as behavioural problems.

Organic (including genetic) accounts of subnormality
are often used as explanations of functional accounts, as
before 1944 physically handicapped children were categorised with (subsequent) ESN children as 'defective', and
professionals thus had a precedent for attempting to identify organic causes to account for poor functioning.   The
1946 Ministry of Education pamphlet suggested that one
explanation of retardation was 'limited ability', which
may have an 'innate basis', and an explanation of poor
functioning in terms of poor genetic endowment is popular.
However, genetic accounts are seldom used alone, social
accounts are used as reinforcement, 'frequently, inherent
limitations are reinforced by environmental ones'
(Gulliford, 1969, p. 15).

Interestingly, it is the medical profession who stress
social rather than organic accounts of educational subnormality.   Stein and Susser's study (1960) stressed the
factor of social selection for the category of ESN.
'Culture, social class and family function profoundly
influence the diagnosis and management of the ESN child.'
They suggested that genetic studies which appeared to
suggest family tendencies towards mild subnormality may
not be valid in the light of their findings.   The Court
Committee on Child Health Services, published in 1976
('Fit for the Future ...', 1976), also rejected organic
explanations of ESN-M children.   'Two-thirds of slow-
learning children do not show any signs of central nervous
system pathology.'

It is psychologists who have tended to stress organic
accounts of ESN children (Osler and Cooke, 1965; Stott,
1966), and it does seem relatively easy to demonstrate
tautologically (as the section in chapter 2 on the
children demonstrates) that children ascertained as ESN-M
may have medical conditions which can then reinforce their
categorisation, but which may in fact be shared by
'normal' children in ordinary schools.

Psychological accounts of ESN children are not particularly prevalent.   They are often used to explain behavioural accounts.   A child who seems disturbed, odd,
bizarre or troublesome, may be accounted for in terms of
psychological or emotional disturbance.   Children for
whom psychological accounts are given are more likely to
fall into the 'maladjusted' category and be offered psychological or psychiatric treatment; although the 1946
pamphlet did suggest that a cause of retardation might be
psychological maladjustment.   Psychological accounts are
often used to reinforce a social account.   A child's
educational retardation is attributed to emotional disturbance due to poor parent-child interaction (Davis, 1961)
or the parents are not providing an encouraging environment (Hunt, 1973).

The most popular accounts of ESN children have always
been social.   It was in elementary schools set up for
working-class children that children unsuitable for education in these schools were first discovered, and it was in
the London School Board's poorest districts that the first
schools for special instruction were set up during the
1890s.   The influence of the eugenics movement in the
early twentieth century linked low social class with a
variety of social 'evils', including mental subnormality,
and helped reinforce beliefs that such subnormality was a
prerogative of the lower social classes.   The influential
work of Cyril Burt also reinforced these beliefs.   Burt
considered (1935) that every civilised society faced a
problem in dealing with their social problem classes, who
comprised: 'the dull, the backward, the unemployed, the
habitually delinquent'.   Burt's widely read books and
membership of government committees probably helped
influence many practitioners towards the belief that there
was a natural relationship between the lower social
classes and educational subnormality.   Post-war research
in the sociology of education, demonstrating the social
factors impinging upon the intellectual development of
children, probably also reinforced beliefs in the lower
educational capacities of the lower social classes
generally (see chapter 7).

Low socio-economic status, cultural and linguistic

deficiencies, poor socialisation techniques and preparation for school, adverse material factors and 'disorganised' families have been among environmental factors used
in research on ESN children to 'explain' functioning and
behaviour.   Social accounts have historically been so
persistent and pervasive that their plausibility as an
explanatory tool is seldom questioned.   It is taken for
granted that low social class attributes are natural
factors in accounting for ESN-M children, and that one
function of special schools is to help children to overcome their class-linked attributes.

> The special school can be regarded, for the majority of
> children who come from low socio-economic groups, as
> the stimulating environment which may promote intellec-
> tual growth. (Williams, 1965)

> Cultural and adverse material factors, which play a
> large part in mild mental handicap, are a minor
> influence in severe subnormality. (City of Liverpool
> College of Higher Education, 1977)

Accounts indicating a deficiency in the normal schooling provided for some children have been sporadically
offered in conjunction with a functional account.   The
1946 pamphlet mentioned 'unsatisfactory school conditions'
as an explanatory factor as to why some children failed to
achieve, but it would be unreasonable to suppose that
practitioners would criticise their own institutions when
a variety of other accounts are available.   The notion
that schools may help to account for a child's subnormality is not popular and, as Squibb (1977) pointed out, many
people now have a vested interest in discovering backward
children:

> There is a backward and remedial industry.   There are
> academics, publishers, child guidance clinics, psycho-
> logists, testing centres, school departments and
> teachers who exist because backwardness exists, and in
> whose interest, career-wise, it is to discover more and
> more backward children.

Statutory accounts of ESN-M children are likewise
seldom offered by practitioners, but can be discovered in
the relevant government acts and circulars.   Section 34
(1) of the 1944 Education Act laid the duty on local
education authorities of ascertaining children in their
area 'suffering from any disability of mind or body'.
Section 34 (5) deals with the certification procedures by
which children may be compelled to attend special schools
and no change in these 'enforceable procedures' was
recommended by the Warnock Committee in 1978.
Intuitive accounts of ESN children are most likely to

offered by parents.   The parents 'know there is something
wrong with him'.   But Booth's work (1978) has shown how
the intuitive speculations of parents have to be confirmed
by professional opinion - a child's 'slowness' has to be
turned into evidence of permanent disorder before intuitive accounts can be broadened.

Tautological accounts are, interestingly, quite fre-
quent among professionals.   The whole concept of 'special
educational need', upon which the Warnock Report is based,
is tautological as far as ESN children are concerned.   An
ESN child or child with learning difficulty is described
as a child in need of special education.   This presup-
poses that there is a consensus upon which an ESN child
can be recognised, but apart from the functional account
that a child has learning problems, no such consensus can
be deduced from the literature on ESN, nor from this
study.   Likewise, it is logically dubious to prescribe
for a 'need' if no causal account of how the need comes
into existence is offered.   Apart from a brief social
account which 'makes children unable to benefit from education in the normal sense', the Warnock Report ('Special
Educational Needs', 1978) makes no attempt to examine
causal factors pertaining to ESN children.   The Report is
based on the tautology that children with learning difficulties are the children who need discovering as having
learning difficulties.   Moreover, more children need
discovering more frequently.   They need referring,
guiding or assessing by more professionals.   More schools
need more special classes and more categories of special
educational treatment are to be offered.   It may well be
that the Warnock Report, described by Vaizey (1978) as a
'magnificent and important report', represents the cul-
mination of a caring society's efforts to provide for all
special needs.   But it is sociologically important to
note that for the category ESN or 'Child with learning
difficulty' (CWLD), the care is being applied to a group
of lower social class children, with the threat of enforceable procedures and that there is no consensus in the
variety of professional accounts as to what the ESN
category actually comprises.

SOCIOLOGICAL ACCOUNTS OF EDUCATIONAL SUBNORMALITY

Professional accounts of ESN children appear to be natural
to the professionals because they are held to be grounded
in nature.   Despite the ways in which the accounts are
used (see chapter 9), their naturalness has become a
taken-for-granted characteristic and they would all be
recognised as 'common sense' by the layman.

A sociological account must begin by taking professional accounts of categorisation as problematic, and must
attempt to produce alternative coherent accounts that are
recognisably sociological.   If the epistemological status
of the category ESN is questioned, the empirical grounds
upon which a child can be 'recognised' as ESN become
problematic.   This study attempts to demonstrate the
social construction of the category by examining the
accounts offered by professionals on which they judge
children to be ESN, and their accounts of the decision-
making processes.   The study indicates that the accounts
are not, in fact, as natural as they appear to be, and
that constructing the category is not necessarily a matter
of smooth 'team-work' between professionals, but more a
matter of their competing claims for professional status.

It is the status of the professional judgments, and the
power implicit in these judgments, which legitimates the
complex procedures which make the category ESN an objective reality.   The study tries to show that the variety
of accounts and complex procedures used to categorise ESN
children are not chance, haphazard developments, but that
they fulfil distinct social functions connected to the
control of what is perceived to be a substantial social
problem.

The creation of the category is based upon the typifi-
cation of educational subnormality as a social problem.
However, social problems are themselves social inventions.   Definitions of social problems are produced by
specific groups who have an interest in promoting a
particular definition.   Everett Hughes (1971) noted that:
'Professionals do not merely serve, they define the very
wants they serve.   Thus, the old dictum that the professionals fulfil the basic wants or desires of people and
society is much too simple.'

In defining educational subnormality as a problem and
continually constructing the category by their judgments,
the professionals put themselves in a particular relationship to the social structure.   They are acting as legitimating agents in excluding a particular proportion of the
population from normal education.   The special education
which this category of children receives does, in fact,
fit them as suitable for the lowest status occupations
that a technological society can offer.   As Sharp and
Green (1975, p. 222) noted:

Educational institutions have a crucial role to play in
the reproduction of socio-economic systems that depend,
at one level, on the production of human capital
through the inculcation of knowledge and skill, and at
another level, on the social transmission of varying
levels of ignorance.

Thus the professionals are helping to reproduce a part of the lower social class. Educationally subnormal children are predominantly drawn from the 'problem class', as Cyril Burt put it. Controlling potential 'problem classes' is part of the perennial problem of order in any industrial society. Any potentially troublesome section of the population must be controlled in legitimate, ostensibly non-violent, ways. The education system, as Bourdieu has pointed out, has taken over the function of legitimating control and power relations between classes (Bourdieu and Passeron, 1977). Educational achievement certifies certain occupational roles. Total non-achievement, in the form of total exclusion from the normal education system, can be regarded as a powerful form of social control. Categorising children as ESN (or children with learning difficulties) and isolating them in some form of 'special' education, can be regarded as a form of symbolic violence which has the function of controlling a poten-tially troublesome section of the population, and of 'reproducing' a particular section of the class structure. Thus, from this perspective, it is not surprising that lower social class children are the ones predominantly categorised as ESN.

The above kind of sociological account and the vocabu-lary it uses is, of course, dependent on relatively recent developments within the sociology of education. It has become commonplace to note that the emergence of an alter-native paradigm, incorporating a variety of alternative approaches, and methodologies, has liberated sociologists from a reliance upon scientific positivism and quantita-tive methodology. The normative view of society, typified by functional and conflict theories, has been augmented and broadened by a variety of interpretative approaches, particularly stemming from phenomenological traditions. Within the newer framework it is possible to regard social knowledge and social categories as artifacts, socially created, rather than as given, objective, 'true' categories. Phenomenologists, as Eggleston (1974) has pointed out, have particularly stressed: 'The ways in which reality is perceived in social situations as an artifact, a creation of all participants in a social situation, which, however perma-nent it may appear to be, may be re-defined and therefore changed.'

However, set in a purely phenomenological context, this study could be accused of doing nothing more than documen-ting the obvious, i.e. that professionals have social power to construct categories in which their decisions continually place people who are deemed 'less intelligent'

and they then produce plausible accounts of what they are
doing.

Phenomenological perspectives, as Archer (1974, p. 14)
has pointed out: 'seek to eliminate references to structure and culture by reducing the environment and its
influences to a series of negotiated inter-subjective
constraints.'

The use of both phenomenological and structural perspectives as a context for this study does not constitute
a defence of eclecticism.   Rather, while acknowledging a
profound debt to the empirical possibilities opened up by
the 'new' directions in sociology and by being able to
'take as problematic' categories that were previously
'taken for granted' (Seeley, 1966) the study constitutes a
critique of the ultimate limitations of phenomenological
perspectives.

Sociological phenomenologists are generally opposed to
the mechanistic interpretation of society, either social,
cultural, economic, biological or political (Mead, 1934;
Schutz, 1962; Blumer, 1962; Douglas, 1971; Cicourel,
1973).   Following Mead, they stress that man engages in
symbolic communication and becomes a creative agent of
construction through his acts.   In this way social structure is thought to develop as an intellectual construction - a result of the consciousness of people who acquire
a 'sense' of social structure through their own socialisation, and by their own interpretation of the world the
social structure is produced and reproduced.   But this
process does not necessarily produce an objective social
structure, since man and society are seen, in this
tradition, as creating a permanent dialectic relationship.
Society is seen as a process of interpretation of individuals engaging in interaction.   It is this which 'is' the
social structure (see Hiller, 1973).

Phenomenologists are occupied with the micro-world -
social action is regarded as people endowing the world
with conscious meaning, then reinterpreting and negotiat-
ing with others new structures of meaning so that the
'subtle texture of meaning constitutes social reality'
(Sharp and Green, 1975, p. 20).

However, there are serious problems posed by a purely
phenomenological analysis of any given social situation.
First, as Karabel and Halsey (1977) have noted, the empirical research that has been done within the context of the
'interpretative paradigm' largely impresses by its 'fre-
quent banality'.   The old charge against sociologists,
that they are doing no more than document the obvious -
may be invited by the extreme relativity of phenomenological approaches.

Second, and more serious, it can be held that the social world is 'more than mere constellations of meaning' (Gellner, 1968). The world does not necessarily possess the characteristics that the knowing subjects endow it with and may possess others of which they are unaware. Out of the negotiations and reinterpretations an entity can be held to develop - a real world with an objective social structure. Phenomenological approaches tend to situate people within a structure that is supposedly meaningful to them, and then fail to place social encounters within a macro-structure, which may indeed ultimately be the product of the consciousness of individuals but which, nevertheless, can be held to exist objectively. It is mainly in their reluctance to accept an objective social structure that phenomenological approaches become inadequate in explaining the structure and inter-connectedness of social relationships, which include constraints on people's actions. The relationship between a person's consciousness and the social structure may very well be the meanings he applies to the structure, as a result of his own socialisation, and thus, without recourse to the notion of false consciousness, people can sincerely hold beliefs which are both a product of, and reinforce, a particular type of social structure. However, Max Weber noted that there are structural arrangements conducive to the development of certain kinds of beliefs within individuals, and these affect the way in which the world view of a person is shaped. 'The Protestant Ethic' (Weber, 1930) demonstrated that certain forms of social structure can only accommodate certain forms of consciousness. For example, it can be held that in a society stratified by class the consciousness of social participants will probably include beliefs which rationalise inequalities, and in a meritocratic society inequalities may well be rationalised in terms of qualities such as 'intelligence', which are perceived to be intrinsic personal qualities.

This study holds that the real world does possess an objective social structure and that structural perspectives are necessary to make accounts of consciousness meaningful in a truly sociological way. It would be nice, of course, to be able to demonstrate direct links between beliefs which inform judgments and decisions, the actions performed on the basis of decisions (in this case the assignment of children to categories) and the observable class structure. However, all this study does is to attempt an empirical demonstration that judgments and decisions create and perpetuate categories, and then note that logical links can be suggested between forms of thought (beliefs behind decisions) social actions, and structural forms within a society.

A third critique of phenomenological perspectives concerns the neglect of the dimension of power.   Given that
an objective social structure exists, unequal distribu-
tions of power mean that the beliefs held by people with
power affect the decisions they are able to make about
other people with less power.   Power may take the form of
the ability to coerce others, through symbolic displays of
violence, into acting in ways, or accepting decisions,
which they do not necessarily want to.   Thus, at the outset of this study, a review of 'official' literature on
ESN children showed that there is a current ideology held,
which assumes that a consensus exists about what constitutes an educationally subnormal child and how he should
be treated, and that there are mutually acceptable definitions shared by all those concerned with ESN children,
including the parents.   In reality, it seems that there
are groups of professional people, who, while not in consensus over definitions of ESN, still manage to define the
reality of educational subnormality for others, because
they have power to enforce their definitions and decisions.   To say this is not to deny that one attribute of
educational subnormality may very well be 'dullness',
whether this is defined functionally, statistically or in
other ways.   What is sociologically important is that the
quality 'dullness' and subsequent categorisation as ESN
are only brought together and imposed upon a particular
group - the children of manual working-class parentage.
The ideology of consensus can be shown to break down when,
for example, professionals attempt to impose a definition
of ESN, with the consequent attribute of 'dullness' upon
the children of middle-class parentage.
Despite this critique, phenomenological perspectives do
provide a context for the empirical part of this study.
Data concerning the kinds of accounts offered by the professionals interviewed in this study, are used to demonstrate the way in which the epistemological status of the
ESN-M child comes to be created as a social reality.
The notion of the social construction of reality - the
phenomenological perspective used in this study - is that
developed most systematically by Berger and Luckmann in
their book with that title (1966).   Initially Berger and
Luckmann drew their ideas from Husserlian and Schutzian
phenomenology.   Particularly they used Husserl's concep-
tion of knowledge as wholly rooted in the 'lifeworld' -
a place in which individuals share intersubjective meanings and related to each other through these shared meanings.   They also drew upon Schutz's 'phenomenology of the
social world', in which Schutz develops Max Weber's concern with interpretative sociology (the study of social

behaviour by interpreting its subjective meaning as found
in the actions of individuals in the social world).
Schutz's aim was to: 'Interpret the actions of individuals in the social world and the ways in which individuals give meaning to social phenomena.'   Berger and
Luckmann regard social reality as a construct of meaning,
rather than having any natural reality.   Thus, any
reality exists only in so far as it has a meaning for the
participants who subscribe to that reality.   Their theory
of the social construction of reality starts from the
point of view that it is the intersubjectivity of face-to-
face relationships which is the basis of social reality,
and this intersubjectivity is mediated by language.   They
analyse the subjective and objective reality of society in
terms of the relationship between subjective meanings and
objective 'facticities' - intersubjective constructs which
are created by a continuing process of interaction.   The
central analytic categories which Berger and Luckmann use
to explain the relationship between the objective world
and subjective meanings are institutionalisation, legitimation and internalisation.   The origins of institutionalisation are to be found in the realisation that all
human activity is subject to habit, and actions repeated
frequently become cast into patterns.   Once established,
institutions, by the fact of their existence, control
human conduct by setting up predefined channels of communication.   Legitimation 'explains' an institutional order
by reference to its cognitive validity and its normative
design.
   But it is through internalisation that society comes to
exist both as an actively objectified and subjective
reality.   There is a mutual identification between people
- they not only live in the same social world, they participate in each other's social being.   The socialisation
process creates the conditions for internalising the
objective social world.   Thus as an example, Berger and
Luckmann quote the 'lower class child who absorbs a lower
class perspective on the world' (p. 151).   It may be the
absorption of a particular 'lower class' perspective on
the world that is a precondition for the way in which some
people come to accept professional judgments that they
have subnormal children - and it is the legitimation of
professional judgments, which as a whole institutionalise
the categories of subnormality.
   However, in addition to the legitimation of professional judgments, a most powerful tool that those who ascertain educationally subnormal children have at their
disposal is the legitimation of subnormality as a social
problem.   Subnormality only became recognisable as a

social problem in the nineteenth century - and then only
the more severe forms of subnormality.   It was not until
the twentieth century that educational subnormality
attained the status of a social problem, and gave rise to
the remedial industry noted by Squibb (1977).

Foucault (1967) has demonstrated, in his study of madness to 1800, that for a long time insanity and idiocy
were part of everyday life, and 'fools and mad men walked
the streets'.   Eventually madness became perceived as a
social threat and the mad were enclosed in asylums.   The
asylum movement spread to include the subnormal who also
began to be enclosed and 'treated' during the 1800s.
Madness and subnormality achieved social problem status in
the same manner.   However, the way in which a social
situation attains the status of a social problem is itself
a subject for study, as Spectre and Kitsuse (1977) have
demonstrated.   Social problems can be regarded as social
situations which attract the attention of other people as
needing 're-adjustment or remedy' (Case, 1924).   They
have a subjective, moral element in that they violate
norms (Fuller and Myers, 1941) or threaten an established
order or they can be generated by the interests of particular groups in society (Mauss, 1975).   Spectre and
Kitsuse themselves describe social problems as 'claim-
making activities'.   'The emergence of a social problem
is contingent upon the organisation of activities assert-
ing the need for eradicating, ameliorating, or otherwise
changing some condition.'

They hold that any theory of social problems should
address itself to the activities of any group or groups of
people making claims on others for ameliorative action.

Spectre and Kitsuse actually use as an example of the
way in which specific vocabularies come to be used in the
definition of a social problem, the history of the concept
'mental retardation' in the USA.   They note that the way
in which groups vie with each other for control of the
definition of a social problem is often expressed through
language - the vocabulary of the 'winning' group being
adopted and institutionalised.   Thus, in the USA the
'moron' became an administrative category representing a
shift from medical to psychological models of subnormality.   Similarly, in England and Wales, the shift from the
term 'educable defective', in 1944, to 'educationally subnormal', represented a move away from a medical definition
of the social problem under consideration.   The history
of the concept of education subnormality, briefly documented in chapter 1, can be regarded as a history of competing definitions of an emergent social problem, which is
still in the process of definition.   Indeed the social

construction of the social problem which is currently
termed educational subnormality is in a permanently
dynamic state.

Nevertheless, the professionals involved in this
dynamic activity of defining and categorising the ESN are
whether they are conscious of it or not, in the business
of reproducing a particular element within the social
structure and performing a particular social service in
terms of the control of a potentially troublesome social
group.   This group is troublesome in the sense that while
in the twentieth century the education system inflates
demands for higher and higher levels of skill, a larger
and larger part of the school population will be unable to
meet the required levels and will have to be categorised
as backward, or ESN.   It is also troublesome in the sense
that on a day-to-day level teachers will constantly find
that children who cannot or will not conform to learning
and concomitant behavioural standards in the classroom
are a problem.

The elusive character of professionalism and professional judgment has been examined by Larson (1978).   She
considers that 'professional identity' in the twentieth
century derives largely from residual values of 'free'
nineteenth-century professionalism, which was in turn
linked to liberal capitalism.   The (essentially middle-
class) privileges of the professionals depend upon the
retention of these values and their ability to create
enough mystique about their work to preserve their
privileges and status.   Thus, although in the twentieth
century professionals sell their labour to employers and
conform to bureaucratic practices, they manage to preserve an aura of mystery about their work.   The judgments
of professionals are supposedly based upon their possession of special knowledge and skills and Larson would hold
that professional 'mystique' can in fact exert a form of
ideological control over people.   Without the mystique of
professional judgment, it is doubtful whether parents
would continue to accept that their children are indeed
subnormal and should be excluded from normal education.
Legally enforceable procedures can be regarded as
developing to cater for the minority of parents who do not
accept the 'mystique' of professional judgment.   Indeed
it is doubtful whether, if the Warnock recommendations
are implemented and despite an emphasis upon catering for
the 'special needs' of children, the professionals who
ascertain subnormal children will be able to persuade the
much larger group of parents who will be involved, that
their children should be excluded from a full, normal
education.

The professionals are performing the social service of legitimating the exclusion of numbers of children from the education system and recommending them for a special education, which fits them for low-status, low-paid occupations in times of economic stability, unemployment in times of recession.   The legitimating device by which this is accomplished is the claim that the children 'could not benefit' from normal education because of intrinsic qualities.

It is at this point in this sociological account that a structural perspective must be introduced in an effort to relate the categorisation created by professional judgments, to the creation and maintenance of part of the class structure.   From a phenomenological perspective the reality of the 'ESN child' may be created by the intersubjective accounts, beliefs and decisions of professionals, but at the same time the professionals can be regarded as causal factors in the structural process of reproducing a class.   It has been suggested by protagonists of interpretative sociology that explanations on the level of meaning and on the level of cause are in principle irreconcilable (Winch, 1958).   Nevertheless, without an attempt to reconcile the two this study would remain on the level of banality noted by Karabel and Halsey.   The phenomenological perspectives are inadequate in explaining the social use made of the category of ESN.

The traditional perspective of the sociology of education - structural functionalism - was not considered to be particularly useful for this study, since the major assumptions of this perspective have to do with consensus produced by normative value systems in a society, and this study began by taking as problematic the normative construction of the ESN category.   Out of other varieties of structuralism, the perspective formulated by Bourdieu and Passeron (1977) appeared to be the most useful, illuminating particularly the subtle relationship between the education system, represented in this study by the professionals, and the class, control (and race) dimensions of the ESN category.   Bourdieu and Passeron's work is concerned with the function of the education system in legitimating and perpetuating the current social order by making social hierarchies appear to be based on gifts, merits or skills.

Now Bourdieu and Passeron have argued that the importance of institutionalised knowledge and qualifications lie in social exclusion rather than in any technical or humanistic advance.   They argue that educational selection has replaced real capital as a seemingly more democratic currency for reproducing social class relations

in modern society.   Educational advancement or exclusion
is controlled by ostensibly 'fair' meritocratic testing.
But the education system demands a cultural competence,
during these testing procedures, which it does not itself
provide.   An advantage is given to families who possess
'capital' and who can pass this on to their children.
Social class and cultural 'reproduction' are linked processes, with the ostensibly democratic education system
certifying achievement or non-achievement.

The families of children who come to be categorised as
ESN have little or no cultural capital or cultural competence to pass on to their children because of their own
class position, neither do they have economic or social
capital to pass on.   Indeed the cultural and economic
'disadvantage' of the parents of the ESN is a recurring
theme in the literature.   By legitimating the withdrawal
of their children from the normal education system the
reproduction of a part of the lower social class is
ensured.   To those who claim that the children have shown
themselves to be unable to benefit from normal education,
Bourdieu and Passeron would reply that the relative
autonomy of the education system enables it to conceal the
social functions it performs, and to misrepresent the
objective truth of what is happening.   Thus by claiming
to provide for the 'special needs' of a group of children
the education system can misrepresent the fact that it is,
in reality, solving a problem of social order by excluding
a potentially troublesome group of children whose 'handicaps' are social, cultural, and familial, leading to
educational handicap, and that by giving these children a
'special education' the system is in fact ensuring its
smooth running and reproducing a part of the lower social
class.   As Bourdieu and Passeron (1977, p. 192) note:
'A system which helps to reproduce the structure of class
relations indeed serves "society" in the sense of the
"social order".'

However, the major value to this study of Bourdieu and
Passeron's structural perspective lies in the use they
make of the concept of culture, and their notion of the
'cultural arbitrary' (1977, p. 5).   It is the cultural
beliefs of professionals that lead to their accounts and
decisions and categories, and these lead logically to the
placement or replacement of some individuals within the
lowest part of the social class structure.

The concept of cultural arbitrary illuminates a logical
analysis of how professionals come to be assisting in the
reproduction of the class structure.   It is not sufficient merely to assert that professionals belong to a
dominant social class, and that because they are in a

position of power vis-à-vis their clients, their decisions
must be accepted, the two-fold nature of 'arbitrariness'
must be asserted.   The professionals not only have power
to 'impose' - they also select from a range of possibilities and decide what shall be 'imposed' on others.
Thus (p. 195): 'to believe that the meaning of any element in the education system is exhausted merely by
relating it directly to a reduced definition of the
interests of the dominant class,' is not an adequate
explanation - the nature of the cultural arbitrary must be
adequately understood.

The 'interests' of the dominant class' are partly com-
posed of the beliefs and meanings which are shared and
which help to define a group's culture.   The choice of
meanings may appear to be arbitrary when one considers
other possible cultural variations.   In fact the arbitrary nature of the culture is understood when it is
understood that 'cultural facts' owe their existence to
the social conditions in which they were created.   This
is another way of putting Weber's point that the structural conditions in a society limit forms of consciousness.   Bourdieu and Passeron assert that dominant groups
can develop their own cultural arbitrary and, because of
superior power relationships, can impose their cultural
arbitrary on to others.   But the manner in which dominant
groups impose their cultural beliefs and meanings must
conceal the fact that the groups do have power to impose
their arbitrary.

The dominant group must ensure that the 'arbitrary' is
accepted as legitimate authority.   Any violence must be
symbolic and manifest itself as a right to legitimately
impose upon others.

Now the professionals who make decisions about ESN
children are members of a dominant social group whose
'cultural arbitrary' includes specific beliefs about the
inferior cultural competence of lower social groups.
These beliefs can be empirically documented: for example,
socio-economic status and lack of 'intelligence' have
always been regarded as linked attributes within the
belief system of those who classify subnormal people.
'Stupidity', as Cyril Burt observed in 1935, may not be
the 'inevitable result of poverty, but poverty is its
commonest concomitant.'

Whatever humanistic rationalisations may exist in the
form of civilised concern over people who are deemed to be
below 'normal' educationally, categorising people out of
the education system is done by professionals acting upon
their cultural beliefs, and they are able to impose their
beliefs through their superior power position.

The power of the professionals, in this case, rests ultimately upon legal coercion.   Parents who object to the categorisation of their children and to special schooling, can be coerced by law.   However, as Bourdieu and Passeron note, dominant groups seldom use open coercion.   This study demonstrates vividly that professionals can impose their beliefs by 'persuasion'.   The persuasion works as a symbolic form of coercion partly because the cultural understandings of the parents as an inferior social group include acknowledgment (however unwilling) of the superior status and power position of the professionals.   A group of parents presented with the information that their children 'cannot cope' with an education system might reasonably ask that the system should change to allow the children to cope.   Instead, the impositions of the values of professional people based on their cultural arbitrary, have, since the 1890s, legitimated the view to parents that their children should rightly leave the system.   It is worth noting that it has never been part of the cultural understandings of either group that 'special' education is an education.   From this point of view there has never been any possibility that special ESN schools could be regarded as anything other than stigmatised schools.

The study also demonstrates that the cultural beliefs of professional people currently include beliefs about the capabilities and behaviour of other racial groups.   The professionals have power to act upon these beliefs, and the observable result is that a disproportionate number of West Indian children are categorised as ESN and subsequently enter the British class structure at the lowest possible level.

The study therefore seeks to demonstrate that there is no normative consensus amongst the professionals about what constitutes an ESN-M child, and that beliefs about qualities other than 'educational' are used to account for the categorisation: that formal procedures which are officially designated to produce categorisations are supplemented by 'informal' procedures during which professionals can reinforce their characterisations of the child and his parents - the parents being involved in the process as 'cultural inferiors';   that rather than the official 'smooth team-work' between professionals which supposedly processes the children, constructing the category is part of an historical struggle for status assertiveness on the part of different professional groups groups: and that the relationship between the construction of the category ESN-M by the professionals and the social structure is that their dominant cultural beliefs and power position have the effect of 'reproducing' the children of the lower social class in their inferior social and cultural position.   This latter is regarded as a major function of education systems in the twentieth century.   The system is used to make social hierarchies appear to be based on intrinsic qualities of 'intelligence' and 'competence'.

The categorisation of certain children as ESN-M serves social order in two ways.   First, it serves order within the education system by removing troublesome children, and second, it serves order in the wider society by legitimating the reproduction of a troublesome section of the population as an inferior stigmatised group.

But the sociological account suggested here is no more plausible than professional accounts.   The major aim of any sociological account is to open up new ways of thinking about social processes and social categorisation. The following empirical study has been undertaken with precisely this aim in mind.

1 An initial overview of the concept of ESN–M, the politics of IQ and the West Indian 'grievance'

The first chapter of this study is initially concerned
with an historical overview of the emergence of the concept of educational subnormality.   The concept is traced
through the separation of idiot, imbecile and feeble-
minded - later educable defective - children through the
post-war definitions of ESN to the post-1971 distinction
of ESN-M (mild or medium) and the subsequent 1978 (suggested) change of terminology again, to 'child with learning
difficulty' ('Special Educational Needs...', 1978).

Literature documenting the emergence of provision for
the mentally defective or subnormal has tended to concentrate on the descriptive detail of the Acts, commissions
and provisions involved, set within an ideology of humanitarian progress (Pritchard, 1963).   Recognition, and
classification of, and provision for, more and more people
as handicapped, defective or subnormal is regarded as enlightened advancement, and an obligation placed upon
civilised society to care for its weaker members.   In
contrast to this view, it can be held that the social
categorisation of weaker social groups always serves the
specific interest and purposes of the dominant definers
and categorisors.

During the nineteenth century the medical profession
developed a sustained interest in subnormality, and
clinical definitions of various types of subnormality
became the prerogative of medical men.   After the 1870
Elementary Education Act educationalists began to define
a problem of the feeble-minded in schools, and the notion
developed that a 'special' education, rather than a normal
education, should be offered to selected children,
eventually under threat of compulsion.   This meant that
the educational administration and the teaching profession
developed an interest in defining the defective but educable child.   The early twentieth-century period of

consolidating definitions of educational defect or subnormality paralleled the development of the science of
psychology, and eventually it was the new profession of
educational psychologists who came to have a major share
in the decision-making processes by which children come to
receive a special education.

The twentieth-century history of the concept of educational subnormality can be viewed in terms of the vested
interests of various professional groups, each attempting
to influence the definition of the concept and the
assessment processes in various directions.   In this way,
it becomes easier to understand the successive re-workings
of complex definitions of subnormal but educable children.
The creation of ancillary professional groups and their
claims to be involved in the decision-making have further
affected the discovery and assessment of ESN children.
More professionals now have strong professional vested
interests in the discovery of more children in need of
special education.

Yet the decisions and actions of professional groups
are themselves influenced and constrained by beliefs and
ideologies current within a society, and beliefs about
subnormality, within industrial society, have always been
problematic and contradictory.   The basic contradiction
stems from the structure of industrial society itself.
The profit motive within such a society dictates that as
many members as possible be productive.   To be profitable, the economy cannot tolerate idle members and those
classed as defective (along with paupers and the unemployed, with whom subnormality has always had a close
connection) must work if possible, and not be a charge
upon the state.   This is a theme running through the
literature on subnormality and the treatment of defectives
from the opening of the first idiot asylums.   In addition, the religious ethic which validates the moral value
of productive labour in industrial society has always made
it possible to present the care, control and directed
employment of defectives as a Christian and humanitarian
duty.   Yet the preparation of a normal productive 'educated' workforce in elementary schools, was seen after 1870
to be impeded by the presence of troublesome defectives.
The contradiction to be resolved for the past hundred
years has been the control of a potentially troublesome
group by the provision of separate institutions and
schooling, while keeping the cost of such provision low,
and encouraging as many of the group as possible to be
productive and self-sufficient.

The problem of the validation of defective or subnormal
children was partially solved by the development of

psychometric techniques and IQ testing.   IQ provided a
seemingly objective legitimation for categorising certain
children into special education, and the measurement of
intelligence by means of standardised IQ tests has been
part of the assessment procedures since the 1930s.   This
chapter devotes a section to an examination of some of the
political uses towards which IQ has been put, to suggest
that it is not necessarily the objective scientific tool
of 'diagnosis' that practitioners sometimes present.
Although IQ is an easily comprehensible vehicle of
diagnosis to describe 'what is' an ESN child, testing
techniques have probably played a larger part in legitimating the increased power of psychologists in the
decision-making processes than anything else.

    In a final section to the chapter, the history of the
West Indian 'grievance' that 'too many' of their children
are referred, assessed and sent to ESN-M schools, is
documented.   The history of the development of the concepts of defective and educationally subnormal children
records individual resistance, but no articulate group
resistance to classification.   The protest of the West
Indian community is the first protest to have arisen on a
group level.   It is the West Indian demand for clarification of 'what is' an ESN-M child that has provided an
important impetus for this study and the study attempts to
document possible reasons for the over-referral and the
significance of the categorisation as ESN-M for the
position of black children in Britain.

SUBNORMALITY BEFORE 1944

Understandings about subnormality have varied historically
according to specific cultural value systems and the
treatment of the subnormal has varied throughout the ages
from harsh persecution to occasional reverence.
Confucius (551-478 B.C.) referred to the 'weaker-minded'.
Hippocrates (460-377 B.C.) described forms of cranial
anomalies that lead to retardation, and bishop Isidorus
Hispalensis (560-636) referred in his dictionary to
'amens' - one who has no mind at all - and 'demens' - one
having retained part of the mind.   The Greeks exposed and
killed idiots and deaf children;   the Hebraic Law and
Christian ethic exhorted aid for the handicapped, but it
was a businessman rather than a clergyman who opened the
first English hospice for blind men in 1329.   During the
reign of Edward I the distinction had been made between
the 'idiot' and the 'lunatic'.   Financial consideration
dictated this distinction;   if a man was found to be an

idiot, the Crown could take permanent possession of his
property.   Martin Luther denounced the subnormal as
godless but in the early seventeenth century St Vincent
de Paul was providing for the handicapped at the (later)
Bicêtre.   By the end of the seventeenth century the
doctrine of Realism, with its emphasis on the nature and
use of the senses, and inductive methods in education, and
the study of the nature and acquisition of knowledge,
meant that those who failed to acquire knowledge were
objects of interested scrutiny.   The influence of
Rousseau's individualism on prevailing conceptions of
childhood - notably that education should be based on the
nature of each child and his capacities (1772), led
logically to an interest in individual difference, including the difference of subnormality.   Itard's experiments
(1894) in the training of Victor, the 'Wild Boy of
Aveyron' are generally considered to be the first scientific attempts at the education of the subnormal and the
work of Itard's pupil Seguin later influenced Binet and
Simon (1914) in their construction of the first intelligence tests.   However, it was the influence of medical
men that was predominant in the idiots' asylums opened
during the early nineteenth century, in Germany, Switzer-
land, America and England, although Seguin, who had become
superintendent of an idiots' school at Bicêtre, emigrated
to America in 1842 and became superintendent of the new
Massachusetts School for Idiots and Feeble-minded Youths.
In England, Doctor Andrew Read opened the first idiot
asylum at Highgate in 1847, with the Duke of Cambridge and
Duchess of Gloucester as patrons.   By 1870 five idiot
asylums were established, offering medical 'treatment' and
training and being reluctant to take 'pauper' defective
children. (1)
   The seventeenth-century movement to confine paupers and
the unemployed in workhouses had also drawn in 'defective'
people.   But the presence of grossly defective people
interrupted the smooth functioning of forced labour in the
workhouse, and set problems for the Guardians.   Pritchard
records (1963, p. 57) that in 1815, a Lancashire mill-
owner was persuaded by a London workhouse to take one
idiot child to every twenty supplied to his mill.   The
move for asylums for defective poor children was intended
largely to remove their troublesome presence from workhouses.   Accordingly, the Metropolitan Poor Act (1867)
empowered the Poor Law Board to establish asylums for
pauper idiots.   Four more asylums opened, and in 1878 the
inmates of the Hampstead Asylum were moved to Darenth.
This asylum illustrated early on the principles of cheap
provision and the work ethic.   By 1887 only half of the

children were receiving any form of instruction, and the
cost of education was low 'because the school staff is
starved'.   Meanwhile, workshop blocks were used so that
as many inmates as possible were productive.   The medical
superintendent at Darenth, as Pritchard noted, made the
decision that every child was reaching its highest educational potential (Pritchard, 1963).

These asylums mainly took children whom, under the 1886
Idiots Act, were divided into imbeciles and idiots.
Meanwhile, a further group, the high-grade defectives or
feeble-minded, were being discovered.   They were discovered in England both by medical men and by the schools at
more or less the same time.   A sub-committee of the
Charity Organisation Society, whose composition included
several doctors, visited asylums and campaigned on behalf
of 'improvable idiots'.   The secretary of this sub-
committee, Sir Charles Trevelyan, a former governor of
Madras, was credited with the first use of the term
'feeble-minded'.

Although auxiliary schools had opened in other European
countries during the 1880s for children who were 'intellectually weak ... poorly endowed in perception, memory
and reason' (Klemm, 1891, p. 78), (2) it was the introduction of mass elementary education in England in 1870 that
brought numbers of children who experienced difficulty
within a formal education system to the attention of the
school authorities.   Many of these children would have
passed unnoticed before the introduction of formal schooling, but these dull children could not keep to the
required standards and interfered with the system of payment by results.   The fore-runners of the ESN - feeble-
minded children - were 'discovered' by the education
authorities, not necessarily for humanitarian purposes,
but because they were troublesome to the smooth running of
the education system.   A medical officer to the London
School Board reported in 1897 that of every seventy
children in Standard I at school, twenty-five 'were almost
entirely ignorant.   They misbehaved, learned nothing or
truanted' (Pritchard, 1963).   Some schools established a
Standard O, where 'the feeble-minded were joined by the
physically handicapped, partially sighted and delicate
children, and ... even imbeciles' (Pritchard, 1963, p.
117).

The problems posed by feeble-minded children were
officially added to the more obvious problems of the blind
and deaf in 1886, when a commission to investigate the
needs of the blind had its powers extended to investigate
the deaf and 'other cases as from special circumstances
would seem to require exceptional methods of education'

('Report of the Royal Commission on the Blind, the Deaf, the Dumb ...', 1889). This was the first recognition that universal education would not proceed smoothly until special provision was made for the feeble-minded. Lord Egerton's commission frankly used the argument of economic expediency to advocate special education. If left uneducated, blind, deaf and educable imbeciles would become a burden on the state, and if not educated, they would swell a 'great torrent of pauperism'. The commission recommended residential training for imbeciles and that feeble-minded children should be separated from ordinary children in school and given 'special' instruction, although this was not made specific. The Egerton Commission included several medical men, and the evidence given by another doctor, Dr Warner, to the commission was influential in encouraging School Boards to provide special education. Warner had a vested medical interest: he considered that 'weak-minded' children could be detected by physical indications, and his survey in the London School Board and Poor Law Schools found one per cent of such children. The Charity Organisation Society published Warner's work (Charity Organisation Society, 1893) and supported his conclusions. Papers published by another Doctor, Dr Shuttleworth, medical superintendent of the Lancaster asylum, also advocated special schools as 'the remunerative industry of restored pupils might justify them (Shuttleworth, 1888).

Thus, by the end of the 1880s, the feeble-minded were regarded as an educational and economic problem, and the notion of 'special' schooling had been put forward by medical men and by a commission chaired by an aristocrat, with the economic justification that educational provision for these children would ultimately benefit the state.

The Education Department appeared reluctant to take up the recommendations of the Egerton Commission and it was the actions of a Major-General Moberley, chairman of the London School Boards' sub-committee on blind and deaf children, who in 1890 persuaded the Board to instruct the School Management Committee to 'prepare a scheme by which special instruction may be provided in special schools or classes, for those children who, by reason of physical or mental defect, cannot be properly taught in the ordinary standards or by ordinary methods' (Pritchard, 1963, p. 120).

The Board recommended to the Education Department that provision be made in the Code, for schools giving special instruction, with no definite curriculum being laid down. In July 1890 the Department sanctioned the establishment of such schools. The first three schools for special

instruction were started in London's poorest districts.
Children were admitted after examination by a team com-
prising the Board's medical officer, school inspector and
head of the special school.   This notion of a 'team'
decision seemed inevitable, given the discovery and
interest in feeble-minded children by both medical and
educational personnel at the same time.   The rivalry of
interest seemed to favour the medical men slightly from
the outset, despite the fact that few school boards at
this time employed full-time doctors.   In Leicester Dr
Warner claimed to have seen the first boy classed as
feeble-minded (sent to him for being troublesome in ordinary school), but the Leicester School Board inspector,
Mr Major, asserted that he had first noticed feeble-minded
children and claimed that he alone selected children for
the first Leicester special school, on the basis of educational criteria.   In Birmingham the first two special
classes established were filled by children selected by
the teachers of these classes, while in Bradford a medical
officer, Dr Kerr, was responsible for the selection of
children.   He was of the opinion that if teachers of
ordinary schools were allowed to select children, they
would attempt to get rid of all their dull children.   In
Brighton Dr Warner was invited to select children for the
first special school, and in Bristol a doctor was consulted as the first Bristol classes took physically handicapped children as well as feeble-minded (Pritchard,
1963, p. 127).

The 'ad hoc' development of special schools and
classes, had thus been undertaken by School Boards during
the 1890s, but the expense and lack of central direction
made it inevitable that the Boards, particularly the
London Board, with the largest number of children in
special schools, should press for more central provision
for defective children.   The Charity Organisation
Society, with its medical influence, also lobbied MPs,
sponsored a National Association for promoting the Welfare
of the Feeble-minded, and published several reports
stressing the need for action by the Education Department
(Charity Organisation Society, 1893).   Dr Francis Warner
published a second report in 1894 showing four classes of
'defect' all requiring special education.

In 1896 the Department set up a Committee on Defective
and Epileptic Children under the championship of the chief
schools inspector, the Reverend Sharpe.   The Committee
consisted of two more educationalists, two doctors and a
representative from the Charity Organisation Society.
They were to enquire into the education of 'feeble-minded
or defective children' and report on means of discriminat-

ing between educable and non-educable children (Education Department, 1898).

The medical influence on the assessment of children requiring special education emerged paramount from the recommendations of this Committee, published in 1898.   It was the doctors on the Committee who suggested a distinction between imbecile and feeble-minded children that led to an official classification of a group of children capable of 'education' to be self-supporting, but too 'defective' to receive this education in ordinary schools. The Committee preferred the term 'defective' to 'feeble-minded' children, and the children were to be those: 'not being imbecile who cannot properly be taught in ordinary schools by ordinary methods.'   This group included physically handicapped children until 1944.

The medical witnesses to the Committee were of the opinion that only doctors were capable of distinguishing between imbecile and defective children - and defective and normal children, although it was conceded that teachers' opinions could be sought and it was intended that head teachers or inspectors should make a preliminary selection of children thought to be in need of special schooling.   The only teacher on the Committee, a woman, was presumably not prestigious enough to press the case for equal teacher participation in decision-making and Pritchard (1963, p. 139) conceded that it was partly the prestige of the medical witnesses that brought about the medical victory. (3)   Thus, by 1899, the duty of recommending the best educational provision for a child lay with a doctor, but normal schools had secured a means of transferring their troublesome children.   Attempts to compel parents to send their children to special schools had been made during the 1890s, but at this time parents could send their children to voluntary schools which did not come under the control and regulations of the local education authorities until 1902.   The recommendations of the Committee were swiftly put into effect with the passing of the 1899 Elementary Education (Defective and Epileptic Children) Act.   Pritchard (1963, p. 150) considered it praiseworthy that 'a class of children who had hitherto been neglected received official recognition', but alternatively it is unlikely that provision would have been made for these children unless normal schools had supported this particular way of removing troublesome and dull children.   Also the medical profession had now obtained a new area of competence.   It was a doctor who signed a certificate to say whether a child was capable or incapable of receiving benefit from instruction in ordinary schools if thought to be feeble-minded.   The 1899

Act expressed the familiar contradiction that, while it
was agreed that defective children should be educated
separately, it must not cost too much.   The Chancellor of
the Exchequer himself expressed fear that if the definition of 'defective' were not carefully settled, many
authorities 'especially in Ireland' would discover too
many defective children.   In order to cut down expense
the 1899 Act enabled, rather than required, authorities to
provide for their defective children.

The Committee on Defective and Epileptic Children also
made the first suggestions as to the curriculum of the
special schools;   the emphasis was to be on manual work,
with the provision of vocational training for the older
children.   During the early twentieth century there were
moves towards the greater segregation of defective
children from the ordinary school system.   Dr Eichholz,
an HMI and qualified doctor, was appointed in 1900 to
advise the Education Department on questions pertaining to
defectives.   Eichholz linked moral depravity to pronounced mental defect and recommended segregation in country
schools with manual labour for these children.   This was
a foretaste of the influence of geneticists and eugenicists whose work led to popular acceptance that defective
children were a danger to society.   The work of Galton
(1889;   1909) on the heritability of mental characteristics, in England, and Dugdale's 'genetic' study of the
Juke family (1877), and Goddard's Kallikak family study
(1912), were used to link mental defect with crime,
pauperism, prostitution and unemployment.   Dr Tredgold,
a doctor and lecturer in mental deficiency, whose influential 'Text-book of Mental Deficiency' (1914) ran to
seven editions, was a member of a Departmental Committee
on sterilisation, and considered that 90 per cent of
defectives 'come from psychopathic stock ... and are
potential carriers of defect' (p. 492).

Tredgold proposed euthanasia for idiots and imbeciles
and the sterilisation of defectives not merely to prevent
propagation, but to check 'depraved and bestial propensities' (p. 493).   Tredgold was influenced by the strong
eugenics movement in the USA and approved of legislative
proposals, carried in some states, for the castration and
sterilisation of the feeble-minded.

Two women members of the National Association for
promoting the welfare of the feeble-minded, both celebra-
ted as pioneers on behalf of the defective children, were
also exponents of the segregation of defective children.
Mary Dendy, a member of the Manchester School Board,
campaigned for a 'medical man' to 'weed out' defective
children, and set up an association for the permanent care

of the feeble-minded.   Children were to progress from the
first country residential school for the feeble-minded -
set up by Manchester - to an adult industrial colony.
She was able to influence the curriculum of this school
in the direction of manual work, writing being particularly dangerous, as it allowed adult men and women to
communicate.   Ellen Pinsent, a School Board member in
Birmingham, personally selected children for special
schools, became chairman of an after-care committee in
1901, and campaigned for the provision of industrial
colonies.

The movement towards the segregation of defective
children for life, may have also been influenced by the
early development of mental testing, and the assumption
that a child shown to be of low intelligence on a test,
never increased that intelligence.   Binet himself was
ambiguous on this point (Binet and Simon, 1914).   But the
move may also have been linked with a rise in unemployment, which made it harder for defective school-leavers,
to find work, since employers preferred the leavers from
normal education.   The early products of 'special'
education were thus used as a form of replacement labour,
to be used in times of high employment.

By 1904 there was sufficient anxiety that the education
of the feeble-minded might be financially unjustified if
their labour was not subsequently used, and that without
work they might pose a severe threat to social order, for
a Royal Commission on the Care and Control of the Feeble-
Minded to be set up.   The Commission noted at the outset
of its 'Report' (1908, vol. 8, p. 3) that:

> of the gravity of the present state of things there is
> no doubt ... there are numbers of mentally defective
> persons, whose training is neglected, over whom no
> sufficient control is exercised, and whose wayward and
> irresponsible lives are productive of crime and misery
> ... and much continuous expenditure wasteful to the
> community.

The Royal Commission was chaired by another aristocrat -
the Earl of Radnor - and of the eight other members three
were doctors, two were lawyers.   Mrs Ellen Pinsent was
also a member and pressed enthusiastically for the regis-
tration and segregation of defectives - on the grounds
that unemployed special school leavers meant that 'the
years of special and expensive education were probably
entirely wasted'.   The Commission firmly endorsed the
position of medical officers in the discovery and examination of defective children.   Without doctors 'the opinions which teachers form may be of little or no service in
dealing with mental defect' (p. 91).   The major recom-

mendation was that a medically dominated Board of Control
be set up to be responsible for all types of defective,
including educable defective children.   Education
authorities were to report any possible defective children
to doctors, and parents would be compelled to take their
children for medical examination.   Once in special
schools, 'the simple occupations of the earliest years
should develop into systematic industrial teaching, while
the scholastic teaching should become entirely subordinate' (p. 103).   The Commission supported the appointment
of medical officers to education authorities, in order to
carry out medical inspections of all children (this became
statutory in 1907).   They considered that doctors would
thus be able to carry out the observation of children to
try and distinguish between 'mental defective' children
and those who were merely 'dull and backward'.   The
authority should then provide for the latter group in
ordinary schools.

The recommendations of the Royal Commission represented
the high point of medical domination of the procedures for
assessing defective children.   If the care of all defective children had indeed passed to the Board of Control, a
whole new medically dominated bureaucracy would have
developed with far-reaching consequences for the education
of all subnormal children.   However, not all recommendations of the Commission found their way into the Mental
Deficiency Act of 1913.   In the intervening years,
educationalists had had time to realise their own interests in retaining control of as many children as possible
in education, and 175 authorities had made some provision
for feeble-minded children.   The 1913 Act gave education
authorities the duty of ascertaining which children aged
7-16 were defective, and, of these, which were incapable
of education in special schools.   These children alone
were passed to the local Mental Deficiency Committee,
responsible to a Board of Control.   The 1914 Act made the
1899 provision compulsory - education authorities now had
the duty of providing for defective children who were not
passed to the Mental Deficiency Committee and the 1921
Education Act laid a duty on parents to cause a child
certified as 'mentally defective' to attend a special
school or class recognised by the Board of Education.
Section 54 of this Act enabled the authority to compel
parents to send their children to special schools.
Section 55 defined defective children as those who 'not
being imbecile and not being merely dull and backward ...
are by reason of mental defect incapable of receiving
proper benefit from the institute in ordinary public elementary schools'.

By the 1920s the stigmatisation of defective children as a category set apart from normal children had, historically, reached its most pronounced point.   Subsequently, in the twentieth century, attempts have been made to reduce the stigma and blur the overt control functions of 'special' education.   The 1913 Act had defined four categories of defect - idiots, imbeciles, feeble-minded and moral imbeciles - that is, defective people with criminal propensities, and this statutory link between the feeble-minded and moral depravity reinforced popular understandings of mental defect.   However, the case histories reported by the Royal Commission indicate strongly that the 'depravity' supposedly displayed by defectives consisted largely of poverty, lack of economic self-sufficiency, poor health and troublesome behaviour. Nevertheless, the 1913 Act referred to feeble-minded adults as requiring 'care, supervision and control for their own protection or the protection of others'.   The stigma was further intensified by the legal requirement that children be certified as mentally defective. Children ascertained after a medical examination to be educable defectives were certified by an officer of the Education Authority to qualify them for admission to a special school, although if they were discharged from the special school the certificate had to be returned to the parents.

During the 1920s medical officers working for education authorities were anxious to consolidate their new area of competence, particularly with regard to how many defective children there were to be discovered in the school population. (4)   The new profession of psychology was also seeking a foothold in the assessment procedures, as the rise of the mental testing movement had been closely bound up with measuring subnormality.   Educationalists now had two vested interests in classifying more exactly which children could be termed defective - a profession of special school teachers had developed with skills and competence in dealing with defective children, and normal schools were using the referral procedures to refer troublesome children and thus assist the smooth running of normal schools (Crowley, 1936).

The first two of these interests were brought together when the Wood Committee on Mental Deficiency was set up in 1924 by Dr Newman, the chief medical officer to the Board of Education (Board of Education and Board of Control, 1929).   This committee decided to extend its deliberations to include all defective people, and the Board of Control joined the Education Committee in financing the enquiry - the indefatigable Mrs Pinsent representing the

Board of Control.   Of the other ten committee members,
four were medical officers, two - including the chairman,
Arthur Woods - were in the medical branch of the Board of
Education.   The only teacher was head of a colony school
and also an inspector for the Board of Control.   Teachers
of educable defective children were not represented, nor
were teachers of normal children, and they subsequently
disagreed with major recommendations made by the
Committee.   Cyril Burt, the first psychologist to be
appointed by an education authority and now Professor of
Education at London University, was also a member.   It
was his influence and recommendations as to the definition
of subnormal children that subsequently radically affected
the assessment procedures, and advanced the claims of
educational psychologists to share in the assessment
processes and validate procedures by psychometric testing.

The Committee also relied heavily on the report of an
enquiry by Dr Lewis, appointed medical investigator to the
Committee.   Lewis encapsulated all vested interests in
one person.   He was a medical doctor, had worked as a
school teacher, and lectured in educational psychology.
The findings of his report served all interests, but
particularly psychological interests, since he administered group intelligence tests to discover subnormal
children.

The Lewis investigation covered six selected rural and
urban areas and aimed to discover the incidence of defective children of all types.   As regards feeble-minded
children, he considered it 'impossible in many cases to
decide whether a young child is feeble-minded or merely
backward, whether its retarded development is due to poor
mental endowment ... or bad home conditions' (Board of
Education and Board of Control, 1929, part 4, p. 59).
Nevertheless, he estimated that 104,509 children aged
7-16 years (in England and Wales) were feeble-minded - a
figure calculated from the incidence rate for his investigation areas.   In order to discover these feeble-
minded children, Lewis asked head teachers to put forward
the names of children they considered retarded.   Here
Lewis encountered one of the early sources of conflict
between teachers and educational psychologists.   He
complained that teachers put forward children backward in
attainment, whereas he wanted children retarded in the
current psychological understanding of 'general intelligence'.   However, Lewis then administered group IQ tests,
based on the Binet-Simon scale, standardised by Cyril
Burt.   Individual tests were also administered, again
standardised by Burt.   Lewis informed the Committee that
'For the measurement of innate general intelligence,

fairly efficient psychological tests have been devised.
In almost all civilised countries such tests now form the
main ... criterion in the diagnosis of mental deficiency'
(Board of Education and Board of Control, 1929, part 4).

The Wood Committee urged that the educable and defective child and the dull and backward child should no
longer be regarded as separate, but 'envisaged as a
single group presenting a single educational and administrative problem'.   This was the group subsequently termed
ESN.   The children were to be discovered largely by means
of mental testing;   the certification procedures should be
abolished for this group and special schools should be
presented to parents 'not as something both distinct and
humiliating, but as a helpful variation of the ordinary
school' (Board of Education and Board of Control, 1929,
part 1, p. 117).   The NUT were opposed to the abolition
of certification;   teachers in special schools reasoned
that the needs of defectives would be submerged under a
larger group of retarded children (National Union of
Teachers, 1930), but the teachers could equally have
feared that without compulsion they might lose their
clientele.   However, they need not have feared for this ⌐
the interests of special educators were about to be considerably furthered by the 1944 Education Act and post-war
development and the interests of educational psychologists
consolidated as their importance in the assessment processes as 'mental testers' developed.   However, the
statutory powers within the ascertainment process remained
medical under the 1944 Act, a situation unchanged in 1979.

SUBNORMALITY AFTER 1944

The 1944 Education Act went some way towards bringing
special education under the general educational framework
and reducing the segregation of defectives.   The Act
altered the legal categorisation of children who had
previously been termed mentally deficient or feeble-
minded, and linked them to a larger group of backward
children - the whole to be known by subsequent regulations
as the educationally subnormal.   Williams (1965) considered that 'educational sub-normality is a different
concept from mental deficiency;   it is a descriptive
category rather than a diagnosis', and the 1944 Act can
perhaps be regarded as a major effort by educationalists
to move as many defective children as possible out of
medical domination and firmly into an educational aegis,
albeit a 'special' education.   Classifications of mental
subnormality are illustrated at this point by Table 1.1.

TABLE 1.1 Classifications in mental subnormality England and Wales - historical classification

1886-1899	idiot	imbecile	feeble-minded		
1899-1944	uneducable mentally defective		educable mental defective or feeble-minded		
1944-1971	unsuitable for education in schools severely subnormal		educationally subnormal		
1971-present	educationally subnormal (severe S.)		educationally subnormal (mild M.)		
Suggested Warnock categories 1978	children with learning difficulties (severe)		children with learning difficulties (moderate/mild)		
For comparison					
IQ on Stanford-Binet test range	Below 20	20-49	50-70/75+		
American education sub-division	1 custodial/dependent 2 uneducable	trainable (TMR) mentally retarded	educable (EMR) mentally retarded		
American Association of Mental Deficiency	profound mental retardation	severe mental retardation	moderate mental retardation	mild m.r. IQ below 68	borderline m.r. IQ below 83
Soviet distinction	ZND 'Zone of next development'				

The relevant sections of the 1944 Act are section 8(c)
wherein the duty of securing provision for any pupil
suffering from a 'disability of mind or body' is laid upon
local education authorities, and section 34(1) which laid
down the duty to ascertain which childeen in an authority
from the age of two years required special educational
treatment.   The LEA was given powers, under this section,
to require parents to submit their children for a medical
examination.   Section 34(4) noted that the authority
should consider the advice of the medical officer 'and
any reports or information' from teachers or other
persons, with respect to the 'ability and aptitude of the
child'.   Thus, the model of ascertainment in the Act
remained medical, with only medical doctors given statutory powers in the assessment procedures.   Children who
were considered to be uneducable defectives, before 1944,
were provided for under Section 57(1) of the Act which
gave the LEA the duty of discovering children whose disability of mind 'is of such a nature or to such an extent'
that they be passed to the local health authority.   Section 33 required the minister to define categories of
pupils requiring special educational treatment and make
provision for them.   This section also allowed that where
'it is impracticable' or the 'disability is not serious',
arrangements may be made in ordinary schools.   Hence, in
1945, the Handicapped Pupils and School Health Service
Regulations defined eleven categories of children
requiring special education.   These were the blind,
partially sighted, deaf, partially deaf, delicate,
diabetic, educationally subnormal, epileptic, maladjusted,
physically handicapped, and those with speech defects.
A 1953 amendment linked delicate and diabetic and ten
categories currently remain.   Educationally subnormal
pupils were defined in the 1945 regulations as 'pupils,
who by reason of limited ability, or other conditions,
resulting in educational retardation, require some
specialised form of education wholly or partly in substitution for the education normally given in ordinary
schools.'   The Ministry of Education envisaged from 1945
that the category of educationally subnormal would include
a much larger number of children than those who fell
within the other categories (see Appendix 1 to this
chapter for numbers of ESN children after 1944) and the
1945 definition was intended as 'educational' in that it
included a far wider range of children than those educable
defectives who were previously certifiable.   Nevertheless, the notion of certification was built into the 1944
Act through Section 34(5).   A certificate signed by a
medical officer, defined later under the regulations as

Handicapped Pupils form 1, can be used to secure compulsory attendance at a special school for a child whose
parents object.   This persistence of certification made
nonsense of subsequent Ministry assurances that 'special
educational treatment was not a matter of segregating the
seriously handicapped from their fellows, but of providing
in each case the special help suited to the needs of the
child' (Ministry of Education, 1956, p. 1).   Although
most authorities insist they do not use certification
procedures (Brindle, 1973), the threat of such procedures
takes decision-making about ESN children into the area of
civil rights.   Special education is the only type of
prescribed education whereby a child who has not been
before the courts may be placed in a school contrary to
the parents' wishes.   No statutory mechanism was built
into the Act or regulations for consulting or involving
parents in this decision about their child.   The notion
of certification was also at odds with the idea of providing special educational facilities in classes in ordinary
schools specified in section 33(2) of the 1944 Act.   To
secure the attendance of one child at a special school,
under the threat of certification, while allowing another
child to stay at normal school is a manifest contradiction.   In any event, the wording of the Act allowed LEAs
to evade their responsibilities as to the provision of
special classes in ordinary schools and the whole spirit
of the Act, classifying all children as to 'age, aptitude
and ability', made a move towards provision in separate
schools for the new category of educationally subnormal
pupils inevitable.   From 1945 the notion that any child
who was 'educationally retarded' was a potential candidate
for a special school made a need for the clarification of
the category very important.   However, subsequent
official guidelines and advice have confused, rather than
clarified, the definitions as to who exactly is an ESN
child and what criteria define the category.
     The first Ministry guidelines were laid down in a 1946
pamphlet.   In this document educational retardation was
noted as being caused by 'limited ability' or by 'other
conditions' or by both together (Ministry of Education,
1946).   Limited ability was considered, on the basis of
current psychological knowledge, to have a genetic basis
and was likely to be permanent, although special schools
were thought to play a useful part in training the
children.   The 'other factors' considered to lead to
educational retardation were mainly home conditions, maladjustment and late bed-times, and poor teaching in ordinary schools.   'Over-indulgence and irresponsibility on
the part of parents' was mentioned.   Thus, two groups of

children were explicitly identified here - the innately
dull and backward - but LEAs were told that it was not
necessary to make separate arrangements for the two sets
of children.   'One of the advantages of the new Act is
that no decision as to the cause of retardation may be
given before the child is given special educational
treatment.'   Thus, every retarded child was potentially
ESN and the cause need not be taken into account.   As a
rough guideline to how many children and which children
should be classed as ESN the pamphlet spoke of a 'large
body of opinion' who favoured giving special educational
treatment 'if the child is so retarded that his standard
of work is below that achieved by a child 20% younger than
he is' (Ministry of Education, 1946, p. 19).   An IQ of 55
was suggested as a cut-off point at which a child cannot
be educated in a special school and teachers were urged
not to be sentimental over referring 'detrimental or low-
grade' children to the mental health authorities.   One
criterion for ineducable children was suggested - 'children of so low a degree of ability often have undesirable
personal characteristics or even appearance'.   Also 'if
a child behaves in so disorderly a way, or has such objec-
tionable habits ... that it is impossible to correct his
behaviour by the usual methods of school discipline' he
should be referred as ineducable.   Thus, educationally
subnormal children, appropriate for special schools, were
not, in 1946, to be children whose behaviour or appearance
was considered inappropriate to teachers;   they were to be
children with IQs of between 55 and 70-75 who were of
innately low intelligence or functioning at 20 per cent
below their age level but did not present behaviour
problems.   Six to nine per cent of all registered pupils
less seriously retarded, 'for other reasons' may be
retained in ordinary schools for special educational
treatment, but in 'good schools drawing from suburban
areas' the proportion of retarded children may be small.
     In fact, the numbers of pupils referred, assessed, and
sent to special schools, increased rapidly between 1946
and 1955.   One hundred and forty-two more ESN schools
were opened for almost 11,000 more ESN pupils, and there
was a shortage of ESN schools.   Since there was no
mechanism for monitoring who the children were who were
being referred and sent to special schools, the question
remained whether the ineducable with behaviour problems,
the 'innately dull' and the 'retarded' were in fact being
separated.   There was no guidance issued to teachers as
to how they were to distinguish between the three categories, and although no research exists on this point, it
appears that, as Crowley had noted in the 1930s, teachers

tended to refer children on the basis of retardation plus
behaviour problems (Crowley, 1936).   There were hints of
this in a subsequent Ministry pamphlet in 1956.   'It has
become less difficult to place the really troublesome
educationally subnormal boy or girl, whose mental disability is complicated by behaviour difficulties and
perhaps a record of delinquency' (Ministry of Education,
1956, p. 13).   Also by 1956 the notion of special classes
for children in ordinary schools had given way to an
acceptance that educationally subnormal children needed
help ' which ordinary schools cannot give'.   If no
guidance was available for educationalists in deciding
which children were ESN at this time, the medical officer,
who had the duty of making the actual decision on the
child, was expected to give a clear decision.   Section
15(a) of form 2 HP (report on a child examined for a disability of mind) required the medical officer to state
that in his opinion 'the child is/is not educationally
subnormal'.   The medical officer was required to fill in
a form commenting on the home conditions of the child,
with no requirement that he/she should visit the home,
and had the option of filling out part 2 of the form on
intelligence tests, rather than a psychologist, in
addition to completing part 3, reporting on a medical
examination of the child.   The medical officer's ability
to complete the section on intelligence testing rested on
him/her having completed a three-week training course on
the administration of one of the two major intelligence
tests in use.   Thus, in the 1950s (through to the 1970s),
a flow chart of decisions made under the suggested procedure would be as shown in Figure 1.1.

In the early 1970s Brindle (1973) found in a study of
thirteen LEAs in the West Midlands that there was some
confusion over the use of 'formal procedures' - some
authorities referred to 'formal procedures' as simply
filling in forms 2 and 3 HP, while others thought the
statutory 'certificate' 1 HP was a formal procedure.
The Ministry of Education itself seemed unclear about this
issue.   Circular 11/61 (Ministry of Education, 1961b)
welcomed the fact that the ascertainment of children for
special education was apparently being done without recourse to 'formal procedures', that is 1 HP under Section
34 of the 1944 Act, but went on to note that there is, in
law, no need for 'formality about the offer of a place in
a special school ... or about admission if the parents
accept such an offer', by which the circular was referring
to the completion of forms 2 and 3 HP.   This 1961 circular was one of a number of attempts in the 1960s and early
1970s to further define educationally subnormal children.

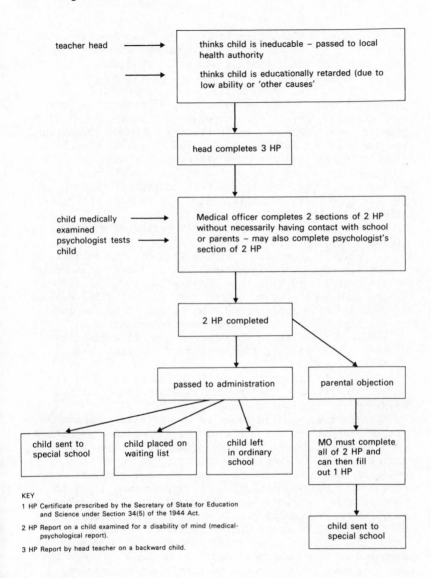

KEY

1 HP Certificate prescribed by the Secretary of State for Education
   and Science under Section 34(5) of the 1944 Act.

2 HP Report on a child examined for a disability of mind (medical-
   psychological report).

3 HP Report by head teacher on a backward child.

FIGURE 1.1 Decision-making in ESN education 1945-75

It noted that ESN children include the 'temporarily retarded as well as the innately dull, who may suitably receive some or all of their special education in ordinary schools as well as those who need to attend special schools.'

A 1964 pamphlet on slow learners commented that 'no attempt is made to define, classify, or categorise backward children, nor is special education looked on as a form of education peculiar to special schools' (Department of Education and Science, 1964), and a report in 1965 noted that the 1944 Act drew attention not only to children who may need to be taught in special schools, but to the far larger numbers who need additional help while remaining in their ordinary school (Department of Education and Science, 1965).

A 1969 definition encapsulated a series of contradictions by noting that

educationally subnormal pupils include both children who are educationally backward (i.e. their attainments are appreciably less than those of average children of the same age) whether or not they are mentally retarded, and also children of average and above average ability who for various reasons are educationally retarded (i.e. their attainments are not commensurate with their ability). (Department of Education and Science, 1969)

The 1946 vague notion that children can be backward for 'other conditions' persisted in the 1969 notion of backwardness for 'various reasons'.

By this time a child could be educationally backward with a high or low IQ; he could be ESN without requiring special schooling, or could be of above average ability and still require special schooling. No cause need be established for a child's retardation, but teachers were expected to distinguish different degrees and types of backwardness. Special education was not to be looked on as a form of education peculiar to special schools, but children could be certified as requiring special schooling. Definitions of educational subnormality were supposed to be educational but only medical officers had any statutory powers in the ascertainment procedures. An ESN child may or may not be distinguished from a backward child who may remain in ordinary school. In the 1940s he was not initially intended to be a troublesome child, but troublesome children had tended to be referred as potentially ESN. Formal ascertainment procedures were to be used sparingly but there was confusion over what exactly constituted a formal procedure. No one throughout this period, 1946-70, had attempted to find out exactly what ESN schools were doing in terms of goals,

organisation or curriculum.   One point that does emerge
clearly is that the optimistic view that a large group of
children had had their educational needs catered for - a
continuation of late nineteenth-century humanism towards
the feeble-minded - had little justification.   Tansley
and Gulliford (1960) represented this view when they
wrote, 'the category "educationally sub-normal" defines a
group of children in terms of their educational need and
not in terms of medico-legal-type.'

With no criteria as to how teachers should define an
educational need, and with the legal designation of an ESN
child being the responsibility of a medical officer, it is
difficult to see how children were being defined on the
basis of educational need.   The most one could say was
that a set of procedures had been developed which isolated
a particular group of children into separate schools, the
major characteristic of these children throughout the
hundred-year period discussed here being that they were
predominantly the children of semi- or unskilled manual
working-class people.

The persistent connection of subnormality with the
lower working class, stemmed from the early 'discovery' of
feeble-minded children in Board schools in the poorest
districts, assisted by the fact that middle- and upper-
class people were able to provide privately for their dull
and defective children (5) and given a spurious respecta-
bility by mental testing and the eugenics movement.   It
was further entrenched during the 1960s with the introduction of the notion of 'cultural disadvantage' in the USA
and Britain.   The crudity with which the early connections were made is probably best exemplified by Tredgold's
(1947) unpleasant assertions concerning the 'dregs of the
nation', and linkages between subnormality, crime,
pauperism and unemployment.   This theme also preoccupied
Cyril Burt in the 1930s - dealing with the 'social problem
class', which was a 'momentus question which every
civilised society must face' (Burt, 1935, ch. 3).

By the 1960s 'cultural disadvantage', documented by an
enormous literature in the USA and Britain, was being used
to explain connections between socio-economic status and
educational attainment generally, and was also being used
to explain the relationship between social class and
children categorised out of the normal education system
into special education.   Once a cultural disadvantage
explanation for children who were not of 'low innate
intelligence' but observably retarded at school had been
posited, it could be acknowledged that these children
tended to be predominantly lower working class.   As
Gulliford wrote in 1969, ESN children are 'the most

educationally handicapped children as a result of a combination of factors.   The factor of social disadvantage is
prominent in at least half of the cases', and P. Williams
(1964) went so far as to claim that ESN schools could be
regarded as 'culturally stimulating environment' which may
promote 'intellectual growth' for ESN children from low
socio-economic groups.

By 1970 a campaign mounted by educationalists and also
by parents (6) led to children who had been termed ineducable mental defectives prior to 1944, severely subnormal
and 'unsuitable for education in school' after 1944, being
integrated into the special education system.   This move
represented a further victory for educationalists,
particularly the now considerable bureaucracy concerned
with 'special' education - against medical domination.

The Mental Health Act of 1959 had recommended that
these children should receive education and training, but
in 1970, by the Education (Handicapped Children) Act these
children were formally brought within the education
system.   Section 57 of the 1944 Act, whereby ineducable
children were the responsibility of the Health Service,
was repealed and the children were placed under the local
education authority.   About 32, 750 children were involved who had previously been catered for in training units,
hospitals and special care units (Department of Education
and Science, 1971b).   They were children with severe and
often multiple defects.   The DES, in a report on 'The
Last to Come In' was enthusiastic about the integration of
mentally handicapped children with educationally subnormal
children.   The severely handicapped were to be known as
ESN-S (severe) in contrast to ESN-M (mild).   The report
noted that 'the inclusion of mentally handicapped children
in the category ESN gives recognition to the fact that
mental handicap is a continuum.'   This notion of a continuum of defect had been developing alongside the historical attempts to impose administrative and legal classifications on subnormality in hierarchical grades.   Various
reports had acknowledged the artificiality of rigid distinctions, and then proceeded to define arbitrary
categories.

Since ESN-S and M were now counted together for some
purposes, the total number of ESN pupils appeared to
expand dramatically in the year 1971-2 (see Appendix 1 to
this chapter) and in 1975 there were around 1,600 schools
and 132,000 pupils in ESN-M and ESN-S schools.   Thus, the
category ESN in 1971 officially included a range of
children from virtually non-functioning children to
retarded children of above average ability.

A DES report on special education in April 1973 purpor-

ted to be 'A Fresh Look' at the situation.   The report
deplored the use of statutory categories of handicap,
which are 'now believed by many people to encourage the
pinning of a single label on each handicapped child,
which hinders proper consideration of an individual's
often complex disabilities', but there was no suggestion
that the statutory categories be removed.   Instead, five
authorities were recruited to pilot a 'descriptive list
based on educational needs' alongside the statutory
categories.   A DES letter to chief education officers in
November 1973 concerning the placement of immigrant
children in special schools, displayed no doubts that a
statutory category ESN-M existed, and that West Indian
children were disproportionately represented in the
category.   While this letter did not question the
category, it did for the first time introduce a criterion
for teachers in deciding which children to refer as in
need of special education.   The criterion was that if
teachers could not cope with the learning difficulties or
the discipling of immigrant children, they should refer
the children as in need of special education.   1973 was
also the year that a committee to review definitions,
treatment and care of handicapped children, was set up
under the chairmanship of Mrs Mary Warnock.

By 1975 the DES had prepared a Circular (1975a)
designed 'to clear up uncertainties and confusion which
surround the subject of ascertainment, and to provide a
fresh statement of what is involved in discovering which
children require special education, and in recommending
what form it should take.'

The implications of Circular 2/75 are clearly that the
DES considers an educational model of assessing children
in need of special education to be preferable to a medical
model.   However, the educational model envisaged is
heavily oriented towards an educational-psychological
assessment.   The DES had since 1944 made statements to
the effect that decisions should be educational;   the
medical officer had been retained as the only statutory
decision-maker via Section 34 of the 1944 Act.   In the
Circular, nineteen years after the inception of form HP 1
- 'the prescribed certificate' for children whose parents
object to their 'treatment' at special school - the DES
does criticise the form as having gone further than
Section 34 required 'by calling on the Medical Officer to
make what are really educational judgments' (Department of
Education and Science, 1975a, para. 3).   However, 2/75
not only retains the 'certificate' to be signed by a
doctor, but also requires that all children assessed for
special education be notified to their own GP.

The Circular introduced new forms in place of the handicapped pupil (HP) form, as 'standard forms are still desirable in the interests of handicapped children moving from one area to another and to ensure that the insights of doctor, educational psychologist and teacher' are made available when children are being considered for special education.   The new 'special education' (SE) forms 1-3 are intended to replace HP forms 2-4.   Thus, SE 1 is for completion by a teacher or head, SE 2 by a school doctor (not necessarily a senior clinical medical officer), SE 3 by an educational psychologist, and SE 4 is a new summary form.   A pilot study carried out by several LEAs in 1973 recommended the introduction of SE 4.   This study was considered successful in that a description of the child's handicaps and needs helped, particularly in cases where a conference of professionals was necessary, or the 'authority's office staff' are considering a school placement, or when the child's case is to be reviewed (Department of Education and Science, 1975a, Appendix B, para. 6).   The form is a 'summary and action' sheet and intended for completion by an 'experienced educational psychologist or adviser in special education' who, 'after seeing the child and after consultation with medical or other professional staff' convey to the LEA a recommendation about special education.   The introduction of SE 4 represents a concrete demonstration of the power position of educational psychologists in the assessment processes for special education, by 1975.   SE 5, however, still leaves the medical officer with a statutory 'certification' procedure, but instead of specifying the category (ESN) the doctor certifies that a child is 'suffering from a disability of mind or body'.   Although the circular promises to review these statutory provisions for certification and perhaps amend the legislation, certification procedures still continue in force and can be used if a parent objects to special education.

The Circular still leaves confusion as to what exactly constitutes a 'formal procedure'.   In paragraph 5 of Circular 2/75 formal procedures refer to the certification necessary to force a child's attendance at special school, and paragraph 23 refers to the section of the 1944 Act (38-2) under which aggrieved parents can make an appeal to the secretary of state.   When the Circular uses the word 'informal' it is refe-ring to all the procedures apart from the certification form, i.e. an 'informal' medical examination still requires SE 3 to be completed.   As the discussion in the City of B's procedures will indicate, some professionals regard all the forms as 'formal'.

Parents receive cursory treatment under the suggested

new procedures.   Although the Circular recommends that
they should be involved at all stages of the assessment
process, their opinions sought, and their rights
explained, there is no machinery built into the procedure
for involving parents, no form on which parents can record
their opinions, and the forms as they are presently constituted, tend to stigmatise parents rather than consult
them as equal participants (see chapter 7).

The decision-making procedures suggested by Circular
2/75 are illustrated in Figure 1.2, although local authorities have interpreted the suggested procedures in
different ways.

In 1976 the government decided to incorporate a section
on special education into the 1976 Education Act, an Act
designed primarily to enforce comprehensivisation in all
areas of England and Wales.   The relevant section, Section
10, substituted for Section 33(ii) of the 1944 Act, a
clause which appears to change the legal emphasis from
special educational treatment in special schools, to the
provision of special education, for all categories of
handicapped children, in ordinary county and voluntary
schools.   Section 10 lays down that pupils shall be
educated in special schools only if they cannot be given
efficient instruction in ordinary schools, or if the cost
of instruction in ordinary schools would cause 'unreasonable public expenditure'.

The secretary of state, when questioned about Section
10 ('Special Education - Forward Trends, 1977) noted that:
The principle of integrated provision for the education
of handicapped children is not new, and we firmly
adhere to it, but special education in ordinary schools
has not been clearly defined.   Section 10 gives
opportunities to think about what it entails and to
ensure that future arrangements spring from informed
judgment both of need and provision.

The integration principle referred to here by the
secretary of state, dated from the Wood Committee's
recommendations, and to some of the hopes expressed in the
1946 pamphlet, although this pamphlet was itself ambivalent over special education being provided in ordinary
schools.

Section 10 still remains to be implemented, but it does
throw the role of existing special schools open for
debate.   The secretary of state has said that she envis-
ages that they will have a more varied future - perhaps
becoming resource centres to help the provision of
special education in ordinary schools, but it has been
left to the Warnock Committee to debate and make recommendations on this issue.   The implications of Section 10

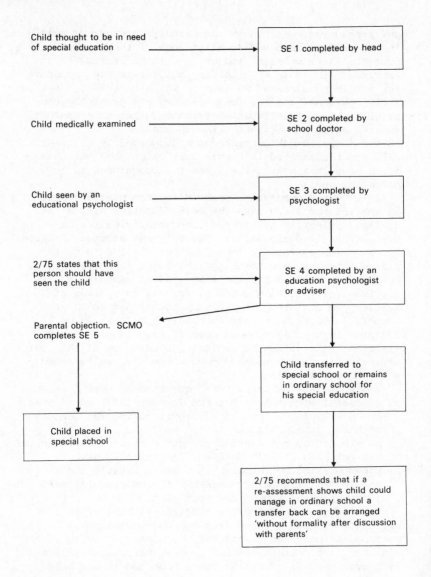

FIGURE 1.2   Decision-making in ESN-M education as suggested by Circular 2/75

are at present unclear, but legally the existing procedures for special educational assessment and placement
remain unchanged until the Section is implemented.   The
major questions which it raised concerned the difference
between ESN children requiring special education, and
'remedial' children in ordinary school, with the training
of staff and the issue of curriculum, and with the future
role of special schools - all of which have been scruti-
nised by the Warnock Committee.   The DES attempted to
assess local authority reactions to the new procedures
suggested in Circular 2/75 and the new SE forms by sending
a circular to local education authorities in June 1977.
One of the aspects they wished for information on, was
whether the 'emphasis on informality', as they described
it, had resulted in any closer involvement of parents in
the assessment process (Department of Education and
Science, 1977).

The manner in which the changing definitions of subnormal but 'educable' children have worked during the
twentieth century, to encompass more and more children,
have not been subject to much scrutiny, either by
academics or practitioners.   One plausible contention,
which deserves more consideration than can be given here,
is Pritchard's (1963) suggestion that as a society
becomes more complex and technological, so the dividing
line between normality and subnormality will be drawn
higher and higher.   It seems eminently reasonable to
assume that the increased numbers put forward and assessed
as suitable for a 'special' rather than a normal education
are a direct result of the twentieth-century demands for
universal literacy and the acquisition of skills which the
more 'backward' children are not able to acquire.
Pritchard's work also embodies the liberal assumption that
provision for the subnormal represents the enlightened
advancement of a civilised society.   Bourdieu's contention - that the economic growth of twentieth century
industrial societies demands 'mass-produced, guaranteed,
interchangeable products' (Bourdieu and Passeron, 1977,
p. 148) - might also be offered as an explanation for an
increasing number of children coming to be excluded from
'normal' education.   It is better for the education
system that children who cannot be 'guaranteed' to gain
some kind of skill or credentials should leave the system
and move into a special (i.e. non-credential awarding)
education.

However, this chapter so far has sought to demonstrate
that there might be yet another explanation.   The changing definitions, classification and statutory provision
have partially been the result of influence by the vested

interest of various professional groups, particularly
medical influence being superseded by education-psycholo-
gical interests in the late 1970s.   The educational
interest represented by normal schools provides a clue to
one actual purpose of the exercise in ESN provision -
normal schools have used the special educational system as
a means of removing children who exhibit learning and
behaviour problems.   Thus, an alternative explanation for
the twentieth-century expansion of the category which
eventually became ESN can be that the smooth development
of the normal education system has required that troublesome children be categorised out in this way.   Children
have increasingly become ESN, less for their intrinsic
qualities, than for their interruption of the smooth
running of the normal system.   This explanation makes
understandable the need to further extend the category to
cover children who are not ESN in the terms of the 1945
regulations but are 'backward', 'remedial' or 'disruptive'
within the normal school system.   After 1945 it quickly
became apparent that the division between ESN and
'remedial' was untenable.   Gulliford, who, with Tansley,
used the term 'slow-learning child' in 1960 noted that
'the line between these ESN children and those who remain
in ordinary schools is not clearly defined and varies
according to local need and provision' (1969, p. 14).

The need to clarify this distinction had become acute
by the 1970s.   While the creation of even larger numbers
of separate special schools had been legitimated from the
1930s by the influence of the Hadow Report (Board of
Education, 1926) and the separation of children according
to 'age, ability and aptitude', by the 1970s, the
'equality thesis' (7) had brought children formerly
selected by 'brightness' back into a common school.
Justice now required that children segregated by dullness
should also be brought back.   However, this suggestion
has posed severe problems for the vested interests within
both normal and special education.   Normal schools, in
order to do their job effectively, need to remove their
troublesome children.   They have traditionally done this
by recourse to special ESN-M education and more recently
by developing withdrawal, guidance and suspension units.
Special education, having developed a whole sub-profession
with a vested interest in retaining its clients is not
anxious to lose its area of competence.   The National
Union of Teachers in particular, having built into its
constitution an advisory committee on special education,
would, in the 1970s, as in the 1930s, 'like to see provision for special education increased rather than diminished' (Devlin, 1977;   Segal, 1974, ch. 14).

Suggestions for overcoming some of these problems are
contained in the Warnock Report, published in 1978
('Special Educational Needs ...', 1978), although to date
neither Section 10 of the 1976 Act nor the Warnock
recommendations have officially been put into practice.

THE REPORT OF THE WARNOCK COMMITTEE, 1978

The Warnock Committee urged the merits of a more positive
approach to special education, aimed at overcoming the
'disability of body and mind' enshrined in the 1944 Act,
and the whole stigma of defect and handicap.   Accordingly
they searched for a new basis for the framework for
special educational provision.   One of the major recommendations of the Committee was that the categories of
handicap laid down by the 1945 Handicapped Pupils Regulations be abolished and the concept of a large number of
children with 'special educational needs' be substituted.
Their estimate of children within the school population
exhibiting, at some point in their school career, these
special educational needs, was one in five, or 20 per cent
of the school population.   Even though this description
is intended to cover all categories of 'handicap' it is a
notable extension of the 1946 guidelines which considered
that 1 per cent of children may be assessed as ESN but
8-9 per cent, less seriously retarded, remain in ordinary
schools.
     Despite the recommendation to abolish the statutory
categories, the Committee noted that 'for the sake of
convenience, descriptive terms will be needed for
particular groups of children who require special educational provision' (paras 3-26).
     Thus, educationally subnormal children are to become
'children with learning difficulties' and this descriptive
category is to be widened to include children who are
currently assessed as ESN, and those at present described
as 'remedial' and remaining in ordinary schools.   At a
stroke, Warnock has removed the fifty-year-old uncertainty
about the difference between ESN children and remedial
children. (8)   Warnock has also taken the view that the
concept of special education 'embraces educational help
for children with emotional or behaviour disorders who
have previously been regarded as disruptive' (paras 3-38).
Thus, thirty years ago, ESN children were not necessarily
to be considered as behaviour problems, now children with
learning difficulty may legitimately be regarded as
behaviour problems.   Further, the Committee note that 'in
some deprived inner-city areas, many schools already

contain a very high proportion of children with mild or moderate learning difficulties or emotional or behavioural disorders' (paras 7-38).

'Children with learning difficulties' are to be divided into mild, moderate, and severe. Children with mild difficulties are those for whom remedial teaching in ordinary schools has been thought appropriate, and 'we see these children as forming the largest portion of all those who ... require special educational provision' (paras 11-49). Children with moderate learning difficulties are to be those currently described as ESN-M, 'the children showing these difficulties constitute the largest group of children at present in special schools and a large proportion of children in many ordinary schools for whom special education is needed'. Children with severe learning difficulties are those currently classed as ESN-S. Although only brought under the Education Services in 1971, the Committee note that the education of these children has been developing in scope and purpose.

The suggested procedure for the discovery and assessment of children with special education needs is illustrated in Figure 1.3.

The suggested Warnock procedure for discovery and assessment of children with special educational needs takes account of all handicapping conditions, but this should not obscure the fact that the great majority of children who are discovered and assessed as having special educational needs will be the old ESN category plus remedial and disruptive children. The Committee does note that 'the difficulties of the large majority of children who are likely to require special educational provision, however, will become apparent for the first time in school, and their needs will therefore have to be identified in that setting.' The school-based states of assessment procedures are suggested as follows: a class teacher who notices that a pupil is 'showing signs of having special educational needs' will consult the head. This is Stage 1 and the head will collect all the information he can about the child. In this task he will be assisted by two types of personal folder which Warnock suggests all schools should keep on all children. The first folder will contain records of the child's school performance, absence, notes on family, diagnostic tests, results, etc. This should be available to parents. A second folder will contain 'the results of professional consultation and sensitive information given in confidence about a child's social background and family relationships'. This will be a confidential folder and access to it will be controlled by the head teacher. At Stage 2

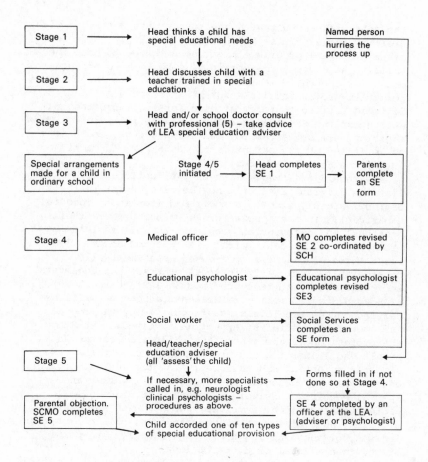

FIGURE 1.3 Decision-making in special education as
suggested by the Warnock Report

the head will consult with the teacher and a teacher with
training and expertise in special education.   At this
stage a special programme might be arranged to help the
child.   At Stage 3 the option will be to make arrangements for the child in the school or to refer the child
for multi-professional assessment at Stage 4 or Stage 5.
If it is decided to refer a child for multi-professional
assessment the SE form procedure will be initiated.   Two
additions are suggested for the SE procedure, an SE form
to be filled out by parents, and an SE form to be filled
out by the Social Services.

At Stage 3 presumably most of the 'children with mild
learning difficulties' will now be catered for in their
ordinary school, either in their old (re-named) remedial
department, or in a special class or unit, where their
emotional and behavioural problems, as well as learning
problems, will be dealt with!   As Warnock notes: 'The
first three stages of school-based assessment allow for
considerable flexibility in local or school arrangements
and would not be suitably defined in law' (paras 4-39).

Beyond Stage 3 multi-professional assessment will be
carried out at two levels, distinguished by the degree
and amount of specialist expertise involved.   At Stage 4
the professionals who assess the child will be the local
people who, under the old procedure, generally saw and
assessed potential ESN children, i.e. the medical officer,
educational psychologist, teacher, social worker and
special education advisory teacher.   At Stage 5 more
professionals will be involved, perhaps with narrower or
different specialisms, i.e. neurologists, clinical psychologists, or those having a wider geographical responsibility than a local or district level.

It seems likely that the old ESN-M category will mainly
stop short at Stage 4, the children with severe physical
and mental handicap being assessed at Stage 5.   However,
in order to keep the procedure as 'educational' as
possible, rather than medical, Warnock suggests that
multi-professional assessment should take place at a
centre within the community other than a hospital.

The Committee single out two groups of children 'for
whom the assessment of special needs will call for
particular sensitivity' - Welsh and Gaelic-speaking
children, and children from ethnic minorities.   In one
paragraph out of 415 pages the Committee deal with the
issue of vital concern to the West Indian community by
noting that: 'Any tendency for educational difficulties
to be assessed without proper reference to a child's
cultural and ethnic background and its effect on his
education can result in a category of handicap becoming
correlated with a particular group in society' (paras 4-51).

They do not think the procedures should be varied for ethnic groups - that as long as the child's cultural background is considered and the parents consulted, assessment will not be viewed with suspicion, but 'as offering the possibility of enhanced educational opportunity for their children'.

At any of the five stages children will be offered one of ten types of special school provision, the first four in ordinary schools:

(i) full-time education in an ordinary class with any necessary help and support;

(ii) education in an ordinary class with periods of withdrawal to a special class or unit;

(iii) education in a special class or unit with periods of attendance at an ordinary class and full involvement in the general community life and extra-curriculum activities of the school;

(iv) full-time education in a special class or unit with social contact with the main school;

(v) education in a special school (day or residential) with some lessons at a neighbouring ordinary school;

(vi) full-time education in a day special school with social contact with an ordinary school;

(vii) full-time education in a residential special school with social contact with an ordinary school;

(viii) short-term education in hospital or other establishment;

(ix) long-term education in the above (viii);

(x) home tuition.

In (iii), education in a special class or unit, the Committee recommend that although there will be difficulties, 'they see scope for making arrangements of this kind for children with a wide range of difficulties and disorders, including emotional and behavoural disorders' (paras 7-12).

Which children, then, does the Warnock Committee envisage will, in the future, be assessed beyond Stage 3 and require special education in special schools?   There are three groups of children identified in paras 6-10.

(i) children with severe or complex physical, sensory or intellectual disabilities who require special facilities, etc., which ordinary schools could not provide.

(ii) children with severe emotional or behavioural disorders whose behaviour is extreme, unpredictable, and may cause severe disruption and inhibit the educational progress of children in ordinary school;

(iii) children with several, less severe disabilities, who are likely to thrive in a more intimate educational setting of a special school.

It might appear, then, that children from the old
'categories' of blind, deaf, physical handicap, epileptic,
plus the children who were 'severely subnormal' from 1971,
plus some of the old category of 'delicate' children and
speech defects, might remain in their existing special
schools and there would be relative unambiguity over which
children fell into group (i).   In group (ii) the old
'maladjusted' type of child, plus ESN-M children with
behavioural and emotional problems will presumably require
special schools, and group (iii) would seem to cover many
of the children at present categorised as ESN-M.

Briefly, then, what does the Warnock Committee consider
an (old) ESN child to be from 1978?

*They consider that he should not be officially classi-
fied with a statutory label, but should, for convenience,
be described as a 'child with learning difficulties'.   As
a CWLD he may have educational problems of a long or short
duration;   he may have emotional or behavioural problems
which may be caused by innate characteristics, the home
environment or school.   He may need 'discovering' at
Stages 1-3 and keeping in ordinary school although perhaps
in a special class or unit;   he may need 'assessing' at
Stages 4-5 and sending to a special school.   No cause
need be established for the educational difficulties, but
in chapter 1 the Warnock Committee are in no doubt as to a
major cause of difficulties:* 'We are fully aware that
many children with educational difficulties may suffer
from familial or wider social deficiencies', and 'show
educational difficulties because they do not obtain from
their families or their social circumstances the quality
of stimulation or the sense of stability which is necessary for proper educational progress.'   Thus, the
familiar connection between low social class and subnormality is once again elaborated in a government report.

A more flexible framework for assessing children's
special educational needs is suggested, which will entail
the production of two more forms to be filled in (6 not 4)
and at least six professionals seeing a child who pro-
gresses to Stage 4, with a necessary close liaison
between medical (including hospital) personnel, schools,
local education offices, social services, child guidance
and psychiatric services, and parents.   Since, in this
present research, it was discovered that under the old,
less flexible procedure, it took two years, on average,
for three professionals to assess a child and fill in
three forms, the suspicion that this more flexible procedure might be somewhat idealistic, is generated.   A
further addition to the flexibility is the notion of a
'Named Person' whose duty it will be to hurry the

procedure along as much as possible.   The Named Person
for children under five will generally be a health
visitor, and for school-children, their head teacher.
    The Warnock Report ('Special Educational Needs ...',
1978), with its emphasis on the future employability of
'handicapped' children, also illustrates the dilemma
noted at the beginning of this chapter - that the economy
needs as many profitable, and as few idle, members of
society as possible.   Chapter 10 notes that: 'the
resources spent on further education and training facilities and support for these young people ... will in the
long term reduce their dependence on the social and health
services and thus the cost to the community of supporting
them' (p. 163).

THE POLITICS OF IQ

The development during the twentieth century of a mental
testing movement has been of enormous importance to the
assessment processes for special education.   IQ has
provided a seemingly objective validation for hierarchi-
cally graded categories of subnormality and for assigning
children to special schools.   Psychologists, in developing, refining and administering mental tests, have come to
influence the selection processes within education which
validate grades of 'dullness', and most textbooks on subnormality (for example, Clarke and Clarke, 1965, p. 11),
describe an ESN child as a child obtaining an IQ score of
between 50 and 70 or 75.
    It is important to trace briefly the way in which IQ
developed as a tool of validation to legitimate the
categorisation of certain children out of normal education, particularly as it is the mastery of this area of
competence that has led educational psychologists to their
current influential position within the decision-making
processes.   The DES Circular 2/75, while recommending
that assessment procedures should move more from medical
to educational domination, does equate 'educational' with
educational-psychological.   It is also important to note
that the historical development of IQ testing has always
taken place within a political context which has assumed
and attempted to validate the 'inferiority' of certain
social classes and races.
    IQ has never existed as a pure 'scientific' concept;
most interpretations of IQ data have demonstrated political overtones and policy implications.   It is suggested
in this study that beliefs about the subnormality of
working-class and black children held by decision-makers

will be affected by the historical development of the IQ concept, and that it is not generally recognised how morally repugnant some of this historical development has been.

IQ tests were used in Europe and America to establish the 'fact' that by and large 'the distribution of I.Q. score conveniently parallels the social order' (Rose, Hambley and Haywood, 1973), and that there are consistent differences between the IQ test scores of black and white children (Jensen, 1969).   Arguments about the supposed genetic endowment between different races and classes have retained considerable importance in discussion about the stratification systems of Western industrial societies.

Since the revived controversy over the genetic compo- nent of 'intelligence' in the 1970s (Block and Dworkin, 1977) many psychologists have claimed that they do not rely solely on test results to recommend ESN schooling, and that they base assessment on a child's current and future educational and social needs, amongst other considerations. (9)   Nevertheless, Presland (1970), listing thirteen factors which he considered an educa- tional psychologist should take into account when recom- mending ESN schooling, placed 'intelligence leve' first, and thirty-six of the forty study population children in this research had been administered an IQ test.

The notion behind psychometric measurements - that important predetermined (by a combination of genetic and environmental influences) qualities are being tested, and that test results carry implications for the future educa- tional placement of a child - is an implicit part of the assessment procedure for special education.   In itself, this belief is unremarkable.   It accords with Binet's beliefs which led him to develop the first intelligence test in 1905.   Intelligence, to Binet, was the ability to 'judge well, comprehend well, to reason well' (1909). The goal of Binet's test was to retain a child in a normal school rather than send him to one of the then newly established French special schools.   Binet never himself considered intelligence to be a fixed quality - but by 1909 he was already complaining of the 'brutal pessimism' of some recent philosophers, who had 'given their moral support to this deplorable verdict'.

In Britain, nineteenth-century beliefs about the innate inferiority of working-class and black people, in terms of intelligence and temperament, were given a spurious res- pectability with the publication of Galton's book, 'Hereditary Genius', in 1889.   Galton believed that the place of each class and race was inevitably determined by heredity.   He regarded emigration to the colonies as a

means of 'cleaning up' England, and was made 'ashamed of
his own species' by the failings of blacks, whom he
described as 'childish, stupid and simpleton-like'.

It was a student of Galton, Cyril Burt, who was
appointed as the first full-time psychologist in England
and Wales, in 1913, and Burt's influence was paramount
both in determining the actual IQ 'score' in grading subnormality, and in continuing to reinforce the notion that
it was the lower social classes who were more likely to be
subnormal.   As a London County Council psychologist,
Burt worked on the problems of mental measurement (1917,
1929, 1921) and was particularly concerned to define the
children who, under the 1921 Education Act, were not
educable defectives, but merely dull and backward.   It
was in concentrating on further educable gradations that
psychologists were able to define an area that was
apparently 'non-medical' and develop their influence.
The publication of Burt's 'Mental and Scholastic Tests'
preceded his appointment to the Wood Committee in 1924.
Dr Lewis, who undertook the investigation on which the
Committee relied heavily in its recommendations, used
tests standardised by Burt, and adopted his 'mental
ratio'. (10)   The Committee's recommendations publicised
the notion of 'mental ratio' or IQ and suggested 'scores'
for subnormality, and these scores have now become part of
the commonsense understandings of many practitioners
(Squibb, 1977).   Thus, the Committee reported that:
'Speaking generally, it may be said that a person with a
mental ratio of between 50 and 70 per cent is probably
feeble-minded' (Board of Education and Board of Control,
1929, part 1, p. 12).

However, in their recommendations for schooling, they
used the term 'retarded' rather than feeble-minded, and
recognised a larger group of 'backward' children whose
mental ratio might reach 85 (p. 144).   While the Wood
Committee noted that financial considerations might
dictate that the 'backward' children remain in ordinary
schools the creation of the ESN category in 1945 was
considered to encompass the two groups.   The 1946 guidelines on special educational treatment mention an IQ score
of between 55 and 70 for ESN day-school children and
recommended that, 'A child with an I.Q. over 75 should
rarely find his way there' (Ministry of Education, 1946,
p. 22).   The suggestion in this pamphlet that ESN
children may also be regarded as retarded by more than
20 per cent of their age also came via the Wood Committee
from Burt's writings. (11)

It was Burt's writing that popularised the notion of IQ

as fixed, innate and constant, and he supported his
hereditarian case with his influential twin studies.
Despite Kamin's (1977) reworking of the twin studies,
which led to the conclusion that 'on analysis the data
are found to contain implausible effects consistent with
an effort to prove the hereditarian case', Burt's
influence on definitions of subnormality cannot now be
cancelled out.   In his influential works on 'The Sub-
Normal Mind' and 'The Backward Child' Burt demonstrated
that his undoubted concern with the welfare of children
was linked with his own elitist beliefs about the lower
social classes and subnormality.   He considered in the
1930s that the (then) certifiable defectives were only a
fringe of a much larger population: 'the portion which is
sometimes termed the social problem class - and includes
the dull, the backward, the unemployed, the habitually
delinquent - in fact all who are sub-normal in whatever
direction' (1935, ch. 3).

He considered that the problem of dealing with this
subnormal group was a momentous question which 'almost
every civilised society must face in the near future'.
Both educable defectives and backward children were to be
tested as to their 'inborn capacity' on intelligence
tests.   Burt was in no doubt that subnormality and
criminals, chronic paupers, and unstable persons, were
closely linked.   He considered that low-grade populations created slums, and that transporting people to an
improved environment would have no effect as they would
soon reproduce their original slum conditions: 'Our own
investigations in London show that town and country alike
are dotted with local centres of dullness and deficiency'
(1935, p. 154).

Burt himself recognised the likelihood that children
from poorer working-class homes were more likely to be
'certified' than children from a 'better' environment, but
he explained this as a poor environment dragging an
already dull child down and he considered that 'stupidity
is not the inevitable result of poverty though poverty is
its commonest concomitant' (1935, p. 124).

Although Burt was consistent in his assumptions that it
was the lower social classes who were defective, and dull,
he never espoused the eugenics movement.   He did, rather,
stress the notion of regression to the mean, to suggest
that intelligence might be improved in families of low
intelligence, rather than cause social degeneration.

However, Burt has been a major academic influence on
decisions currently made about subnormality, and his
persistent linkage of innate low intelligence, social
problems and low social class, form part of a historically

developing popular assumption that it is 'natural' that
the subnormal are likely to be working class. The notion
that race, as well as class, could provide an hereditary
disadvantage, was popularised in Britain by Eysenck, a
pupil of Jensen who, in turn, had studied with Burt.
Eysenck (1971), while being convinced that 'one important
reason for the existence and composition of the lumpen
proletarian may be the genetically determined low intelligence of those who have descended into it', also believes
that genetic factors account for many of the intellectual
test differences observed between racial groups.

In Europe the eugenics movement or 'race-hygiene' as it
came to be called was very strong. Its ideological
foundations can be traced to Calvinistic notions of pre-
destination and in Nietzsche's ideas of a Superman.
During the 1930s sterilisation programmes were directly
related to 'low intelligence', which was measured on tests
which included such questions as 'Compose a sentence out
of the words - war, soldier, fatherland.' The notion
that the inferiority of certain social and racial groups
is responsible for 'social decay' is still propagated in
Germany in the 1970s (Lorenz, 1973).

In America, the influence of eugenicists on intelligence testing was crucial to the whole notion of IQ. The
original Binet tests were imported into America and standardised at Stamford University by Professor Terman - a
supporter of the eugenics movement. Terman's preface to
the 1916 edition of the tests promised that:

> In the near future intelligence tests will bring tens
> of thousands of high-grade defectives under the sur-
> veillance and protection of society. This will
> ultimately result in the curtailing of the reproduction
> of feeble-mindedness and in the elimination of an
> enormous amount of crime, pauperism and industrial
> inefficiency.

Terman's high-grade defectives (70-80 IQ range) were
'very common among Spanish Indians and Mexican families
... and also among negroes ... their dullness seems to be
racial'. He was of the opinion that the whole question
of differences in mental traits should be taken up by new
experimental methods, that is testing procedures, and that
these would reveal: 'enormously significant racial differences in general intelligence ... which cannot be wiped
out by any scheme of mental culture' (1916).

The children with low intelligence were to be segregated into special classes and not allowed to reproduce.
His subsequent writings on the 'menace of feeble-mindedness' and methods to 'curtail the increasing spawn of

degeneracy' are reminiscent of the 1930s Nazi propaganda.
It is worth noting here that almost every child tested in
this present study was administered the Stanford-Binet
test, sometimes known as the Terman-Merrill.   Associa-
tions between feeble-mindedness, pauperism, crime and the
working class are evident in the work of other early users
of the Binet tests in America.   Goddard, famous for his
'Kallikak' family study, argued cogently that social
equality could never exist because of the proven wide
range of mental capacity.   As Kamin (1977) has pointed
out, to Goddard the feeble-minded, paupers, labourers in
hobels, and unemployed coal miners were scarcely disting-
uishable.   Professor Yerkes, who worked with Terman and
Goddard on the army intelligence tests of the First World
War, was of the opinion that economic status and feeble-
mindedness were related.   'A true diagnosis of feeble-
mindedness should never be made on the basis of I.Q. alone
... we must inquire further into the subject's economic
status' (Yerkes and Foster, 1923).

At the time of writing Yerkes was chairman of the
committee on the inheritance of mental traits, of the
Eugenics Research Association.   The notion that feeble-
mindedness, morally defective behaviour, social dependency
and a variety of social problems were attributable to
genetic inheritance was strong enough, in early
twentieth-century America, to support the passage of
sterilisation laws through seventeen State legislatures,
prompted by such early 'scientific studies' as Dr Flood's
reports on 'The therapeutic castration of twenty-six
Massachusetts male children'.   A Bill put to the Michigan
State Assembly provided for the castration of criminals
convicted for a third time.   The rise of the mental
testing movement at this time convinced some legislators
that 'science' would be able to decide which orphans,
paupers, and criminals might be prevented from reproduction in order to create the kind of society that Terman
(1916) envisaged at Stanford: 'If we could preserve our
State for a class of people worthy to possess it, we must
prevent, as far as possible, the propagation of mental
degenerates.'

Early American mental tests were also used to promote
the passage of immigration laws based on the assumption
that immigrants from south-eastern Europe were genetically
inferior to those from north-west Europe, and to rationalise the inferiority of black Americans, since the First
World War tests had supposedly demonstrated that blacks
consistently scored lower on IQ tests than whites.

Brigham, Psychology Professor at Princeton, re-analysed
the army data on immigrant intelligence, and worked out

that as the proportion of Nordic blood decreased and
Alpine and Mediterranean blood increased, so the intelligence of immigrants decreased.   He considered that the
Nordics were: 'rulers, organisers, aristocrats, and
usually Protestants ... the Alpine is the perfect slave',
and that 'the decline of American intelligence will be
more rapid, owing to the presence here of the negro'
(1923).

He recommended that immigration to the USA should be
carefully selective.   An Appendix to the House of Representatives' Committee's report on 'Immigration and
Naturalization' in 1923 illustrated the prevailing acceptance that mental tests could be used to determine who was
socially and morally, as well as intellectually, superior.
The Slav and Latin races were linked in this appendix to
pauperism, crime, sex offences and dependency, and the
opinion was expressed that: 'We must protect ourselves
against the degenerate horde ... we must apply ourselves
to the task with the new weapons of science....   It is
now as easy to calculate one's mental equipment as it is
to measure height and weight.'   Also in 1923, a study by
a Professor Pintner on 'Italians in America' noted that
the median IQ for Italians was sixteen points below that
of the average American IQ.   No suggestion followed this
study, that Italian 'IQ genes' were inferior.   However,
in a resurgence in the late 1960s of 'scientific' attempts
to prove certain groups mentally inferior, the suggestion
was made that because blacks consistently score fifteen
points below the average white population, this finding
might have some genetic significance.   In his much
publicised article in the 'Harvard Educational Review'
(1969), Jensen commented that: 'No one has yet produced
any evidence based on a properly controlled study to show
that representative samples of negro and white children
can be equalised in intellectual ability through statistical control of environment and education.'

The 'Harvard Review' article produced a vigorous
debate, particularly when Jensen's view were supported and
elaborated by Professors Hernstein and Shockley (Hernstein, 1973; Shockley, 1971).   The Society for the
Psychological Study of Social Issues criticised Jensen's
views and claimed that there was also no evidence to
support the view that there is an innate difference
between members of different racial groups.   This view
endorsed the four UNESCO statements issued between 1947
and 1964 that: 'Available scientific knowledge provides
no base for believing that groups of mankind differ in
their innate capacity for intellectual and emotional
development' (UNESCO, 1951).

Jensen published the article again together with
defence of his views in 'Genetics and Education' in 1972,
but in 1973 made his views on 'Educability and Group
Differences' more clearly articulated.   He argued that
race and social class differences are more social than
'scientific' problems, but that scientific knowledge, that
is, mental testing, should be brought to bear upon understanding group differences.   He noted that mental retardation tends to become concentrated 'in particular
families, neighbourhoods, and communities, and a whole
class of problems arise from the sheer fact of the concentration itself'.   He worried that the social concentration of a low level of intelligence might create a
'substantial source of population variance in I.Q.', much
the same worry that Professor Terman had voiced earlier in
the century over 'degeneracy'.   Jensen is also sure that
'social classes are breeding populations differing in gene
frequencies, especially for genetic factors related to
ability' and was as doubtful that low social class IQs
could be raised by compensatory education programmes as he
was that black IQs could be thus raised.

His book is devoted to essays rebutting arguments that
inequality of schooling, teacher expectations, language
deprivation, culture-biased tests, or even a poor physical
environment have much to do with lower IQ and professed to
be worried about the 'massive expenditure of limited
resources on misguided, irrelevant and ineffective
remedies' of trying to make social and racial groups more
equal in test and academic performance.

Part of the refinement of mental measuring techniques
has included a recognition that tests which were a product
of a particular culture, and are standardised on particular social or racial groups, could not be culture-free or
culture-fair.   Anastasi and Foley noted in 1949 that
'intelligence tests measure certain abilities required for
success in the particular culture in which they were
developed.'   Vernon's (1969) work described in some
detail attempts to develop tests applicable to non-Western
cultures.   He considered it particularly important to
develop culture-fair tests, since 'cross-cultural comparisons are unavoidable when members of different cultural
groups ... are in competition for the same schooling or
jobs' (p. 229).   Nevertheless, he concluded that even the
use of non-verbal tests, such as Progressive Matrices or
Kohs blocks, are not effective in demonstrating factors
which underly any deficiency or superiority in any particular ability.   He argued for the need to develop locally
constructed tests within non-Western cultures.   Against
this, the argument has developed that sub-tests would

serve no useful purpose as it is impossible to distinguish between innate and learned skills (Block and Dworkin, 1977).   In the USA the application of 'Western' tests to black people for vocational selection purposes was ruled illegal after the 1964 Civil Rights Act, and in 1971 six black children brought a case against the California Department of Education, claiming that they had been assigned to special classes for the educationally mentally retarded on the basis of culturally and racially biased IQ tests.   A temporary injunction was issued in 1975 barring the use of IQ tests for EMR placement in San Francisco ('Times Educational Supplement', 20 October 1978).

In England and Wales the question of culture-fair testing was raised during the late 1960s largely in connection with the over-referral and placement of 'immigrant' children in ESN schools.   The DES recorded (1971a) that although 'the great majority of immigrant pupils in the ESN special schools of one authority registered IQs (on the Stanford-Binet test) of 80 or below ... these results were not representative of their true ability', and doubted whether it was worth pursuing attempts to measure innate potential.   On the basis of evidence provided by Vernon, the DES noted that no test could be culture-fair or decisive, but that verbal and non-verbal tests should continue to be used to provide 'useful clues to areas of disadvantage'.   Vernon particularly mentioned the Terman-Merrill and Weschler Intelligence Scale for Children tests as suitable.   Despite complaints from the West Indian community (documented below), the children of immigrant parentage have continued to be tested on tests standardised on white 'Western' children.   The Assessment of Performance Unit at the Department of Education and Science has not openly pursued the development of culture-fair testing, although the National Foundation Educational Research were commissioned to review the possibilities.   Hegarty and Lucas (1979), in carrying out this commission to 'pursue culture-fair assessment' suggest that tests based on the notion of learning ability, would seem more promising than tests of 'intelligence' and have produced test materials aimed at providing detailed assessment of children's learning ability, to be administered by psychologists, and teachers.

The history of the use to which mental testing and the IQ concept has been put does tend to conflict with the humanistic belief that psychometric testing is helpful and necessary.   Teachers in Britain tend to stress environmental explanations for the under-performance of some social and racial groups in schools, but there seem to be

underlying beliefs about the genetic potential of the
groups.   For example, Brittan, in 1976, reported that
teachers in her sample perceived West Indian children as
being of low ability partly because of 'innate characteristics'.
   A sociological account of the use of psychometric
measurement must point out that the claim that mental
testing constitutes 'objective science' rests on dubious
foundations.   The historical development of testing would
suggest that the procedures have been used to rationalise
sets of beliefs about the inferiority of lower social
class and black people.   Rex pointed out in 1972 that an
analogy to Jensen's claims would be to transport a group
of white Americans to West Africa, enslave them for 200
years, then administer tests standardised on West Africans
and compare the results.   This illustrates the inherent
absurdity of purporting to measure intellectual differences as though 'other things were equal' in the social
world.

WEST INDIAN CHILDREN AND EDUCATIONAL SUBNORMALITY

The final section of this chapter documents the concern
which began to be expressed from the mid-1960s that West
Indian children were being disproportionately assessed as
educationally subnormal and sent to special schools, and
discusses the significance of this issue.   Appendix
2 to this chapter illustrates the 'over-placement'.   In
order to discuss the 'over-placement' of West Indian
children it is necessary here to suspend investigation
into the nature of the category ESN-M and accept it as
given, but to remember that it is a stigmatised 'undesirable' category to be placed in.
   The large number of immigrant children (12) who were
being admitted to special schools was first officially
noted in a 1966 Inner London Education Authority report.
In September of that year the percentage of immigrant
children in ILEA ESN day-schools was 23.3 per cent compared to 13.2 per cent in the authority's primary and
secondary schools.   The 'immigrant' children were largely
of West Indian origin.   By September 1967 the proportion
had risen to 28.4 per cent.   The ILEA undertook a survey
of twenty-two ESN schools in May 1967, asking head
teachers about the language difficulties, intelligence,
attainment and social behaviour of their pupils, and also
about the apparent misplacing of pupils.   The result of
this survey was presented in a further ILEA report (1967).
This report noted that the schools felt that a misplace-

ment was four times more likely in the case of immigrant
children and that the methods and processes of ascertainment were the major reasons for this misplacement.   The
special schools also felt that many of the pupils were
referred to them primarily for behavioural, rather than
educational, reasons.   The report concluded with some
recommendations for alternative, more suitable, provision
for immigrant children, but that until this could be found
ESN schools must continue to provide for 'even those
(children) of relatively high I.Q.'   This was an internal
ILEA report, but copies were circulated.   The failure to
make the report public contributed to West Indian anxiety
that their children were not being fairly treated and in
1969 the North London West Indian Association met the
chairman of Haringey Local Education Authority to discuss
the issue.   In January 1970 the NLWIA lodged a complaint
of racial discrimination with the Race Relations Board.
The Board reported in 1971 that there was no evidence of
an 'unlawful act', but suggested that the intelligence
tests used did not effectively distinguish the ESN from
those who were 'educationally deprived'.   During the year
1971 the Race Relations Board suggested that the DES
should discuss the ESN issue with the Community Relations
Commission, as they had noted that Townsend and Brittan's
(1971) recent research had documented an over-representation of West Indian children in ESN schools on a national
level.   In their 1972 report the Board noted that the DES
had promised fresh guidance to local authorities on the
ESN issue.

A Caribbean Education Association, later the Caribbean
Education and Community Workers' Association, had been
formed in 1970, and a conference held in August that year.
At this conference Bernard Coard spoke on the problems of
West Indian children in ESN schools, and re-drafted this
paper to be published as 'How the West Indian Child is
made Educationally Sub-normal in the British School
System' (1971).   Coard's polemical paper received a good
deal of publicity.   He suggested that cultural bias and
low teacher expectations resulted in the referral of
larger numbers of children as possibly ESN than was war-
ranted, and that the IQ tests used contained built-in
cultural and class bias.   He also pointed to the low
self-esteem and self-image that black children acquire in
a hostile white society.   Coard suggested that no immigrant child should be placed in an ESN school without at
least two years' education in a 'normal' British school.

The West Indian concern over the placement of West
Indian children continued to be voiced in the 1970s,
through the columns of the monthly journal 'Race Today',

and in evidence to the Government Select Committee on Race
and Immigration.   Barbar Omar published a short article
in the journal 'Race Today', which points out the permanent stigma that is attached to being 'labelled for life'
as ESN.   In 1973 a Birmingham special school head teacher
contributed to the journal's on-going interest in the ESN
issue by arguing that special schools could help West
Indian children, and that migration experiences, family
instability, child-minding, and possibly genetic 'anomalies' contributed to their failure.   This article was
bitterly attacked the following month by two black writers
who accused the head of 'pseudo-scientific formulation
based on popular and racist genetics'. (13)   In February
1974 an article on 'The Black Explosion in Schools'
pointed out that the issue of 'too many' black children in
ESN schools had become the battleground for a more general
controversy over the failure of the school system to
incorporate and educate West Indian children (Dhondy,
1974).

This article criticised both the genetic explanations
offered for poor black and working-class school performance, and the liberal ideology of deprivation, and
pointed out that other historical factors are at work in
the process of separating out 'clever and stupid, educable
and ineducable'.

By August 1975 a black parents' movement had been set
up in London, and a further article in 'Race Today', on
The Black education movement and the struggle for power
(Who's educating who ..., 1975) argued that the ESN issue
had been instrumental in demonstrating to black parents
that it was the schools, and not their children, who were
responsible for under-achievement and lack of progress,
and that black parents were now concerned to marshall
expertise which would be concerned with the educational
problem of the black child through the formation of a
national association.   By 1977 the West Indian Standing
Conference was asking the DES for permission to set up
separate black schools, as distinct from the black supple-
mentary schools which have been organised around the
country since 1970.   The black pressure group which has
emerged around the ESN issue overstates its case, as
pressure groups are bound to do - an editorial in 'West
Indian World' (September/October 1977) claimed that in
ESN schools West Indian children outnumbered all other
children 'five to one' and asked 'who is responsible for
steering our children down the bottomless pit of educational oblivion?'   In fact, DES statistics in 1971 indicated that West Indian children outnumbered other immigrant children four to one.   Asian children have always

been notably under-represented in ESN schools in proportion to their numbers in the total school population.
   The evidence to the Select Committee on Race and
Immigration for their 1973 report on 'Education' and the
1976 report on the 'West Indian Community' also indicated
the extent of the West Indian Community's anxiety about
the classification of their children as ESN and their
determination to alter the situation.   Evidence from the
Caribbean Educationalists and Community Workers noted in
1973 that 'many [West Indian children] are packed off to
ESN schools on the basis of very inadequate assessment
procedures.   Very little consultation between the parent
and the authorities takes place.   Many parents are given
inaccurate information as to the nature and purpose of ESN
schools.   Many children are wrongly assessed and are sent
for reasons other than educational subnormality' (Select
Committee on Race Relations and Immigration, 1973, vol. 3,
p. 824).   The evidence went on to describe ESN schools as
'educational dustbins' and to demand a change in the
assessment system.   Evidence by Ealing Community Relations Committee noted the large number of West Indian
children assigned to ESN schools and low 'streams in
normal schools' and concluded 'this relegation is fraught
with social and racial dangers for which the present
educational system must share much of the blame' (1973,
vol. 2, p. 374).   A memo from the Brent Education
Committee to the Select Committee noted the authority's
concern with the high proportion of children in ESN
schools (vol. 2, p. 232).   This memo was, interestingly,
attacked by Mr Butta, a West Indian, in a further memo to
the Committee.   He argued that he expected working-class
children to be disproportionately represented in ESN
schools, and since West Indian children were mainly from
working-class homes and from an 'inferior' school situation in the West Indies, he was not surprised to find West
Indian children thus classified (vol. 3, p. 849).
   Sixteen official bodies gave evidence about ESN classification to the Committee for the 1973 report, indicating
the extent of concern over the issue.   The DES evidence
defended the over-representation of West Indian children
on the grounds that the definitions of ESN took account of
'other factors beside innate limitations of the mind'.
The secretary of state for education, then Mrs Thatcher,
argued in her evidence that 'We have probably not yet got
the right method of assessing their abilities, bearing in
mind the background from which they come' (vol. 3, p.
647). (14)   The 1973 report based its understanding of
numbers of West Indian children in all special schools on
the figures for January 1971.   At that time 5,500 immi-

grant children, of whom 3,850 were West Indian, were in
all special schools.   In November 1973 the DES sent a
letter to all chief education officers on 'the educational
arrangements of immigrant children who may need special
education'.   An appendix attached to this gave the
figures for January 1972 as shown in Table 1.2.   This
letter attempted some explanation of the high proportion
of West Indian children sent to ESN schools, and
mentioned dialect English, and teachers who cannot cope
with the learning problems and disciplining of these
children in normal schools, as possible causes.   This
letter specifically rejects the suggestion made by Bernard
Coard - that no child should be placed in an ESN school
unless he has had two years' normal schooling in England -
and instead suggests annual reviews of the placement of
immigrant children, with a 'new test of intelligence'
being administered by an educational psychologist in
uncertain cases.

By 1976 nine official bodies had given evidence to the
Select Committee on Race and Immigration, on the ESN
issue, for a report on 'The West Indian Community'.   The
Committee noted in this report that: 'It was clear that
the West Indian community is disturbed by the under-
achievement of West Indian children at school and continues to be seriously disturbed by the high proportion of
West Indian children in ESN schools' (1976-7, vol. 1).

They noted a witness from the West Indian Standing
Conference who reported that 'this was one of the very
bitter areas'.   The DES gave evidence to the Committee
that there was tending to be a decrease in the number of
West Indian children sent to ESN special schools, particularly at the lower end, and that several authorities now
make no attempt to place children if the parents object.
However, they were unable to back this statement with
evidence as the collection of official statistics had
ceased in 1973.   The Committee recommended in the final
report that: 'Statistics of children of West Indian
origin attending ESN schools be obtained, published, and
carefully monitored' (1976-7, vol. 1).

The two major points which emerge out of the above
documentation are, first, the West Indian community has
emerged as a significant pressure group, the first in the
history of ESN classification, to question the actual
category of 'ESN' and the 'right' of education authorities
to place their children in ESN schools.   Second, for the
West Indian community the ESN issue has taken on a symbolic function, in that it symbolises the general under-
achievement of West Indian children in the English educational system.

TABLE 1.2 Numbers of immigrants in special schools in January 1972 (England and Wales)

	All children	Non-immigrant children	All immigrants children	West Indians	Indians	Pakistanis
Maintained primary and secondary schools and all special schools	8,486,629	8,206,757	279,872	101,898	56,193	30,620
All special schools	122,283	115,628	6,655	4,397	658	443
Special schools for ESN-M	60,045 (0.7%)	56,139 (0.68%)	3,906 (1.3%)	2,972 (2.9%)	284 (0.5%)	169 (0.5%)

Note   1972 West Indians are 76 per cent of all immigrant children in ESN schools and 5 per cent of all children in ESN schools

1972 Immigrant children constituted 2.4 per cent of the total school population.

Source Adapted from DES table, in letter to chief education officers, November 1973

The actual number of West Indian children in ESN-M
schools in 1977 is probably under 3,500, and there is
certainly some evidence both from other research
(Saunders, 1973) and from this study that some West Indian
parents regard the special school as being helpful to
their children.   But the general concern with the poor
performance and under-achievement of West Indian children
generally has been closely connected with the ESN issue.
Evidence from Brent West Indian Standing Committee encapsulated this point in the statement to the Select
Committee:

> Do not go away with the impression that our major
> interest is with the ESN schools.   We are concerned
> about them, but we are concerned more with the point
> that the majority of youngsters who have been to the
> so-called normal schools come out having achieved as
> little on the academic side as the children who went to
> the ESN schools. (1976-7, p. 135)

The arrival of black children of colonial origin into
British urban schools and an education system dominated by
a white elitist ethos posed problems both for the children
and for the system.   Over the past fifteen years racial
discrimination and a growing popular racism have made it
difficult to promote a liberal ideology wherein all
children are treated equally.   The media publicity given
to the writings of Jensen and Eysenck, and a consequent
resurgence of genetic explanations for the poorer educational performance of black children, have contributed to
West Indian anxiety that their children were destined,
through educational failure, to inferior status and
employment.   The rejection of paternalism and a growing
militancy amongst some sections of the West Indian Community focused on the education issue, and particularly on
the ESN issue, as an area of direct confrontation in which
pressure group opinion could be mobilised.   The evidence
given by black groups and individuals, and by some white
groups, suggests that their understanding of how children
are assessed and classified as ESN was, not surprisingly,
uninformed.   The West Indians' case is based on the sup-
position that ESN schools are for children of low innate
intelligence, that IQ tests are not suitable for testing
black children, and that teachers' expectations in normal
schools work against black children.   The Department of
Education and Science could validly make the point that
definitions of ESN were not solely concerned with low
intelligence or IQ testing, but with 'other factors'.   As
the history of the concept ESN demonstrates, the authorities, given the confusion over 'other factors', could not
be accused of misplacing any particular group of children.

If black children were sent to ESN schools with high IQs
or because they posed discipline problems for ordinary
teachers, rather than on any educational need, the
authorities were, on the basis of the definitions, quite
within their rights. / Since the West Indian community, as
a pressure group, have begun to demand more clarity over
the criteria for ESN school placement, they do constitute
a historical 'event' in the saga of subnormality, in that
they are the first group to organise to protest about
definitions and classifications, whereas previous parental
protest has been on an isolated individual level.

APPENDIX 1 STATISTICS OF ESN PUPILS 1950-76

Full-time pupils in ESN schools ESN-Mild (medium)			Attending ESN class in normal school	
Girls	Boys	Total		Total
1950	5,968	9,205	15,173		
1955	9,011	13,633	22,644		
1960	13,175	19,640	32,815		
1965	17,099	25,571	42,670		
19 9	19,598	30,333	49,931		
1971	20,847	31,996	52,843		
1972	-	-	60,045		
1974	21,284	32,096	53,353	9,851	63,204
1975	21,017	31,727	52,744	11,117	63,861
1976	21,173	32,599	53,772	13,064	66,838

Source   DES, 'Statistics', vol. 1, 'Schools 1974-76',
         HMSO.

Notes
  1 These figures exclude ESN children awaiting placement,
in independent schools, receiving education other than at
school.
  2 In the DES statistics for 1972-3, totals for ESN
pupils were not sub-divided into ESN-M and ESN-S.
  3 In the twelve months up to January 1976 a survey of
special educational provision in maintained primary and
secondary schools was undertaken.   Special classes in
ordinary schools were attended by 21,000 'handicapped
pupils' of whom almost two-thirds were ESN.

APPENDIX 2

Total numbers of children in maintained primary and
secondary schools and total number of children in ESN
schools/classes

	'Normal' school (1)	ESN school/ classes (2)	(2) as a % of (1)
1968	8,190,745	48,818	0.59
1969	8,391,756	49,931	0.59
1970	8,597,451	51,768	0.60
1971	8,800,843	52,843	0.60
1972	9,032,999	(60,045)	0.66
1974	9,560,060	53,353	0.55
1975	9,617,474	52,744	0.54
1976	9,669,000	53,772	0.55

Total numbers of West Indian children in maintained
primary and secondary schools and total number of West
Indian children in ESN schools/classes

	'Normal' school (1)	ESN school/ classes (2)	(2) as a % of (1)
1968	89,988	-	-
1969	106,126	-	-
1970	109,963	2,551	2.3
1971	107,136	2,896	2.7
1972	101,898	2,972	2.9

Source   Adapted from DES, 'Statistics in Education',
         1969-76, vol. 1, 'Schools', and letter to chief
         education officers, November 1973.

In 1972 West Indian children constituted 1.1 per cent
of all children in maintained primary and secondary
schools but constituted 4.9 per cent of all children in
ESN-M schools.

It will be seen from the available statistics - 1970-2
- that while the total number of children in ESN-M
schools constituted less than 1 per cent of the total
population in maintained primary and secondary schools,
around 0.6 per cent in fact, the percentage of West
Indian children in ESN-M schools rose from 2.3 per cent
to 2.9 per cent, 1970-2, as a percentage of the total
numbers of West Indian children in maintained primary and
secondary schools.

These statistics were based on the DES formula that

West Indian children were 'immigrant' and an immigrant
pupil was defined as:
(i) a child born outside the British Isles to parents
whose country or origin is abroad, and
(ii) children born in the British Isles whose parents have
lived here for less than ten years.

The collection of statistics was officially discon-
tinued in 1972, and there is no published information on
numbers of children of West Indian parentage in British
schools.

Any further statistical information must consist of
speculation based on unofficial estimates by individual
local education authorities.   The DES has recently
ventured the opinion that the numbers of West Indian
children referred, assessed, and placed in ESN schools is
decreasing;   this information may be because some
authorities, e.g. Brent, now do not place children at all
if there is a parental objection, but it is not known how
accurate this is.   There was some speculation that
numbers in ESN schools as a whole were falling, but the
numbers for 1974-6 can hardly be described as a 'trend'
in this direction.

Estimates of the number of children of West Indian
parentage in schools currently vary between 125,000 and
150,000.   However, if the number of West Indian children
is assumed to be 150,000, and the number in ESN-M schools
is assumed only to have risen in four years by 28 to
3,000, this is still 2 per cent of West Indian children
in ESN-M schools as compared with 0.5 per cent of
children from the total school population in ESN-M
schools.

In addition, the figure for 1972 shows that 4.9 per
cent of all children in ESN schools were of West Indian
origin whereas they constituted only 1.1 per cent of the
total school population.   In 1972 there were still, in
effect, over four times as many West Indian children in
ESN-M schools as there 'ought' to have been.   There
'ought' to have been no more than 600 children, if they
were not to have been over-represented.   (This would be
a proportionate 1 per cent to their 1 per cent in the
total school population.)

APPENDIX 3   CHRONOLOGY OF EVENTS CONCERNING SUBNORMALITY
1870-1977

1869   Charity Organisation set up.   Sir Charles Trevelyan
       a member.
1870   Elementary Education Act established compulsory

primary education.   Robert Lowe's 'revised code'
was in operation.   Children had to pass through 6
'standards'.

1875   Trevelyan first used the term 'feeble-minded'.

1886   Idiots Act distinguishes between lunatics, idiots
and imbeciles.

1888   Dr Shuttleworth's paper on The education of children
of abnormally weak mental capacity, 'Journal of
Mental Science', vol. 34 - appeal for special
schools to be set up for these children.

1889   The Royal Commission on the Blind, Deaf and Dumb
included feeble-minded children in its brief.

1890   London School Board prepare a scheme for special
schools and special classes in ordinary schools.

1892   First special class opened in Leicester.

1893   Charity Organisation reported on 'The feeble-minded
child and adult' and pressed for special schools.

1895   London opened first special class and special
school.

1896   National Association for promoting the welfare of
the feeble-minded set up.

1896   Committee on Defective and Epileptic children
distinguished the feeble-minded as candidates for
special schools.

1898   Committee on Defective and Epileptic children reported.   Medical officers were to be responsible for
admission to special schools although head teachers
and inspectors were to be consulted.   Children
would be 'selected' by teachers for a medical examination which parents could attend.   The term
'mental defective' was introduced.

1898   Dr Eichholz appointed to Board of Education.   He
suggested classifying children into three groups -
imbeciles and depraved, handicapped and epileptic,
backward.

1899   Elementary Education (Defective and Epileptic
Children) Act.   School Boards enabled to make provision for defective children.

1904   Royal Commission on the Care and Control of the
feeble-minded set up.

1908   Royal Commission suggested that special schools
should come under the Board of Control rather than
the Board of Education, and that local Mental
Deficiency Committees should provide manual training
for the feeble-minded.

1913   12,000 'defective' children in 177 schools.   175
Education Authorities had made some provision.

1913   Cyril Burt appointed by London County Council as
their first psychologist.

1913   Mental Deficiency Act.   Education authorities given
the duty of ascertaining which children aged 7-16
were defective.
1914   Elementary Education (Defective and Epileptic
Children) Act.   Authorities required to make provision for their defective children.
1914   13,563 children in special schools.
1921   Education Act.
1924   Wood Committee set up.   Joint Departmental
Committee on Mental Deficiency.
1926   First Child Guidance Clinic opened in London.
1927   Mental Deficiency Act.
1929   Wood Committee reported - recommended that a larger
group - the retarded - should be catered for with
defective children in a new type of 'special' elementary school.
1939   17,000 children in special schools.
1944   Education Act - laid duty of securing provision for
pupils suffering from a disability of mind or body
on LEA.
1945   Handicapped pupils and school health service regulations laid down eleven categories of handicap
(modified in 1953, 1959 and 1962).   HP forms introduced.   ESN category introduced.
1946   'Special Educational Treatment', Ministry of Education Pamphlet no. 5, defines ESN children on educational criteria.
1956   'Education of the Handicapped Pupil 1945-55',
Education Pamphlet no. 30.
1961   Circular 11/61.   'Special Educational Treatment for
Educationally Sub-normal Pupils', Ministry of
Education.
1964   'Slow Learners at School', Education Pamphlet no.
46, DES.
1965   'Special Education To-day', Report on Education no.
23, DES.
1968   Summerfield Report, 'Psychologists in the Education
Services', DES.
1969   Circular 15/69.   Special schools.
1970   Circular 15/70.   The Education (Handicapped
Childrens) Act.
1970   Education (Handicapped Childrens) Act.
1971   Report on Education no. 69, 'The Last to Come In'.
1970-1 Race Relations Board investigates Haringey LEA as to
the number of West Indian children ascertained as
ESN.
1971   Bernard Coard's essay published, 'How the West
Indian child is made educationally sub-normal in the
British school system'.

1971   'The Education of Immigrants', DES Education Survey
       13 includes a chapter on immigrants and special
       education.

1973   'Special Education - A Fresh Look', Report on Educa-
       tion no. 77, DES.

1973   'Education', Report of the Select Committee on Race
       Relations and Immigration.   Sixteen official bodies
       gave evidence on immigrant children in ESN schools.

1973   Circular 4/73.   Staffing of special schools and
       classes.

1973   November - letter to chief education officers on the
       educational arrangements for immigrant children who
       may need special education.

1973   Warnock Committee set up to report on handicapped
       children.

1974   DES, 'Educational Disadvantage and the Needs of
       Immigrants', cmd 5720, recommendation 19 - that an
       enquiry be set up to look into the number of West
       Indian children in special schools.

1975   Circular 2/75.   A fresh look at 'The Discovery of
       Children Requiring Special Education and the Assess-
       ment of their Needs'.

1975   HP forms replaced by SE forms (non-statutory).

1976   Education Bill - provides a substitution for Section
       33(2) of the 1944 Act and lays duty of LEA to pro-
       vide special education in normal schools unless it
       is impracticable.

1977   Letter to chief education officers asking for
       comments on SE forms.

1978   April - Warnock Committee reports.

2 Methodology, local authority and children

The choice of a methodology for a sociological study is
inevitably bound up with the nature of the problem which
the researcher has chosen to work on.   Although sociology
can now draw upon two paradigms - the positivistic and the
phenomenological (Kuhn, 1962), and the variety of methodologies which have become 'permissible' as a result of
advances within the sociology of science and the sociology
of knowledge, the need to explain why particular methodologies were, or were not, adopted is still important.
However, it was clear at the outset that the classical
research process described in many text books (for
example, Lazarsfeld and Rosenberg, 1955), outlining an
ideal-typical situation in the physical sciences, (from
theory to operationalised hypothesis to data collection to
logical deduction to disprove or not disprove the hypothesis) would not be applicable to this particular study.
The researcher was anxious to avoid a charge succinctly
made by Glaser and Strauss (1967).   'So often in journals
we read a highly empirical study which at its conclusion
has a tacked on explanation from a logically deduced
theory.'
  This study is a highly empirical study.   It starts
with a problem and a set of questions, and uses selected
sociological concepts and methods to illuminate the
problem.   It has attempted to adapt a particular method
(semi-structured interviewing) so that intuitive rather
than deductive statements can be made, that is, the method
of collecting data should provide some immediate insight
into the problem.   In a sense, the method is the study.
As Baldamus (1977, p. 27) has noted: 'The interlocking
between methodological inventions and discovered facts is
in sociology closer than in any other social or physical
science.'   The choice of methodology was influenced by
Denzin's (1970) view that it is the empirical world which

sets the tone, shapes the theories and indicates the uses
to be made of research. It is the empirical world which
provides the ultimate evaluation of the research act.
If researchers are unsuccessful in their attempts to
explain the nature of the social world, their work is,
sociologically speaking, a failure.

The problem in this study appeared to be the dynamic
one of how complex industrial societies deal with that
section of their population which comes to be called subnormal, and more especially, with the increasing numbers
of mildly subnormal who find difficulty in coping with the
educational, technological, and social demands made on
them, but who are usually able to function at an economic
level that is beneficial to the society. (1)   The treatment of the subnormal is a public problem, the bureaucratic machinery which must be developed to identify,
educate, train, and employ, subnormal people is a policy
problem, and the beliefs and subsequent actions of the
policy-makers about subnormal people is a sociological
problem.   If justification for this statement is
required, actions resulting from norms, values, and
beliefs, are the legitimate subject matter of sociologists
which add to the cumulative knowledge about the social
world which sociologists are building up (Baldamus, 1977).

The questions in this study took the form of immediate
'practical curiosity' in an area where answers appeared to
be confused or nonexistent.   Who defined a mildly educationally subnormal child?   What criteria for definitions
and classifications were used?   What were the perceptions
and beliefs of the people who had power to classify?
Were the procedures official and rigid or 'ad hoc' and
intuitive?

Previous research on educational decision-makers has
taken the form of descriptive analytic case studies of
specific groups, usually set within an historical context (for example, Birley, 1970; Lee, 1963; Fowler et
al., 1973), but few studies have followed through a
specific educational process wherein the decisions of
several professionals were required.   The two studies
which eventually influenced the methodology of this study
were first Kogan's studies (1971; Kogan and Van der
Eyken, 1973) of the perceptions of five decision-makers,
in which the subtleties of the management of educational
decisions, the exercise of power, and the discretionary
negotiations which form part of educational decision-
making, were examined through tape-recorded interviews.
The second study was Cicourel's study of the 'Educational
Decision-Makers', whose 'advice' and 'guidance' determined
whether students at high school should go on to college or

not (Cicourel and Kitsuse, 1963).   Cicourel's method was
to interview (tape-recording and using a semi-structured
questionnaire) three groups involved in the process
(students, parents and councillors) and to illustrate, by
analysis of the interviews, the management of decisions,
which included persuading some students that they were not
suitable for college.   There seemed a suitable analogy
between this process and the special educational process,
part of which involves persuading parents that they have
subnormal children.

After some unstructured interviewing of professional
people involved in the ascertainment of ESN-M children,
it was decided that the methodology of the study should
take the form of interviewing, using semi-structured
schedules, all the professional personnel who were involved in making decisions on a specific group of children as
they passed from normal to special education.   Interview
schedules were prepared, the first four cases studied were
treated as pilot cases, and the interview schedules
amended.   Two of these were subsequently included in the
study.   Tape-recording was attempted with preliminary
interviews, but abandoned in favour of shorthand recording
of replies.   Head teachers, educational psychologists,
medical officers, heads of special schools, and the
parents of the children were to be interviewed, as these
were the people mainly involved in the decision-making
processes of referral, assessment and placement in ESN
schools.   'Others' who had made a decision on the
children were also to be interviewed informally (social
workers, psychiatrists, etc.).   It seemed sensible to
start by isolating a study population of children who had
been assessed as ESN-M or who were in the process of
assessment, and to interview the people who had made
decisions on them rather than interview samples of professional people and parents separately.   In this way two
objectives could be pursued; the professionals could be
interviewed on a general level, asking about their perceptions and beliefs, and then asked separately how they
acted in particular cases.   Thus a 'check' would be
available on the general statements made.   Second, this
method enabled the collection of case-study information on
particular children to provide data on what sort of
children were referred and assessed as ESN-M.

A large LEA was approached in April 1975, but it was
not until January 1976, when the study had been formulated
in its present shape, that a formal approach for permission to carry out a study was made.   The chief educational psychologist was initially approached, since it was
decided to select names of children from the files kept by

psychologists at the Child Guidance Clinics.   After discussions with the senior administrative officer for
special education, and the permission of the senior
specialist in community medicine (child health), to
approach doctors, selections of cases for interviewing
began in March 1976 and continued until January 1977.

It was intended to take twenty children from each of
two Child Guidance Clinics in the LEA, since this would
theoretically entail 200 interviews, if five people were
involved in making decisions on each child.   In fact,
since the same doctor or psychologist had seen several of
the children and occasionally the same head teacher had
referred two or more children, 104 interviews were carried
out over the nine-month period, with thirty heads of
normal schools, ten heads of special schools, eight educational psychologists, six medical officers, forty parents,
and ten 'others' (two psychiatrists, two social workers,
two remedial teachers, one speech therapist, one GP and
staff at an assessment centre and an educational guidance
unit).   The two Child Guidance Clinics selected out of
the five in the city were located in the north-west and
east of the city.   As the study progressed and thirty
children had been followed, twenty-eight of manual
working-class parentage, it was decided to take the final
ten children from a third clinic in a suburban area to the
south-west to see if this produced more children of non-
manual parentage.   In fact, children taken from this
clinic were also manual workers' children, living on
suburban council estates.

The forty children in this study are referred to
throughout as a study population, rather than sample. (2)
A statistical sample, as a part of a population, is
generally considered to need to be representative of the
population, although as Moser and Kalton (1971, p. 63)
point out, a decision to cover only a sample rather than
the whole population, means leaving the field of certainty
and moving into that of inference.   The forty study
population children satisfied the researcher's specifica-
tions that they had all been referred (or re-referred) to
one of the Child Guidance Clinics as possibly in need of
special ESN-M education, and had either been placed in a
special school or were in the process of assessment.   In ·
order to ensure a representative sample every child in the
city so referred should have had an equal chance of selection.   In fact, the confidential nature of records kept
on the children dictated that statistically representative
selection could not be made.   Educational psychologists
at three clinics who expressed a willingness to co-
operate in the research were asked to provide the names of

children who satisfied the general criteria.   The selection of the children was then dependent on the choice of
the psychologists.   However, lack of representation of
the children was not considered to be detrimental to the
study, since it was not intended to make generalised
statements about the children, but to discuss the mechanics of the decisions made on them.   There was no way
of discovering whether these decisions were representative
or not.   The methodology, then, corresponds to what
Glaser and Strauss (in Denzin, 1970, p. 105) have called
'theoretical sampling', whereby questions are asked about
categories and their properties in order to suggest inter-
relationships into a theory.   The intention here is to
describe decision-making processes, infer the beliefs and
values upon which decisions were made, and suggest consequences.   There is no claim to 'verify' or 'prove' in a
statistical sense.   Rather, the study is an analysis of a
social process and its consequences.

Initially the professional people involved with each
child were noted.   The administrative divisions within
the local education authority, by which the city is divided into geographical areas served by different specialists, meant that children from each clinic had been seen
by the same two or three psychologists and doctors.
Approaches to the head teachers, psychologists and doctors
were made by telephone;   the parents were sent a short
letter asking if the researcher could visit at a specific
time, and a visit was made whether or not a reply was
received.   Several of the parents were anxious that their
child had apparently been 'singled-out', but after the
nature of the research had been explained, none refused to
discuss their involvement in the process.   When the five
Asian parents in the study were interviewed, an interpreter accompanied the researcher to prevent language difficulties interfering with the parents' full understanding
of the research.   The research was thus dependent upon
the educational psychologists producing 'suitable' cases.
Several cases were discarded as unsuitable, for example,
the child was at a school for physically handicapped
children.   One boy was followed through who should not
strictly speaking have been included - he had eventually
been sent to an educational guidance centre.   The psychologists were not specifically asked for 'immigrant
children' but since one clinic area included West Indian
and Indian settlements, and another a Pakistani settlement, fourteen out of the forty cases were West Indian or
Asian and four were 'other immigrants'.

The interview schedules used are appended at the end of
this chapter as Appendix 1.   As far as possible, the

questions were phrased in the same way for all respondents
and replies recorded on the interview schedules.

The parents' schedule proved the most difficult to draw
up and went through several changes during the initial
pilot studies.   The major problem was designing questions
that were understandable to the parents.

A checklist was added to the schedule assessing the
parents (in the judgment of the researcher) as to whether
they were deferential towards the education system,
apathetic towards the system, ignorant or knowledgeable
about the system.

If the child in question was present when the visit to
the parents' home was made, further comment on the child
in his home setting was added.   Thirty-eight of the forty
children were observed either during the home or the
school visit.

The 'other' professional personnel who had had contact
with and made a decision about the child were interviewed
on the 'factual' basis of: 'At what point were they involved in the decision-making process on the child?   What
did they contribute?   Were they in communication with
other professional people and parents?'

When the data collection was finished, the material was
organised as follows.

The files of interviews with head teachers of referring
schools, with educational psychologists, with medical
officers, with heads of special schools and with parents
formed the basis for chapters 3-7 of this book.   The
interview schedules were analysed and other material, for
example notes made during initial conversations, observational notes, were also used.   Since the questions on all
the interview schedules were open-ended, replies to all
the questions had to be coded in order to produce any
tables or to generalise in the text.   Since the numbers
in all the groups were relatively small, data 'lost'
through coding has been presented qualitatively - in the
form of whole replies being reproduced.   The comments
made by the professional personnel on the general interview schedules were cross-checked, where appropriate, with
the schedules recording their statements on the study
population children.   At the end of each chapter several
case studies of children are appended to illustrate the
way in which all the professional people went about making
their decisions on particular children.   In the parents
chapter, the case studies illustrate the way the parents
were involved and consulted in the referral and assessment
process.   For chapter 8, all the material referring to
the eighteen 'immigrant' families was temporarily extracted from other files and the case studies used as a basis

for discussion of the wider issues relating to immigrants, special education and the reaction of the education system as a whole to the presence of black children. Irish children are not considered as a group in this study, although some data on Irish children appear in the text.   Questions on Irish children were originally included in the interview schedules as Irish children (both Northern and Southern Ireland) appeared to be heavily represented in ESN referral in the city.   However, it was eventually concluded that they ought properly to form the basis for a separate study.

Much of this data collected on the children is not used in this study although it was essential to understanding the kind of families and children about whom the decisions were made.   It is available as a basis for a descriptive-analytic study of forty 'ESN children'.   It was very tempting to carry on following through the children who were in the process of referral, assessment and placement. The whole process is a dynamic and lengthy one - the twenty-two non-immigrant children placed in special schools had waited, on average, for two years during referral and assessment.   However, this was not a longitudinal study of the children and collection of information on the children involved ceased in January 1977. Those children still in the assessment process were thus 'frozen' at a point in their processing.

One set of decision-makers who were not formally interviewed as part of this study were the administrators - the officers and clerks who collate the information and decisions made on the children and officially 'place' the children in special schools.   This is a notable omission, and was made because of difficulties of formal access to the administrative personnel and because there was already sufficient interviewing to be undertaken in the allotted time.   However, an attempt has been made to rectify this omission in part, by explaining how the administration are officially intended to carry out their duties, in the following section.

THE LOCAL EDUCATION AUTHORITY AND SPECIAL EDUCATION

After the creation of the Inner London Education Authority under local authority re-organisation, the City of B became the second largest education authority in England, and despite a slow decline in the overall population of the city, the number of children in school continued to increase.   In 1975 there were approximately 122,000 children attending the city's 366 primary schools, 93,000

attending 112 secondary schools and approximately 4,000
children attending 42 (all types) special schools.
There were 11,200 teaching staff and a further 1,600
ancillary staff, and the net expenditure in the city was
over 86 million pounds for the year 1975-6.   The changeover from selection by 11+ to comprehensive schooling
became a focus for intense party-political and parental
debate from the mid-1960s, but by 1972 the City Council
had initiated a process of planning a change to comprehensive schooling by grouping all secondary schools into
eighteen separate geographical units or consortia.   By
1976 the consortium system was more or less in operation,
with only seven 'grammar' schools remaining, and under the
system each secondary school receives an intake of pupils
on a wide 'neighbourhood' basis, parental choice being
allowed between the five or six secondary schools in each
consortium.   The affairs of each consortium are organised
by a committee consisting of head teachers, the district
inspector, Further Education College principals, and a
primary school head representative.   Most consortia
invite heads of special schools within the area to attend
meetings.   One of the major aims of the consortium system
is to work towards a uniform curriculum in the first three
years and to share facilities and resources between
schools so that no child is 'disadvantaged' in terms of
taking courses for which his school is not equipped.
   The city is well-provided for with a variety of types
of special school, the most recent being a new campus
containing an ESN and physically handicapped school, which
opened in 1976.   Numbers and types of special schools in
the city are shown below (day and residential):

ESN	18
Physically handicapped	4
Maladjusted	4
Delicate	5
Hospital schools	5
Deaf/partially deaf	2
Partially sighted	2
Variety of handicaps	1
Seaside school	1
Total	42

Several of the ESN schools in the city began to
'integrate' severely subnormal children during the mid-
1970s but despite the provision for most types of handicap
the problems of classification as to which 'type' of child
actually arrives at specific schools remains.   Delicate

schools, in the opinion of several professionals interviewed for this study, could easily become 'ragbag'
schools, where children who do not readily fit into any
category, may be sent.

The numbers of children attending ESN schools has risen
steadily until the last three years, as Table 2.1 shows.
This is in line with the national trend and perhaps
reflects the provision of ESN schools and places, which
make it possible to classify and place more children.

TABLE 2.1 Numbers of children at day and residential ESN
schools in the City of B

1962	1,439
1963	1,387
1964	1,417
1965	1,413
1966	1,409
1967	1,404
1968	1,456
1969	1,519
1970	1,546
1971	1,561
1972	2,002
1973	2,015
1974	1,989
1975	2,138
1976	2,115
1977	2,006

Source City Statistics Office.

The percentage of children placed in ESN-M schools
would appear to be slightly higher than the national
figure. In 1975, ESN-M children constituted 0.9 per cent
of the total number of children in maintained primary and
secondary schools in the city. There has been a decrease
in referrals over the past three years, again in line with
a national trend, and in 1977 the number of children began
to drop. There are a variety of explanations, but no
actual evidence to explain the drop in referral and thus
placements.

There are seven sections which make up the Education
Department in B, the Special Services Branch being one of
them. This Branch is responsible for the management of
special schools and the educational needs of 'handicapped
and other disadvantaged children', the psychological and
child guidance services, the remedial teaching services.
The chief psychologist is thus responsible to the senior

administrative officer of the Special Services Branch, who
is responsible to the chief education officer, who is in
turn responsible to the Education Committee of the
Council.   The Education Committee delegates a special
schools sub-committee to oversee the management of special
schools and the affairs of the Special Services Branch.
A working party of head teachers, advisers, and administrators was formed in 1972 and they recommended the
setting up of two 'educational guidance' centres and three
units for suspended pupils.   The guidance centres deal
with 'pupils whose behaviour in their own school has been
so disruptive as to hinder seriously their own or other
pupils' educational or social progress' (City of Birmingham, 1972).   Pupils may be admitted immediately to the
centres and remain on their own school roll; they may not
be admitted if already ascertained as in need of special
education, but some professionals have suggested in this
study that the centres may be becoming regarded as
another 'type' of special schooling.

The city has certain charismatic figures who have
extended their influence over the sphere of special
education.   The name of Dame Ellen Pinsent was important
for the development of special schooling in the early part
of the century and one of the city's ESN-M schools is
still named after her.   After the war, one of the head
teachers of a suburban ESN school worked with a senior
lecturer at the city's University School of Education,
and together they produced a book on the education of
slow-learning children (Tansley and Gulliford, 1960) which
one reviewer claimed 'should be a standard text-book for
all working with ESN children'.

Tansley went on to write an influential book on
remedial reading, and an infant reading scheme which
became widely adopted as a remedial reading scheme (1967).
He eventually became City Inspector for Special Education,
retiring in 1975 before the implementation of Circular
2/75.   Gulliford continued to write on educational
failure and special education, became joint editor of the
journal 'Special Education', worked on committees for
handicapped children, and eventually became the country's
first Professor of Special Education.   The School of
Education runs an MEd course for educational psychologists, a diploma in special education, and a post-
experience BPhil(Ed) course which includes courses in
special education.   A large proportion of the professional personnel currently working in the city have
received some part of their training here, on courses
that are psychologically and social-problem oriented
(School of Education, 'Prospectus', 1976).   Tansley and

Gulliford (1960) have consistently noted the difficulties
of assessment for ESN schooling, and the possibilities of
'misplacement' and have supported the integration of as
many 'slow learners' as possible into the normal school
system.

It is not unusual for some of the backward children in
ordinary schools to be achieving less than their con-
temporaries in the ESN school ... we incline to the
view that the ESN school should expect to provide for
a proportion of (children who should have been provided
for in other ways) but we cannot be certain on this
point until there is a more comprehensive provision of
special educational treatment in ordinary schools.
(p. 11)

Tansley's enthusiastic support for the integration of
as many children as possible who had 'special needs' in
the normal school system had had permanent effects for the
city.   In 1973 he published his reasons for the undesirable segregation of such children.   These included: the
limited staff and resources of normal schools; the doubtful psychological criteria for assessment, which he
considered were based on 'low expectations based on
pessimistic psychological theories'; lack of attention to
teacher training; and the assumption that special schools
offered something 'special' rather than simply smaller
classes.   Since this type of comment called into question
the role of most of the other professional personnel
dealing with special education in the city, it was not
surprising that Tansley's views incurred some hostility
from various quarters.   Nevertheless, after a pilot study
in 1971 of twelve schools in a high-immigrant area of the
city to identify children 'at risk' from educational
failure, a scheme was produced for Special Educational
Treatment (SET) in infant and junior schools, whereby
teachers could be taught to administer a screening test to
all children in school. (3)   The screening devices were
intended to identify 'children with special needs' which
were to include children with 'learning and behaviour
problems', and to provide a rough differential diagnosis
of each child's needs.   The procedures included teacher
questionnaires asking for teacher assessment of each
child's physical and sensory development and behaviour
characteristics.   Children found to be 'at risk' were to
be withdrawn from their classes and given intensive pro-
grammed treatment.   The Education Committee decided in
1972 that these procedures should be spread throughout the
city and in-service training courses, run initially by
Tansley, and the Remedial Teaching Service, began.   The
training has been continuing since this period, consortium

by consortium.   Two teachers from all primary schools in
each consortia are trained to administer the tests and
Tansley noted in 1973 that 'the work they are doing is
having a great influence on their own schools'.   However,
a small piece of research carried out by Lindsay in 1975
produced the following comment:

> The screening instrument could not be considered a
> useful method of screening children.   Measures of
> reliability and validity, and the large percentage of
> false positives and false negatives, suggested that the
> use of this instrument to identify children at risk of
> having learning difficulties is not warranted.

In the course of this study, head teachers were asked
if they had staff trained in the Tansley SET to attempt a
rough assessment as to whether this might affect ESN
referrals, i.e. did teachers feel better able to cope
with 'educational failure' in the young children?

The three departments who are concerned with decision-
making in special education are the Special Services
Department, the School Psychological Service and the
School Health Services.   The personnel who take responsibility for the decisions are the senior administrative
officer (special services), the chief psychologist, and
the senior specialist in community medicine (child
health) (formerly the principal school medical officer).
The post-war involvement of medical personnel dates from
the 1948 National Health Act and, as noted in chapter 1,
the 1944 Act (Section 34) specified the duty of local
authorities to involve medical officers in the process of
ascertainment for special education from the age of two
years.   Administratively, the city is divided into five
areas, each with a special services casework clerk responsible for collating the files on children in their area.

The year 1976, when interviewing for this study was
carried out, was a transitional period during which the
recommendations of Circular 2/75 were being discussed and
put into effect, and a changeover to the new SE forms
implemented.   Local education authorities have considerable autonomy to interpret central government recommendations and this allows for the development of different
procedures in the referral and assessment process in
special education.   Some of the city's psychologists, in
particular, had been critical of some aspects of the
referral and assessment procedures for special education
since the early 1970s.   The appointment of a new chief
psychologist, and a chief administrative officer who had
previously been an educational psychologist, meant that
the city took the duty of implementing the new procedures
very seriously and there were 'extensive consultations

with both educational and medical staff involved' (City of
Birmingham, 1976).   A pilot study of the use of the new
SE forms was carried out in late 1975 at one of the Child
Guidance Clinics, and psychologists in particular were
encouraged to comment critically on the new procedure.

In January 1976 the Education Committee, bearing in
mind the pilot study of SE forms, agreed to the replacement of forms 1-5 HP with 1-5 SE(B).   These B forms were
the original DES forms modified to suit local needs, and
SE 3 in particular took the form of a report based on
suggested categories.   Notes for guidance on the use of
these forms were drawn up in consultation with the chief
psychologist and the community specialist (child health).
Two procedures were envisaged - those where a child would
first be referred to an educational psychologist attached
to a Child Guidance Clinic, and those where the child was
first referred to a medical officer.

In the Notes for professional staff of the Education
and Health Service the administrative procedures were laid
down as follows:

Referral may be made by schools, other agencies, or
parents, but the normal practice in B. will be that
children apparently in need of special education
because of learning or behaviour difficulties will be
referred to a psychologist in the first instance,
whereas children with actual or suspected physical or
sensory handicaps will first be referred to a medical
officer.

A city educational psychologist summarised the two procedures in the form of flow charts, see Appendix 2 to this
chapter.

The procedure ideally envisaged by the administration
would seem to be as follows.   If the referral is to a
psychologist, he will interview and test the child and
complete SE 3(B).   The head teacher will then be
'invited' to complete SE 1.   The original SE 3 will go
to the central administration (Special Services) where
the casework clerk for the part of the city where the
child lives will open a file and register arriving documents on the child.   The head teacher's original SE 1 and
a copy of SE 3 go to the medical officer via the central
medical files.   If the medical officer decides to examine
the child, this is done and SE 2(B) completed and sent to
Special Services with a copy to the psychologist.   If
there is no need for a medical only the front sheet of
SE 2 is required.   If the psychologist and medical
officer are in agreement, the notes then suggest that
SE 4(B) is completed by the psychologist, who will recommend to the authority what action should be taken on

behalf of the child and his/her difficulties.   If the
medical officer and the psychologist disagree, a case
conference will be arranged by the Special Services Branch
and the Services of the Staff Inspector (special education) called upon to make a recommendation.   The administration will then formally arrange for a child to attend a
special school if recommended, but Placement Panels are
envisaged for pupils 'for whom no placement has been made
or offered within a reasonable time of recommendation
having been made (usually three months)'.

If the first referral is made to a medical officer the
child will be examined and SE 2(B) completed.   The head
teacher will then be invited to complete SE 1;   the
original SE 2 goes to Special Services and a copy to the
psychologist;   the original SE 1 goes to the psychologist
through the Central Psychological Clinic.   The senior
psychologist decides whether the child should be psychologically tested (giving priority to ESN and maladjusted
pupils), and SE 3 will be completed.   The original SE 1,
3 and 4 then go to Special Services.   If the child is not
psychologically examined prior to special school admission, the front sheet only of SE 3(B) is completed.   SE 4
will be completed by the chief psychologist or one of the
special education inspectors, and in the event of medical
and psychological disagreement a case conference will take
place.

There is a brief paragraph in the guidance notes to the
effect that parents must be involved at an early stage in
the assessment procedure, and discuss the referral with
the head teacher or other referring agency: 'Other than
in the most exceptional cases parental consent for
referral must always be obtained in advance.'

The notes also mention that it is within the Education
Committee's power to require admission to special schools,
through formal certification, but that the notice to
parents 'requiring them to submit their children for
medical examination in connection with admission to
special schools' is no longer required.

These new procedures are intended to give effect to
three principles set out in Circular 2/75.   These were,
first, the preferred use of an educational rather than a
medical model for advising on children's special educational needs;   second, that professionals should engage in
full consultation;   and third, that parents should be
involved at an early stage.

Notably absent from the recommended procedures in the
City of B are reference to consultations with the head
teachers of referring or special schools - the impression
that there is a power struggle between psychologists and

medical personnel to dominate the assessment procedures at
the expense of involving the school personnel, was, as
this study indicates, felt by some of the head teachers.

Also absent from the recommended procedures is detailed
comment on how parents should be involved, apart from a
note on SE 1(B) that 'the parents should have been interviewed and the child's difficulties discussed with them
well before this form is completed'.   There is no form or
report where parents' views or comments can be recorded.
The medical 'diagnosis' on SE 3(B) requires the MO to tick
handicaps concerning 'ability to care for himself' and
'behaviour and emotional development' without any requirement that the child should be seen in his home setting.
A third absentee from the advice on procedures is any
comment on evaluation of the results of placing a child in
special school and any recommendations on follow-up procedures, re-examination or transfer back to normal school.

Of the professional personnel who were asked by the LEA
for comments on the changing procedures during 1976, the
psychologists were the most critical and their comments
centred mainly on three aspects: the confusion over the
description of 'formal' procedures as used by the DES in
Circular 2/75, the on-going controversy between the medical and the educational models, and the consideration that
special school placement in B might become administratively dominated (Conference proceedings, 1976).

On the first point, although the DES apparently regard
only the use of compulsory procedure (SE 5) as 'formal',
some psychologists regard the other four SE forms as a
static procedure which will 'preclude their usefulness in
anything other than the most formal assessment situation'.
They would like the assessment and treatment of children
to be regarded as a dynamic process including 'on-going
liaison between professions' rather than the discrete
examinations suggested by the forms.   As one psychologist
noted:

> Crucial to this issue is our view that special educa-
> tion does not represent the end of the assessment line.
> It constitutes a stage, albeit a large one, in the
> assessment of a child's status and needs, which must
> continue throughout the period of special school
> provision. (Conference proceedings, 1976)

On the second point, early guidelines produced in 1976
had suggested that in the event of disagreement between
MOs and psychologists both should complete a copy of SE 4.
The final recommendations were that the staff inspector or
chief educational psychologist should fill out SE 4.
This would seem to represent a victory for the educational-psychological model.   However, the psychologists

are well aware that the senior clinical medical officer is still legally the only person entitled to 'certify' a child using SE 5.

On the third point, administrative domination, one psychologist commented that: (4)

The administrative procedures seem unnecessarily wasteful. A more efficient and less costly procedure would be to avoid copies to Special Services Branch until the professionals involved have completed forms SE 1, 2, 3 and 4. That is, when those collaborating at a local level have decided that special schooling is necessary.

The psychologist thought that while professional evaluation was taking place the administration would not be in a position to comment on a child's needs and should only enter the decision-making process when a decision to recommend special schooling had been made.

The note that 'Special Services place child in accordance with SE 4 recommendation' (Conference proceedings, 1976) was regarded by educational psychologists as being somewhat optimistic. Within the procedure a casework clerk at Special Services would still actually be involved in contacting special schools and the administrative procedure then becomes 'secretive' in the sense that the administration was not obliged to reveal what criteria were used to place a child.

Despite the attempted implementation of new procedures suggested by Circular 2/75 within this particular LEA, this study indicates that the personnel involved in the referral and assessment processes still do not feel completely satisfied. As one professional noted: 'The confusion comes about when people don't know what criteria to use for ascertainment, not what forms to fill in' (Conference proceedings, 1976).

It will also be noted in this study that, despite complex administrative processes, a good deal of 'informal' contact goes on between professionals, which can have various consequences for the processes.

THE STUDY POPULATION CHILDREN

The task of describing the forty study population children cannot be undertaken in any detail here - they comprise 'case studies' of forty children of whom twenty-eight have been officially classified as ESN and twelve were in the process of having their special educational needs assessed.   They are also forty individuals who have their own reactions and opinions about the process they have

undergone or are undergoing.   Thirty-eight of the forty
children were observed and spoken to, either at home or at
school.   Some general characteristics of the children are
noted here and several case studies described in more
detail.   The families of the children are by and large
described in the chapter on parents.   The information
given here relates as far as possible to the children,
although there is some overlap.   Twenty-two of the
children in this study are 'indigenous', that is born in
England, although four had one parent born in the Republic
of Ireland.   Nine of the children were of West Indian
parentage, seven born in England and two born in Jamaica;
three of the children were of Pakistani parentage;   two
Indian;   one Turkish;   one Italian-Indian;   one half-
Pakistani and one half-Ukrainian.   Two of the Asian
children were born in Pakistan;   three were born in
England.
    The 'intelligence testing' of potentially ESN children
on standardised tests is part of the assessment process
for special education.   Thirty-six of the children had
been tested on either the Stanford-Binet or the Weschler
Intelligence Scale for Children (WISC) test and their full
IQ recorded in their file at the Child Guidance Clinic.
Three children were awaiting their interview with the
psychologist, and one child had not been tested.   The IQs
of the children were in the range 43-81, and Table 2.2
shows that a clustering around IQ 60-75 was noticeable
for this population of children.

TABLE 2.2   Full IQ scores of study population children

IQ	Number of children
85-80	3
79-75	3
74-70	9
69-65	6
64-60	6
59-55	4
54-50	2
Below 50	1
MA only given	1
RA only given	1
Awaiting testing	3
Not tested	1
Total	40

Although IQ score is considered to be important in the decision to send a child to ESN school, three parents whose children's IQ scores were 64, 70, 70 respectively, were currently objecting to the idea of special schooling and up to January 1977, when collection of information ceased, were not being pressured too much over the issue. Three children with IQs of 67, 70 and 72 had not been sent to special school, in two cases the heads of normal school were willing to keep the children, and in one case the psychologist would not recommend special schooling. These three children were all 'immigrant'.   One child in the study population whose IQ was given as 43 was an Indian child and the psychologist said: 'These results suggest she is of inferior intelligence, however, I would not take these results at face value as she does not speak much English.'

As noted in the Introduction, explanations for the educational backwardness of some children classified as ESN-M can be described as organic; (5)   birth injuries, faulty pre-natal development, subsequent childhood illness or accident, are all considered to contribute to organic causes of backwardness.   The mothers (fathers in five cases) of the children were asked about the birth and subsequent illness/injury to the children, and their comments were noted.   Six of the forty children were reported to be premature births, and three mothers mentioned oxygen starvation.   One mother attributed her son's backwardness to the following: 'Some of his brain cells died in the split second before he got the oxygen. He was a premature baby too;   all my babies click-off at eight months.'

In four cases the mother reported that she had been ill during the pregnancy, one with thyroid trouble, one with toxemia, two with arthritis, and four reported that the child had had a difficult birth or a handicap at birth. In all, sixteen children - 40 per cent of the study population - had some kind of reported birth handicap. Thirty-two cases of subsequent illness or injury were commented on by the mothers.   These were as shown in Table 2.3.

No percentage is calculated here as several mothers mentioned more than one thing.   One girl had been particularly unfortunate.   Her mother had suffered from thyroid trouble and undernourishment during pregnancy and has a speech defect.   The mother said:

She's been unlucky; when she was six she was run over. Her granny tried to save her and broke her own leg and died soon after.   I was that upset.   She's got a bit of eye damage from the accident.   At eleven she had to have an operation on her 'private' and her brother died when he was little too.

TABLE 2.3 Illness/injury of study population children
reported by parents

Operation/hospitalised in early childhood	6
Convulsions after birth	3
Enuretic/urine infection	3
Eye defect	7
Poor speech	6
Frequent colds	3
Asthmatic	2
Traffic accident	2
Total	32

This mother had recently miscarried a child and was
objecting to medical advice that she should be sterilised.
Another child, a Pakistani, had convulsions soon after her
arrival in England.   Her mother described the problems
thus: 'She was okay until she came to England.   Then one
day she fell down and couldn't see or hear. She's been
in hospital plenty.'   This girl also had been involved in
a traffic accident.

One mother, whose husband was a teacher, explained her
son's backwardness as due to: 'His troubled childhood;
he was often ill, and his grandfather died just when he'd
got fond of him.   He reads the last letter of words
first.   It's mixed cerebral dominance or something.'
Another mother reported that she never really wanted the
child: 'I almost starved myself when I was carrying him,
to try and get rid of him I suppose.   Well, I've read
since that that could affect his brain.'   This child had
been a premature baby.

The backwardness of another child was attributed by a
psychologist to a medical problem after birth: 'He had a
period of low blood sugar during the first few days of
life.   This could have caused some permanent damage to
his intellectual function.'

Five of the children had been separated from their
parents for over a three-week period.   One West Indian
mother, whose child had been born with a heart murmur,
said that her child had been badly affected when she had
a breakdown and he was in a children's home for six
months: 'He really fretted for me.   He and I had always
been close.'

Five mothers reported that their children had temper
tantrums, and one child was a suspected battered child.
The father of this child said he was 'disappointed' in
her: 'She was our most perfect baby but as she grew you
could see her mind was wrong.'   He admitted 'whacking' his

children but thought parents should be allowed to whack
their children 'otherwise they get into trouble when they
grow up'.

It was noticeable that the five Asian children in this
study all had some kind of illness or handicap.   One
child had a club foot;   two had had convulsions when
young;   one was premature with oxygen starvation and one
had 'funny teeth so he was slow to talk'.   This is similar to other research findings concerning Asian children
in ESN schools (Saunders, 1973).

The children nearly all came from large families.   The
forty families had produced a total of 185 children
between them;   only three children are 'only' children and
four have seven or more siblings.

TABLE 2.4 Number of siblings of study population children

Siblings	Study children
0	3
1	5
2	3
3	7
4	8
5	8
6	2
7	3
8	1
Total	40

Nine of the children have siblings in some kind of
special educational or child care.   Three children have
two siblings, each at ESN school;   one boy has a brother
at a deaf school;   another has a brother attending a
speech therapy clinic;   one boy has four siblings who have
been taken into care;   one has a brother in a community
home, and another boy has a brother attending sessions at
the Child Guidance Clinic.   Two of the children's parents
attended an ESN school themselves.

The children were first referred to the Child Guidance
Clinic at the ages shown in Table 2.5.

Thus, although it is commonly held that children tend
to be referred around the school transfer ages of 7 years
and 11 years, this study population were referred fairly
consistently throughout their junior school period, and
five were referred during their second year at secondary
school.

TABLE 2.5   Age of referral of study population children

Number of children	Age
1	4
3	5
4	6
7	7
5	8
7	9
6	10
1	12
5	13
1	14

Eight of the children were 're-referrals'.   That is, they had previously been referred to a Child Guidance Clinic as in need of some form of special educational treatment, and four of these children came from families designated as 'problem families' by the Social Services Department, and had had contact with other social agencies.   One boy had been referred in 1973 for disruptive behaviour at school.   The psychologist recommended special remedial attention in ordinary school and 'reviewed the case periodically'.   In 1975 the boy moved to another school and the head referred the boy again for disruptive behaviour.   The case was transferred to the Child Guidance Clinic serving that particular school and the boy was placed in a residential ESN school shortly afterwards.   Another child, a West Indian girl, had originally been referred in 1968 at the age of five. She was sent to an ESN school, and after a parental request and a review of her case, was returned to normal secondary school at the age of eleven.   However, she was then re-referred by her secondary school in 1975.

The reasons given by the referring agency (usually the normal school) for the referral of the study children were as shown in Table 2.6.

Thus, only eleven of the children were referred solely for educational backwardness.   The other cases were regarded as multi-problems, usually in the terms that a problem at home or of aggression was contributing to a general educational backwardness.   The kind of comment head teachers made illustrated this point:

He 'stood out' at infant level by his inability to concentrate.   He was sulky and played with bits of string.   Eventually he did some truanting and became obstreperous.

TABLE 2.6   Reasons for referral of study population children

Low intelligence	3
Educational/backward at school	8
Educational/disruptive behaviour	5
Aggressive disruptive behaviour	7
Home problems/backward	4
Medical problems/backward	3
Home problems/truancy	6
Retarded speech and language	3
Attention-seeking	1
Total	40

I tolerated him for nearly all his primary school life. The class teacher reported he was an uncontrolled child, punching and stealing.   In the end I went over the psychologist's head and got the medical officer in to examine him.

He had several handicaps, one leg shorter than the other and no co-ordination;   a slow learner with the added problem of no English.

Twenty-eight (70 per cent) of the study population children were attending ten special schools (nine ESN, one delicate school).   Of the remaining twelve 'pending' children, three parents were refusing to allow their children to be sent to ESN school;   one mother had recently been persuaded to allow her child to attend and one boy had recently been accepted by the remedial department of the local comprehensive;   two cases had been passed to the remedial teaching service;   one boy was being kept at his primary school, despite a recommendation by the psychologist for ESN-M school;   another boy was being kept at secondary school as a new head had arrived who was willing to keep him;   one boy was waiting for a placement, one for psychological testing, and one was still at his primary school as the psychologist would not recommend special schooling although the school wanted the boy transferred.

One result of the historical categorisation of subnormal people by physical signs is that a commonsense view prevails that children who are subnormal should have a different appearance to 'normal' children.   This assumption is made for mildly as well as severely subnormal children.   This criterion may still implicitly play a part in the judgment of professionals.   Eyes, in particular, are singled out to illustrate subnormality.   Descri-

bing one of the study population children, a psychologist
said: 'You know, he looked different.   He had no sight
in one eye.'

Comments on the physical appearance of fourteen of the
children were made in interview by professionals.   Five
were noted as physically small for their age;   three were
noted as having eye defects;   one girl was described as
obese (she undoubtedly was, but seen together with her
large mother and grandmother, she appeared less obese).
Two Asian girls were noted as having a tendency to microcephaly;   one West Indian boy was noted as having peculiar
pigmentation on his face;   and another West Indian girl
was described as 'unfortunately rather ugly'.

While the status of ESN-M children places them firmly
in a 'social problem' class, observation of the individual
study population children during the course of the
research did call into question 'who defined' the problem.
The case of Ken illustrates a family who Cyril Burt
(1937, p. 154) would undoubtedly have placed in the social
problem class yet to the child in question the problems
were more reasonably his own parents, his socio-economic
background and the professionals who were paid to help
him.

Ken, aged eleven, lives with his mother and two sisters
on a new council estate which has already acquired the
reputation of being a dumping ground for problem
families.

His mother left home for eight months when he was
two, and his father has constantly blamed the mother,
saying it caused Ken's backwardness.   The father also
hit and bullied his mother, who is a thin, tense,
nervous, defenceless woman, and eventually he left
home to live with a neighbour's wife.   This became
known on the estate and Ken felt very ashamed.   His
mother frankly cannot cope;   she lives on social
security, cannot keep the house or children clean, and
lets the little girls - aged six and eight - suck
babies' bottles.   She smokes incessantly and worries
that she will 'lose' the children, although she takes
her worries out on Ken.   At the time the researcher
visited, Ken was crying because she had just sold his
puppy, claiming it was 'biting baby' (the six-year-
old).   Ken presumably can't be sure either of his
parents' love for him or that he will be allowed to
love anything.   He has to wear second-hand clothes and
was incontinent until quite recently.   He had an eye
operation as a child and is noted as having 'cross-
eyes'.   Thus, he can't be too happy about his own
appearance and self-image.   His head teacher referred

him at age seven years because he made little school
progress, soiled himself and was 'made a butt by other
children because he was dopey'.   He was sent to an ESN
school but was re-referred to the Child Guidance Clinic
two years later as being 'disruptive and trying to set
things on fire'.   This was about the time his father
took up with the neighbour's wife.   A psychiatrist saw
Kenneth and his mother and said that Ken was anxious
and confused, and the family needed social work help.
Ken recently transferred to a boys' secondary ESN
school.   The head there thinks a residential school
might be best for him, as although he's quiet he still
wets himself.

On the other hand, professionals can be in dispute as
to whether a 'problem' exists, as the case of Bashir
demonstrates:

Bashir is a cheerful nine-year-old Indian boy, tall for
his age, who lives with his parents and three sisters
in an old terraced house opening straight on to the
street in a re-development area of B.   His house has a
minimum of furniture, but is very gay, blue-flowered
wallpaper, yellow paint and pink-flowered settee
covers.   The interpreter thought the family was a
'real peasant' family.   The father said he came from
the Punjab in 1957 but speaks hardly any English;   the
mother speaks none.   Father has worked at a foundry
nearby since he arrived, but has heart trouble.
Bashir's main problem would appear to be that he is in
charge of communications between his parents and
British society.   He translates and interprets for
them.   His parents are not particularly bothered about
his intelligence and school attainment, over which
there is some argument by the professionals.   The
school regard him as a 'worry';   he makes little
progress, especially at reading (in English), and has
twice been referred.   The psychologist who tested him
gave him an IQ of 70, but regarded his problem as one
of reading and will not recommend him as ESN.   He
thinks the boy does quite well considering his main
language is Punjabi and his parents don't speak
English.   At the time of studying, the school was
getting more irate with the psychologist, but Bashir
was cheerfully unaware of the 'problem' he was causing.

The study now moves on to examine in some detail the
way professionals set about making decisions in the
assessment processes for ESN-M children.

APPENDIX 1   INTERVIEW SCHEDULES

Referring school schedule

A1   1   Can I check what sort of school this is and how
         big?
     2   How many staff and ancillary workers do you have?
     3   Do you have a large staff turnover?
A2   1   What sort of resources and facilities do you have
         in the school?
A3   1   How long have you been head here?
     2   Where were you before?
B   1   What sort of things do you refer children to the
         Child Guidance Clinic for?   (As possibly in need
         of special education.)
C1   1   Do you usually use forms or do you depend on more
         informal contacts?
C2   1   Do you use the old HP or the new SE forms?
C3   1   Do you think the new forms will work better?   If
         yes, why?
D1   1   Do your staff usually bring to your attention
         children who have special difficulties and perhaps
         need special education - or do you decide which
         children need it?
     2   Do you think the head teacher's role in sending
         children for assessment is important?
D2   1   How do you see the job of the educational psycho-
         logist in assessing children you have referred to
         him?
     2   How do you see the job of the MO in checking
         children referred for special education?
     3   How do you see the role of Special Services in the
         referral and placing process?
     4   Do you contact parents before you refer a child?
         If yes, how?
     5   What part do you think parents should play in the
         assessment and placement process?
E1   1   Do you think it is better to keep a child at his
         normal school if possible?
E2   1   What sort of things do you think an ESN school can
         do for children that ordinary schools cannot do?
F   1   Do you have contact with any special school?   If
         yes, specify: what schools, what sort of contact.
G1   1   What sort of problems do you think West Indian
         children have that you have come across?
G2   1   What sort of problems do you think Asian children
         have?
G3   1   What sort of problems do you think Irish children
         have?

Referring school individual case schedule

In the case of ...
1 Why did you decide to refer ... to the Clinic?
2 Did you discuss ...'s problems with anyone before you
   made the referral?
   other teachers
   MO
   parents
   others
3 Did you fill out a 3 HP form or a CG 5 (or an SE form)?
4 Do you think ... will do better in a special school?
   If yes, why?
5 Have you had any contact with a special school about
   ...?
6 Have you discussed ...'s change of school (or possible
   change) with the parents?
   (If West Indian or Asian.)
7 Do you think being West Indian/Asian contributed to
   ...'s difficulties?

Psychologists' schedule

A Can I start by asking how you came into educational
   psychology?
   1 Was your first degree in psychology?
   2 Where did you study for your first degree?
   3 What sort of further (post graduate) training have
      you had?
   4 Where did you do this further training?
   5 How long have you worked as an educational psycho-
      logist?   In B?   For other local education
      authorities?
   6 Have you worked in special education in any other
      capacity than as an educational psychologist?
B 1 Do you think Circular 2/75 represents an important
      change in the ascertainment process for children
      needing special education?   In what way?
   2 Did you use the old HP forms to any extent or did
      you depend more on informal contacts with people?
   3 Do you think the proposed B SE forms will work
      better than the old forms or the DES version?
      If so, why?
C 1 How important do you think the role of the psycholo-
      gist is in the assessment process of children
      referred to the clinic?
   2 Do you think the psychologist's decisions are becom-
      ing more or less important in the assessment process
      (and the placement process)?

D   1   How important is the MO's involvement in the assess-
        ment process?
    2   Do you think the MO's decisions are becoming more or
        less important in the assessment process (and place-
        ment process)?
    3   Do you think it's a good thing that MO's can some-
        times refer children themselves and see them before
        an educational psychologist?
    4   How do you see the role of Special Services in the
        assessment and placement process (including the role
        of the Staff Inspector)?
    5   What part do you think parents (should) play in the
        assessment and placement process?
E   1   Do you think it's better to keep a child at his
        normal school if this is at all possible?
    2   What things would influence you to recommend a
        change of schools (to ESN)?
    3   What do you think ESN schools can do for children
        that ordinary schools cannot do?
    4   Do you think referring schools are often anxious
        that children with behaviour problems should leave?
F   1   Have West Indian children whom you have had contact
        with had special problems?
    2   Have Asian children whom you have had contact with
        had special problems?
    3   Have Irish children whom you have had contact with
        had special problems?

Psychologists' individual case schedule

    In the case of ...
1   Were you the first professional person to see ...?
2   Can you remember whether you filled in an HP or SE
    form for ...?
3   Can you remember if you had any informal contacts with
    other people involved in ...'s case?   E.g. phone calls
    to Special Services.
    (If child is placed)
4   Did you try to find ... a special school place
    yourself?
5   Were you and the MO in agreement over the case?
6   Do you think ... will do better in ... school than in
    his last school?
7   How did you find out that ... had a special school
    place?
    (If West Indian or Asian)
8   Do you think that being West Indian/Asian contributed
    to ...'s difficulties at school?

Medical Officers' schedule

A 1 Could I ask you about your background and training?
   2 How long have you been a medical officer?
   3 Have you worked in other medical areas before you
      became a schools' MO?
   4 Do you think the Health Service area re-organisation
      will affect your work with children needing special
      education?
B 1 Could you tell me what part the MO plays in examin-
      ing children referred for special education?
   2 Do you usually see children before an educational
      psychologist sees the child?
   3 How do you see the role of Special Services and
      other people involved with children in need of
      special education?
   4 Do you think the SE forms will be more useful than
      the HP forms?
   5 Do you write informal reports rather than rely on
      forms only?
C 1 What do you think ESN schools can do for children
      that ordinary schools cannot do?
   2 If children have relatively serious handicaps, do
      you think they should be educated separately from
      children who are classed as ESN (M)?
D 1 Do you think West Indian and Asian children have
      special problems in England?   I.e. medical prob-
      lems?   Cultural problems?   Educational problems?
   2 What sort of problems have (a) West Indian and (b)
      Asian children had that you have come across?
   3 Do you think Irish children have any special
      problems?

Medical Officers' individual case schedule

   In the case of ...
1 Did you see ... before an educational psychologist?
2 Did you agree with the psychologist's assessment of the
   case?
3 Did you fill in an SE or HP form on ...?
4 Did you write any other reports or have contact with
   anyone about ...?
   (If placed)
5 How did you find out that ... had been placed in ...
   school?
6 Do you think he/she will do better in ... school than
   in his/her last school?
   (If West Indian or Asian)

7 Do you think being West Indian/Asian contributed to
   ...'s difficulties?

Receiving school schedule

A1 1 Could you say something about the history of the
       school - when was it built, how big, etc.?
    2 How many staff and ancillary workers do you have?
    3 Do you have a fairly settled staff?
A2 1 What sort of extra resources and facilities do you
       have here that ordinary schools don't have?
A3 1 How long have you been head here?
    2 Where were you before?
B1 1 Could you tell me how children come to be placed in
       your school?
    2 Do you have to take every child suggested as a
       pupil?
    3 Do you have a waiting list?
C1 1 How do you see the job of the educational psycholo-
       gist in assessing children referred to him/her?
    2 How do you see the job of the MO in checking
       children referred for special education?
    3 How do you see the role of Special Services in the
       placement process?
D1 1 Do you think the new SE forms will work better than
       the HP forms?
    2 Do you depend on informal contacts (e.g. phone) for
       getting information on children?
E1 1 Do you have contacts with the schools who refer the
       children who come to your school?
    2 Do you see parents before their child comes to your
       school?
F1 1 What sort of things do you think that special
       schools can do for children that ordinary schools
       cannot do?
G1 1 Do you think West Indian children have any problems
       that make them likely to be referred for special
       education?
    2 Do you think Asian children have any problems that
       make them likely to be referred for special educa-
       tion?
    3 Do you think Irish children have any problems that
       make them likely to be referred for special educa-
       tion?

Receiving schools' individual case schedule

    In the case of ...
1 When did you first know ... was coming to your school?
2 Do you know who referred him/her as needing special
   education?
3 Have you seen ...'s parents.
4 Do you think ... will get on here better than in his/
   her last school?
5 Could you tell me who you have had contact with
   about ...?
   last school
   MO
   educational psychologist
   Special Services
   other
   (If West Indian or Asian)
6 Do you think being West Indian/Asian contributed to
   ...'s difficulties at his/her last school?

Parental schedule

A Description and details of house, family and sample
   child
   1 Description of area and house.
   2 Description of parents and family (including
      father's job or registered unemployed, mother's job
      if any).
   3 Ages, care and condition of children.
   4 Birth and development history of sample child.
B Understandings about 'normal' education in B
   1 Is ... primary/secondary school the only primary/
      secondary school ... has been to in B?
   2 Have you been to the school recently?   (Who did you
      see?)
   3 What are the teachers like at ... school?
   4a What sort of things do you like about the school?
   4b What sort of things do you dislike about the school?
(Put these questions in past tense if child is already
placed in special school.)
C Understandings about 'special' education in B
   1 Do you know what special schools are supposed to do
      for children?
      (If child placed or going to special school)
   2 Have you been to see ...'s new school (and what do
      you think of it)?
   3 What are the teachers like there?
   4 Do you think ... will get on better in his new
      school (what will the school do for him)?

D   Parental involvement and consultation in the referral
    and assessment process
    1   Who told you ... needed special help (and when)?
    2   Were you asked to take ... along to see a psycholo-
        gist at the ... clinic?
    3   Do you think the psychologist was helpful to ...?
    4   Were you asked to take ... to see a medical doctor?
    5   Did the doctor tell you or ask you anything about
        ...?
        (If child placed)
    6   Did you get a letter from the education authority
        telling you which school ... was to go to?
E   Beliefs about multi-racial education
        (If West Indian or Asian)
    1   How does ... get on in school, being ...?
        (If child goes or went to a multi-racial school)
    2   How does the school get on teaching black and white
        children together?
Check Assessment of parent/parents.
            Deferential towards education system.
            Apathetic towards education system.
            Ignorant/knowledgeable about the education
            system.
Further Comment
            On child and family.

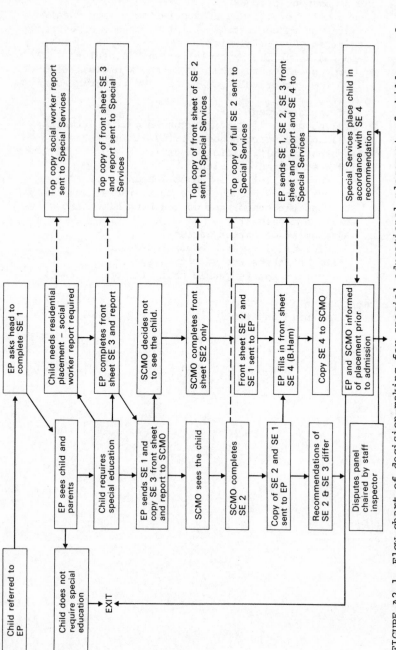

FIGURE A2.1 Flow chart of decision-making for special educational placement of children referred initially to educational psychologist

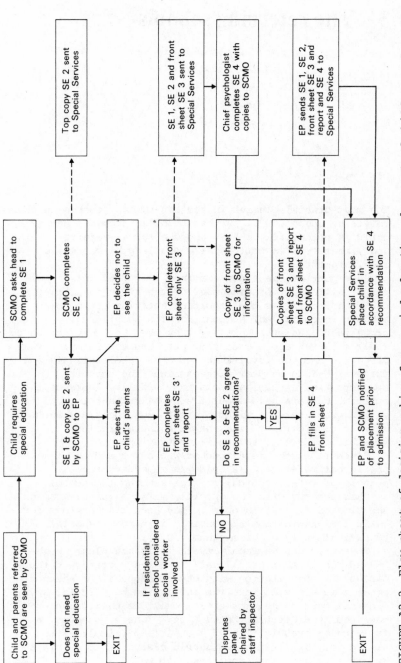

FIGURE A2.2 Flow chart of decision-making for special education placement of children referred initially to senior clinical Medical Officer

3   The referring schools

The most crucial element in the assessment process is the
referring school.   It is the school's judgment that a
child is potentially ESN-M, and the formal referral by the
head, that sets in motion the whole lengthy process of
ascertainment.

This part of the study examines thirty of the schools
which initiated the assessment of the study population
children and raises the important question as to how
schools recognise and account for ESN-M children.   What
criteria do head teachers say they use when they decide to
refer children and how do they perceive the formal
processes and the involvement of other professionals and
parents?   This chapter also examines the schools'
contacts with special schools and, finally, looks at the
cultural beliefs held about the problems that the children
of immigrant parents might present in schools, so as to be
able to consider any links between these problems and
possible referral into special education.

Since it is the head teacher who has the duty of making
the formal referral, the head was regarded, for the
purpose of this research, as representing the school.

This accords with the Special Services guidelines for
the City of B: 'It is open to any Head Teacher to refer a
child for examination as possibly in need of special
education' (City of Birmingham, 1976).

However, on a national level, it is not clear whether
DES advice is that heads shall make the referral on their
own, or in consultation with other teachers, or whether
other teachers will take the initiative.   Circular 2/75
does not mention head teachers, only 'teachers' and on
page four the Circular notes that: 'where, however, a
full-scale investigation of a child's difficulties is
called for the first steps should always be to obtain a
report from a teacher who knows him well'.

Form SE 1, according to the Circular, is for 'completion by a child's teacher(s)'.   In this study head
teachers were interviewed to enquire into their overall
views of the referral process, including whether they
consulted with other teachers, and were then asked
specifically how they had dealt with the individual study
population children.

Given the degree of power and autonomy which British
head teachers exercise in their schools, it seemed
reasonable to suppose that they were the people who
actually made the decision to refer a child.   The important but unusual aspect of this decision is that while it
is crucial in the initiation of a complex, lengthy and
expensive process, it is only a small and relatively unimportant aspect of the role of the head teacher.   For
example, in Bernbaum's study (1973) of three hundred and
fifteen headmasters, not one mentioned referring children
into special education as a specific task.

Research on the role of the head teacher has pointed to
two distinct headmaster styles - a 'paternalistic-
traditional' as against a managerial style, although whatever style the head adopts Waller's remark probably still
holds true that: 'Schools are typically organised on some
variant of the autocratic principle' (1932).

Bernbaum's account of the growth of the unique position
of the British head teacher, and his own study of heads
(1973; 1976), led him to conclude that few heads wished
to relinquish a traditional formulation of their own role.
On the other hand, supporters of the managerial role have
argued for the management training of heads, and the
application of management techniques to schools (Taylor,
1968; Colgate, 1976; Marland, 1975), and Cohen (1970)
concluded that schools become less personalised and more
bureaucratised with size.   Primary school heads, about
whom there is little research information, are generally
considered to retain a paternal style of headship, as a
consequence of learning their role 'on the job', but
despite appearances of 'democratisation' retain a
traditional centralised authority pattern and feel a need
to involve themselves personally in every aspect of school
life (Coulson, 1976; Cook and Mack, 1972).

In this research it was assumed at the outset that
primary school heads would be more likely to adopt a
paternalistic style, be more personally involved, and
consult more with parents, while secondary heads were
assumed to be more likely to adopt managerial styles and
delegate the referral tasks to some extent.   This turned
out to be the case.   The differences in the way in which
heads perceive their own role affects the amount of

consultation with colleagues and parents which takes place
when they refer a child.   This point was particularly
illustrated by the question asking heads about their
actual consultation procedures before referral;   secondary
heads did turn out to rely on their heads of schools or
departments.   However, just as in other school affairs,
the decision-making powers of heads becomes a taken-for-
granted characteristic, so in the matter of referral of
ESN children, heads do take for granted their powers to
make a decision which will eventually remove a child from
the normal school system, and place him instead into a
system which the heads themselves admit is a stigmatised
type of education.

The forty study population children were referred by
thirty-four schools: ten secondary, twenty-two primary,
one nursery and one other type of special school.   Thirty
schools were visited and the head teachers were inter
viewed (in two cases deputies, who were acting heads, were
interviewed).   Of the remaining four schools, one secondary school had disappeared under reorganisation, and one
declined to be interviewed.   The special school was not
considered eligible for this part of the study, and in one
primary school the staff who had referred the child had
all left.   The remaining thirty schools had referred
thirty-six of the children.   These comprised eight secondary, twenty-one primary, and one nursery school.   The
size of school varied from the nursery school with under a
hundred, to a comprehensive with over 1,500.

Eight of the primary schools who referred children had
between two and three hundred children on roll;   ten of
the schools had between three and five hundred children,
and three primary schools had over five hundred children.
The size of the secondary schools varied from under five
hundred to one and a half thousand.

The schools were widely spread around the city, to the
north and north-east, the south-east and south-west and
were located in four of the city consortia.   In external
appearance they ranged from a school with a forbidding
Victorian exterior, surrounded by council demolition areas
and boarded up derelict houses, to suburban schools in
pleasant tree-lined streets.   Most heads were able to
describe the areas they perceived their schools to serve
quite explicitly, both in physical and social terms.

'We are a pleasant estate, but have large family houses
with gardens, so we keep up our numbers as families
move in and out.   We have some problems, but no
problem families.'

'This is an older estate.   It has a lot of one-parent

families, socially disadvantaged families with low
intelligence, a lot of unemployment - some haven't
worked for years.'
Heads intuitively feel they 'know' the area which their
schools serve, even though they seldom live in the same
area.   Thus, one head who regarded himself as committed
to serving a pathological area, spoke of it as 'a slum
area, a high-immigrant area, commerce dies, the indigenous
population move away and there is vandalism and decay'.
The heads were asked what facilities and resources they
had in their schools as it seemed reasonable to assume
that schools with sufficient resources, particularly in
terms of remedial facilities, might tend to refer children
less often than schools with fewer facilities.   This did
indeed turn out to be the case.   Six heads particularly
mentioned their remedial facilities, as catering for slow-
learning children.   'I've got two remedial teachers, a
special remedial room with tape-recorders, a talking page
and so on.'   This head had only referred two children in
four years.   Another head, who seldom referred, had his
remedial children withdrawn for specialist small-group
teaching and several heads specifically mentioned using
the Tansley SET programme (Tansley, 1973).
The heads all mainly felt that their schools had good
resources and facilities, although four heads said they
had old inner-city schools which lacked play-space and
greenery particularly, and one school operated a complicated timetable on a split-site basis.   Heads were in
general enthusiastic about improving the resources their
schools could offer to all children.   One said: 'I'm a
good housekeeper, I have jumble sales to raise money for
resources.'
Fourteen of the schools were 'high-immigrant' schools,
with over 40 per cent of the children being of New Commonwealth origin.   Eleven schools had over 60 per cent of
such children.   The number of children of immigrant
parentage reflects the area that the school serves.   It
is very noticeable, but consistent with demographic data
for the city, that the schools serving outer suburban
areas have under 5 per cent of children of immigrant
parents.   One head said: 'We don't have those sorts of
children here.'   Another said: 'I have a small number of
West Indians.   I treat them all as children.'   Yet
another said: 'I have very few, mainly half-castes of the
second generation', and one head replied, 'We don't have
many, being a Catholic school.'   The schools with a high
proportion of children of immigrant parentage appear to
have quite a good staff-pupil ratio.   It is the outer
suburban schools which have a higher ratio.   This is

consistent with the LEA policy of providing extra staffing
for 'inner area' schools.   The following tables indicate
the ratio of pupils per member of staff, although not too
much reliance can be placed on the information, as some
heads included, or excluded, part-time staff.

TABLE 3.1 Staff-pupil ratio (primary)

Number in school	Number of staff	Number of pupils per staff
90 (45 per session)	5	9
200	7	28.5
200	5	40
210	7	30
220	9	24.4
240	7	34
240	9	26.6
240	9	26.6
250	12	20.8
300	11	27.2
300	11	27.2
310	14	22
360	13	27.6
360	13	27.6
360	11	32.7
400	12	33.3
450	18	25
470	17	27.6
500	20	25
500	15	33.3
570	22	25.9
610	22	27.6

In the one outer suburban school recording forty
children per staff member, the head had recently had a
nervous breakdown and another staff member was expected
shortly.

The referrals came from schools with a high and low
staff-pupil ratio, and in general it did not seem to have
been the case that a lower staff-pupil ratio meant that
schools did not refer children for ESN schooling.

Heads of primary schools were asked whether there was a
high teacher turnover in their schools.   In 1976, the
year the interviews were carried out, the teacher cuts due
to the economic recession were beginning to make themselves felt, and many heads replied that 'now' they did
not have a high teacher turnover.   However, it was interesting that seven of the primary school heads in the high

TABLE 3.2   Staff-pupil ratio (secondary)

Number of pupils	Number of staff	Number of pupils per staff
400	20	20
600	42	14.2
700	42	16.6
700	70	10
860	52	16.5
1,000	70	14.2
1,600	60	26.6
1,800	100	18

immigrant areas still said 'yes', they did have a high teacher turnover.

Of the thirty head teachers interviewed, sixteen of the primary school heads were male and six were female.   Of the secondary heads, four were male and four female. The heads were asked how long they had been heads in the school.   They were fairly long-serving and thus had had time to learn about the area and the children that the school served.   Seven heads had been in the post for over ten years, six for over five years and eight for over two years.   Five had been heads for under two years and four declined to answer.

THE REFERRAL PROCESS

A crucial part of this research was the attempt to elicit from head teachers information as to why they referred children as potentially ESN, and early on in the interviews heads were asked, 'What sort of things do you refer children to the Child Guidance Clinic for?'   The question was phrased in this manner as pilot study cases had shown that the heads thought initially in terms of referring a child to the clinic or to a psychologist, rather than 'as in need of special education'.

The heads overwhelmingly used behavioural and functional criteria in deciding to initiate the referral process.   They felt it was their responsibility to refer children who had functional problems connected with learning, reading and speech, and with behavioural difficulties.   Table 3.3 illustrates the replies the heads gave as to why they referred children.

Some heads replied to this question purely in terms of learning difficulties brought to their attention by the staff.

TABLE 3.3 Head teachers' reasons for referring children
as potentially ESN

Disruptive/maladjusted/behaviour problems	17
No learning progress/educational retardation	15
Reading problems	3
Speech defects	3
Emotional difficulties	1
Social problems	3
Genetic problem	1
Total	43

(More than one answer given.)

'The teacher tells me if a child is slow, dull, not
talking or reading; we take it from there.'

'They fall behind their fellow-pupils ... my staff are
trained to deal with average children, but not this
range.'

Other heads felt they noticed the learning problems themselves initially:

'I notice a problem - the rate of progress is slow, and
if he is in a class of thirty he can't have the
attention.'

'So many of my children are poor learners. I've just
referred eight. I tried to cope with them while they
were in the infants, but that's a mistake.'

This research did not interview the teachers who brought
children to the head's attention, as it was considered
that this was a study in itself. (1) However, whether it
was the class teacher who first brought a child to the
notice of the head, or whether the head took the initiative, most of the heads thought that they could intuitively judge which children were merely 'backward' and
which were potentially ESN.

'Most of the children we say are ESN are just backward,
so I don't refer many.'

'Even if children are backward, I don't refer them
unless they make no progress.'

'I have two remedial classes here, so I refer as a last
resort for learning difficulties and emotional
difficulty.'

One head said he was able to tell quite specifically
which children were ESN rather than 'remedial', and he

tended to refer children quite often.   He noted at the
time of interview that he had just referred eight
children: 'but the psychologist says seven of them are
low average, not ESN'.   However, he disagreed with the
psychologist's decision and remarked that 'children are
lost souls if they don't get remedial help or sent to ESN
school'.

It tended to be schools who had good remedial facilities, in the form of special teachers, extra staff, or a
special room for remedial children (at both primary and
secondary level) who preferred to regard as many children
as possible as backward or remedial, and who only referred
children as potentially ESN as a last resort.

From the interviews with heads, and informal discussion with classroom teachers, it appeared that a major
criterion for deciding who was remedial and who was
potentially ESN, was by comparison with fellow pupils.
Despite the 'semi-official ideology' (Sharp and Green,
1975) of a child-centred approach, recognising individual
differences, which is supposedly prevalent in
English primary schooling, the heads implicitly assumed a
standard of intellectual functioning to which children in
the same class should more or less conform.   Children who
do not 'progress' at a rate comparable to their fellow
pupils may be selected for referral.

Heads usually mentioned more than one reason for
referring children, the most common response being to
connect learning difficulties with behavioural difficulties.   There was no consensus about the relationship
between poor learning progress and behaviour problems.
One said he referred for: 'educational problems rather
than behaviour; behaviour problems are usually of average
intelligence', while another head considered that it was
backward children who became behaviour problems: 'I cope
if the children are not disruptive.   Backward children
are usually disruptive.   It's a vicious circle.'
Another head remarked: 'I've only referred six in
eighteen years.   I was desperately worried about their
work.   Children who are slow learners are not necessarily
behaviour problems', while yet another said he referred:
'if we feel a child is making no progress.   A lot is pure
social behaviour, bizarre behaviour.'   One head said he
referred for 'learning problems, speech defects' and
offered the explanation that, 'it may all be genetics' as
to why some children needed special help.   Another said
he referred for reading problems, and these tended to be
his coloured children.   Seventeen heads altogether
replied to this question in behavioural terms.   Four
heads said they referred

'behaviour problems mainly.   They are usually a
problem at home as well.'

'for continual evidence of unsocial behaviour.'

'maladjustment, not just education problems.'

'disturbed children.   They get more disruptive if they
aren't seen by the clinic.'

Two heads mentioned the clinic's social worker, who could
liaise with the child's home: 'Some children are vicious
with others and need removal if they can't be contained in
a school situation.   I get a social worker's help from
the clinic; educational problems may be well-adjusted of
course', and a head who referred mainly for educational
retardation added that: 'We pressure the clinic when a
child's behaviour is deteriorating.'   One head noted in
his answer to this question that the children of West
Indian origin may need referral.   'I refer several maladjusted children.   These are WI to a man.   There's a lot
of social maladjustment of children who've just come from
Jamaica.'   Only two heads were disturbed at referring
children who did not appear to be educationally retarded,
but who might present problems in school.

One said he had referred a girl who constituted a
problem: 'She's wet at one end and loud at the other;
I've referred her even though she's not dim', and another
head, who was worried about referring for behavioural
reasons, remarked that: 'We have a good try with a child
before we refer him.'

Heads did seem to think that in maintaining order and
control in their own schools, ESN-M schooling is available
'as a last resort' for children who were behaviour problems as well as for those with learning problems.   Four
inner-city heads said that they seldom referred children,
as they were used to coping with problems.   Heads who
felt they had a 'low standard' or a 'large remedial
intake' tended not to refer.   As one secondary head put
it: 'I seldom refer ... I have a remedial teacher who can
assess children and we admit 40 per cent with a reading
age of below nine anyway.'   Heads were asked specifically
what procedures they followed when referring children and
what consultation took place with other teachers.   Twelve
heads said they took the decision to refer a child and
then discussed the matter with staff, while four said they
followed the 'established procedure'.   Eleven heads said
the initiative was taken by the class teacher or remedial
teacher, who brought the child to their attention, and
after discussion the head referred the child.   Three

secondary heads noted that their heads of department took
the initiative in the referral.

Some heads felt they knew all the children well enough
to spot the problems and initiate procedures.

'In a small school like this I know all the children.
I want to be sure they all make adequate progress.'

'I initiate, then we discuss it together.'

'We discuss it, but I know every child and his problems.   I keep files on each child and keep my own
notes on them.'

'We do standardised tests throughout the year and I can
notice the children who are failing.'

'I know all the children and the parents and I can pick
out retarded development.'

'I decide, then I consult the staff.'
The eleven heads who felt that teachers or remedial
teachers drew their attention to particular children
tended to be enthusiastic about their staff and more
willing to delegate tasks.

'The staff bring it to my attention, then we work from
there.'

'The infant staff draw my attention to those backward
at the change to junior level.'

'My staff always come to tell me if they have a child
who isn't making progress; we work together.'

'The remedial teacher tends to see problems arising;
she discusses it, with the teachers concerned and it
moves from there.'

'My remedial teacher is marvellous.   We discuss the
child together.'
Secondary school heads tended to rely on their heads of
schools, departments or deputy heads, to initiate proceedings which accords with the managerial style of school
management noted earlier in this chapter.

'This would come via the heads of schools.   They are
are responsible for pastoral care and educational
problems.   The head of the remedial department tests
the children at certain times.'

'We have established an Integrated Literary Studies

course; even our backward children do it, but if we
feel a child is completely out of his depth the head
of department will discuss it with me.'

Four schools, three of them primary, said they had an
established procedure for checking on all children, and
that this would tend to bring to light children in need of
referral.

'Once a year I send a card asking all the teachers
about children who have problems, down to being backward or smelly.'

'I have pink slips. The staff fill in details of
children's problems on them; this way they feel they
have the support of the head and don't get frightened
by big words.'

Almost two-thirds of the heads in this study saw the
initial referral very much as a decision taken after discussion with the staff, and it is during these discussions that a child's potentiality as a candidate for ESN-M
school is reinforced or negated. Teachers who feel they
can cope with 'backward', 'smelly' or 'problem' children
do not press for referral.

Heads were also asked if they thought the head
teacher's role in sending children for assessment was
important. Heads tended to treat this question as part
of the previous question concerning consultation, and
elaborated on the discussions held between members of
staff before the referral was initiated. Four heads
developed the theme that referrals should be seen in a
wider context than one school and two heads particularly
mentioned that ideas could be developed within their consortium to help the referral process.

'We are hoping the consortium will help develop
remedial work and give us contact with secondary
schools.'

'We have a system of cumulative record cards. I was
on a working party for record cards. The X consortium
drew up the card I use.'

Two of the secondary school heads saw their role as a
rubber-stamp to procedures: 'I just sign forms'; 'I'm
like the pope; I give my blessing to get in touch with
the Services.'

Only two heads felt that it was not sufficient to
simply 'diagnose' a child with problems and make a referral. They thought schools should examine more carefully
what they could offer the children.

'There is a lot more we can do in schools. We should
develop new ideas. We should be able to discuss the

children's problems fully before we refer them to the
clinic.'

'The school may not have adjusted to the child.   I
like to feel we've got our house in order before we
look for outside help.'

By and large heads did not consider their schools as
problematic for the children;   they saw the schools as
attempting to help or 'cope' with problematic children.

There is an obvious difference between the way primary
and secondary schools regard and initiate the referral
procedure.   The secondary schools tend to think that the
referrals should have been done at the primary stage, but,
if they have an organised remedial department, they are
generally willing to try to accommodate backward children.
The heads do tend to adopt a 'managerial' style, in that
they depend more on their subordinates to bring children
to their attention who need special help beyond a
'remedial' stage.   Primary school heads tended to regard
the referral question as very much tied up with the resources their own schools could offer in terms of remedial
work and/or teachers trained specially for assessing or
dealing with backward children.   'Backward' was usually
an intuitive assessment comparing the children to their
fellow pupils.   Therefore children who were considered
'backward' in certain suburban schools might very well not
have been considered 'backward' in inner-city schools.
Several schools mentioned that they felt the Tansley
Special Educational Treatment programme was helping them
to 'diagnose' and deal with slow-learning or backward
children and it was decided to ask all schools whether
they had teachers who had participated in the SET programme to see whether schools which had done so were
referring fewer children.

Ten primary schools had been associated with the programme and they were all quite enthusiastic about their
new skills in testing children and felt they could now
assess possible 'failure' amongst children.

'I've been on the course.   It gave us more ideas at
infant level but we used to do these things
intuitively.   We were able to screen all our first
year;   only two didn't pass the test.'

'Yes, we were one of the first pilot schools for the
SET programme.'

'Two staff went last year.   We found 8-9 children in
our 6+ range failed the test.   They sent a mobile team
to help us.'

'Yes, my top infants are all screened and the children
withdrawn to a special class if they fail the tests.'
Two heads who had not yet been associated with the programme disapproved of it.

'No, we don't do it. I don't approve. I've never
had trouble teaching children to read.'

'No, we haven't done SET yet. I rely on the remedial
service and don't refer many children anyway.'
Of the ten schools who had had teachers and/or the head
do the course, five indicated that they 'now' did not
refer children to the clinic for educational reasons as
much, but that they still referred for behavioural problems. Five schools did not seem to think participation
in the programme had made much difference to their number
of referrals.

Heads were asked about the actual administrative procedures, and what their opinions were of the new SE forms
which in this year have replaced the old HP forms. All
the heads said they were obliged to fill out forms, but
two-thirds said they had a variety of other ways of contacting the other professional people concerned in the
referral.

'Yes, I use forms, but I always phone people.'

'I use everything. I ring them, write to them, fill
in the forms and then ring and say "Why haven't you
done anything?" I harass them.'

'After the referral, usually I phone. The clinic
sends a series of forms on parents' attitudes, scales
of aggression, etc.'

'I have to fill out forms, but I'm never above an
honest fiddle if it's for the child's benefit.'

'I keep in touch by phone as well. It's a short-cut
to get things done.'

'I'm always on the phone. It's a matter of knowing
which person can help.
Some heads felt that the 'ESN' forms tended to be used to
cover other handicaps, and are inappropriate. One head
said that he actually tore up forms which he considered to
be inappropriate. 'I get cross when I phone up about,
say, a child with sickle-cell anaemia, and they send me an
ESN form. I tear it up in front of the phone so they can
hear me.' Heads felt that the most irritating aspect of
the referral process was the long delay that ensued after

referral and form-filling before they were contacted by
other professionals or the administration.   They felt
that 'nothing was being done' and they were seldom offered
an explanation for the delay.   Several heads were vague
about the new SE forms which were being used in the city
in 1976.   Thirteen heads said they were not familiar with
the new form.

'I've only got HPs.'

'don't know about SE forms.   Is it anything to do with
Tansley's SET?'

'I've heard about the new forms but haven't got any
yet.'

Eight heads had not yet made referrals under the new procedures and nine said they had been sent the new forms.
The heads regarded the forms as a necessary administrative
device before the next step in the referral could occur
but were not particularly critical of either the old HP or
the new SE forms.   One head thought the HP form was 'out-
dated' and one said he had had to accept the psychologist's opinion when the psychologist wrote to him that:
'Forms are a hangover from the past when people were
classified.'   Twenty -two heads did not want to offer an
opinion on whether the new forms would be more appropriate
than the old.   Only four said they thought the forms were
more relevant or said more about a child, and one head was
of the opinion that 'forms are only as good as the people
using them'.   Heads felt somewhat aggrieved that they had
not been consulted about the introduction of new procedures.   Despite the importance of the head teachers in
initiating referrals there had been no central communication from the local education authority concerning the
new procedures at the time of interview.   One head said
that the first he heard of the new procedures was a curt
note from a psychologist saying: 'Due to an alteration in
referral procedures you now fill in an SE 1.'

The initial decision by the head to refer a child to
the Child Guidance Clinic as possibly in need of special
help, means that other professional people will then be
concerned with the child and his family.   In some cases
the head may decide to consult other professional personnel before he makes the referral.   The head should also
consult the parents before the referral is made.   This
part of the research was concerned with eliciting from the
heads how they regarded the other personnel and the
parents, and what contact they actually had with them.

THE INVOLVEMENT OF OTHER PERSONNEL

Heads were asked how they saw the role of the educational
psychologist in the referral process.   While the antipathy between medical and psychological personnel has
previously been documented, there is to date no previous
information on the relationship between heads and psychologists.   It was interesting, therefore, to find that
there was considerable antipathy towards psychologists
from the heads.   Table 3.4 illustrates head teachers'
perceptions of the role of the educational psychologist.

TABLE 3.4   Head teachers' views of the role of the
educational psychologist

Tests children	6
Assesses/prepares programmes	6
Offers advice	3
Important but too busy	5
Slow to come - too busy	6
Inefficient - doesn't advise enough	5
Other critical comments	4
Total	35

(More than one answer given.)

Six heads mentioned the IQ testing procedure as a
skill offered by the psychologist.
'When he actually arrives he obviously uses his expertise in applying the tests which he feels are most
adequate for that particular child.'

'He has a battery of tests that I can't apply.   He
tests the child mentally.'

'They do tests and we hope they'll give us some idea of
a child's potential.'
One head felt that testing was not the answer to her
problems: 'I want help and advice from them and I only
get tests and get told what I know....   This child is
disturbed.   I know that.'   Six other heads saw the
psychologist's role as the 'assessment' of children, with
a view to preparing special learning programmes for the
schools to carry out.   By and large these heads felt that
children should remain in the normal school if possible
and if the school could cope.   One of the heads had the
impression that it was her school's duty to cope with difficult children as there was a shortage of ESN schools.

'I see him as a specialist to do an assessment of the child and give me a programme for the class teacher to carry out.'

'He is in a position to come to a conclusion of his own without being biased by the teacher.... It's often difficult for a teacher to put into practice what he suggests.'

'They have a wider panorama of children with problems and can help us assess whether we can cope.... There aren't enough ESN schools so they should provide programmes to help staff.'

Five heads stressed that the psychologist was important but too busy to do much good.   This theme of the 'overworked' psychologist recurred several times.

'It's a very important role but they are too busy.   X is a good chap but he's only learning.'

'We only have one in this area.   I keep referrals down so as not to overwork him.'

'We had a directive that they were overworked and we shouldn't refer unless the child was chronic.'

'Our last one was marvellous, but now they are overworked and never come.'

Another theme that recurred was that of the 'slow process'.   The educational psychologist was seen, correctly as chapter 4 indicates, as the person holding up the process of transferring a child out of the school once the school had asked for help.   The secondary schools were almost unanimous in their criticisms of the educational psychologist.

'I'm tremendously disappointed with the work of the Child Guidance Clinic.   We've been trying since September to get a child to ESN school.   Why aren't these cases resolved at primary level.   We have two-year cases waiting.'

'We never get help from them.   We always have to wait so long.' (from a head who tries not to refer)

'They are too slow.   A referral takes a long time, then they give you that hateful phrase "this child should remain in his normal school".'

'The whole procedure is cumbersome.   Nothing gets done unless I'm constantly on the phone.'

Also, 'inefficiency' was a theme:
> 'There should be two hundred more of them in the city -
> they aren't efficient enough to be of any use.'

> 'It's no bloody good referring children.   It takes so
> long.   Whatever good there is in the clinics is
> impossible to show, while the bad is magnificent.   The
> clinic hasn't got the resources to scratch the surface
> of the problems.'

Three heads saw the psychologist in a supportive role and
felt that they had a good relationship with their local
Child Guidance Clinic.
> 'I'd like to see him as a supporter of the whole
> school, staff as well.   We can have a working lunch
> and chats about the children informally.'

> 'We deal closely with them.   I can't speak too highly
> of them.'

> 'The Child Guidance Clinic is for consultation and
> support.'

One head replied that he 'didn't have much to do with
them'.   Another head approved that he could send maladjusted children to the clinic to 'chat' with the psychologist, and one head confided: 'We have to be ever so
careful with them.   Some of them think we don't know
anything about children.'   Another head felt they baffled
his staff with long words.

Heads were asked how they saw the role of the senior
clinical medical officer in the assessment process.   Some
heads did not appear to know that the SCMO had a duty to
examine children in need of special education.   Twelve
heads, including six secondary heads, said they had no
contact with an SCMO.   Another said he saw duplicates of
letters written by medical personnel and another said he
'got the doctors' comments via the psychologist'.   Five
heads said they called in the school MO before they
referred a child.
> 'We usually try and engineer it so that the MO sees the
> child and the parents.   We say, "Doctor what do you
> think of so and so?"   Usually the doctor has some good
> comments about the relationship between the child and
> the mother.'

> 'I try to eliminate physical causes first as a reason
> for backwardness, so I always call in a doctor.   Dr X
> is our school MO and Dr Y our senior.'

> 'I've got a close relationship with the medical

personnel, MO, school nurse and health visitor.   I
call them in to see to problems.'
Two heads mentioned that under the new procedure a child
could be referred and seen by a doctor before being seen
by a psychologist.   Heads did not regard the medical
examination of the child in the same light as they regarded the psychologist's interviews, and some seemed unaware
that parents not attending the medicals, or long waits for
medicals, could delay the procedures of moving the
children into special education.

Asked about possible contacts with the Special Services
administration, fourteen heads said they had no contact
with them, and one head confused them with the Social
Services Department.   Eleven heads saw the role of
Special Service as administrative: 'They do the forms,
find the places, and send me the letters'; 'They send the
papers on' and one head produced a guideline document sent
out to schools on how to use the various services available (e.g. school psychological services, social services)
and said Special Services sent out these kinds of documents.   Heads were not particularly critical of the
administration; their major criticism for the delays in
the assessment process and thus in the removal of certain
children from their schools, was directed at the psychologist.   Several heads regarded Special Services as an
'emergency service' if children were being ill-treated or
in physical danger at home.

The involvement of parents in the referral and assessment procedures has always been regarded by professionals
as a matter of some sensitivity, as the formal procedures
laid down by Section 34 of the 1944 Act were designed
with possible parental objections to special schooling in
mind.   Circular 2/75 noted that in fact parents normally
recognise the need for special education for their child
'provided they are involved in decisions from an early
stage' and that 'parents should be brought into consultation even before ... the time when medical and psychological investigation takes place'.   The Circular does not
go into detail as to how this consultation is to take
place, but usually the person who initially consults
parents about the possible need for special schooling for
their child is the head teacher of the child's normal
school.   Therefore, it was considered important in this
study to ask heads about the extent and type of consultation they had with parents.   Circular 2/75 also hinted
that lack of information to parents about the legal basis
of assessment might smooth the path of initial consultation with parents - 'which can be arranged quite informally without reference to the legal basis for the medical
examination'.

Heads were asked if they contacted parents before they
referred a child.   Twenty-five heads replied that they
did (or in the case of secondary schools, a deputy or head
of school contacted the parents);   four heads replied 'not
always' and one head replied, 'I try to keep parents out
of school.'   Several heads phrased the contact with the
parents in terms of 'I send for them'.   One head said he
'invited' parents, and another said, 'I tell the parents
the doctor will be here to see their child;   they can come
if they like.'

One head felt diffident about contacting parents
because 'the label "special school" is a handicap;   so
many parents are reluctant because it's a social slur'.
Another head confided that if the parents wouldn't co-
operate, 'We try to wear them out.'

The heads were then asked what part they thought should
be played by parents in the assessment and placement process.   This left heads free both to say what they thought
'ought' to happen, and to comment on their actual procedures.   Five heads stressed that the parents must agree
to the referral before they actually make it.

'We are not allowed to have the children tested without
the parents' permission.'

'If you don't have the parents behind you, you can't
move.'

'A parent has to agree;   it's not allowed to send a
child to special school without the parents' consent.
I do it tactfully.'

Fifteen heads said that they must or 'should' consult
parents before they make the referral, and most said this
in terms of 'persuading' parents to agree to referral.

'To my mind the only way is to consult them before you
send their children around.'

'I sow the seed - it's an absolute must - to discuss it
with parents.'

'I go and visit the parents.   This impresses our Asian
parents particularly.'

'The earlier they are involved the better.   They can
come in at a late stage and say they don't want their
child to go to special school.'

Two heads said they showed the record cards of the children to the parents to demonstrate how backward their
children were, and eight heads spoke specifically in terms
of 'persuading' the parents to co-operate in the referral
process.

'I say I'm going to ask the experts for help.   They
usually accept my opinion.   They sometimes think their
child will go to a daft school.'

'I tell the parents their child is naughty - difficult.
We have a good old chat and they usually co-operate.'

'We suggest to the parents the child needs "help" and
we need "guidance";   that way we get 100 per cent co-
operation.'

'We broach the idea we are concerned with lack of progress and how do you feel about special school if
there's a place.   We make it sound as if there's an
element of success in getting a place.'

Since heads were also asked how they had actually dealt
with the particular children in the study population, it
was interesting to compare what they said 'should' happen
with what actually did happen in particular cases.

'The head of X school replied that he liked to think
that 90 per cent of the cases he had referred had been
because the parents wanted him to.   He said it was
vital to keep the parents in the picture while making a
referral.   In the case of Lucy C., he said the mother
would not recognise that Lucy was a dull child and took
some persuading that she needed special schooling.
Eventually she realised that Lucy would probably get
pregnant before she was sixteen if she wasn't looked
after.   I arranged for her to visit the special
school, and then she agreed for the child to go there.
We got her there before the situation became
desperate.'

The head of Y comprehensive replied that her head of
year and head of lower/upper/middle school saw the
parents, but that she was available if parents really
wished to see her.   The head of middle school said
that he had seen Barbara B.'s mother, who was a con-
scientious, religious, West Indian mother, who talked
coherently about her problems with her daughter.   However, she objected to the stigma of special school.

'I had to put pressure on them - a reasonable amount of
pressure - as I really thought Barbara should go to X
school.   I could have threatened to expel her.   I've
got her brother here;   he's remedial but okay'.

In the case of Lucy the head's persuasion of the mother
had taken the form of suggesting that the child's 'dullness' would lead to pregnancy;   in the case of Barbara the
pressure was more overt and the threat of expulsion was
hinted at.

ESN-M SCHOOLING

In view of the discussion, which was widespread by 1976,
over the integration of 'handicapped' children in normal
schools, rather than the provision of special schooling,
heads were asked about their perceptions of the value of
ESN-M schooling, as compared with normal schooling, for
children with learning and/or behavioural problems.   Over
half the heads were adamant that some form of special
schooling was required to deal with children of limited
ability, or those who could not be controlled in normal
school.   Primary heads in particular expressed anxiety
that their teachers would not be able to cope with certain
types of children:
   'My younger staff have problems with slow learners.'

   'If you have big numbers in the school you have to
   refer, the teacher's haven't got time to deal with
   problem children.'

   'My teachers and I know all about these children, but
   we get to a point where we don't know what to do with a
   child.'

   'We get more problem children now.   It's because we
   keep more weak babies alive and we have to deal with
   them later.'

   'Some teachers would have nervous breakdowns if they
   had to cope with ESN children.'

   'We'd like to keep the children but our teachers aren't
   trained and we have too large numbers.'
Secondary schools tended to have established remedial
departments which could contain ESN children.   Four
secondary heads felt they should try and keep the children, but even they had reservations.   'They may be better
off at the barmy school, as I've heard it called.'   Secondary heads also put more emphasis on the behavioural
aspects:
   'If a child is really violent and aggressive, we can't
   keep him, so we have a case conference.'

   'If the child can't be controlled in a normal school
   the ESN school should take him.'

   'There are some children we would like to see moved as
   quickly as possible.   We reach our limit of being able
   to educate them.   They need time, which is something
   we haven't got.'

On the other hand sixteen heads felt that if the school
could 'cope' it was better that children with learning
problems should remain in the normal school.

> 'Unless it's essential, the children should be kept in
> normal school.   I try not to refer.   I keep children
> an extra year in the infants and things like that.'

> 'If a school doesn't have a high standard then they can
> keep children here who in a better school would stand
> out.'

> 'Yes, if you have teachers who can work with the slower
> children.'

> 'Yes, they are better now.   We have a remedial unit
> which works marvellously.'

There was a feeling amongst heads of inner-city schools
particularly, that backward children did not 'stand out'
in their schools in the way that they might have done in
suburban schools - the schools having a lower 'standard'.
One head in particular was of the opinion that ESN-M
schools could not do anything for children that an inner-
city school could not do.   One head of a Catholic school
was adamant that ESN schools were for 'strange types' and
no child from her school would go if she could help it.
The heads' diverse opinion on the value of special schooling reflected the current debates on the 'integration' of
children in need of special education in normal schools,
as against their 'segregation' in special schools.   Head
teachers' evidence to the Warnock Committee on this point
had tended to favour the segregation of children in
special school ('Education', 28 August 1975, 19 September
1975).   Since by the act of referral heads were setting
in train the procedures which could exclude a child from
normal education, they were asked what they thought ESN
schools could do for children that normal schools were
unable to do.   Table 3.5 summarises heads' views on this.

TABLE 3.5 Heads' views on the functions of ESN-M
schooling

Trained teacher/expertise with slow learners	8
Smaller classes/individual attention	13
Small units for anti-social children	4
Better than segregation in normal school	2
Nothing	6
Total	33

(More than one answer given.)

Eight heads thought that ESN-M schools could provide expertise with slow-learning children, to a greater degree than remedial teachers in normal schools were able to provide.   Their views as to the extent of this expertise tended to be somewhat idealised; one head said they had: 'a better staffing ratio and specialised knowledge.   The staff have all done a one-year special course.'   In fact, few ESN-M schools have many specially trained staff.   In this study no school had more than three members of staff who had completed a special education course or qualification, although a high proportion of staff were planning to take advantage of the growing number of in-service courses being started.

The most popular view about the value of ESN-M schools was that the smaller classes make more individual attention per child possible.

'They have a good pupil-teacher ratio and can give extra attention.'

'Special schools can give small group teaching.'

'It boils down to a smaller ratio.   Five children per adult.   They get what they are lacking at home ... individual attention.'

This latter head had similar views to the head teacher in Sharpe and Green's study of 'Mapledene' School (1975). He had both a child-centred perspective on education, and a social pathological view of the homes of the children. However, a view prevailed among heads that their schools were not equipped to give individual attention on the scale needed by particular children.   The 'attention' noted by heads was not necessarily academic attention. Four heads specifically saw ESN-M schools in terms of the control of anti-social children:

'They have small working units for children who become aggressive and anti-social.'

'The schools do a great job and the teachers have a tough time.   Maladjusted children need a regime.'

'If children can't be controlled in the normal school the ESN school should take them.'

There was a general tendency to assume that however much attention the children received, they were educationally 'beyond the pale' - the value of ESN-M school did not lie in any educational aims in the accepted sense, but in social adjustment and social control.   It is on the basis of this kind of perspective that it becomes possible to speak of special education as being a 'non-education' in

terms of the academic goals generally accepted in (some)
normal schools.   The heads were also aware that any
values ESN-M schools might offer could be offset by the
public image of ESN-M schools.   'They give extra help,
but some people still see these schools as no good.'
However, two heads thought that the children were stigmatised even more by remaining in special units attached to
the normal school.   'I know there are some schools that
have ESN units attached to them on the campus.   If
worked properly this could be all right, but often I
think they're worse off than being in an ESN school.'
This is interesting in the light of the current post-
Warnock enthusiasm for 'integration'.   Six heads did not
think that ESN-M school could offer children anything that
normal schools could not offer.

Despite all heads offering an opinion on the value of
ESN-M schooling, when asked what contacts they had with
the schools, fourteen heads said they had no contact with
the school generally although several felt it was a
failure on their part:

'I've never been round a special school.   We should
have more contact.'

'I'm part of an experiment in community education, so
I've had a chance now to contact all sorts of special
schools.   I haven't been to an ESN one yet but I
should go.'

Ten primary school heads said they had no contact with ESN
schools.   Of these schools three were 'high-immigrant'
schools, five were suburban schools and two were RC
schools.   Another RC head said he didn't really have contact, but he had actually driven the child in question to
the ESN school for a visit.

Four secondary heads said they had no contact with
special schools; several did have contact.   In one case
the head of the remedial department was married to an ESN
head.   Another secondary school head had taken six pupils
back from the local ESN school.   Another head said she
invited ESN heads to consortium meetings.   A fourth secondary head has an 'informal arrangement' to discuss
children with the local ESN head.

Seven heads said they had informal contact by telephone
with special schools, but wished there was a more formal
mechanism by which contacts between normal and special
schools could be maintained:

'In D.'s case I phoned two special schools as the
papers had gone astray.'

'I phone, but it's a limited interchange.   It's a pity
we can't get a bigger interchange.'

'We have very little contact, but enough to ring up
heads of special schools.'
Six heads felt they had informal contact amounting to
'arrangements' with special school heads.

'I contacted the head of our neighbouring school - the
deputy came down and had a look at one or two children
we were worried about and gave his opinion....   Within
a week the kids were in.   It was marvellous.'

'I knew the previous head of X school very well.   We
had a private arrangement over one boy.   He let him
come back to me for a trial six weeks and it worked
very well.'

'The head [of ESN schools] knows that if I express concern the child needs help.   I liaise in the same way
that I do with the local immigrant centre.'
In general the heads do regard ESN-M education as 'outside' normal education, with goals more related to control
and adjustment rather than academic.   Although some heads
expressed the view that there 'ought' to be more contact
and information flow between special and normal schools,
they were not particularly enthusiastic to take the lead
in this.   ESN-M schooling is a stigmatised form of
schooling, rationalised as 'education', but the heads are
aware that this is not the major goal, and do see the
schools as places where children who present learning and
behaviour problems (particularly the latter or both)
should go as speedily as possible.

CULTURAL BELIEFS ABOUT IMMIGRANT CHILDREN

There are differing perceptions of the significance which
schools and teachers attach to cultural and racial diver-
sity, and the kinds of problems that children from different cultural and racial backgrounds might present for
schools when they arrive as immigrant children or are born
to immigrant parents in Britain.   The cultural base of
schools in certain areas of the country has changed
rapidly over the last twelve years, and children from the
dominant culture are often numerically a minority in these
schools.   The limited research available on the perceptions of teachers about their pupils, once they are working within a changed cultural framework (Brittan, 1976;
Giles, 1977) has suggested that teachers tend to operate
within a framework of stereotypes, which are reinforced,
rather than negated, by the response from the pupils.
Brittan, for example, noted that the teachers in her

sample perceived West Indian children as of low ability
and creating disciplinary problems.   Giles found that:
'Teachers' stereotypes and expectations do influence the
way they behave towards West Indian students and have an
influence on the interaction process', and Edwards (1978)
concluded from her research on teacher attitudes towards
West Indian speech that: 'Teachers differ little from the
rest of society in the stereotypes which they hold of
minority groups....   They also discriminate between
working class and West Indian speakers and evaluate the
working class guise more favourably than the West Indian
guise.'

In this research heads were asked whether West Indian,
Asian (and Irish) children had particular problems that
might affect their education.   Table 3.6 illustrates the
heads' views of the problems of West Indian children.

TABLE 3.6 Heads' perceptions of the problems of West
Indian children

Learning process slower/poor concentration	9
Language problems/dialect	5
Not keen on education	3
Volatile/boisterous/extrovert	8
Aggressive/troublesome	7
Family problems/working mothers	6
Sickle-cell anaemia	2
Don't have many problems/WI children	8
Total	48

(More than one answer given.)

This question elicited a variety of responses from heads,
particularly those heads in areas of high West Indian concentration.   There was a strong feeling among heads that
the learning process was slower for West Indian children,
that they lacked the ability to concentrate for any length
of time, and that they would tend to under-achieve and be
'remedial'.

There was an implicit assumption that these qualities
which they attributed to the children were somehow
'natural' qualities, although only one head specifically
mentioned genetic inheritance:

'They are bound to be slower.   It's their personalities.   They lack concentration.'

'I've got a small representative bunch.   They are a
slow, docile, low-functioning lot.'

'I've had their parents here crying for me to keep
their children.   They want them to have a good education, but they'll only get CSE Grade 5.'

'A lot of WI children have undoubted difficulty in
concentrating for a length of time that we assume to be
reasonable.'

'They are slower than the Asian children - not as
bright.'
Several heads made overt comparisons with Asian children
who were felt to be 'naturally' brighter and also had more
home support.   Three heads elaborated on their opinion
that West Indian children were 'less keen' on education
than other groups of children.   Here particularly they
were sometimes unfavourably compared with Asian children.
'It's mainly their attitude [to education].   We are
getting rid of our top older boys who have been
influenced by older boys.'

'They are less keen on education than Asians.'

'It's such a transition for the kids.   One minute they
are sitting under a banyan tree waiting for breakfast
to fall on their heads, the next minute they are in a
cold wet place full of walls and cars.'
Five heads thought that language problems or dialect
speech might impede the progress of West Indian children.
'Many of them have a language problem, largely because
... well, they speak two languages - English and
dialect.'

'They have language-dialect problems.'

'West Indian patois is a handicap.'

'We have been saying for years the WI have a language
problem.   I felt the Department of English as a Second
Language had the wrong end of the stick concentrating
on Asians.'
Despite the conclusions Edwards came to, the heads did not
mention any negative evaluation by the school, of the
children's speech, as affecting their performance.   Eight
heads mentioned that West Indian children were more volatile or boisterous than their other pupils and that this
could disrupt the normal classroom activity.
'Many of them are extremely extrovert.   They tend to
be very noisy, which can be upsetting in a class where
individual or group work is going on.'

'West Indians are boisterous and less keen on education
than Asians.   This is well known obviously.'

'The children are mainly born here now but the temperament of the West Indian children is more volatile, disruptive, easily stirred.'

'They are the usual problem; hyper-active and anti-
authority.'

'A racial characteristic is that West Indians are
voluble.   Their fights look like riots.'
Seven heads also considered that the boisterousness of
their West Indian pupils could become aggressive,
especially amongst older pupils.   Four of the secondary
heads in particular were worried that their adolescent
West Indian pupils might be influenced by 'black power'
groups in their area.
   'We are a black power area and it's very dangerous....
   The black power people destroy kids, especially the
   less able.'

   'They are violent.   A "none of you whites are going to
   tell me what to do" attitude.'
Three primary heads were quite explicit in their views on
the aggression of West Indians:
   'They can get very nasty and aggressive but we try with
   them.   If I referred every West Indian with temper
   tantrums I'd refer them all.'

   'I have some who are a danger to other children and to
   staff.   It's because West Indian parents thump hell
   out of their kids....   They want their kids to grow up
   to be good citizens, but don't know how to make it
   happen.'

   'The Jamaicans are the trouble....   They are so
   impudent....   We have children from the worst family
   in the Midlands here.   They are always in trouble:
   stealing, mugging.   They threw a woman off a 'bus and
   broke her teeth.   A Police Inspector told me that.'
[A primary head who regards 'the coloureds' as one of
her major problems.]   She also said:

   'Enoch Powell is right.   He has an avid love of his
   country, as many people have.   There are enough immigrants and there is going to be trouble.'
The heads ostensibly view the aggression of their black
pupils in the same manner that they perceive white

aggression;   it is a basic problem of social control -
particularly of working-class children.   However, their
reactions to black aggression, even at primary school
level, do have built-in racial assumptions and rationalisations.   Without making explicit political connections
the heads are uneasily aware that the aggression of some
black children is not the same as white children's disruptive and aggressive behaviour.   The aggression is a
threat to white people in general, and 'black power' is
regarded as a threat from which young black children must
be protected.   However, the heads in the study were
unanimous in their view that West Indian parents wanted
their children to benefit from education and do well at
school.   Nevertheless, six heads specifically mentioned
family problems that they felt held the children back
educationally.   Three heads mentioned that the West
Indian family was 'different'.

> 'The West Indian family is different.   There is
> trouble for them when they come over here.   Things are
> not like they are in Jamaica - the West Indian men
> expect the women to work and bring up a family.'

> 'Their home environment is different.   The parents are
> very strict.   My West Indians are co-operative and
> have bright children.'

Several heads noted their views on stricter discipline in
West Indian homes, and in one case the head considered
that this was taken to illogical extremes.   'The kid
gets the same belting if he drops a fork or robs a bank.'
Two heads complained about working West Indian mothers and
shift working: 'The parents are glad their children are
getting an education, but they can't give much help....
They need to stop working shifts and see something of
their kids.'   Two heads also mentioned that West Indian
children tended to suffer from sickle-cell anaemia.   One
head answered: 'They don't have special problems.   I
teach them all to be courteous.'   The secondary school
heads in areas with a high concentration of West Indian
parents had given a great deal of thought to the problems
they considered West Indian children currently presented
in their school, and gave lengthy answers.   One head had
suggested that a meeting of West Indian parents concerned
about their children's education should be called, and a
committee formed.   (In 1977 the Society for the Advancement of Multi-Cultural Education was formed in the area by
the head of the department for teaching English as a
second language, and meetings with West Indian parents
have been held.)

Heads were also asked what sort of problems they

thought Asian children had as far as education was
concerned.   This did not elicit the lengthy answers that
the question about West Indian children did.   Table 3.7
illustrates heads' views of Asian problems.

TABLE 3.7 Heads' perceptions of the problems of Asian
children

Language/communication	7
Family/cultural problems	7
Non-English-speaking mothers	3
Assessment problems	3
None	5
Few here	5
Total	30

Five heads mentioned that Asians were 'well-motivated to
learn' when asked this question, but one said that it was
'a myth that Asians were more interested in education than
the West Indians'.   The problems which heads considered
Asian children presented were largely concerned with
language, and with family and cultural differences.
    'Their problem is in mastering the language, particu-
    larly the idioms and the comprehension.   They can
    usually read well, but their level of understanding is
    below par ... it also takes a long time to get over to
    them that reading is for enjoyment.'

    'A lot of the children won't talk - communicate.
    Where do we go if the child won't talk?   But once they
    get over our stupid English language they usually do
    well.'

    'Language is the main problem, but we have an Asian
    teacher who can act as interpreter.'

    'I can remember when they came with no English, but now
    we have the Immigrant Centres and they come with quite
    a lot.'
Some comments on the family and cultural differences were
concerned with 'good' parental support, which was considered to be carried too far.
    'They get good family support but are over-protected.'

    'The families have ambitions for the children and give
    them coaching in the evenings.   I don't really approve
    of that.'
The arranged marriages for girls were mentioned as a

problem by two heads and by and large Asian girls were
considered to have more problems of adjustment than Asian
boys.   One head said: 'I've nothing against people
keeping their own culture, but it slows the children at
school.'   Non-English-speaking families were considered
to be a problem by three heads: 'Our Pakistani parents
are mainly peasants from Mirpur.   They don't speak
English and don't know what's going on', and three heads
also mentioned the problems that Asian children presented
for assessment as in special educational need.

> 'There are real problems of assessment....   I haven't
> referred any Asians.'

> 'The psychologists are not experts with Asians.   Their
> tests are not good.'

The heads were also asked whether Irish children presented
any specific problems, although, as noted, Irish children
were eventually excluded from the study.   Six heads
replied that they did find the Irish children a problem,
and were quite vehement in their views on Irish children:

> 'A lot have been 'demolished' (the houses) and they've
> gone, thank heaven.'

> 'You get the Irish tinker variety - they live like pigs
> and are the worst group for ability, attainment and
> honesty.'

> 'Thank God I don't get any Irish or tinkers.   They are
> awful.'

Otherwise heads tended to reply that the Irish children
attended nearby RC schools and the three RC schools in the
study did not find them any problem.

CASE STUDIES OF HEADS' DECISIONS

After the head teachers had given a general response to
the questions raised by the interview schedule, they were
asked specifically about the decisions they had made on
the particular child in question.   The following case
studies indicate why heads had referred a particular
child, who they had consulted during the referral, whether
they thought the child would do better in a special
school, whether they discussed the referral with the
parents, and, finally, whether a child being West Indian
or Asian affected the referral.
1 The head of H Infants School, a pleasant outer suburban
school serving mainly private semi-detached estates, had
referred David in April 1974, when he was seven years old.
She said,

'He was a small and immature child.   He made no progress even though he was kept in the infants an extra
year.   He stood out like a sore thumb;   he was
emotional, could be difficult, he couldn't cope with
himself.   Two of my staff were very good with him.
It took a year to get him to eat dinner properly.   He
had poor co-ordination and turned to jelly on the
climbing frame.'
She said David would obviously be better off in a special
school, as they had smaller classes.   She was 'rather
upset' that the head of the special school had not rung
her about David, and while we were talking discovered
some papers she should have 'sent on'.   She had only
seen David's parents at parents' evenings and felt David's
problems were compounded by the fact that he and his
younger brother were 'afterthought' in a grown-up family.
'The mother is emotional as they usually are when they
are older.'   This case illustrates the way in which heads
implicitly compare children making 'no progress' with
other children, particularly if the child cannot keep up
with his age group.   This head, although head of a
pleasant, suburban school, thought that teachers in normal
schools should not be asked to cope with slow learners
because of large numbers in a class.   If the child had
attended an inner-city school he might not have been referred.   The head also had strong views on the fact
that 'nowadays we keep more weak babies alive' and that an
increase in problem children could be traced to this.
The case also illustrates the way in which the 'tipping-
point' of referral came when the child showed that he was
not only slow, but emotional and difficult.   Although
this head said she consulted her staff before referral,
she had never visited an ESN-M school, although in this
particular case she felt the head of the ESN school should
have rung her.   Although she thought that parents should
be contacted before a referral, she had not specifically
spoken to the parents, apart from seeing them at a parent
parents' evening, but she had formed a theory as to the
'inherent' emotional characteristics on which David's
problems could be blamed.

2   The head of St A.'s School, an RC school in an inner-
city re-development area, had referred Bertram at the age
of eight.   He said:
'I think that's a good age to refer.   He'd been a pest
since he came to the school but we like to give them
time to settle.   He's disruptive and constantly seeks
attention.   He makes class teaching a misery.   We
discussed him at several meetings and got a language
master for him to help his reading.'

The head had discussed Bertram's problems with his mother.
'It's a one-parent family.   She looks after him to the
best of her ability, but her English isn't much good.'
He felt that being West Indian had contributed to
Bertram's difficulties, mainly because he was an only
child in a one-parent family.

This case illustrates the way in which disruptive
children tend to be referred in the hope that they can be
removed from the school.   In this case the class teacher
felt that Bertram was too troublesome to cope with and
was pressing for his removal.   It was interesting to
note that while the child, who did in fact have a solitary
life at home, was pressing for human attention, the school
provided him with a machine!

3   The head of R Junior and Infants School, an inner-city
primary school, had referred Karl in 1975 after he had
made seventy-seven attendances out of a possible 274.   He
said:

'His brothers were already in ESN school.   They came
from B school.   I thought that school had got fed up
with them.   I filled out a 3HP.   I don't often refer.
My teachers come and say they've got an ESN child, but
they don't know what they are talking about.   All
backward kids aren't ESN.'

The head said he consulted with his staff over referrals
but remarked that, 'Teachers can be as weird as anyone
else.'   He said he had contact with the local ESN school
and had had a 'private arrangement' over one boy.   'I
pressed for Karl to go to a residential school to get him
away from his very inadequate family.   He'll do better in
special school if he attends - he was never here long
enough to make friends or links.'   He was very critical
of the parents.   The family was a long-term 'problem'
family, well-known to the Social Services, and the EWO.
The mother was a crippled woman and the family moved
around the inner city frequently.   'We wore them out.
They are a really low quality family.   I only met them
once.   My teachers saw them mainly.   They had delib-
erately opted out of their responsibilities.   Bernstein
would have produced a restricted, restricted code for
Karl!'   This case illustrates the way in which the heads
of inner-city schools feel that they can distinguish
between 'backward' children who can remain in their
schools which have a lower standard, and potentially ESN
children.   This head felt that the referral was his
decision and responsibility despite pressure from
teachers.   He had a social pathological view of the
surrounding area and some of the families of his children.

Karl's family particularly were considered a problem to a
variety of social services. The parents were very
reluctant to have another of their sons sent to ESN
school, but were persuaded by a process of 'wearing-out'.
It was interesting that the head employed academic educational theory in his diagnosis of the family problems.
The work of Bernstein was evoked to rationalise views of
the family pathology.

The major conclusion from an analysis of the referring
schools and heads concerns the way in which schools recognise and define what they consider to be potentially
moderately educationally subnormal children in need of
special help. Although heads were aware that in 1976
recommended changes of procedure (use of forms) were being
implemented, few heads were aware of, or had read, the DES
Circular 2/75 or were taking much part in the current
debate concerning the diagnosis and assessment of children
in need of special education - despite the fact that it is
largely their decision which sets in train the whole process. Their view of the referral was a logical pragmatic response to their 'professional' understanding that
certain children were beyond the capacity of 'normal'
school to cope with them. This understanding operated
when children exhibited a given level of problems of an
'educational' or 'behavioural' nature. The level at
which the problem was regarded as abnormal and beyond the
capacity of the school was measured in terms of available
school resources, ability of teachers to cope and comparison with class-mates. Heads felt intuitively that
they could make a distinction between pupils who were
merely 'backward' and pupils who were potentially ESN-M.
Such children were variously described as 'slow learners',
'poor learners', 'pretty poor', 'make no progress', or had
reading handicaps or speech defects and/or who exhibited
behaviour problems that disrupted the classroom
activities.
   There was no consensus amongst the heads in this study
as to whether a potentially educationally subnormal child
was necessarily a disruptive behaviour problem, except in
so far as the symptoms of educational retardation were in
themselves sometimes regarded as a problem in the classroom, but there was a very blurred line between what was
regarded as an educational problem and what was regarded
as a behavioural problem. Some heads equated ESN
children with 'bad', 'disruptive', or 'maladjusted' behaviour. Other heads regarded a 'true' ESN child as not
necessarily disruptive. This difficulty in separating
the educational problems of particular children from

behavioural problems which might disrupt the daily
activities of a normal class may be one reason for the
number of children referred as in need of special education who have become classified as moderately educationally subnormal rather than maladjusted.   It has previously been suggested that in the absence of clear
referral criteria, the selection of the ESN-M school
population has depended to a significant degree on inadequate or difficult behaviour within the 'normal'
school.

The heads in this study were divided in their views on
the segregation of ESN-M children in special schools as
against their continuing in the normal school.   Most
heads felt that ESN schools had facilities and resources
for dealing with slow-learning or disruptive children, and
that normal schools did not have teachers who could cope
with the children.   Heads who felt they had sufficient
staff or remedial facilities, or other aids (e.g.
Tansley's SET) thought that the children should be kept in
the normal school, with ESN schools used as a 'last
resort'.   Some heads in inner-city schools felt that they
had a general 'low' standard of achievement which made it
impossible to keep slow-learning children.

A second conclusion concerns the way in which school
heads regard the involvement of other personnel in the
referral process.   By and large, they expressed dissatisfaction with the psychologists, but felt psychologists had
special skills for assessing and helping children that the
schools did not possess.   They had considerable expectations of the Child Guidance Clinics which were not fulfilled.   Psychologists were held to be 'too slow' or 'too
busy' and were regarded as a scarce resource.   The decision by the psychologist to 'see' and assess a child was
regarded by heads as a step that could not be by-passed in
the process.   The medical officers were regarded by heads
as less important than the psychologists, although some
heads felt they should eliminate possible physical causes
of backwardness before psychological testing.   The heads
all thought parents 'ought' to be consulted over the
referral process, and by and large they fulfilled their
responsibility to discuss the referral with parents.
However, they did not fully understand the importance
which parents placed on this discussion for providing
information.   Some heads were more concerned to 'persuade' parents not to object to special education than to
inform them.   They thought parents had more stereotyped
ideas about the 'daft' school than parents actually had.
Parents want to visit the special schools and see what
they are like, but the lack of contact heads reported with

special schools may make this difficult for heads to arrange.   Two-thirds of the heads consulted their staffs before referral - primary school heads tended to be more paternal in their approach to the referral, often feeling quite personally involved in the child's problem and occasionally reacting emotionally as well as 'professionally' to the situation.

The third conclusion concerns the cultural beliefs that heads hold about the children of immigrant parents, and West Indian children in particular.   The heads were undoubtedly genuinely concerned with the kinds of problem they felt that these children exhibited, but the cultural beliefs they held did conform to the beliefs described in previous research as 'stereotyped'.   West Indian children in particular were thought to display educational and behavioural problems, compounded by family differences. Asian children were not considered to have so many problems as West Indian children, but their language problems, compounded by family and cultural differences, and the difficulties of assessing children from other cultures, were mentioned.   Given the ways in which heads 'recognise' potentially ESN-M children (intuitive understanding that the educational and/or behaviour exhibited by a child is beyond the capacity of a school to cope with), it seems likely that West Indian children, in particular, might be considered by the schools as being potentially ESN-M, more so than other groups.

4   The educational psychologists

The first psychologist to be employed by a local education authority was Cyril Burt, appointed in 1913 by the London County Council. Although LEAs employed educational psychologists increasingly from the 1930s there is still no statutory definition of the function of the educational psychologist in England and Wales. (1) The employment of educational psychologists, Child Guidance Clinics, and school psychological services all stem from the ancillary powers which derive from the 1944 Education Act.

In this study the statutory powers of the medical officers in the ascertainment process were resented by the educational psychologists, who expressed anxiety that educational decisions could be made by medical personnel and felt that their own non-statutory position was ambiguous if, as Circular 2/75 indicated, they were supposedly equal partners in the process. (2) At the same time the psychologists now felt that the two professions might both find a bureaucratic administration attempting to overrule their decisions. (3)

In 1965, 150 local education authorities employed 414 educational psychologists and twelve made alternative arrangements. This gave an approximate ratio of one psychologist to 20,000 children. The Summerfield Committee examining 'Psychologists in the Education Service' in 1968 recommended a ratio of one psychologist to 10,000 children, and the Warnock Committee in 1978 recommended that enough educational psychologists should be trained to give a ratio of one psychologist to every 5,000 children ('Special Educational Needs ...', 1978). It is thus an expanding profession, but one which, as this study indicates, is little understood and tends to mystify other professionals, as well as the parents of the children with whom the psychologists deal.

According to the Summerfield Report the particular

contribution which psychologists can make to the education
service derives from their specialised study of psychological science and its application to education and other
aspects of human development.   The major method adopted
by the pioneer psychologists in applying their science was
mental testing, and a major impetus to develop and improve
techniques for assessing the ability and intelligence of
children was provided by the need to select children for
the newly opened schools for the feeble-minded, in the
early part of the century.   One of the duties of Cyril
Burt in 1913 was 'the examination of children who presented problems of special difficulty' and Burt's primary
objective in classifying children was 'the discrimination
of ordinary from special school cases' (1921).

Just as Cyril Burt linked the learning problems of
children with their home and family background, the
Summerfield Report noted that when a child has special
psychological needs or problems 'these involve an interaction in him of both family and school - the first concern of the educational psychologist is to contribute to a
resolution of these problems'.

The importance of mental testing as a major aspect of
the work of educational psychologists has tended to over-
shadow other aspects of their work, and from the 1960s
educational psychologists were at pains to point out that
they were not simply 'IQ bashers' but that their work has
other aspects.   The Summerfield Committee noted that
people were unclear about the role of the educational
psychologist - the 'games and puzzles lady', as one child
was recorded as addressing an educational psychologist -
and sought evidence from various bodies about the nature
of the work considered proper for the psychologists.   In
evidence, the Association of Educational Psychologists
considered that psychologists had three major tasks:
1 to assess the psychological and educational development and needs of children;
2 to work as members of Child Guidance Clinics;
3 to contribute to discussion of educational policy
   where useful.

The British Psychological Society considered that the
'specialised study of psychological science and its
application to education' was the main contribution of
educational psychologists, and the Summerfield Report
devoted a whole chapter to the demands made on educational
psychologists not immediately associated with schools, for
example: children's departments, juvenile courts, probation work and pre-school services.   The Summerfield
Committee also sent out a questionnaire to LEAs employing
educational psychologists, which produced a picture of the

kind of work they generally undertook.   This emerged as
follows:
1   Psychological assessment
    (a)   in child guidance clinics
    (b)   in schools or homes.
2   Writing psychological reports.
3   Treating children
    (a) in child guidance clinics
    (b) in schools or homes.
4   Discussing individual children
    (a)   with teachers
    (b) with others.
5   Discussing other matters with teachers in schools.
6   Organisational and administrative duties.
7   Travelling.
(Adapted from Table 2B.13, Summerfield Report.)
    Educational psychologists themselves are in dispute
about the practice of their science.   Moore (1969) and
Curr (1969) suggest that educational psychologists should
have teaching qualifications and experience in order to
close the 'gap between present-day psychological knowledge
and its concrete implications for techniques in education'.   Herbert (1973) argues that regarding educational
psychologists as well-qualified teachers may lead the
teaching profession as a whole to regard them as 'super-
teachers or confidence tricksters'.   Using Piaget's
notion of 'experimental pedagogy' he suggests that psychologists should observe or participate in the classroom and
in the child's home, in order to learn how a child learns
and interacts rather than simply testing his achievements.
Evidence concerning the work which educational psychologists actually do in practice has been elaborated by
Brindle (1973) and Bhattacharyya (1974) in postgraduate
theses, and aspects of the changing role of the educational psychologist can be found documented in Williams
(1974, Carroll (1974) and Burden (1976).
    The four procedures which the Summerfield Committee
considered formed the core of methods used by educational
psychologists were appraisal and evaluation, investigation, action, and communication.   Appraisal and evaluation involves selecting the problems of individual groups
of children which can be dealt with by psychological
rather than other personnel, for example: psychiatrists
or social workers.   Problems which fall within the competence of the psychologist are those concerning development and progress, behaviour and adjustment, education and
guidance.   Investigation involves collecting as much
information about the child as possible; action includes
making specific decisions about the action that might be

in the best interests of the child.   'The range of
decisions available varies from place to place and in
individual circumstances.   Parental attitude might
influence a decision, so may the lack of a special school
of a particular kind' ('Psychologists in the Education
Service ...', 1968, p. 60).   Action also includes treatment, either working with school and teachers or alone.

Communication is important as it is the means by which
psychologists collect data on which they base decisions
and the channel through which their recommendations are
implemented, either in discussion or written reports.

A persistent theme in writings on the work of the
educational psychologist has been the notion of 'team-
work'.   The Summerfield Committee stressed the inter-
disciplinary work with other professionals to identify
handicapped and slow-learning children.   Circular 2/75
recommended team-work between educational psychologists
and medical doctors to observe children 'over a period of
time, in an educational setting ... and learning programmes can be devised with the teachers concerned which
may lead to a modified assessment of the child's need for
special education' (DES, 1975a).

The notion of educational psychologists as part of a
'multi-professional assessment team' is now enshrined in
the Warnock Report.   The Warnock Committee had their own
view of the special contribution of educational psychologists in the future.   First, their specialised knowledge
of observational techniques and assessment procedures will
be needed to help heads and teachers develop school-based
assessment at stages 1-3 of the suggested new procedures.
Second, they will be needed to assess the needs of individual children at stage 3 and at stages 4-5, either in
school or as a member of a multi-professional team, and
third, their professional skills will be needed if the
proposal to monitor whole age-groups of children during
their school life was to be taken up ('Special Educational
Needs ...', 1978).   Although Warnock recommended that
Section 34 of the 1944 Education Act be amended to
require the 'multi-professional assessment of children of
any age', they did not suggest that any of the functions
of educational psychologists should be made statutory and
written into the law.

There is no clear pattern for the organisation of
services under which educational psychologists work.   The
majority work within Child Guidance Clinics, which owe
their present structure to the Underwood Report ('Report
of the Committee on Maladjusted Children', 1955) which
suggested that a comprehensive child guidance service
could be provided by educational psychologists working

together at clinics, and coming under both educational and
medical administration.   According to the Summerfield
Report the majority of educational psychologists are male,
aged under forty, and although there is no statutory
requirement for their training, usually have an honours
degree in psychology, several years' teaching experience
and postgraduate diploma or degree in educational
psychology.

In answer to the question 'What do educational psychologists do?' it appears that they work within a 'scientific' model which utilises mental testing, observational
techniques and discussion as its main diagnostic tools.
The major tools of 'treatment' for children are learning
programmes, individual therapy and 'advice' to home and
school.   The continued overlap with a medical model,
illustrated by the use of the word 'treatment' with its
medical connotations and also perhaps by the use of drug
treatments in Child Guidance Clinics (see, for example,
Sampson, 1976), still makes it difficult to establish a
practice of educational psychology which is clear-cut and
divorced from medical connotations.

The City of B has a long history of utilising the
services of psychologists in various capacities for dealing with children and their families exhibiting problems
of an educational, behavioural and emotional nature.
Dr Auden, the senior medical officer of the city in 1908,
argued the case for a psychological service for school-
children and the establishment of a University Psychology
Department which would work in close connection with the
city schools, and the first Child Guidance Clinic was set
up in the city in 1932.   In 1974 a joint DES/DHSS
circular required local authorities to draw up a plan for
child guidance in their area (DES, 1974).   B set up a
working party with representatives from child health,
psychiatric services, psychological and social services
who were in agreement with the recommendation of the
Circular, which noted that:

> The schools' psychological service, the child psychia-
> tric service, the social work service, the child health
> service, are seen as constituting a network of services
> each having its own independent organisation and
> function, and its own premises in the community, but
> having joint working arrangements.

There is some indication in this study that the psychologists, in particular, are concerned that the bureaucratic procedures which operate do impede communications
between the various services and which they feel to not
always work in the best interests of the children.

At the time of the research interviews the number of

educational psychologists employed by the authority was
twenty-two.   The psychologists were based at one of the
five (six after the 1974 reorganisation took place) Child
Guidance Clinics in the city.   The chief psychologist
operated from the central area clinic, where a central
index of all case records was kept.   The clinics had a
senior psychologist and one or two others, and a psychologist over retirement age still worked at the central
school medical clinic.   The LEA also used the services of
several psychologists based at the centre for child study,
at the university.   The persistence of Dr Auden had been
rewarded: the city psychological services did indeed have
close links with the university, and five out of the eight
psychologists interviewed in this study had taken a higher
degree there.

Two of the psychologists interviewed for the study were
over and nearing retirement age.   One of these was
female.   The other six did in fact conform to the image
of the educational psychologist suggested in chapter 2 of
the Summerfield Report:

He is a young man under 40 years of age who is employed
by the local education authority....   The preparation
for his job was lengthy....   While working as a
teacher he applied for admission to courses of postgraduate training in educational psychology....   In
the selection his personal qualities were assessed,
especially his capabilities for sympathetic and understanding relations with children and other adults.

Five of the psychologists had a first degree in psychology, two had joint honours degrees - psychology and
another social science - and one had a first degree in
theology.   This last was an interesting man nearing
retirement age whose career had begun in holy orders.
He had worked for fourteen years at a training college in
India, then taught for four years at Dar-es-Salaam
University.   He finally left because 'Tanzania was
getting too doctrinaire - too socialist'.   The other nonconformist to the Summerfield image was a brisk, white-
haired lady, who described herself as 'the oldest employed
psychologist in the city'.   She had taken her degree in
Vienna, in a Freudian climate, and had studied child
development under Bühler.   She was proud to have been 'in
at the start of IQ testing'.

Seven of the psychologists had taught, mostly in
special schools.   One had taught in a school for maladjusted children, two in ESN-S schools, and one had
remedial teaching experience.   Another described his
teaching career in an approved school, a boys' school
which went through comprehensive reorganisation and a

primary school as 'a traditional route you know, initial
degree, four years' teaching, then a postgraduate qualification'.   Another described his teaching career as
follows: 'a year with an inner-city remedial class, a
nice middle-class school, then a year at X school for
emotionally disturbed children; that was a killer.'

Five psychologists had graduated with a Masters degree
in educational psychology from Birmingham University.
One had travelled to Belfast for a postgraduate qualification, and one had left Belfast for a London qualification.
One had qualified before the war in Vienna.

Since this study depended on the goodwill of the educational psychologists in selecting suitable cases to be
followed through, from the files in the Child Guidance
Clinic, several visits were made to the clinics to talk
informally with the psychologists, and during the course
of the study a more formal interview, using the semi-
structured schedules, was carried out.   The informal
visits also made it possible to understand the way the
clinics operated.   The professional skills of the psychologist appeared to be used in a variety of ways.   The
procedures were that incoming cases were allocated, after
consultation, to one or more of the personnel operating
from the clinic, for example: to the psychiatrist, social
worker, remedial teacher.   Amongst the cases allocated to
the psychologist were those of children referred for
assessment for special education.

PSYCHOLOGISTS' PERCEPTION OF THEIR ROLE IN THE ASSESSMENT
PROCESSES

The point has been made above that the role of the psychologist within the education service still remains somewhat
ambiguous.   How important did the psychologists interviewed in this study think their role was in the assessment process?   In answer to this question, four psychologists thought their role was important because of the
'specialist knowledge' possessed by the psychologist.
One thought the role important because psychologists
could employ IQ testing procedures, and one thought the
role no more important than the other members of the
'team' who assessed the children.   Two answered this
question in terms of hostility to the current system of
referral and assessment.   As far as the 'specialist knowledge' was concerned, the psychologists stressed that they
had an 'educational role' to play:

'I think it's an essential role in that we are working
within an educational framework....   We have knowledge

of learning theories, education theories, testing, and
so on. We are in a good situation to look at issues
of educational assessment and placement.'

'For ESN schools our role is of major importance
because it's an educational matter - we are the most
qualified to make judgments on the educational needs
of the child and the facilities schools can offer.'

The younger psychologists tended to regard themselves
as part of a team, which presumably should augur well for
the Warnock Committee's recommendations of team-work in
multi-professional assessment:

'The educational psychologist is more a member of a
team - ESN heads really want a psychological assessment
if a child has been failing in (ordinary) school....
One is going through strategies to see whether or not
it's because he's slower than other children or if
there are other factors. We may pull in other members
of the team - the social worker - to help.'

The two psychologists who were against the current
procedures thought that the process worked to the detri-
ment of the children's needs:

'I don't think it's possible for us to assess a child
for special school - there are no special school
children - only schools who've rejected children.'

'I'm against the system at the moment; we should
operate a service to encourage schools to work for
themselves rather than to get us to test children.'

The psychologists were asked whether they felt their
role was becoming more or less important, particularly
after the recommendations of Circular 2/75 which stressed
the 'educational' importance of the psychologist. Six of
psychologists thought their role was indeed becoming more
important under the new procedures, and that their
decisions were being taken as seriously as the medical
and administrative decisions:

'Yes, we are more important as against the local
authority administration ... but we have to look at
how our decision-making ... is tied in with the head
teachers' expectations.'

'It's more important now the medical officer's role is
being questioned in this area; the educational psychologist's role is central to most cases. He's the best
qualified to make educational placement decisions.'

'Our decision-making is still not quite clear with the
authority, but the involvement of the psychologist

seems to be more recognised and people are expecting us
to be advisors.'
Two psychologists felt that they were either ignored or
'used' by teachers:

'In theory with the change in procedures our role
should be more important, but in reality our decisions
may not be important - people ignore us.'

'The more psychologists at the clinic, the more
children get referred - the more staff here the lower
the tolerance in schools; if we weren't here the
teachers would cope.'

The psychologists were asked whether they thought
Circular 2/75 did represent an important change in the
suggested procedures for ascertaining children as in need
of special education. Six psychologists thought the
suggested procedures in the Circular did represent a
change, but for a variety of reasons and with some reservations. One thought that an emphasis placed on the role
of the psychologist in the Circular had: 'Brought nearer
a mandatory status for the educational psychologist.' In
fact the Warnock Committee has not followed up any hint of
this in the Circular and they have made no recommendations
as to the mandatory status of psychologists.

Three psychologists thought the Circular represented a
move forward because it stressed the educational rather
than the medical component of assessment:

'The DES is saying that it should move over to a more
educational decision-making, and medical officers can
contribute by giving statements on the child's medical
needs.... It gets away from the notion that there is
a once and for all assessment of a child.... It
implies that assessment, placement and treatment are
all part of a continued sequential strategy.'

Several psychologists saw the Circular as helping to
negate the image of a 'fixed diagnosis' for life, of a
child as ESN, and one or two wondered if the 'informality'
that was mentioned in the Circular would extend to moving
children more easily in and out of special schools without
going through the procedures of filling in forms. One
psychologist who favoured this procedure thought there was
a trend towards placing some children in this kind of
'informal' manner which the SE forms would not reverse.
He said: 'People think that if a child is assessed as ESN
he's ESN for ever more - it's not a sentence for life - we
have to get away from heredity - teachers and administrators are working with a psychology that's twenty years out
of date.'

Two psychologists did not think the new procedures

suggested by Circular 2/75 were important;   one because
'it won't change much in this city - it might if the
advice was implemented though', and another thought the
Circular did not represent 'what was going on, on the
ground'.   'They are always looking for a formula but we
don't want one.   I'd like to see the old approach replaced by a problem-solving approach - a case decision -
decisions should arise out of work on a case, not out of
forms.'
    The psychologists were asked whether they thought the
new SE forms were an improvement on the old HP forms.
During the years 1975-6 one of the city Child Guidance
Clinics had conducted a pilot survey in the use of the SE
forms.   The opinions of the professionals who filled out
the forms had been sought, and there had been much discussion and criticism, particularly for SE 3.   One
psychologist was of the opinion that 'SE 3 has been anni-
hilated', but in fact the city eventually produced its own
version of SE 3 which still allowed the psychologists to
write a full report, and all the psychologists interviewed
approved of this version of the new form as an improvement
on the old HP form.
    'The old HP form was a kind of necessary evil one had
    to go through for all the rest to get done.   They were
    the administrative key that one had to turn to unlock a
    place in special education.'

    'The HP was part of the structure in the city - you
    read through the information and often it was out of
    date or totally inadequate ... so you went about
    collecting your own information which was relevant and
    meaningful.'

    'The HP came after the 1944 Act with no real change
    since the days when children were certified as mentally
    handicapped - there is a danger, of course, that the
    SE will be little different - it may still mean psycho-
    logists producing scores.'
    The psychologists stressed that they used 'other proce-
dures' than testing and interviewing to assess the children referred to them.   One noted that: 'We learned to
get round the HP forms and we'll learn to get round the SE
forms.'   Another elaborated on the way in which he
gathered information to supplement what was to be written
on the old HP forms:
    'I got information primarily from the school....   One
    would get information on social factors by talking to
    the parents.   Some of the categories on 2 HP - about
    family factors - were horrific, because the information

was just subjective impressions - very loaded.   When
we decided a child needed ESN schooling we were
supposed to fill in page 2 or 3, that bit about IQ
tests;   well, we put a line through that and wrote
"See attached report".'
One of the psychologists who had piloted the SE forms in
the city commented:
'The DES version of SE 3 was a bad one - there are some
doubts about whether it was formulated by a psychologist....   They are trying to get away from the
horrific practice of a psychologist producing an IQ and
saying "this child needs an ESN school" - you know, the
three-line report business.'
The psychologists were generally worried that the SE 4
form would be filled out by a professional who had not
actually seen the child, and they all thought that SE 4
should be filled out by an educational psychologist:
'SE 4 is a key document - it ties in all the rest and is
the big administrative base centrally;   it should be fill
filled in by an educationalist, or an educational psychologist.'
In this study the psychologists, of all the professionals interviewed, were the most concerned about the
nature of the administrative procedures under which they
had to operate, and two psychologist were very critical of
the whole assessment process and the administrative procedures.   They felt that the needs of the children were
subordinated to the procedures.   On the whole, the
psychologists welcomed the new procedures suggested by
Circular 2/75 and the new SE(B) forms, but they were
perhaps more sensitive than the other professionals about
the tentative nature of an assessment process that turns a
'normal' child into an 'ESN' child.   It may be that the
very qualities which make a good educational psychologist
- sympathy and sensitivity, as noted in the Summerfield
Report - predispose the younger psychologists in particular to anxiety and awareness of the ambivalent nature of
their job.   In contrast, the older psychologist at the
school clinic was more confident about the role of the
psychologist and the importance of IQ testing.

PSYCHOLOGISTS' PERCEPTIONS OF THE ROLE OF THE OTHER
PERSONNEL IN THE ASSESSMENT PROCESS

The resentment demonstrated by some educational psychologists concerning the statutory nature of medical officers
and their possible over-involvement in the assessment
process for special education has been noted above.   How

did the psychologists in this study perceive the involvement of medical officers?

One psychologist was adamant that too much medical
involvement meant that the procedures could not be
considered to have changed at all: 'As long as there is
the smell of a medical decision we will all be working
under the old terms.'   Another psychologist thought that
the role of the medical officer was not particularly
important in the assessment process as 'in 80 per cent of
the cases they are a rubber stamp.'

However, six psychologists were of the opinion that the
role of the medical officer was important although three
qualified their opinion by indicating that the senior
clinical medical officers should keep to a medical role
and not trespass on what the psychologists regarded as
their educational territory:

'Medical assessment is important but they shouldn't be
involved in anything else.'

'I don't think they should question our decisions
except on medical grounds.'

'They are important in the initial screening of physical attributes but annoyingly irrelevant if they
duplicate information, especially if they do IQ tests,
and if they don't pass information on to us.'

One psychologist thought that the medical screening
procedures in the school population needed a general
overhaul: 'The whole school medical service should formulate more efficient processes for screening children as
they come through school.'

Four of the psychologists thought that the decisions of
the medical officers were becoming less important and
three others stressed the 'team' decision.   One of the
psychologists would like to see the team idea taken as far
as working in the same building:

'I would like to see Dr A have an office here in the
clinic, then things could be done on a local level and
the decisions could just be communicated to a central
base....   I don't think psychologists can make decisions in the [ESN] area themselves - some kids might
need a full neurological examination.'

All the psychologists approved of the involvement of
school medical officers and SCMOs in the referral process,
in that the head teacher could contact them about a particular child, rather than referring the child straight to
the Child Guidance Clinic, but once the assessment process
was under way, they did not want medical personnel making
educational decisions.

The psychologists were asked how they saw the role of
the Special Services Branch in the whole process of
assessment and placement.   The administration received
some quite severe criticism from some of the psychologists, who felt that the mechanics of bureaucracy could
impede or negate the influence of decisions made by
professionals:
   'They are administrators and not involved in schools -
   we make careful decisions on a child and some sixteen-
   year-old clerk decides which school to send a kid to.'

   'Their role should be to deal with the paperwork and
   find a school for the child, but they take their role
   far beyond this and do naughty things.'

   'They do a good job, trying to match the papers to the
   provision; they have a statutory responsibility to
   find places.   But I think the feel they are the
   authority and not just officers of the authority, like
   we are, and accountable to the people we are supposed
   to be serving.'

   'The [assessment] decision is a mutual kind of decision
   between psychologists and medical officers and I think
   Special Services can be a great obstacle to this.'
One psychologist dismissed the Special Services Branch
with the comment that: 'I'm not bothered about the
office, it's just a paper-crunching machine.'

PARENTS

The psychologists were asked what part they thought
parents should play in the referral, assessment and
placement process.   All the psychologists thought the
parents had some part to play and only one said he didn't
often see parents, as he hadn't got time, and he left that
sort of thing to head teachers.
   Several psychologists expressed worry about the current
non-involvement of parents in the decision-making process:
   'I think they should play a primary role but the situation doesn't allow it.   I try to set up an arrangement
   between the parents and the head of the special school,
   but in fact decisions tend to be made and then the
   parents get consulted.'

   'I think parents should be involved at the outset but
   even I am guilty of not practising what I preach.   I
   discuss with parents before I fill the forms out; it's

vitally important to get a picture of the home before I
make the recommendations.'

'I think they should play an important part; it's
their child that is being poked and prodded by the rest
of us, and the onus is on the professionals to make it
clear to parents what their rights and responsibilities
are.'
Several psychologists saw parents as potential problems
in that they might object to their children going to
special school, but they were divided over their approval
of the use of 'certification' procedures:
'If the parents don't agree I've considered the certification process, although I don't see the point of
sending a child to a school the parents disapprove of.
My parents are usually frightened and anxious and we
try to explain that he should go to a school that can
cater for his needs.'
Another psychologist thought he would be 'play-acting'
if he insisted on the certification procedure: 'I had a
parent who said "No" three weeks ago.   It creates enormous problems and perhaps if I were convinced that special
education was the be-all and end-all in terms of improving
the child's educational performance, I'd be more insis-
tent.'   One psychologist noted that early consultation
with parents was important: 'Otherwise resentment on the
parents' part can persist throughout a child's school
career.'
The psychologists, despite their sensitivity, did in
fact think of parents as possible impediments to the procedure, particularly the placement of a child in a special
school.   However, they were grateful that the city did
not insist on certification procedures: 'If our authority
was the sort that insisted, that could throw a different
light on the parental interviews and we'd have to make
them aware of it [certification].'

HOW THE PSYCHOLOGISTS RECOGNISE A POTENTIALLY ESN CHILD

Psychologists are ideally working within a 'scientific'
model providing an objective assessment of the special
needs of a child on which a decision can be made about
special schooling.
The psychologists were asked what things would influence
them to recommend a change of schools for a child.   Six
psychologists mentioned qualities within the child as a
major reason for recommending a change of school, stressing intellectual functioning and social/emotional adjustment:

'The major thing would be attainment, that's what it's supposed to be about - intellectual functioning.'

'Consistent failure, if I thought a child becomes so different in his ordinary school that he's more or less put himself there [in ESN school].'

'If I thought a child was suffering emotionally at ordinary school - having peer group and social problems - I'd recommend a change.'

'My perception of what a child feels - you can ask him or infer this - would help me recommend a change.'

Four psychologists also stressed the competence of the ordinary school in dealing with the children:

'I'd look at the school's adaptability. I'd suggest things were done in the classroom and see what rate of progress he made - if none, I'd make a decision.'

'If I thought the school couldn't cope, I'd recommend a change.'

Only one psychologist mentioned IQ as the first consideration amongst many: 'IQ score, attainment, parental attitude, social adjustment, temperament, quality of schooling - at both normal and special school, pupil-teacher ratios, personal and educational background, illness and attendance and so on.'

Another psychologist said he tried to draw a distinction between 'cultural disadvantage and organic handicap' although this was sometimes difficult. He mentioned children with hearing loss and said: 'Middle ear infection is common in certain socio-economic groups - this tends to hit at six months and five years, critical stages in terms of educational implications.' He was also worried about the use of IQ tests: 'Our special schools are full of - no, have a percentage of - children who have scored low on some verbal IQ test - a test which does not put working-class kids in a very favourable situation.'

The psychologists were asked if they thought it was better to keep a child at his normal school if possible. Six of the psychologists thought that if the ordinary school could cope this would be best for the child, but that special schools were there as a last resort:

'I'm not convinced special schools are special, I don't necessarily see them as benefiting all kinds, but they are a haven.'

'When presented with a problem kid, I try to see how he could stay at normal school. If all else fails, I think in terms of special schools.'

TABLE 4.1   Educational psychologists' accounts of potentially ESN-M children

	No. of replies
Attainment/intellectual functioning	6
Social/emotional adjustment	3
Competence of normal school	4
Cultural disadvantage/parental attitude	4
Organic handicap	2
IQ	2
Total	21

(More than one answer given.)

One psychologist said he took a bundle of referrals back to the ordinary school and tried to show the teachers how they could handle the problems.

The psychologists stressed that the 'suitability' of the special school was important in recommending a change of school, and one psychologist was of the opinion that 'now the procedure was non-rigid' cases sent to special schools were reviewed and thus the decision had become less important.   Another psychologist anticipated the Warnock recommendations with an eloquent plea for units in ordinary schools:

'What we need is a more flexible arrangement in the ordinary school system - more small units in most cases, although perhaps this is a bit protective.... I've tested kids who have IQs of 50 but because the special provision is quite good in their ordinary school and we can get special programmes going down as far as nursery units, I'll go along as far as I can to keep them in the ordinary school "system".'

The psychologists were asked what they thought ESN schools could do for children that ordinary schools could not do.   Three of the psychologists felt that they could help a child to achieve in a limited sense: 'ESN schools can provide children with experience of success that they don't get in the ordinary school - they can individualise learning programmes and show concern for all aspects of a child's behaviour.'   And they stressed that the school could provide care and concern for the child's 'total' personality:

'They provide a more protected and sympathetic environment, at least that's what they are supposed to do; they are not just concentrating on attainment but they get the kid to be socially competent outside the school setting.'

'Special schools usually care more for the kids....
There is more appreciation of a child's identity,
pressure is taken off him to achieve - there are no
exams.'

One psychologist thought special schools provided a
'haven for rejected kids' and another thought they offered
the opportunity to find the 'right educational environment' for a certain type of child.   Three psychologists
were critical of the current functions of special schools:

'They work towards establishing an inferior status in
society - that's what they do that ordinary schools
can't do.   It's a labelling process - a stigma thing
which is very sad.   I'd rather see small ordinary
schools give special provision.'

'You can almost hear the drawbridge go up and down -
bang.   The child is in an ESN school.'

One of these psychologists noted that: 'If there is
nothing special about special schools it's worrying, but
the trouble is we don't evaluate the effects of special
school.   We don't set expectations so we never learn
about our own placements.'

The theme of special provision in ordinary school as
preferable to special ESN school, was a recurring theme
amongst the comments of four of the psychologists.   One
considered that while children with an obvious organic
handicap may need special school, 'there may be a group
who are culturally disadvantaged who need some kind of
... hot-house class where they could get intensive
remedial teaching'.

The psychologists were asked whether they thought
children with behaviour problems tended to be referred as
ESN by ordinary schools.   By and large, the psychologists
thought this did happen, but saw themselves as able to
circumvent the process:

'Normal schools often refer children they want to be
rid of.'

'Yes, you go in to implement their wishes that a child
shall be removed - it's uphill work to persuade the
school to cope.'

'I think in the past schools used to be anxious about
children moving who had behaviour problems....   There
still are a few rogue schools where the children's feet
don't touch the floor if they cause problems.'

'Often the schools are saying - for God's sake move him
- he's causing merry hell.   In some of these cases we
can say - sorry, it's a problem you have to cope with.'

'We may have to say - I'm sorry this child is a
nuisance but what he needs is more appropriate
teaching.'

The psychologists were very conscious that schools
differed in their willingness to cope with children:

'The school can make it happen if they want to. Some
heads will keep difficult children; some regard them
as the scum of the earth and want them out. There is
a criterion of acceptability in each school.'

'If a head is enthusiastic and can cope with children
he will manage.'

One psychologist was quite vehement in his condemnation
of secondary schools in particular:

'Secondary schools are notorious for their rejection -
they are like the army or police force. It's rare to
get a secondary school who can cope with kids - all
these suspension units, etc. are all the same. If
they want to get rid of the kids "appropriate placement" is the glib phrase used.'

Thus the psychologists, whom head teachers of ordinary
schools see as part of a process which removes the child
from the school, do in fact see themselves as turning the
referral back if necessary.

This probably accounts for some of the ambiguity with
which heads of normal schools view psychologists. The
heads refer children and expect a process to begin which
removes the child from the school. The psychologists are
not always popular if they do not accelerate the process -
the psychologist who 'took a bundle of referrals' back to
the school to persuade the teachers to cope was not
popular with the head or teachers in the school. He was
nicknamed 'Yogi Bear' and generated a mixture of amusement
and hostility in several schools.

Finally, the psychologists were asked whether they
thought that West Indian and Asian children had any
special problems that might make their referral more
likely. As with the referring schools, the psychologist
commented more widely on the perceived problems of West
Indian children than Asian children.

Six psychologists mentioned different child-rearing
methods and socialisation practices on the part of West
Indian parents as creating problems for the children,
although one psychologist thought this was a similar problem for white working-class children: 'They have all the
usual social factors, the subcultural factors, different
values, different normative systems operating, but
probably no more difficulties than children from a
working-class culture in schools which reflect middle-
class goals.'

TABLE 4.2   Educational psychologists' perceptions of the problems of West Indian children

Child rearing/socialisation different	6
Behaviour problems	3
Language/communication	3
Culture shock/social adjustment	2
Assessment problems	3
School rejection	2
Low social class/heredity	1
Total	20

(More than one answer given.)

Another psychologist thought child-rearing practices made for 'changes in development schedules'.   He said: 'You might see a boy at the age of five with a very low level of language and assume that he was always going to be low on the language side and not going to progress educationally, then you see the same child at seven or eight and he seems to have come on enormously.'

Another thought the parental background constituted 'a whole plethora of factors': 'You can't talk about a West Indian immigrant; he may be well or poorly educated - come from a rural or an urban background.'   Several mentioned the home discipline as a problem:

'West Indian children are culturally handicapped in the English school system - they suffer from West Indian discipline in the home - the parents beat them.'

'While physical care may be adequate, even fussy, the parents may show extremely limited emotional insight and occasional physical cruelty.'

And one psychologist said that: 'West Indian children are deprived of toys.'

Three specifically mentioned that West Indian children may have behaviour problems but they referred to this more delicately than the referring schools:

'A problem is West Indian boys acting out behaviour that in psychiatry is called "lacking in control" - there is a good case on theoretical grounds to get the schools to treat them as parents do, to get a more consistent thing going.'

The possible culture-shock and social adjustment of children who were actually immigrant into the country was noted by two psychologists, particularly in regard to girls: 'West Indian girls - we come across cases where they make a reasonable adjustment on arrival from the West

Indies, then about 12-13 they start running away.   I
don't know what factors are operating here - delayed
culture shock, adolescence?'

One psychologist said he fought shy of placing any
immigrant children in ESN school unless he could demonstrate 'organic deficit or significant adjustment
problems'.

Language and communication were mentioned as a problem
three times, particularly communication: 'Silence is a
barrier - we are not communicating, not using the same
concepts.'   As previously noted, communication is considered very important in the work of the educational
psychologist, and psychologists also felt lack of communication created assessment problems.   Assessment problems were specifically mentioned three times, twice in
'culture-free' terms, once in 'cultural disadvantage'
terms.

'I've had West Indian immigrant kids who've done well
in ESN schools and been transferred back.   It makes
you think the tests aren't culture-free and the kids
are being dumped there.'

'Testing creates problems for West Indian children even
though they are a good guide a child's functioning.
I had a West Indian boy - IQ 66.   He went to a
special school and got help.   Later I tested him - IQ
99 - and he's gone back to ordinary school.'

'From the point of view of intellectual assessment
there are big problems of assessment, like separating
cultural disadvantage from organic or intrinsic
factors that are less remedial.'

The mention of 'intrinsic factors' was the only reference
by psychologists to possible innate factors.   One of the
psychologists who thought assessment created problems was
also of the opinion that 'we don't get the cream of the
West Indian population here.   The low income groups come
- that's perhaps why we get so many referrals, and I don't
discount heredity'.

Only two of the psychologists mentioned heredity and
'intrinsic' factors as a problem for West Indian children,
and two psychologists considered that rejection by the
ordinary school constituted a problem for the children:
'It's the school's screaming at you to get the kids out -
it's nothing to do with ESN - the kids go to a special
school because they are trouble, either backward or
behaviour.'

The psychologists did not perceive children of Asian
parentage to have as many problems as children of West

Indian origin, and three psychologists said they had not
recommended any Asian children for ESN schools.

TABLE 4.3 Educational psychologists' perceptions of the
problems of Asian children

Language	4
Assessment	2
Haven't sent any to ESN schools	2
Haven't tested any	1
Schools expect too much	1
Total	10

(More than one answer given.)

Language problems were mentioned four times, leading
particularly to cognitive differences:
'Their socialisation processes result in different
language structures which lead to different cognitive
structures - they have to deal with their own language
at home and having to think in two different ways -
they may only have one concept or word for some things
we have several for.'

'They have their own language which they are very good
at and all their basic domestic concepts - full,
empty, boiling - are perhaps fixed in their own
language, then they come into school at five as non-
English speaking and they get this split. We teach
scientific concepts in one language - they have their
concepts in several, or dialects.'
One psychologist thought that some Asian families were:
'Real peasants, and there is culture shock when they come
to this country'. Another mentioned that Asian children
'can't play with toys or puzzles'.
Two psychologists mentioned the assessment process as
not being geared to Asian children, but three psychologists had never recommended an Asian child for ESN
school, and one had never tested any. One psychologist,
who made a practice of encouraging schools not to refer
children, thought one particular Asian child had benefited
from his policy: 'I tested one the other day. He'd
benefited from the fact that I'd not been in that school
for a year. I might have sent the poor little bastard to
an ESN school earlier.'
The psychologists were also asked whether Irish children had any special problems, although it was later
decided not to include the Irish in this study. Two

psychologists did not see many Irish children, but six
said that they thought Irish children did have problems
which might make them more likely to be referred for ESN
schooling.

One thought Irish children had similar problems to West
Indian children - 'they are deprived and not too bright'.
Another thought that it was 'spurious that people pick out
coloured immigrants when the Irish present the most consistent problems'.   One psychologist thought that because
the Irish were 'closer to our culture than black culture'
the cognitive structures of the children were 'not so
different from working-class Brummies'.

Another psychologist thought that occasionally the
educational deprivation of Irish families marked them out
as the most deprived group: 'You may get a total lack of
schooling and unsurpassed parental ineptness.'

In informal conversation with the psychologists,
anxiety about the nature of the job of the educational
psychologist was mentioned several times.   One said: 'It
worried me a lot to what extent educational psychologists
can be sucked into a system which is promoting existing
structures - psychologists may differ on this but I'm
worried about the structures and the way they are
working.'

The whole nature of the decision-making process was
thought to be unsatisfactory by four of the psychologists.
Two specifically mentioned the rigidity of procedures
stemming from the 1944 Act which they felt the new procedures suggested in Circular 2/75 would not change.   They
stressed the inflexible nature of the system which made
transfer out of an ESN school difficult.   One said:
'I'm not that confident of my own decisions - I wish we
could have informal procedures with parental approval -
we could move children in and out of special schools
without papers being shuffled around by clerks.'

This uneasiness with the present system may stem from
the kind of person who is selected to train as an educational psychologist.   If, as the Summerfield Committee
suggested, selection procedures look for 'sensitive'
people, younger psychologists in particular are not likely
to be dogmatic people readily accepting classificatory
systems and rigid procedures.   This point was illustrated
by the comment of one psychologist:

'The decisions we make are based on our personal
beliefs as much as on psychology but we make political
decisions all the time.   I object to the traditional
classification of people - the static model, children
are dynamic, but people label them for life.... It's
what a child does in the future that matters.'

Nevertheless, psychologists do work and make decisions within the current framework, and they have real power within the system to accelerate a child's removal from ordinary school and placement in special school, or they can reverse the process and help to keep the child in normal school.

THE PSYCHOLOGISTS AND THE STUDY POPULATION CHILDREN

The eight psychologists had interviewed thirty-eight of the study population children; thirty-six of the children were tested and an IQ given, using either the Stanford-Binet intelligence test or the Weschler Intelligence Scale test for children and in some cases other tests were also administered. Two boys were not tested - in one case the psychologist said he had 'given up testing West Indians as the tests are not culture-free', and in the other case the boy was being 'rushed' into a special school and he had two brothers there so no IQ test was thought necessary.

In seventeen cases the psychologist said he was the first professional person to see the child after referral; in four cases the psychologist could not remember if he was. In seventeen cases the psychologists said they were not the first professionals to see the child. In three cases the child had been referred to and seen by a medical officer. In six cases the case was taken over from another psychologist; in two cases the speech therapist had seen the child first, and in one case each, a social worker, remedial teacher, assessment centre and a suspension conference had seen the child. In one case a GP had first seen the child and in another case a delicate school had previously seen the child.

The children were referred between 1974-6 during the changeover of forms. In eighteen cases the psychologists said they had filled out an SE form and in twelve cases an Hp form. In six cases no form had yet been filled out and in two cases the psychologist could not remember. The psychologists were asked if they remembered having contact with other professional people in any way over each case. In fourteen cases they had had contact with the referring school, either in person or by phone; in six cases they had had contact with the head of the receiving school; in a further six cases they had had contact with the medical officer, in two with a therapist, in three had phoned the office, in four had contacted a social worker, in one had conferred with a psychiatrist and in one had attended a suspension conference.

The psychologists had been in agreement with the

decision of the medical officers in twenty-two of the cases, although several said they had no contact with MOs and one said, 'She was a pretty ancient medic so just acted as a rubber stamp'.   In six cases the psychologist said he didn't know about this and in seven cases the question was not applicable.

Despite their anxieties over the tentative nature of their recommendations expressed in the general interview, in twenty-four cases the psychologists said that the children they had recommended for special school would do better there.   In four cases the psychologists thought that the child would not do better:

'He's not ESN but his ordinary school thought he was a moron and wanted him out.'

'He did better at his normal school.'

'She didn't need child guidance help or special school.'

'He doesn't go there - he plays truant.'

An omission to this part of the research was to ask the psychologists directly what contact they had had with the parents of the children they saw.   However, six psychologists mentioned that they had had 'trouble' with particular cases as the parents did not want the children to go to special school:

'They were worried; they thought the girl was going to be "put away" for life.   They'd once had a dog taken away from them and saw this in the same light.'

'I feel a bit guilty about this case - the parents didn't want the boy to go - he was their only one at normal school and they were proud of this.' (The boy who was not tested)

Finally, the psychologists were asked whether being West Indian or Asian had contributed to the difficulties of the fourteen West Indian and Asian children.   Of the seven West Indian children who had been seen by the psychologists (the two boys waiting to be seen were West Indian), there was agreement that 'being West Indian had contributed to their difficulties'.   Of the five Asian children, three psychologists said being Asian had contributed to their difficulties, but in two cases they were not so sure.   In one case the child was 'very handicapped' and in another case 'it's a very nice family'.

CASE STUDIES

The following case studies illustrate the way in which
educational psychologists actually worked with the children and made decisions.   The decisions were based on
their own beliefs about the children and their parents,
and were sometimes taken without full information.
Although three of the studies illustrate the power the
psychologists wield in the assessment process, the first
case study strikingly documents the way in which articulate, middle-class parents can 'deflect' a decision and
affect the process in ways that none of the working-class
parents seem able to do.
1   The psychologist at X clinic saw James, a ten-year-old
boy, early in 1975.   He noted that James was from 'a good
socio-economic and academically advantaged background'.
James had been referred in July 1975 by the head of his
junior school.   The boy had come from the infants as a
non-reader, but the junior school had kept him as the head
'hardly ever referred children' and had a special remedial
room and two remedial teachers in his suburban school.
The psychologist said that 'in both the verbal and performance scales of the WISC, James is only able to display
borderline ESN/dull average....   He has a high level of
anxiety and lacks concentration.'   He recommended that
James should go to an ESN day-school with possible transfer
to the remedial stream of a secondary school later on.
However, James's parents objected to the idea of ESN
school in a forceful and articulate manner and after a
parental interview the psychologist said, 'It seems
obvious that James will need special school provision at
some stage but in view of the borderline psychometric
results [IQ 70] and the high level of anxiety and the
provision at his present school, he should be left at his
ordinary school and reviewed'.   The psychologist thought
James's father was a college lecturer as at the parental
interview he had heard the father say he had a lecture
shortly.   In fact the father was a final year teacher
training student at a local college of education, who had
changed his career from electrical repair man.   (He later
obtained employment at a local school.)
 A year later, in June 1976, the psychologist visited
James's school and found he had made little progress over
the year.   The parents had remained unwilling to let the
boy go to special school and the head was willing to keep
the boy until he transferred to special school.   On this
visit the psychologist advised the head that the boy
should go to a secondary school with a good remedial
department and he also wrote to the secondary schools

transfer system recommending a particular school.
However, the parents wanted the boy to go to another
school and in the September James was transferred to the
school of his parents' choice.

In the semi-structured interview with this psychologist, he had said 'in reality our decisions may not be
important - people ignore us!'   The decisions do seem to
have been 'ignored' in this case, but James came from the
only white middle-class family in this study, whose
articulate determination to keep their son out of special
school, and knowledge of the school system, may have
influenced the decision-making process.

2   A psychologist saw Ayub, a six-year-old boy of Turkish
parentage, who had been referred by the speech therapist.
The head of Ayub's school had also written to the psychologist expressing concern over the boy's language difficulties.   In the interview the head had said that Ayub's
family was 'Greek or Polish or one of the European
countries'.   The psychologist saw Ayub, and tested him,
a month after his referral in December 1974.   His score
on the Reynells Language Development Test was 2-6 years
and his IQ was given as 67.   The psychologist said that

> Ayub is a plump, well-cared for little boy of Turkish
> origin, who showed himself both lively and loud in the
> classroom ... where he can be a disruptive influence.
> His social behaviour is immature and unsettled ... his
> general intellectual level suggests an overall retar-
> dation and formal problems are to be expected ... he
> has difficulty with English but makes an effort to
> express concepts.

The psychologist did not recommend Ayub for a special
school as his own inner-area school was willing to keep
him and give special pre-reading and number work.   After
a review visit six months later the psychologist said that
'Ayub has shown considerable improvement in intellectual
and social behaviour and language....   The school has had
a beneficial effect on Ayub'.   The psychologist did not
interview the parents or visit the home - if he had done
so he would also have found that Ayub's fifteen-year-old
brother, currently doing seven 'O' levels, had decided to
take Ayub 'in hand' and stop his mother 'spoiling' him at
home and speaking Turkish to him all the time.   This case
perhaps illustrates the power which psychologists have in
the decision-making process.   If they do not recommend a
child for special school the process generally goes no
further, although schools can press the psychologist or
circumvent his decision by referring directly to the MO.
In this case a boy with an IQ of 67 was not recommended
for special school.

3   The case of Kevin is illustrative of several points
made in this chapter.   First, the psychologist demonstrated some antipathy to the medical officer.   He also
demonstrated the idiosyncratic nature of the job of the
educational psychologist, in that, seeing himself as a
case-worker, he took it upon himself to do social work
with the parents.   Although he regarded special schools
as 'havens' his remarks about Kevin illustrated that he
thought they were also places to control 'mischievous
children'.
    The psychologist at Y clinic, in his own words, 'invi-
ted himself in on a voluntary basis' to see Kevin because,
'I thought the case was being badly handled by the
medics.'   Kevin was a nine-year-old boy when he was
referred in 1974.   A psychologist at X clinic (not interviewed in this study) had tested Kevin, given his IQ as 63
and his reading age as nil, and recommended him for ESN
school.   The SCMO had written to the psychologist at Y
clinic asking him for a report on Kevin.   The psychologist visited the parents, the first of several visits, and
wrote to the SCMO that 'the parents take a traditionally
working-class view that we would be removing the boy to
the daft school and this would mark him for life.'   He
also wrote to the parents that Kevin was 'not mentally
retarded but a slow learner'.   (The father of this family
was a transvestite - when interviewed at home he was
wearing women's clothes and make-up.)   The psychologist
also asked the clinic social worker to visit the family to
'see what can be done to help this family survive', and
contacted a special school to reserve a place for Kevin.
The boy was eventually suspended from his ordinary school
- his class teacher said that she wouldn't teach him any
more as he was 'physically violent, overturning chairs,
slamming doors, will not obey instructions, resorts to
temper tantrums', and he started at ESN-M school in
September 1976.   The psychologist said he had given a lot
of support to the parents and visited them often, but he
thought Kevin would do better in special school as he 'was
the focus of a lot of conflict at home and school ... and
was becoming mischievous'.   In the semi-structured interview this psychologist had seen special schools as a
'haven for rejected children' and saw children going to
special schools 'because they are trouble' for ordinary
schools.   He also thought there should be a 'client'
relationship with the families as in social work.   Thus
psychologists can intervene in the assessment process -
apart from testing - to move a child into special school -
in this case by 'social work' methods.

4 The case of Pete is illustrative of the worry voiced by
the psychologist that the administration might fail to act
on their recommendations.   Although this was considered
to be a straightforward case, with little need to persuade
the parents, the decision by the psychologist was not put
into effect for a year.

The psychologist at Z clinic saw Pete, a six-year-old
boy, at school shortly after his referral by both the
speech therapist and the head teacher in January 1974.
Six months later he wrote asking the parents to bring Pete
to the clinic, tested him and gave his IQ as 51 and said
that he was 'retarded in expressive and motor areas of
language'.   The psychologist regarded this as a routine
case and 'put him through the channels', filling out an
SE 3 in 1975 after he had made a home visit and 'did what
he could to put the mother's mind at rest'.   Almost a
year later the boy was still at his ordinary school and
the psychologist said that he wrote to the chief education
officer asking why the boy had not been placed.   The
administration wrote back that there had been a delay in
receiving the medical report, and that the school nearest
to the family had a waiting list.   Eventually the boy was
placed at this school, after the psychologist had, in
fact, left the authority for another job.

Although the psychologist regarded this case as
routine, he had an unintended effect on the family.   The
mother, wife of a long-distance lorry driver and feeling
'neglected', said in interview that the personable young
psychologist had attracted her very much and she had had
romantic dreams about him!

As a major conclusion, the educational psychologist
emerges as a crucial figure in the decision-making
machinery by which children move from normal to special
school.   In the previous chapter it was noted that
referring heads operated on intuitive understandings that
certain children, potentially ESN, are beyond the capacity
of the normal school to deal with them.   The children are
passed to the psychologist, who, according to official
clarification is working within a scientific model and
possesses certain skills which the schools do not possess,
which will enable him to legitimate the schools' judgment.
The schools expect the psychologist to operate certain
procedures which will remove a child from the school if
he is really problematic, particularly if he is disruptive, although occasionally they accept help and advice
from the psychologist which allows the child to stay in
the normal school system.

How do the psychologists recognise a potentially ESN

child and how are their procedures distinguished as
scientific as against intuitive?   They do operate certain
procedures, mental testing techniques and interviewing of
the child;   they usually have contact with his family and
his teachers, and they consider that an ESN child is
recognisable by low attainment, low intellectual functioning and low IQ.   To the psychologists an ESN child is not
necessarily a behaviour problem and the psychologists
recognise an area of conflict with ordinary schools here,
as the schools may want children removed as ESN or under
some other label, if they are disruptive.   Thus, psychologists do see factors intrinsic to the child as causing
him to be 'ESN'.   However, they also consider that
factors extrinsic to him can create an ESN child.   The
ESN child may be culturally disadvantaged and is usually
working class;   he may have an organic handicap such as
mild deafness.   To arrive at these conclusions the
psychologists are dependent for information on other professionals.   Also, in their own judgment, an ESN child
can be one whom an ordinary school has rejected and wants
removed, and one who will perhaps be better off in a
special school in terms of social adjustment, social competence and experience of 'success'.   An ESN child will
not have to compete in examinations, will be prepared for
manual work and may have a stigma and inferior status conferred on him.   With one exception, the psychologists are
not particularly happy about the 'scientific' nature of
their work or the administrative structures within which
they operate.   In the interviews with the psychologists
the crucial factor which seemed to work against a
'scientific model' was the idiosyncratic nature of the job
of the educational psychologist. / Because there are no
definite statutory functions the personality and beliefs
of individual psychologists can affect the way they work
and the kinds of decisions that they make.   Thus, they
appear to operate at one level on intuitive theories
informed by their own commonsense as well as by academic
theories of child development.   One psychologist thought
that children were better off in normal than special
schools and delayed his visits;   another psychologist
operated on social work, client-based understandings, and
involved himself completely in the home and family of the
children he assessed.   Another psychologist accepted the
traditional 'static' model of a child's IQ and diagnosed
children as ESN on the basis of tests;   and another
operated on the belief that a dynamic model, looking at a
child's future development, was preferable.
    The case studies perhaps illustrate the idiosyncratic
nature of the psychologist's job.   One study shows a

psychologist acting on the belief that his decisions may
be ignored, so that that situation actually comes about.
In another case he made a decision without full knowledge
of family circumstances which kept a child with an IQ of
67 out of special school; but in a third case, a psychologist's belief in full involvement with the home and
dissatisfaction with medical personnel led to a decision
to place a boy which the school wanted rid of at any cost.

With no 'standard' sets of beliefs to inform their
practices, educational psychologists do have considerable
freedom to make decisions on the basis of their own
beliefs, for which they are not accountable, given their
professional autonomy.   The ill-defined role of the educational psychologists allows them to make decisions on
the basis of their personal definitions of their role.
This may have two consequences, first, the permitted
idiosyncracy may be one reason why it is difficult to
obtain statutory recognition of the job of the educational
psychologist, and second, it makes their decisions on
children very difficult to question and puts them in a
powerful position in the area of assessment.

A second conclusion concerns the way in which the
psychologists perceive the administrative structure within
which they work and the other personnel.   Of all the
professionals interviewed they were the most concerned
and critical of the current assessment processes and
administrative procedures.   This may have been connected
to the kind of person selected to train as an educational
psychologist: one who would use his 'sympathetic and
sensitive' qualities to question the tentative nature of
the assessment process and whether his skills were in
reality 'scientific' or were part of an administrative
process which needed to rationalise separating some
children out into special schools.

Thus, they worried that medical personnel might make
decisions which they considered to be educational, perhaps
because within a medical model a decision more easily
becomes a 'diagnosis' which legitimates 'categorising'
children - a process some of the psychologists feel uneasy
about.   However, they did regard medical officers as
fellow professionals, with a specific role to play in the
assessment process.   They were ambivalent in their attitude to parents, expressing concern at the current lack of
involvement of parents in the assessment process, and at
the same time viewing parents as potential problems if
they raised objections to special schooling. . They were
enthusiastic about the new procedures suggested by
Circular 2/75 and the new SE forms, as definite improvements on the old HP forms, and they anticipated the

Warnock Report's recommendations by their enthusiasm for more provision in ordinary schools for children who currently were removed to special schools.

The third conclusion concerns the beliefs that the educational psychologists held about the special problems of the children of immigrant parentage. As with referring heads, psychologists perceived West Indian children to have far more problems than Asian children, with child-rearing and socialisation problems being most important. Assessment problems and rejection by the ordinary school were noted more often than behaviour problems, which suggests that psychologists do not hold such stereotyped beliefs of West Indian children in terms of their behaviour, which they regard as a product of factors extrinsic to the child.   Children of Asian parentage are not perceived as having similar or as many problems as West Indian children.   Language and assessment problems were mentioned but psychologists did not test or recommend many Asian children for ESN school, largely because small numbers of Asian children are referred by ordinary schools.   The psychologists accepted as 'natural' the situation that, in multi-racial areas, they will be called upon to assess mainly West Indian children and recommend them for special school.

5 The medical officers and other personnel

As part of the historical development of the whole process of ascertainment for special school, medical officers, as noted in chapter 1, were closely involved before the beginnings of a School Health Service in the early part of the century.

Under the Mental Deficiency Act of 1913, local education authorities were required to ascertain and certify children aged 7-16 years, who were defective, 'educable defective' children were to remain in the care of the local education authority. School medical officers were to play the primary role in this ascertainment and certification process. Under the 1944 Education Act the requirement for a medical examination to determine whether a child was handicapped became statutory, and thus the School Health Service retained the responsibility for ascertainment. The 1948 National Health Act established a tripartite health service for children - but the School Health Service remained under the aegis of the local education authority, with the principal medical officer being responsible to the chief education officer for matters concerning the health of schoolchildren.

The reorganisation of the Health Service in 1974 effectively meant the transfer of responsibility for the school health services from local education authorities to Area Health Authorities, of which there are ninety in England. The former principal school medical officers became senior specialists in community medicine (child health) and other specialists in community medicine included the senior clinical medical officers (SCMOs) and clinical medical officers, who have responsibility for the ascertainment of children in need of special education. The specialists in community medicine (child health) still nominally work for both the Area Health Authority and the local education authority and at present in the City of B

the senior specialist is still responsible to the chief
education officer for the health of schoolchildren in a
given area.   The Area Health Authority is responsible for
providing school health services to its matching local
education authority and for providing services which
include: provision of medical staff, nurses and therapists at ordinary and special schools, arrangements for
medical examinations, including examination of children
thought to be in need of special education, immunisation,
advice to parents, teachers and local education authorities on the nature and extent of handicapping conditions
significant to a child's education, and counselling
services to pupils.   The specialist in community
medicine (child health) in the City of B was of the
opinion - early in 1976, that reorganisation had resulted
in 'total muddle'.   Since the day-to-day running of the
Area Health Authority is based upon Districts, some confusion has certainly been generated in administrative and
geographical spheres.   For example, the City of B has
five Health Districts, each of which has an SCMO accountable to the senior specialist in the ascertainment process
for special education, and thus to the chief education
officer.   However, the suggestion has been made that
SCMOs should be made responsible to district physicians
who have no responsibility to the education officer.
Also in B the five Districts do not correspond to the old
pattern of school clinics, the central District now contains four school clinics, the southern area only one.
    The Warnock Committee carefully refrained from comment-
ing on 'the wisdom or otherwise on the re-organisation of
the health services ... except to say that ... re-organisation made co-operation at the local level more rather
than less difficult' ('Special Educational Needs ...',
1978, p. 227).
    The reorganisation was intended to result in a compre-
hensive service in which the School Health Service would
be integrated with other child health services to cover
all health services for children, but, while the Court
Committee studied and made recommendations on this issue
('Fit for the Future ...', 1976), the integration of child
health services has not happened.   In this research
several cases illustrated the lack of communication
between services.   One child was being seen and assessed
independently by the District hospital team and by the
Child Guidance Clinic, neither knowing this for some
months.   The Court Committee recommended, perhaps to
obviate such cases, that 'the child health services and
the education service must see themselves as engaged, to a
large extent, on different aspects of a common task'.

However, the educational and medical aspects of the
ascertainment process are proving more rather than less
difficult to reconcile, as the introduction of more professionals and specialists, each claiming professional
autonomy and recognition, is growing.   Circular 2/75
emphasised the inter-professional character of discovery
and assessment for special education and stressed the
educational nature of the decision.   The Court Committee
recommended the formation of District Handicap teams,
based in District hospitals, to provide diagnostic,
assessment and treatment services for children with all
kinds of handicap.   The Warnock Committee attempted to
reconcile the two sets of recommendations by suggesting
multi-professional assessment at their Stages 4 and 5,
which would take place at a centre outside a hospital.
They wrote:

> We recognise that there would be considerable similar-
> ity between the assessment at our stage 5, and assess-
> ment by district handicap teams.   Such teams have
> already been established in some areas ... and we
> recommend that where a district handicap team exists it
> should be augmented where necessary so that it can
> carry out amongst its functions the assessment of
> children with special educational needs. ('Special
> Educational Needs ...', 1978, p. 62)

The Court Committee devoted a whole chapter to 'Handicap'
which illustrates a major problem for the medical services as they play their part in the discovery and
assessment of children with special educational needs.
This is that while the medical specialist services are
unarguably necessary for the diagnosis, discovery,
assessment and 'treatment' of children who fall within
most of the old 1945 categories (blind, deaf, epileptic,
etc.) and for severely subnormal children, the majority of
the children their chapter is discussing are mildly subnormal children, including, if the Warnock recommendations
are taken up, remedial and disruptive children.   Now the
Court Report notes that the prevalence of 'slow-learning'
children amongst unskilled manual workers' children is:
'many times that found in children from other social
groups....   Two-thirds of these children do not show any
signs indicative of central nervous system pathology.'
The major 'symptoms' shown by these children are that they
are predominantly children of fathers in social class five
and 'it is well established that families that are socially disadvantaged - poor, over-crowded, unskilled, ignorant, in ill-health or socially incompetent are at special
risk of having children who are mildly mentally
retarded' (p. 240).

Thus the majority of children who are being discussed in both the Warnock and the Court Reports suffer only from the 'pathology' of low social class.

The recommendations of Warnock and Court have largely yet to be implemented, and the MOs in this study were interviewed before the Warnock Report was published. What sort of medical personnel were implementing the assessment procedures in B in 1976, and who did they consider were 'ESN' children?

Four SCMOs and two MOs were interviewed for this study. The SCMOs had seen and medically examined twenty-three of the study population children. The MOs had medically examined five of the children and one child had been medically examined by a district physician. The senior specialist was initially interviewed in order to obtain permission to approach the other doctors, and a medical officer who had been carrying out research into the assessment of ESN children was also interviewed. There was also some correspondence with a district physician who declined to be interviewed. All the doctors were female and three commented on the status of their branch of medicine which resulted in its being predominantly female.

'It's an inferior branch of medicine; we do a vital job but are regarded as part-timers - we need more recognition for the job.'

'This job attracts women. There is no career structure so young men don't come into it.'

One of the medical officers was 'immigrant' from Australia, one from India, and one from Ireland and three others were Scottish. One doctor had initially trained at Sydney University and later taken a three weeks' course in the administration of psychological tests at Bristol University. The Indian doctor had trained in India and had done postgraduate work and the three weeks' course at Bristol. Two doctors had trained in Ireland - one had then done postgraduate work on 'medical aspects of children with learning problems' at Newcastle and had taken a short course on psychological assessment at Cardiff. The other had taken a Public Health diploma and a short psychological testing course in London. Two doctors had trained in Scotland - one at Glasgow University, followed by training in psychological assessment on a day-release basis - the other at Edinburgh, followed by a course on the administration of psychological tests in London.

All the doctors were therefore 'qualified' to administer the Stanford-Binet intelligence test and to fill out the whole of the old 2 HP forms, 'Report on a child

examined for a disability of mind'.   (Parts 1 and 3 of
this had to be completed by an MO.   Part 2 on 'Intelligence' could be completed either by an MO or an educational psychologist.)

One of the doctors was a young woman who had only
recently started work for the authority, the others had
had considerable experience both in the School Health
Service and in related fields such as paediatrics.   One
of the doctors retired during the year - she had been
employed by the city since 1950 and said: 'Originally
there were only two of us - we had half the city each and
saw all the handicapped children.   Then in the 1960s more
doctors came and got an area each.'   One of the SCMOs was
promoted to senior specialist shortly after this study,
when the current senior left.

The SCMOs who were interviewed were responsible for the
East, South, West and Central areas and had central
offices in the city centre, in a building which housed all
their medical records, including files on children
assessed for special education.   However, they tended to
see children in a variety of places.   Two worked from
hospitals and one from school clinics, as did the MOs.
They had mixed feelings about their working arrangements,
particularly since the reorganisation of the health
service.   One said, 'The central area is ridiculous -
there is no office in my West area so I work from the
centre and actually see children at D Road Hospital.'
Another thought the city would eventually, 'have to do
without community health because of finance', and speculated whether the role of SCMOs might change after the
Court Report.   (The Report recommended the creation of
general practitioner paediatricians, but this suggestion
has not been accepted by the government.)   The doctors'
main worry concerned their records - each doctor has a
casework clerk, and if they saw children out of the
central building the clerk had to retrieve and send the
files out - and in general the doctors did not feel that
their working conditions were ideal.   Up to about 1974
senior clinical medical officers saw potential ESN-M
children, but according to one doctor this created long
waiting lists for examinations, and now 'straight ESN-M
can be seen by MOs.'

The doctors were asked what part they played in examining children referred for special education.   They
stressed that their major task in the assessment process
was 'physical' and that they were not involved with the
child but with his whole family.

'Our role is to assess the child's "physical senses"
and to help the whole family - we must see the "whole
child" - it's part of being a doctor.'

'We could be confined to just a medical role as we see
all sorts of children - asthmatic, ESN, deaf (I
specialise in audiology), but we extend beyond that -
to look at the child in his environment.'
This particular comment was interesting in that the doctor
placed the category ESN with medical conditions.

Two doctors felt that there had been an incursion into
their role in the assessment process by the psychologists.
The older doctor in particular, who had seen the growth
of the schools' psychological service in the city, said:
'I felt the psychologists were taking over from us;
they seldom followed up children as we did.   I felt
someone had to make the final decision and it was the
doctor who was unbiased and could make a fair decision
at a medical clinic.'
On the other hand, the youngest doctor saw her role in
assessing children for ESN school as subordinate to that
of the psychologist.   'I think we should be on the peri-
phery.   We should make sure nothing is physically wrong
but ... medical people know little or nothing about educational decision.'   She said it amazed her to sit in case
conferences and 'see people who weren't concerned with
education deciding which school to send a child to'.

The emphasis the doctors placed on the aspect of their
role termed 'helping parents' may be a function of the
situation whereby children are usually brought to the
medical examination by the parents.   The letter sent by
the Education Department at B until 1974 (see Appendix 1,
chapter 5) told the parents: 'you have a right to be
present at the [medical] examination and we hope you will
do so as it is better for a child if his or her mother
can be there.'   The parents' chapter shows that parents
understood the medical role more clearly than that of the
psychologist, but they did not feel they were given
enough information and became confused when a doctor
introduced educational questions.

The doctors were asked whether they generally saw
children before or after an educational psychologist.
Three doctors said they usually saw children after.
'If the psychologist recommends the child for ESN -
we see them after him.'

'After - I get a report from the psychologist - if the
child is older I hurry.   It's important to get older
children in [ESN schools] or they will be more
retarded.'

'After - if we disagree with the psychologist's assessment, we phone or it can go to a panel.'

One doctor said that in some cases she saw children at
the central clinic before a psychologist and sometimes
afterwards.   Although she was qualified to administer
psychological tests she said she did not do this: 'I
don't use my limited knowledge of tests - I felt I wasn't
a psychologist.'

Another doctor worked mainly with pre-school children
who were usually seen before the psychologist saw them,
and one doctor referred to the 'two methods' suggested
after Circular 2/75 whereby a referral could be made
either to a psychologist or to an MO.   She said, 'I'm
often brought in to facilitate the removal of a child from
school if the psychologist won't co-operate.'

It was noted in the psychologists' chapter that schools
sometimes felt aggrieved by the psychologist's decision
not to move a child and they could use the procedures to
circumvent his decision by referring again to the MO.
This was done in one of the study population cases.   This
procedure would seem to make co-operation between the two
sets of professionals more rather than less problematic.
One doctor particularly mentioned a psychologist who 'had
a chip on his shoulder about doctors'.   It seemed from
this part of the research that doctors were less willing
to regard psychologists as necessary colleages than vice
versa.

The doctors were asked how they saw the role of the
Special Services Branch, and like the psychologists, saw
their task as administrative but were critical of the way
the administration was carried out.   They particularly
mentioned the difficulties of communication.   One said:
'It used to be chaos.   We'd keep ringing Mrs A. [clerk at
special services] to find out what was going on.'
Another described how the administrative procedures had
changed over the years for the doctors: 'When it was
decided that SCMOs should do their own administration
work, we each got a clerk, but I could never keep up with
the work.'

One doctor said that she was thankful that the administration was now in favour of 'straight ESN children being
seen the MOs - they used to keep long waiting lists of
children to be seen by SCMOs'.

The doctors were not as enthusiastic over the new SE
forms as the psychologists.   They did not feel that the
medical information required on SE 2 was sufficient:
'They are daft - they give less information than 2 HP.
SE 2 is marked by an absence of information.'

'It doesn't say on them what's right with a child, only
what's wrong - I ignore the headings and write what I
want.'

'SE 2 is not a good form from the doctor's point of
view - it's meant for teachers - it sets out problems
for a teacher.'

'We can't get all the medical information we want on
these forms - it's just a set of tricks.'

'I write what I shouldn't - I write about behaviour and
emotional problems on the forms - I scribble all over
them.'

Five of the six doctors said they relied on informal contacts as well as filling out forms.   One said that
'although we haven't had a final say in the children's
placements for three years I still phone round'.
Another mentioned that she sometimes had problems with
broken appointments and often wrote letters to parents
herself.   'If that fails, I get "By-laws" to write a
letter', and another doctor said she tries to let everyone
know about her decisions by sending copies of letters to
everyone concerned with the assessment.

What sort of child do the doctors think is an ESN
child?   They were asked what sort of things ESN schools
could do for children which ordinary schools could not do,
and this led to a discussion of an 'ESN' child.

Five of the doctors referred to the smaller classes of
ESN schools, and two mentioned trained teachers.

'They can offer children a lot - they have smaller
classes.'

'The only thing I can see is the smaller classes',
but they were not over-enthusiastic about ESN schooling.
One said:

'The problem with ESN-M schools is the social factor -
a rougher child gets to ESN school.   I feel for
parents who appreciate the difference between a nice
school and a rough school - I wouldn't want my
children to go to an ESN school.'

Two doctors commented on the need to distinguish
between 'low-normal' children who could carry on in
remedial classes and those who should go to ESN schools.
One said, 'I feel my responsibility keenly here.'

One doctor did not think ESN schools could offer much.
She referred to the failure of ordinary schools to help
children and would prefer different arrangements, such as
part-time attendance, to be tried.

There was some difference of opinion on what constituted an ESN child.   The doctor who had been carrying out
research into the assessment of ESN children had developed
a neurological-developmental screening test and said that

potential ESN children scored low on this (Jaffa,
1977). (1)   She had concentrated her tests on children
from the Registrar-General's classes 4 and 5 as she felt
they were more at risk, and had compared the scores on her
tests with scores on Tansley's SET tests (Tansley, 1973).
She found a high correlation between the scores.   Nevertheless, rather than teachers giving the SET tests to
discover children in need of special help, she felt that
MOs could administer her test at the first compulsory
school medical examination and thus identify ESN children.
This doctor was in favour of medical assessment of
children before psychological assessment:
  'It's essential that a doctor sees the child first -
  especially now we are getting more multi-handicapped
  children.   I'm in favour of psychologists being brought
  in, but in any case a very ESN child should see a
  doctor - they can recognise medical symptoms.'
She also thought that an ESN child had an inability to
cope with educational standards, and an IQ of 55-80.
  On the other hand, one of the other doctors did not
approve of Dr J.'s neurological-development tests.   She
said: 'The true ESN child does not necessarily have
neurological problems.'   Another doctor said that an ESN
child was: 'retarded in the three "Rs", finds difficulty
with learning and a low IQ.'   Another said that with the
help of a psychologist she could single out the ESN child
and 'pick up the defects in a child's make-up'.

TABLE 5.1 Medical officers' perceptions of ESN-M
children

Neurological/genetic defects	2
Educational retardation	1
IQ	2
Social/'rough' child	5
Incompetence at normal school	2
Total	12

(More than one answer given.)

  The doctors all agreed that 'ESN' was a separate
category and the children in this category should not be
'integrated' with severely subnormal or other handicapped
children.   In one case the doctor thought integration
could upset the parents of physically handicapped children
'who did not like to think their children were too backward', and another thought integration would lower the
educational standards for ESN children.   However, the

severest criticism came from a doctor who worked closely
with one of the two 'integrated' schools in the city.
She felt that integration was a total mistake because the
custodial and medical treatment aspects of severely subnormal children were being applied to ESN-M children.
She said: 'It's terribly bad - at X school they have
locked doors.   I feel I'm in a psychiatric hospital.'
She has published an article on the problems of drugs in
special schools and she was worried that teachers might be
asking for drugs for disturbed or disruptive ESN-M pupils.
She was particularly worried that the teaching staff were
controlling the drugs prescribed for the children and were
'doling them out enough to take at the week-end'.   (At
this particular school the researcher had sat in on an
interview by the deputy head and the mother of a disruptive ESN-M West Indian boy. The deputy head had urged
the mother to give the boy tranquillising drugs to calm
his behaviour.)

According to the doctors then, ESN children can be
recognised as educationally retarded children with low
IQs.   They do not necessarily have neurological problems,
but are of low social class.   In this they are in agreement with the findings of the Court Report.   ESN children may have 'defects in their make-up' but do not necessarily have other recognisable medical problems. (2)

The doctors were asked whether they thought West Indian
and Asian children had any special medical, cultural and
educational problems.   One doctor said that she did not
find immigrant children presented special medical problems, but five doctors mentioned sickle-cell anaemia as a
major medical problem for West Indian children and a
variety of medical problems for Asian children.

Sickle-cell anaemia is a term used to describe the
presence of an abnormal S-gene within the red blood cells.
As one doctor described the condition at length:
'It's a form of abnormal haemoglobin - it developed in
the African race as a defence against malaria - it's
resistant to malaria but now it's a serious disorder.
If the gene is not homozygous severe anaemia results -
there is no cure except transfusion, and death can
result - it also makes the patient sensitive to cold.'
This doctor went on to explain that black people in the
USA suffered from diseases caused by sickle-cell anaemia
but that a lower incidence was not charted in America and
'it could lessen here'.   Another doctor noted that
although sickle-cell anaemia was a factor, few West Indian
children actually suffered severe medical problems, but
another said it could be very dangerous for children if
they had an anaesthetic.

One doctor said that she found a major problem for
West Indian children to be what she called 'the West
Indian Syndrome' - there were West Indian children who
were 'semi-autistic, non-speaking - psychiatric cases'.

More medical problems were noted as far as Asian
children were concerned.   Rickets, TB, poor nutrition,
pica (a disease derived from lead poisoning) and problems
of communication over the children's health were
mentioned.   'In deprived areas children get pica - it
affects them mentally.   I've got an Asian child under
treatment now for chewing lead paint - probably the mental
subnormality comes first and makes them chew the paint.'

The senior specialist said that Asian children were
increasingly becoming a problem.   Newly arrived children
were examined each week at the immigrant reception
centres, and more were being found to have medical problems.   She wondered if some Asian parents didn't come
over especially to have their children cared for by the
health service.

A nurse at a clinic where one of the doctors was interviewed took up the theme of the medical problems of
Asians.   She said:

'The Asians come in and demand everything - they never
say thank you.   I had a Bangladeshi in the other day -
he had a sunken face and malnutrition but he had ten
children!   You would have thought that when they came
into the country someone would have said "Enough".'
This nurse wondered whether it might be better to move all
the white Rhodesians and South Africans into England and
move all the coloured people out.

The doctors felt that both West Indian and Asian children had problems which could be described as cultural.
One doctor said she thought that when coloured children
came for examination 'they easily got frightened with all
these white faces around'.

The West Indian community was considered to have more
problems than the Asian community: 'The West Indians have
more problems although they are integrating more - they
are more honest, they will flare up, go berserk, call you
names, and then you can talk to each other.'

Two doctors hinted at racial antagonism.   One when she
told the story of a black man 'who threatened to shoot me
for not letting a boy out of X school to go to what he
called West Indian culture'.   Another described a West
Indian mother whom 'I did everything for but complained
and said, "You treat me like this because I'm black".'

The Asians were particularly considered to have
language problems which impeded the assessment process
since parents missed medical appointments because they

could not read letters of appointment, and it was difficult to obtain a child's medical history from a non-
English-speaking mother. One doctor wished there were
some trained Asian speech therapists who could explain the
problems of children's language development to the
mothers.

The West Indians were considered to have more educational problems than Asian children:

'They are an enormous problem. They need special help
and often get sent back to normal school. The complaint about West Indian children and ESN schools does
not hold up.'

'West Indian children have an ebullient nature, sometimes teenagers come over and aren't wanted by their
parents, so it's not surprising they don't do well at
school.'

The Asian children were considered to have language
problems which contributed to their educational difficulties.

THE MEDICAL OFFICERS AND THE STUDY POPULATION CHILDREN

The doctors who had medically examined the study population children were interviewed in a variety of places:
two at district hospitals, one at the central office, two
at school clinics and one at home as she was semi-
retired. Unlike the psychologists, who, with one exception, were largely able to remember the individual cases
they had dealt with, the doctors did not remember all the
cases and arranged for their clerks to send the record
files out to them. The exceptions to this procedure were
the semi-retired doctor, who said she had a good memory
anyway, and one doctor at a school clinic who could not
remember two children very well. She later wrote to say
that one child's records had been transferred to another
authority and one file 'could not be found at the
moment'. In another case the case clerk had confused the
names of two Pakistani children, but the correct file was
eventually found. The doctors made several comments
about the difficulties of keeping complete case records on
children - copies of forms filled out by other professionals and knowing what eventually happened to children.
One said, 'It's informal notes and phone calls that have
kept us above drowning level.'

The doctors were asked whether they had seen the
children before or after the educational psychologist.
In twenty-four cases the doctor had seen the child after

the psychologist; in three cases before and in two cases
couldn't remember.   In one of the twenty-four cases the
doctor said the case had been referred to her by the head
teacher but 'the psychologist got there before me'.

In another case the psychologist had written to the
doctor saying that a boy needed transferring quickly and
there were no medical problems.   The doctor had
apparently taken the psychologist's opinion as correct and
had written back saying that the boy could therefore be
medically examined while he was at the special school.
In the three cases where the doctor saw the child before
the educational psychologist - one was a pre-school child
with a club foot, and in the second case a GP had tele-
phoned a boys' school and the SCMO to say she was worried
about a particular boy.   The SCMO had noted on the boy's
file to 'give him an early clinic appointment' and also
made an appointment for the boy to be seen by a psychiatrist.   In the third case a teacher had taken a girl to
a school clinic and the school doctor there had referred
her to the SCMO.   The SCMO had then written to the educational psychologist, saying: 'As far as I am aware I have
no medical information on this girl.   I have been
approached by the GP and the school with a request for
help regarding her attendance and academic problems and
have agreed to get involved.'

The consultant paediatrician had medically examined and
psychologically tested the child who had also been
referred to the Child Guidance Clinic, and wrote from the
hospital (to the researcher) saying: 'I do not think an
interview will help as far as this child is concerned, she
was referred because of poor school achievement and a
psychological assessment subsequently showed that she
needed ESN education.'

At the time of writing the psychologist at the Child
Guidance Clinic was under the impression that he was being
careful in this case as the parents were against ESN
schooling and did not know the child had been seen at the
hospital.

The doctors were asked whether they agreed with the
educational psychologist in his assessment and recommendation of particular children.

In twenty-two cases the doctors said they had agreed
with the educational psychologist's assessment and recommendations although one doctor said, 'The psychologist
kept saying to me, "What's it got to do with you anyway?"',
and had recommended the child to another special school
than the one the doctor would have suggested.   In three
cases the doctor said she did not agree with the psychologist and in five cases couldn't remember, or it was not

applicable.   In the three cases of disagreement, one was
the case referred to above where the doctor had seen the
boy before the psychologist and had referred him to a
psychiatrist.   She and the psychiatrist both thought the
boy could remain in his ordinary school but the psychologist recommended the boy for special school.   The school
was also pressing for the boy to move as he was disruptive
and the doctors were overruled in this case.   In another
case the doctors recommended ESN school but the psychologist was unwilling to do so as there was parental opposition, and in a third case the doctor said: 'I didn't give
a recommendation on principle.   I was so cross at the
confusion of the changeover procedures and didn't know
what I was supposed to do.'

The doctors were asked about the form they had filled
in on the children referred.   In fourteen cases an SE 2
had been filled out;   in twelve cases an HP form, and
three cases were not applicable or couldn't remember.
The medical information arriving at the special school the
child was sent to (and assuming the forms arrived at the
school) was thus different for the study population children.   The doctors, as noted earlier in the chapter, felt
more confident that the HP forms provided more adequate
medical information.   The doctors were asked if they had
had contact with other people (apart from psychologists,
parents and administrators) over particular cases.   The
replies are shown in Table 5.2.

TABLE 5.2   Other contacts by doctors over study population
children

Special school heads	4
Consultant audiologist/optologist	3
Other hospital	4
GPs	3
Psychiatrist	3
Assessment Centre	1
Social Services	2
None	6
Not applicable	3
Total	29

In one case the doctor said that there had been a 'row'
over the other contacts.   The doctor had referred a girl
to a hospital psychiatric unit and did not inform the
special school that the girl had begun to attend.   The
special school had asked the local Child Guidance Clinic
for extra help with the girl - the parents had become

confused at being asked to take their child to several
places, and the whole case had caused bad feeling because
of the lack of communication.

The doctors had mainly discovered where the children
were finally placed through the administration, although
in several cases what was described as the 'routine
letter' was not in the files, and in three cases the
doctor did not know where the child had been placed.

The doctors overwhelmingly thought that the children
placed in special schools by their decisions would do
better there.   Only in three cases were they hesitant.
In one case the doctor said, 'How should I know?   I only
gave my medical opinion.'

In two cases the children were described as 'not being
all that dim' and had been recommended for review for a
possible transfer back to ordinary school 'in a few
years'.

Finally the doctors were asked whether the immigrant
status of a child had contributed to his problems.   In
the case of the West Indians, the doctors thought the
children suffered particularly from family problems and
dialect problems.   In one case the doctor described her
disagreement with a West Indian mother who did not agree
that her child was ESN: 'She thought the girl ought to
have her laziness beaten out of her.'   Another doctor
said that when she finally saw a social worker's report on
a West Indian family she understood why the boy was backward.   She said: 'More West Indians seem to fall into
this category', and another West Indian boy was described
as having had a 'terrible childhood - a premature baby,
then pneumonia, then child-minded, then sent back to the
West Indies for eighteen months'.   The Asian children
were regarded more as medical than as social problems
since all four of those examined exhibited some definite
'medical' syndrome, for example: a club foot, or microcephaly.   Of the 'other immigrant' children seen, only
one was considered to be a problem because of her immigrant status: 'I thought she was half-Chinese;   the
mother is very excitable and I later found she was
Indian.'

CASE STUDIES

These case studies illustrate the ways in which the medical officers outwardly made decisions on the children.
1 The case of Mary F. particularly illustrates the failure of communication between professionals which can
result in a child being referred around five doctors.

The psychiatrist who saw the child also made a decision
based on inadequate communication and reversed his decision several weeks later.   As psychiatrists' reports did
not appear to be considered overmuch, the initial decision
had no effect in this case.   The family history, particularly the experiences of the father in Northern Ireland,
was not available to all the doctors and there was a somewhat critical reaction to the notion of 'baby-batterer'.

Mary F. had been referred by her school early in 1975
as 'difficult to control - violent'.   The head said, 'I
feel very strongly regarding this [six-year-old] child as
she is continually upsetting other children - biting
furniture, etc.'   The child had also been noted by a
speech therapist after the school doctor, on the routine
medical examination, had pointed out possible speech difficulties.   The family had also been referred to the
local Child Guidance Clinic by a senior social worker who
had also been called in by the school, as the child in
question was a suspected battered child.   The girl was
tested by a psychologist and seen by an SCMO, both of whom
recommended the child for ESN day-school.   The SCMO 'had
a long chat with the parents - the mother didn't want
special education at first but eventually she agreed'.
The child was quickly placed in a local ESN school, but
after a short time this school became concerned that she
was being battered and a cycle of referrals between
doctors ensued.   The SCMO who had originally seen the
child said:

'Dr J. [the school MO] referred Mary to her own GP who
referred her to Dr O. (consultant paediatrician) who
then passed the case back to me - we went in circles.
I told Dr J. to refer the girl to Dr B. (psychiatrist)
but Dr B. said she wasn't going back to that special
school - she felt she wasn't wanted or given a room to
work in.   Well, I knew this school wanted a psychiatrist and I felt terrible.   The head of the special
school suggested Mary go to a residential ESN school
but I felt this was a mistake;   the child would have
to go through the holidays with battering parents.   I
wrote to the head of the Social Services telling him
there should be a care order on the girl.

In the meantime the Child Guidance Clinic psychiatrist had
seen the girl and her parents.   After one interview he
wrote: 'Personally I feel reasonably happy to trust the
father after our talk.'   However, three weeks later,
after a report from the school of further bruising, he
changed his mind and recommended residential ESN school.
The child was placed in residential ESN school two months
later.   The doctors did not appear to know the family

history in this case.   The father of this family had
recently returned from a tour of duty in Northern Ireland
where he had seen several friends blown up.   He had since
left the army and was unemployed.

2   The case of Christine C. illustrates the way in which
the medical officers complied with the psychologist's
request not to pursue a referral while the psychologist
was 'persuading' the mother to allow her daughter to
attend special school.   It was also interesting that
while the doctor did not particularly 'account' for the
girl's background in medical terms, the psychologist was
anxious to pursue this kind of account.
   Christine C. was referred by the head teacher of her
school in 1974; he noted that she 'had fits - convulsions
in infancy'.   The psychologist tested her and gave her an
IQ of 56, although he noted that she had a high score on
the English picture vocabulary test, and said 'Does she
have a higher verbal ability concealed by her fits?'   The
psychologist did not contact the SCMO immediately but
contacted the child's GP, 'to see whether he will pursue
the problem of her convulsions'.   The SCMO said that the
psychologist asked her 'not to pursue this case immediately' and she complied, although she was not sure why.
(The psychologist had found the mother reluctant to agree
to special education and was 'putting in some casework to
prepare her to agree'.)   The SCMO said that eventually
'the psychologist said proceed, and I did'.   This doctor
was one who, in the general interview, expressed concern
at medical people making educational decisions.   She saw
the child and apart from short sight and a history of
convulsions found the child 'quite fit and co-operative'.
She recommended a particular school but the psychologist
had suggested another school which he said was better able
to cope with the fits.   In this case the doctor did not
appear unduly anxious about the child's history of fits.
It was the psychologist who pursued this.   He said, 'I
want to know if the fits are evidence of any disease
process or if they are just a nine-day wonder.'

3   The case of Paul S. illustrates the way in which delays
can operate in placing a child in special school.   The
initial referral was not endorsed by the psychologist for
two years, although a medical officer had pronounced the
boy to be retarded.   Two years later the psychologist was
anxious for the boy to move to special school, but this
time there was a six-month delay whilst papers from a
second medical examination were traced.   There may also,
in this case, have been some 'juggling' with special
school places by the administration.

Paul S. was referred early in 1974, aged 6 years, for
'retarded speech and language'.   He was not seen by the
SCMO until 1976, nearly two years later.   He had, however, been given a medical examination at the local school
clinic in 1974 by an MO who thought that he showed 'retardation in expressive and motor areas of language and has
defective vision - a squint'.   Over the two years the
psychologist gave advice to the school on how to cope with
the boy, but eventually he recommended special education
and rang up the SCMO.   She saw the boy within the month
and recommended him for ESN-M schooling 'at the earliest
opportunity'.   However, there was then a further delay of
six months and eventually the psychologist wrote formally
to special services to ask why the head of the local ESN
school had not received the boy's papers so that he could
be admitted.   The special services clerk rang back to say
there had been a delay in receiving the SCMO's report (the
doctor said she had sent it immediately) and also said
there was a waiting list for this particular school (which
may have accounted for special services delaying the
process rather than the SCMO's report being late).

Medical involvement in the process of assessment for
special education has a history as long as the provision
of special education, and also has a statutory base.   The
doctors in this study did not feel the need to question
their role in the process, as did the psychologists.
They took for granted that a physical medical examination
was necessary before special education was recommended,
and that on this basis they could also recommend a particular type of education and name a school.   They were in
general agreement with the Court Committee's understandings that mildly mentally retarded children were not
likely to suffer from particular medical pathology,
although lead poisoning was mentioned once, but were
likely to be of low social class - an ESN child was a
'rough' child.   They perceived their role as viewing the
'whole child' which in practice meant interviewing the
parents at the medical examination, and since children of
lower social class are most frequently put forward as
potentially ESN, the families they see are predominantly
of low social class.   Their views are presumably thus
reinforced to create this tautology.   The doctors think
that there is a 'true ESN' child, not 'very ESN' or
severely subnormal.   These latter children have a medical
pathology and should not be educated with mild ESN
children.
One doctor went so far as to describe ESN as a
condition analogous to deafness and asthma.   However the

doctors are very much aware of an overlap in the case of
'multi-handicap', where a definite medical condition
exists alongside educational retardation.   The doctors
tend to use 'educational' retardation and 'mental' retardation as synonymous and assume that genetic and environmental causation are inter-linked.   Thus, they are in
agreement with the Court Report that an ESN-M child is
essentially a lower social class child and mild mental
retardation is a characteristic of lower social class.
This image of the ESN child conforms quite closely to
Cyril Burt's description of the 'dull' child in his 1937
book.   By and large, the doctors do not question the
function of ESN schools - they are schools with smaller
classes which ESN children attend.

Although the doctors do not find their involvement in
the assessment process problematic, they are unhappy about
their working conditions, particularly in what they see as
the confusion resulting from the 1974 Health Service re-
organisation, and they feel that this affects their work,
particularly in terms of administration and record-
keeping.   One of their major worries is the problem of
communication.   They feel they are not kept fully
informed of decisions made by the other professionals and
there is some suspicion that the administration might
manipulate them.   They are also aware of the nonsensical
situations which can arise if communication breaks down,
as in the case study where one doctor described a child
being referred around to five doctors.

The doctors are not in favour of the new SE 2 form,
preferring the old HP form, which a doctor could fill out
completely.   The SE forms do in fact emphasise that the
doctor is part of a 'team' in the assessment process,
something which they perhaps find more difficult than
other professionals to accept, given the status and
autonomy of medical qualifications.   They were less
willing to accept psychologists as essential colleagues
than vice versa, although in this research they largely
concurred with the decisions made by the psychologists.
The doctors were also aware that the nature of the
referral process made it possible for them to play a sub-
versive role and collude with schools who might wish to
circumvent a psychologist's decision about a child.   This
would seem to make the co-operation recommended by
Circular 2/75 and the Warnock Committee somewhat
problematic.

On the question concerning the children of immigrant
parentage, the doctors considered that Asian children had
more medical problems, but sickle-cell anaemia and the
behaviour of West Indian children were considered to be

problems.   The doctors were among the few professionals
to directly mention racial antagonism and conflict as a
factor in their dealings with West Indian people and their
view of West Indian and Asian children was perhaps less
'stereotyped' but more medically oriented.   One doctor
was the only professional to raise the issue of West
Indian children in ESN schools and she dismissed the claim
(of too many children placed) as 'unproven'.

THE 'OTHER PERSONNEL'

The process of ascertainment for special education
involves a referring school, an educational psychologist,
a medical officer, a receiving school and the LEA administration.   However, a variety of 'other personnel' can be
involved with the child and his family during assessment.
In this study eighteen of the children were seen by other
professionals at some time during the process of their
assessment and nine of the families were considered to be
'problem' families who had visits from social services
personnel.
    The involvement of other professionals raises a series
of questions, and since there is no previous research on
the relationship of these other professionals to the
assessment process for special education this part of the
study is largely speculative.   The involvement of some of
the other personnel is described and questions which
appear to be important are raised and discussed in the
light of the data presented.   One initial observation
that can be made is that the involvement of the other
personnel adds to the complexity of an already complex
process, felt particularly by the families, who are subject to more people visiting their homes or asking them to
attend for interview at a variety of places.   This is in
addition to medical interviews and visits noted in the
previous part of this chapted.
    The other personnel involved with the study population
children were as follows: the staff of an educational
guidance centre were involved with one boy, the staff of
an assessment centre with another boy, psychiatrists saw
five of the children, speech therapists saw three of them,
remedial teachers from the remedial teaching service were
asked to deal with two of the children, education welfare
officers were involved with three truanting children, two
of the children had been placed on probation and saw their
probation officer, and social workers visited eight of the
families at some time during the assessment of the children.   In several families more than one 'other' was

involved.   One family had a series of social workers, an
education welfare officer and the staff at an assessment
centre concerned about them and their children.   Another
boy was seen by a social worker, probation officer, EWO
and two doctors in addition to his medical by an SCMO.

THE EDUCATIONAL GUIDANCE CENTRE

The involvement of staff at this centre with one of the
study population children is used here to raise what has
emerged as a crucial issue in the definition of 'ESN'.
Chapter 1 indicated that throughout the history of special
education, children who were disruptive and disturbed the
smooth running of classrooms have tended to be referred
as potentially ESN.   Chapter 3 of this study indicated
that there is a very blurred line between what constitutes
an educational problem and what constitutes a behaviour
problem in the classroom.   The category of 'maladjusted'
laid down by the 1945 Handicapped Pupil regulations was
intended as a way of isolating children (in special
schools for the maladjusted) whom schools were totally
unable to cope with, but the numbers of children categorised as maladjusted remained small.   In 1974 only 5,330
pupils were attending maintained schools for the maladjusted.   It seems likely that larger numbers of children
who were a problem in the classroom were referred as
potentially ESN rather than maladjusted.   However, during
the 1970s there has been an increased focus on the problem
of 'disruption' - a problem succinctly posed by Berger and
Mitchell (1978).   'How can we effectively educate and
socialise those who cannot - or will not - with good
grace, accept the traditional tasks of the school.'   The
'ad hoc' answer to this problem has been the unconditional
creation of a variety of withdrawal units, class and
centres, a 'multitude of sin bins' designed to respond to
the demands of classroom teachers that disruptive children
be removed immediately.   Information on the numbers of
units set up is scanty.   In April 1977 a report suggested
that '65 L.E.A.'s are administering at least 250 special
units for pupils who prove too violent or disturbed for
the ordinary classroom - the units are either incorporated
into schools or are educational guidance centres which
offer a teaching alternative to children who might otherwise be suspended from school' (Birmingham Working Party
on Disruptive Pupils, 1976 Report).   This report suggested that the average size of a unit was 20 pupils and that
one aim of the centre was to avoid suspending children
from school.   Greater Manchester was reported at that

time to have two units isolated from school, ten withdrawal sanctuaries, and five tutorial units attached to
child guidance centres.   The City of B, as noted
in chapter 2, had set up a working party - in response to
a 100 per cent increase in school suspensions which
occurred in 1972, who recommended the setting up of two
educational guidance units and three units for suspended
children.   The guidance centres were to take disruptive
children not yet suspended from school and not ascertained
as ESN or maladjusted.   The pupils were to remain on the
register of their own schools and return when reformed.
The working party, which was concerned that suspended
pupils might engage in 'criminal or quasi-criminal
activities while suspended from school' was able to report
in 1976 that the guidance centres 'have been successful in
bringing about certain modifications in the behaviour of
its pupils' and returning them to normal school.   Pupils
who did not respond in this way were removed from the
normal school register and sent to a suspension unit.

There is regretfully no room in this study for an
extended discussion of this new form of special schooling
which has developed, but its importance for any study of
assessment for ESN education is two-fold.   First, and of
immense importance, is that the Warnock Committee has
recommended that the category of 'disruptive' be added to
the existing ESN category or 'children with learning difficulties'.   Thus, these units, centres and classes would
officially become part of special education.   Second, the
relative speed and ease with which children can be transferred to guidance centres, compared to the lengthy
assessment process current for ESN children, could mean
that disruptive but backward children, who might formerly
have been referred as ESN, could be transferred more
speedily to a centre.   This is certainly indicated by the
boy transferred in this study.

Equally, although discussion of the explanations for
the increase in disruptive behaviour in schools is not
possible here, there are, crudely, three major types of
explanation.   The first is a functional explanation
popular with policy-makers and practitioners, equating a
general moral malaise, a breakdown of law and order, crime
and vandalism, with disruptiveness in schools. (3)   The
second is a conflict explanation, at its most extreme
viewing the classroom struggle as an extension of the
class struggle and the provision made for disruptive
pupils as political conformity induced by educational
therapy (Frith and Corrigan, 1977).   A third explanation
is racial, 'racial mixing' being linked with disruption as
early as the 1950s (Mays, 1962, p. 62).   An analysis of

the situation in 1977 by the head of an Educational
Guidance Unit noted that in multi-racial cities in Britain
old educational methods were breaking down and 'disruption
has reached crisis point in many of our big cities where
ethnic problems mingle with bad housing and soaring unemployment' (Dain, 1977).

The head of the centre who took Winston C. had formerly
been head of a maladjusted school.   He said the centre
dealt with children who were: 'obscene, verbal, disruptive and liked confrontation with teachers....   We send
them back to their schools more controlled.'   He saw as
particularly valuable the procedure by which:

'a head can ring me and tell me he wants a child
out....   I can have a child here the same day without
going through the special school referral procedures.
...   There's none of this terrible procedure for
special schools referral that takes so long.'

At the time of interview there were fifteen children in
this centre.   The head described eight as of West Indian
origin, six as of Irish origin and one white indigenous
child.   Two of the children were described as ESN, despite the published article on B's centres which claimed
that: 'children ... whom we consider to be ESN ... we
refer to the child guidance clinic to get them put in the
appropriate school', but the head also noted that:
'these disturbed kids run through the IQ range, the
brighter ones can create more disturbance.'   He said he
usually asked children if they wanted to come to the
centre, and illustrated this by the story of J. - a girl
who said she wouldn't come to the unit.   'A few weeks
later I saw her at the assessment centre.   She was in a
locked room.   I asked her again if she wanted to come
and she agreed.'

The case history of Winston C. is as follows.   Winston
C. is the youngest of nine children.   His parents came to
England in 1961 because they wanted to 'better themselves'
and heard workers were needed here.   They have always
worked in factories, Mrs C. is a machine driller.   The
eldest and youngest children were left in Jamaica but in
1969, at age nine years, Winston came to England.   He had
no special attention in his primary school and was transferred to secondary school barely able to read.   He was
both a behaviour and an education problem during his
secondary school career - the head said that on the school
verbal reasoning test he was ESN (verbal IQ 70) but he had
kept the boy as 'I've worked here fourteen years and
would do anything for these boys'.   At the ages of fourteen and fifteen Winston was suspended from school for
short periods after he had 'lost control' and threatened

teachers and the caretaker.   He also used 'foul language', frequently fell asleep in class, 'switched off' or became 'irrational'.   Reluctantly the head eventually referred him to the Child Guidance Clinic after staff had objected to teaching him.   He was now a large fifteen-year-old and the head noted in interview, 'Whites think of blacks as big and powerful and highly sexed - they are frightened of them.'   Winston was also suspended from school.   His case was passed to an educational psychologist at the clinic who said: 'I'm bothering less and less to test West Indians because our instruments aren't valid.'   He did not test Winston but said he regretted this later. 'It's an important question - whether children who are bad behaviour problems get tested.   The problems could then be re-classified and the kids end up in an ESN school even though the grounds for subnormality are tenuous.' Because he did not get into the ESN process Winston was not medically examined.   His mother said he had been in hospital in Jamaica several times with 'runny ears' and now was deaf in one side.   He also had an accident to his eye.   A meeting on suspended pupils discussed Winston and he was sent to an educational guidance centre - he was now almost sixteen - and after a term he was suspended from the centre for violent behaviour.   He was also placed on probation for threatening two women at a youth club.   The head of the centre said, 'Violence is all part of his personality; he must be contained.'   His mother said he didn't like to be pushed around, especially when he couldn't hear what people were saying to him.   He was sent to a suspension unit 'after a long history of trucu- lence and unco-operative behaviour'.   He liked the head of the unit and co-operated well there until he left aged sixteen and a quarter.   The education authority then had no further interest in the boy, and he had been 'picked up' five times by the police in the year since leaving school.   The deputy head of his ordinary school said he was afraid Winston would murder someone.   Winston had four brothers at home unable to find work, even one with a skilled trade.   They were taking interest in a militant black group in the neighbourhood which studied black- oriented literature and accepted Pan-Africanism as an ideology.

The racial aspects of Winston's case will be further discussed in the next chapter.   What can be noted from the case is the current ambiguous position of the educa- tional guidance centre in relation to special education. The centres are not supposed to take ESN children, but have ESN children in them.   Psychologists are not required to test children before they attend the centres,

although for years they have been required to test similar
children who were both behavioural and educational problems.   Because there is no testing procedure, the extent
to which children are educationally retarded (or gifted)
in the centres, is unknown.   The centres are regarded by
teachers and by the guidance centres as an alternative to
ESN referral, since children can be more speedily removed
from their ordinary school.   Because there is no statutory medical examination, children like Winston, who have
a physical disability which might affect their behaviour,
may go undetected.   Children leaving the centres or units
are not necessarily helped to find jobs or followed up,
whereas the education authority has an obligation to
follow up and help children leaving ESN schools.

The Warnock Committee's recommendations to include disruptive children and make provision for them as children
'with special educational needs' may be a recognition of
what is already happening on an 'ad hoc' basis and may
make for greater administrative convenience, but may not
necessarily work to the advantage of the children.
Children who formerly benefited from psychological and
medical examination may be speedily removed for the convenience of teachers in ordinary schools, without the
benefit of these services.   The recommendation also
confuses, rather than clarifies, the criteria for referral
of children 'with special educational needs' since, as the
study has shown, educational retardation plus behaviour
problems have long been criteria for ESN schooling.

This issue will be taken up again in the conclusions,
but it is of importance to note Warnock's failure to
relate the educational aspects of special education -
about which there can be some normative agreement (e.g.
special schools provide smaller classes) - to behavioural
aspects, upon which there can legitimately be conflict and
a lack of consensus.   The issue of guidance centres, and
units serves to highlight the ambiguity of referral for
'ESN'.

THE ASSESSMENT CENTRE

There are six observation and assessment centres in
B.   They come under the Social Services Department
but teach children on the premises - the teachers'
salaries being paid by the Education Department.   The
centres are intended as places where children may be
brought after a court order has been made, or under
Section 1 of the 1969 Children and Young Persons Act.
The object is to assess the child with a view to a suit-

able placement elsewhere, or for him to be sent home under
supervision.   The deputy head of the centre in which Karl
and his two brothers spent several weeks, said: 'The
authority will pin anything on a child to get him into a
centre if they are worried about him.'   This centre had
been a Boys' Remand Home until 1967 but now 'under the
Director of Social Services provides a full range of
observation and assessment for twenty-four boys aged eight
to fourteen years.'   The length of stay varies, but 'the
aim is for a class conference to be held at the centre
eight to ten weeks after admission to be followed by a
monthly review until placement has been found possible.'
The centres are custodial, the children are locked in, and
parents are only allowed to visit once a week.   The
children are medically examined on arrival, and both
teachers and child care staff prepare reports on them for
the case conferences.   An educational psychologist and
child psychiatrist are availabel if necessary.   If a
child is already attending a special school when he is
remanded to an assessment centre he can continue to
attend if arrangements can be made.

Karl W. and his brothers were placed on a three-week
interim order by a magistrate after they had repeatedly
failed to attend school.   Two years previously they had
been placed on supervision to the probation service for
truancy.   At the time of assessment, one brother was
attending an ESN school, and after the three-week assessment period the deputy head of the centre recommended that
'as the boys came from an affectionate home, we think the
last course of action would be to return them there - a
visiting housemother would be of great help to this family
as Mrs W. is an invalid'.

The boys were all described as ESN although, concerning
Karl, his teacher at the assessment centre noted: 'both
immaturity and lack of schooling are the cause of his
backwardness - his actions are not those of an unintelligent boy and he has shown willingness and ability to learn
while here', and the deputy head passed the papers of the
two boys still officially at normal school to the SCMO.
Karl was medically examined, and seen by the educational
psychologist who recommended him for ESN school.   He was
also seen by a psychiatrist, and sent to the local ESN
school with his brothers, from where he continues to
truant.   Shortly after the interview at this centre a
headline appeared in the local paper, 'Two child care men
suspended' ('Mail', 23 October 1976), and an article noted
that two of the staff had been suspended for cannabis
smoking.   Police had raided the building with a warrant
to search it.

In this particular case it would appear that the deputy
head of the assessment centre made the decision that Karl
needed ESN schooling, mainly on the basis of his brothers
having been assessed as ESN rather than on the class
teacher's report, but the assessment process then ran
smoothly as the psychologist and doctor agreed to recommend the boy for ESN schooling.

THE REMEDIAL TEACHING SERVICE

Two of the study population children referred to the
northern clinic had been passed to the remedial teaching
service.   The head of the service operated from this
clinic.   The remedial teaching staff are responsible to
the school inspector for remedial education, whose post
does not come under the aegis of the special education
administration, but the Child Guidance Clinics were chosen
as convenient centres for the service.   The head of the
service describes the work as follows:
    'There are seven remedial teachers here.   We handle
    referrals for remedial help from schools in 5 of the 18
    consortia in the city.   Two of the staff spend half
    their time in the clinic, teaching children referred
    for behavioural, social or emotional problems.   This
    is done under the direction of the senior psychologist.
    ...   The rest of the staff do peripatetic work in
    school, usually on the request of the head....   All
    consortia heads now get notes on what the remedial
    service does.'
The senior clinic psychologist allocates the children he
thinks may be simply in need of remedial teaching, rather
than potentially ESN, on his own judgment.   The head of
the service said: 'A lot of the referrals to psychologists turn out to be remedial problems', but that there
was 'no standardised system' to decide which child should
have remedial help or proceed to ESN assessment.   Nevertheless, the head felt he could distinguish between a
remedial and an 'ESN' child and felt ESN children should
be 'there' by seven to eight years.   However, he thought
ordinary schools were learning to cope with their 'backward problems before they become behaviour problems'.   He
was very enthusiastic that the Tansley SET will provide a
preventative strategy to help primary schools pick out
their potential educational problem children at the age of
five to six years, and he himself was involved in lectur-
ing to teachers taking the SET course, and running short
in-service teacher training courses at the Child Guidance
Clinic.

The two children in this study passed to the remedial
teaching service were both West Indian boys aged ten and
eight years, who were referred early in 1976.   The
younger boy was referred by the head of his Catholic
school as: 'a likeable boy who needs constant attention.
...   In large groups disrupts by singing loudly or bang-
ing....   Must be the centre of attention.'   His class
teacher considered that 'he has been a pest since he came
to the school....   He's completely disruptive', and felt
that the school had made every effort to teach the boy,
even acquiring a language master to help him read.   The
senior psychologist at the clinic passed this boy's file
to the remedial teaching service and a peripatetic teacher
visited him within the month, gave his reading age as six
years and three months, and gave advice to the class
teacher.   Both the school and the remedial teacher blamed
the fact that the boy was an only child of a single-parent
family for his attention-seeking and the remedial teacher
wrote that 'the boy's limitations must link closely with
the unknown home situation' although she made no attempt
to visit the home.

The mother of the ten-year-old boy had been advised by
the head teacher of his school to refer the boy to the
Child Guidance Clinic as he was 'getting odder and was
disruptive in class'.   Four months later his file was
passed to the remedial teaching service and a teacher
visited the school.   However, the head was not happy with
this arrangement and wrote asking the psychologist to test
the child, although she said he was 'not stupid, but idle
and disruptive'.   The head also thought it was 'no bloody
good referring children - the clinic take so long to see a
child'.   The boy's mother, who had 'A' levels in Psychology and Sociology, was more worried that the boy might
'get into trouble' with bad behaviour at adolescence than
with his reading progress.

The psychologist who passed these children to the
remedial service did not approve of ESN schools and
thought ordinary schools should do more for backward
children.   However, when data collection finished, both
schools were pressing the clinic to go through the assessment procedures which would remove the children elsewhere.
The remedial teaching service did not appear to act in a
decision-making capacity at all in these cases, and the
teachers did as the psychologist asked them.   The basis
on which some children were judged to be remedial and
others put into the assessment process for ESN did appear
to be left to the intuitive judgment of the psychologist.

THE PSYCHIATRISTS

Five of the study population children were seen by three
psychiatrists at some time during their assessment.   The
psychiatrists all worked from a Child Guidance Clinic but
were employed by the Area Health Authority.   They were
all elderly, two retired during the course of the study,
and one who saw three of the children was 68 and worked
part-time.   This psychiatrist, interviewed during the
course of the study, saw his role as involvement in cases
where there were emotional, family or behavioural problems
related to the ESN assessment process, and he saw children
as suggested by the senior psychologist.   He was concerned about what he regarded as a conflict between the
medical and the administrative personnel in the assessment
process, and saw the role of the psychiatrist as a
mediator, 'amongst people who make decisions on children
there are bound to be resentments and jealousies'.   He
said he did not prescribe drugs for children himself but
asked the child's GP to do so if necessary.   'A little
self-control can be built into the child with the help of
drugs.'   The psychiatrist usually asked the parents and
child to attend the clinic for an interview and afterwards
filled out a form for the child clinic file under the
headings: date and problem; family doctor; significant
point in child's history; present environment and family
history; intelligence and social progress; diagnosis and
type of personality; aetiology of problem; treatment
plans and prospects; further comments.

In one case a twelve-year-old West Indian boy had been
referred by his school as backward and disruptive.   The
psychologist gave an IQ of 72 but felt the boy could continue in his normal school 'accustomed to dealing with
below-average children'.   An area social worker, who had
seen the family after the mother had told her the boy was
uncontrollable, suggested to the clinic that he needed
psychiatric help.   The psychiatrist saw the boy and
thought that he was 'a rejected and now aggressive boy -
stresses and rejection in early life have left scars of
resentment, he feels unappreciated and makes demands on
others'.   He recommended a 'few interviews' to help but
later noted that:

> This early impression was based on superficial under-
> standing and without wider knowledge - I can now
> appreciate the depth of the boy's difficulties.   It
> it now my opinion that placement in a residential
> school for maladjusted children is necessary.

In fact, during the year a new head teacher took over at
the boy's ordinary school, who did not regard the boy as
too much of a problem and was willing to keep him.

In a second case, the case of Mary F., the clinic
psychiatrist had seen the child during a long round of
referrals between various doctors, as she was a suspected
battered child.   He spoke to both parents and said: 'I
see no reason to regard them as other than genuine - I
feel reasonably happy to trust the father after this
talk.'   However, within three weeks he changed his mind
and concurred with the decision of the head of the child's
(ESN) school that she needed a residential placement.

In the third case, he had seen a thirteen-year-old
West Indian girl who had been placed in an ESN school,
returned to normal school and re-referred.   A social
worker involved with the family had suggested that the
child needed psychiatric help, and the SCMO had said she
thought the 'child was schizo'.   The psychiatrist saw the
child and sent a note to her GP asking him to provide
drugs for her depressive moods.   Six weeks later he saw
her again but found she had not yet been to the doctor to
get her pills.

In a fourth case a psychiatrist at another clinic saw a
boy whose violent father had left home and whose sick and
anxious mother could not cope with her home, children and
lack of money.   The family was being seen by social
workers and after the boy started stealing and setting
fire to things the SCMO referred him to a psychiatrist.
After an initial interview with the boy she thought that:
'the boy has a poor masculine model and there is therefore
disoriented learning in a boy of low IQ'.

The major conclusion from examining the involvement of
the psychiatrist with the study population children is
that their reports appear irrelevant to the decision-
making process assessment.   The practice of psychiatry
involves theories and models which are not appropriate
within a practical, administrative process, and they
change their reports to fit new information.   When the
psychiatrists are called in to help children after placement in ESN school, their help seems equally irrelevant to
the day-to-day situation of the child.

THE SOCIAL WORKER

Nine of the families in this study were being seen by
social workers.   The city is divided into twelve social
work areas, coming under the Department of Social Services
and its director.   However, social workers also work from
the Child Guidance Clinics, directed by the senior psychologist, and there are also medical social workers from
hospitals.   Social workers from other official agencies

(i.e. one family was visited by a social worker for the disabled) and voluntary agencies who can all be involved in case referral to the Child Guidance Clinics.

Eight of the families in this study were being visited by area social workers, sent by the senior psychologist to gather more information on the family background of the child referred.   Nine of the families were referred to by the social worker as 'problem families'.

The clinic social worker interviewed for this study was involved with the decisions made on a particular boy during his assessment process.   She said: 'In this case the psychologist and I did a joint intervention as the boy was causing difficulty at home....   The parents wanted residential school but I felt a day ESN was better; he has to go home at sixteen so they'd better learn to live with him.'

The psychologist concurred in this, and the boy was sent to ESN day-school.   The clinic social worker said she then 'opted out' of this case as the boy was seeing a probation officer: 'My part in the case is closed when the probation order ends and there is no other social worker, but I can't do anything other social workers can't do.'

In six of the cases the area social worker contacted the Child Guidance Clinic some time during the assessment process to suggest that the family or the child needed psychiatric or psychological help, or in four cases the medical officers or psychologists wrote to the area social workers suggesting that the families needed social work help.   The involvement of social workers with subnormal children is a complex process deserving of separate study and will not be pursued here.   It appears that the decisions of clinic social workers in particular do act as reinforcement to the psychological and medical decisions made on children.

The involvement of the personnel in the decision-making process is important - particularly since the more professional people involved - each working with their own professional autonomy and theoretical models and belief systems - the more complex the process becomes.   Medical, educational, psychological and social work personnel are expected to collaborate and communicate, with little official direction and co-ordination.

APPENDIX 1

Dear Sir or Madam,

The Education Act 1944 - Section 34

The Education Committee have a general duty under the
Education Acts to provide each child with an education
suitable to their ability and aptitude.   They have a
special duty to provide special educational or medical
treatment for children who need special help.
    It is thought that your child ... may possibly be in
need of some special treatment or educational help, and
I am, therefore, to ask you to bring your child to be
examined by one of the Clinical Medical Officers:

        Dr ...
        at ...
           ...
        on ...
        at ...

    You have a right to be present at the examination and I
hope that you will be able to do so as it is better for a
child if his or her mother or father can be there.
    As I have explained, the Education Committee have a
duty to arrange for your child to be examined; I hope
that you will readily agree that it may be in your child's
interest and will be willing to accept this offer of
expert advice.
    If you cannot come at the date and time suggested, I
shall be grateful if you will let me know by letter or by
telephone, so that some other child may have the benefit
of the appointment; I will then suggest some other date
and time to you.

                        Yours faithfully,

Mr/Mrs ...
....
....
....   Authorised Officer

All letters to be addressed to the Chief Officer.
Telephone calls to

6   The special schools

This chapter examines the special schools (1) which
received twenty-eight of the study population children as
pupils, through the interviews with the ten head teachers
involved.   The chapter specifically discusses how heads
perceive their role at the end of the decision-making
process of referral and assessment, when they finally
decide to admit a child into their school, and how they
regard the roles of the other professional personnel and
the parents.   The heads were also asked what they thought
the function of their school was - in terms of what
'special' characteristics they could offer that ordinary
schools could not, and their views on the specific problems of immigrant children were ascertained.   Head
teachers' comments on the part they played in the decisions made on the study population children are recorded
in the form of case studies.
    Questions concerning the function of special ESN-M
schools, and the part played by head teachers of special
schools in the ascertainment process emerged as particularly important during the course of this research.   It
is the head's decision to admit a child, and what goes on
in the school, that shapes the public image of an ESN-M
child.   In the most obvious sense, an ESN-M child is one
who attends or has attended an ESN-M school.
    From the early 1950s sociologists of education,
inspired by egalitarian ideologies, have been demonstrating the inequities of meritocratic selection by 'brightness' for education in separate schools, whereas at the
opposite end of the scale selection for separate schooling
by 'dullness' appears to have gone unremarked.   This
perhaps illustrates the anomalies of sociological claims
to objectivity - sociologists too are influenced by prevailing ideology and fashion in their choice of topic and
accept the position and treatment of certain social groups

as 'natural'. One result of this is that while there is
a large literature on curriculum and pedagogy within
special schools, largely produced by practitioners (for
example Tansley and Gulliford, 1960; Brennan, 1974,
bibliography), there is a paucity of sociological
research. In particular, there are no sociological
answers to the question 'What do special schools do?'
During the course of this research, one head allowed the
researcher to make weekly observation periods over two
terms at his school, and the question of the functions and
goals of special schools became so engrossing that the
research could have developed along the lines of a case
study of a special school. However, it was finally conceded that a special school study was another piece of
research, and the work in the special schools concentrated
on ascertaining the head's perceptions of the decision-
making process by which children arrived in the school,
and their views on the function of their school. It was
thought likely that the heads' decision to admit children
to their schools would rest on their beliefs that the
school could offer something to the child, but that the
decision would also have a pragmatic base - at a time of
falling referral and debate over the function of special
schools, heads are likely to encourage admission in order
to secure their own survival. (2)

To recapitulate briefly on the history of special
schools: the 1889 Royal Commission on the Blind, Deaf and
Dumb recommended that feeble-minded children should be
separated from 'normal' children and receive 'special
instruction', and during the 1890s the first schools for
special instruction were set up. Children suitable for
these schools were to be assessed by a medical officer, a
board inspector and the head of the special school. The
1899 Elementary Education (Defective and Epileptic
Children) act empowered, and the 1914 Act made it oblig-
atory for the local education authorities to provide day
schools and institutions for all mentally defective
children between the ages of seven and sixteen. At the
time of the Wood Report in 1929 there were 180 such
schools in England and Wales, accommodating some 16,750
children. The Wood Committee described the aims of the
special schools for educable defectives as 'the establishment of the child's self-respect, self-confidence and
self-control', and was particularly enthusiastic about the
'instruction in terms of manual work designed to contribute to the general education of the child, and later to
serve ... as vocational training' (Board of Education and
Board of Control, 1929, pp. 54-5). The Wood Committee
also noted one aspect of special school development,

which, sociologically speaking, appears to be very important: they 'possessed the advantage of freedom to adopt
means to the required end' (Board of Education and Board
of Control, 1929, p. 55). The autonomy of special education stems largely from the way in which it was left
relatively free to develop internally. There were no
pressures on heads to prepare children for examinations -
for secondary or further education, or even back into the
normal education system. (3)   What emerged as 'special
education' was largely a product of the decisions of the
practitioners. This point is supported by Jackson who
wrote in 1969 that 'it is regrettable that for over fifty
years most of the special schools in England and Wales
were expected to function with teachers who were left to
learn their craft by trial and error' (p. 2). A Special
Schools Association was founded in 1903 and its journal
and conferences became major vehicles for spreading curriculum practice, and reinforcing existing practices in
special schools. (4)   This pragmatic internal orientation
is currently still in evidence. A new research section
to be added to the Association's journal in 1979 promises
'research which is of relevance to those providing education and care for children with special educational
needs', and a stress on curriculum and pedagogy is again
advocated.

The development of a whole area of special education
inevitably brought about a separation of normal and
'special' education. The vested interests of medical and
later psychological personnel in the development of
special education have been noted in chapter 1, but the
appointment of special school heads and teachers, the
creation of a special school inspectorate, and a 'special'
administrative bureaucracy meant that increasing numbers
of professionals had vested interests in furthering the
separation and laying claim to specific areas of competence in catering for the 'special needs' of certain
children. The separation was noted by some practitioners
with regret. One ex-head teacher wrote that in the 1920s
and 1930s

Special school teachers were felt to have left the main
field of education ... and were looked on as missionaries going into an unknown field.... Teachers in
ordinary schools were glad that some of their profession had elected to do what they felt to be distasteful
- cope with defective children. (Lindsay, 1957)
Despite lip-service paid to the stigma of special schooling, the dangers of segregation and the need to return
children to normal education, the interests of those in
special education ensured that it developed as a separate,

autonomous sector.   The NUT Conference in 1974 passed a
resolution deploring 'the retention of any subnormal - as
distinct from backward - children in the ordinary classes
in primary schools'.   However, the interests of the
practitioners were often felt to be subordinate to those
of the other professional groups.

The role of the special school head in the assessment
process was gradually eroded as medical and later psychological assessment took precedence.   Post-1944 head
teachers of the 'new style' ESN schools did not play a
direct role in the ascertainment of children, although,
acting with the autonomy that all head teachers enjoy in
the English educational system, the final decision to
admit a child to the school does rest with the head.   The
Special Schools Association was powerful enough in 1908 to
oppose the suggestion by the Royal Commission on the Care
and Growth of the Feeble-minded, that feeble-minded
children be moved out of the aegis of education (Jackson,
1970), and the National Union of Teachers set up a Special
Education Committee in 1922.   Nevertheless, the limits of
teacher influence were decisively expressed in the NUT's
response to the 1929 Wood Committee on mentally defective
children.   The Executive regretted that 'Consideration of
a problem of such vital importance was left in the hands
of a committee upon which no representatives of teachers -
in schools for mental defectives or in the ordinary elementary schools - were included' (NUT, 1930).   The union
recorded that it was 'completely opposed' to the major
recommendations of the report - that former educable
defectives and dull and backward children be merged into
the administrative category ESN, and that certification be
abolished.   Nevertheless, the union's opinions were
largely disregarded in the subsequent legislation.   The
opposition to the Wood Committee stemmed from the fact
that if the element of compulsion were removed special
schools would lose their clientele, and teachers their
area of competence.   The union wrote that 'had teachers
been represented on the committee the naive assumption
that parents would be as eager to send their children to
retarded as they are to send them to central or secondary
schools would easily have been corrected' (NUT, 1930).

The designation of eleven 'official' types of handicap,
by the 1945 Handicapped Pupils and Special School Regulations (amended 1959 and 1962), entailed the provision of
a variety of types of special school, although provision
was patchy and dependent on local authority priorities.
Practitioners in ESN-M schools in fact extended rather
than lost their area of competence, as it was the ESN
category which expanded dramatically after the war.   By

1957 a major complaint was that 'the shortage of special school places for ESN is the largest outstanding problem in the special school field' (Report of the Chief Medical Officer to the Ministry of Education, 1956-7, p. 124) and places for 54,000 ESN children were envisaged by 1961. This happened despite Section 33(2) of the 1944 Education Act which allowed for special educational treatment to be given in any maintained or assisted school. The recognition of more 'backward' and 'remedial' children made it inevitable that normal schools should make arrangements for these children in addition to increased referrals to ESN schools, and, particularly in comprehensive schools, what Squibb (1977) has described as the 'remedial industry' began to develop. A Remedial Teachers' Association was forming in 1964, with its own journal, and continued the perplexing overlap between 'remedial' and 'ESN' which almost exactly paralleled the overlap in the 1920s between 'educable defectives' and 'dull and backward' children. The ingenious solution to this problem, suggested in the Warnock Report, is to once again expand the category, as 'a meaningful distinction between remedial and special education can no longer be maintained' ('Special Educational Needs ...', 1978).

However, this suggestion throws into sharp relief the question 'What do ESN-M schools actually do?'

The most common assumptions about special ESN-M schools are that they operate on a more individualistic basis, with smaller classes and staff specially trained to deal with slow-learning children. The maximum class sizes and teacher-pupil ratios for ESN-M were more recently prescribed in DES Circular 4/73, where teaching groups of between 11-13 were suggested (DES, 1973c).

In this research no school had more than three members of staff who had completed a special course or qualification, and it seemed that special school staff have only recently been able to take advantage of the growing number of specialised courses on offer. The teacher-pupil ratio did roughly conform to the DES suggestions.

A second major assumption made about the function of special ESN schools is that they do assist the educational progress of dull children. Evidence on this point to date appears equivocal. Presland (1970), reviewing research for and against this assertion in 1970, was of the opinion that dull children were put at a disadvantage in attending special schools and classes, rather than remaining in the remedial departments of ordinary schools. On the other hand Shearer (1975), in a survey of ESN-M children in Cheshire, considered that the progress of the children was 'reasonably encouraging' compared to their

previous lack of progress in ordinary school.   This point
- whether special ESN-M schools can offer children something that the ordinary schools cannot, particularly in
terms of their educational progress - is crucial to the
current debate on the changing function of ESN schools.

By 1978 the implications of the 1976 Education Act
(Section 10) and the Warnock Report were being widely
discussed and head teachers and teachers appear to be
seeking a new role for themselves and their schools.

Ainscow et al. wrote early in 1978 that since 'mainstreaming' handicapped children had become an accepted
trend, special school staff should be able to move to
ordinary schools to assist their colleagues, and special
schools should develop as a resource for all teachers,
particularly in terms of in-service training: 'There
should be specialist knowledge in the special school
which is not evident in the normal school ... it should
be a centre of theoretical knowledge and practical expertise on curriculum, assessment, teaching methods and
progress monitoring' (Ainscow et al., 1978).

Warnock recommendations concerning their 'wider concept
of special education' and their 'determined opposition to
the notion of treating handicapped and non-handicapped
children as forming two distinct groups' have created a
vigorous debate on 'integration' and called into question
the whole function of special schools.   As a research
editorial in the journal 'Special Education' noted,
'discussion of the integration issue has undoubtedly
aroused anxiety among teachers in special schools' (March
1978), and was of the opinion that 'the role of the
special school as a resource centre with much closer
relationships to the ordinary school must be taken
seriously'.

This debate is seriously hampered by the lack of
research on the functions, goals and organisation of
special schools, which means that there is little actual
knowledge of what these schools have been doing during the
period of their existence.

One unresearched aspect of special schools that is of
great importance to this study and this chapter concerns
the role of the head teacher of the special (ESN) school.

The autonomy of the head teacher in the English education system would seem to be carried to its most extreme
in special schools.   In ordinary schools, despite the
current 'Great Debate' and discussions of a 'core curriculum', there is a general consensus over certain educational aims, for example, educational progress in terms of
literacy and numeracy at primary level, and preparation
for qualifications and skills that lead to further

education or employment at the secondary level.   In
special schools the educational goals are not so clearly
articulated, and may be replaced by other goals.
Gulliford (1971, p. 22) has pointed out that:
    In the education of ordinary children whose development
    is within the normal range, it is appropriate that
    education progress should be the main aim.... In the
    education of children with special needs the first
    priority is to promote the optimum development of the
    child's capacities and personality.
This latter goal, in so far as it is accepted by
special school staff, is, though eminently worthy, vague
and largely unmeasurable and allows for a wide range of
curricular and teaching styles and it is the head
teachers' responsibility to decide just what the goals,
curriculum, pedagogy and organisation shall be in his
school.
    Head teachers, in this study, appeared to be much more
idiosyncratic in using their powers to determine the
goals, organisation and curriculum of their school in
accordance with their own personal style than head
teachers in ordinary schools.   They also consider that
certain aspects of their job are more arduous than in
ordinary schools, for example the larger number of staff
they manage.   Apart from teachers, assistant teachers,
welfare staff, domestic kitchen staff, 'guides' and
parental helpers, they oversee a variety of peripatetic
staff ranging from medical staff to speech therapists.
One head wrote in 1970 that: 'Managing a school for
handicapped children is in many ways more difficult than
running a normal school' (Knowle and Scott, 1970), and he
recommended the introduction of business management
techniques.   The heads in this study did not feel that
they were as accountable to the local education authority
over matters of learning, discipline and parental involvement as the heads of normal schools.   This may be because
the problems of the school, being outside mainstream
education, are regarded as less serious by the authorities, and problems can anyway be more easily attributed to
the child and his background on the assumption that he has
already been judged 'not normal'.   This is not to under-
estimate the problems which special school children and
their families undoubtedly do present to special school
heads - not least because, as previously noted, they tend
to come from that section of the population associated
with a variety of social problems.   The local authority
special schools' administration also seemed more willing
to leave the heads to 'get on with the job' and trust to
their experience and expertise.   Reciprocally, there was

a noticeable lack of reverence for the special schools
branch and inspectorate in the special schools.   When
asked about the role of the local education authority
during the course of the research, one special school
deputy head exclaimed jokingly: 'I'll have to leave;
there's a law of libel.'

   Twenty-eight of the study population children had been
placed in ten special schools.   Nine of the schools were
day ESN-M and one was a residential ESN-M.   Two of these
schools were in the process of integrating ESN-S
children.   One boy, though ascertained as ESN, had been
sent to a delicate school.   For the purpose of this
chapter the ten schools are considered together.
Another boy, a West Indian, whose case is considered in
some detail in chapter 8, had not been 'processed' into an
ESN school, but had been sent to an educational guidance
centre and later to a suspension centre.   The guidance
was visited and the head interviewed, as several professionals felt that these centres and units were taking
children who might previously have been referred as ESN,
and were in a sense a form of special education.   The
number of pupils at the special schools visited ranged
from approximately 62 to 280.   A breakdown is given in
Table 6.1.

TABLE 6.1   Numbers of children at the special schools
attended by study population children

62	delicate school
114	
115	
120	
140	ESN
155	
159	
220	
265	including ESN-S
280	

The oldest school dated back to 1899 when one of the first
special classes in the city was established there.   The
newest school was a purpose-built school opened in 1976
and described by a head as the 'showplace of Europe'.
Another school had been purpose-built as a school for
'defective' children in 1932, but modified twice, and a
fourth school was only nine years old but the head
remarked: 'It must have been built by Poulson - it's
falling down around us.'   One suburban residential school

had originally been part of a mental hospital and took
dull and maladjusted children on a national basis,
however, from 1960 it became residential ESN with an
emphasis on truant and delinquent children.

Eight heads and two deputies were interviewed, first on
a general basis and then about the specific children from
the study population who had been placed in their schools.
It was interesting that while all the heads of ordinary
schools were willing to be interviewed, two special school
heads passed the researcher on to their deputies. For
the rest of this chapter the two deputies will be subsumed under the term 'head' (both are in fact now heads of
other special schools).

The heads were asked how many staff they had at their
school, and they invariably answered this question in
terms, not only of teaching staff, but of all the staff
they managed - nursery nurses, welfare assistants,
domestic and kitchen staff, guides, and in the case of the
residential school - gardening staff. The ratio of
teaching staff to pupils was largely in accordance with
Circular 4/73 on the staffing of special schools and supported the general assumption that ESN-M schools do indeed
provide smaller teaching groups. The ratio of teachers
to pupils varied between 10 and 15. When all staff were
taken into consideration the numbers of children to adults
on the school premises was generally around 5 or 6. All
the heads were of the opinion that they had a 'settled'
staff, that is no rapid turnover, and that when staff left
it was usually for promotion. (5) One head complained
that the welfare staff were his 'biggest headache' but
most heads accepted that they would have more staff
management than heads in ordinary schools. Most were
keen for their staff to acquire more qualifications in
terms of secondment for special courses or in-service
courses, and only one head was disgruntled about his
staff: 'I wouldn't give tuppence for some of them; the
Colleges don't train them properly.'

The heads were asked what resources and facilities
their schools possessed that ordinary schools did not
have. Two heads noted their extra capitation allowance
which allowed them to spend more money on resources.
Three mentioned 'technical aids' - one head being very
enthusiastic about this: 'We have a language master,
television, radio, overhead projector, cassette recorder,
talking page and a minibus.' Three heads mentioned
smaller classes as a resource, and another said his best
resource was his 'good teachers'. The residential head
was very enthusiastic over the sporting facilities his
school could offer - tennis courts, swimming pool,

gardens. The head of the 'showplace of Europe' considered the facilities to be 'fantastic'. He mentioned rubber flooring, strip lighting, soft chairs, a ten-foot-high Wendy house, a sand and water room, and a behaviour therapy unit with two 'quiet' rooms for disruptive children.

Only one head was not complimentary about the facilities and lay-out of his school: 'The corridors are too narrow and there are no spare rooms; the children have a low frustration level and this adds to it.'

The heads of the special schools comprised eight male and two female, and had been head teachers of their schools for some considerable time. Heads of special schools seem on the whole to be older and longer-serving than their colleagues in ordinary schools. Of eight heads, two had been heads for fifteen and thirteen years respectively, three for twelve and ten years, one for nine years and two for over two years. Two of the heads were shortly about to retire. Most of the heads had spent a good deal of their teaching career in special education. Three had previously held headships in ESN schools, and one had left grammar school teaching for an ESN headship. The most original head had spent thirty years in special education after qualifying as an electrical engineer and serving in the navy.

THE REFERRAL PROCESS

The head teachers were asked how children came to be placed in their schools. Three heads answered this question in terms of the formal administrative process:
'I get a formal request from special services, but usually the psychologist or the MO has spoken to me about the child and asked if I can take him.'

'They are submitted to me on a waiting list and I get all the forms sent from the office.'

'They are referred through the office. If I have room I interview the parents and take the child.'
Three heads answered in terms of the referring agents:
'Children get here by a variety of ways; the results of recommendations made by so many people.'

'Psychologists recommend children - they don't recommend unsuitable children so I take those they do recommend.'

'Children are referred by a variety of people - nursery
children by doctors and health visitors.   I even
referred a child myself who eventually came to this
school.'
Four heads answered in terms of the reason, as they
perceived it, for children arriving in their school:
'They come because of educational failure.'   'I get kids
who are throw-outs from other schools.'   The delicate
school head answered more in medical terms: 'I get children for educational retardation and subnormality, but some
children are obvious cases for us, medical - asthma,
cystic fibrosis, occasionally leukaemia.'
These were some hints that the heads did feel sometimes
that their schools were a last resort for problem children
from the ordinary educational system: 'I sometimes think
my school is a dumping ground for the problems of this
city.   It makes me wonder if the educational bureaucracy
exists to help citizens or protect its bureaucracy.'
To test the heads' perceptions of their own autonomy,
they were asked if they had to take every child who was
put forward as a potential pupil.   Only one head gave a
qualified 'yes' to this question: 'Yes - but the decision
is mainly a geographical one - I can postpone entry.'
Nine heads replied in the negative;   two unqualified,
seven qualified their answers, usually in terms of either
numbers of their opinion of the child's problem.

'It depends on vacancies within an age-group - we could
be forced to go up to 20 a class, but I've never got to
that.'

'No, we are limited by the numbers in the school.'

'I don't take every child.   If I think a child has
been wrongly assessed I ask for a further review of the
case: for example, I don't like to take the "cabbage"
- the withdrawn child.'
Two heads used this question to indicate their disapproval
of the integration of ESN-M and S children.   One said
unequivocally: 'I reject a few - usually SSN children.
I think both lots lose out if you mix them.'   Another
head said she found she now had parents asking her to take
their children in preference to the child going to a
school 'integrated' with SSN children.   'Parents have a
right to have their ESN-M children educated separately.'
In general, the heads did see as part of their autonomy
the right to make the final decision to admit a child to
their school.   One head was absolutely adamant that 'the
final decision rests with me'.
Following this the heads were asked if they had a

waiting list.   As previously noted, referrals and placements of children in ESN schools increased steadily until
around 1974, when a drop in referrals became evident.
It was not, therefore, expected that schools would have
waiting lists at this time.   However, two heads gave a
qualified 'yes' to this question:

'I'm one of the few special schools with a waiting
list.   We seem to have more children now failing in
the normal school situation and the ESN schools are
taking them from further down the scale and are full of
tough children now.'

'My middle school has a waiting list - we only take
older children if they are behaviour problems - if we
don't get them 'til secondary age, of course, it means
that someone hasn't done their job properly lower
down.'

The eight heads who said they had no waiting list were
aware that the referral of children was dropping, and this
created something of an anxiety as to the future function
of their school:

'I don't have a waiting list now - my deputy will have
to go shopping for children.'

'No, not now.   The staff inspector came to talk to me
last week about why referrals were dropping.'

There were several suggestions as to why referrals
were dropping - usually connected to the greater willingness of heads in ordinary schools to keep what was
several times referred to as the 'true ESN child'.   By
this the heads appeared to mean a child who was backward
in learning but not troublesome.   Heads felt that the
schools were only passing on the more troublesome children
with severe learning and behaviour problems.   This was
certainly borne out by the interviews with heads in normal
schools.   Catholic schools, for example, did not refer or
only referred children with behaviour problems which they
could not cope with;   inner-city schools which felt they
had a 'low' standard generally, were only referring what
they considered to be severe learning problems, usually
plus behaviour problems.   One head mentioned that the
speedier process by which children could be placed in the
educational guidance units might be one reason for fewer
placements in ESN-M schools.

THE INVOLVEMENT OF OTHER PERSONNEL

Since head teachers are involved at the 'end of the line' in the decision-making process and are presented with a collection of forms incorporating a series of decisions made by other personnel, whom they may not necessarily have had contact with, it was of particular interest to note how the head saw the roles of these personnel.

Asked how they saw the job of the educational psychologist in the referral and assessment procedure, most heads gave a global answer incorporating three points: their general views of educational psychologists; the help and support they got from the psychologists once children were placed in their schools; and the psychologist as 'tester' of children during the assessment process:

'Psychologists are changing now - our last one made good suggestions about teaching and behaviour problems; this is different from the older psychologists who we got in the past who were often just testers.'

'Their role is very valuable.   I wouldn't be so presumptuous as to say I could do their job, but I think they waste too much time testing children who are not ESN.'

'Some psychologists are way out and autocratic - those who have not been teachers usually - they give us a gorgeous programme for a child but don't realise we can't have a one-to-one relationship with every child.'

Three heads were uncomplimentary about the service they get from the educational psychologist:

'We don't get enough help.   The operate a fire brigade service here.'

'They are a useless bunch at our clinic - often they don't know what it's like and try to impose a middle-class solution.'

This latter comment referred to a psychologist who had apparently advised a working-class mother in overcrowded conditions about a rota for domestic chores in which her children could participate.   'The psychologist diagnoses the faults, but only recently has started to tell us what to do - they have not got sufficient practical experience and are somewhat overrated in their abilities.'

On the other hand, two heads appreciated the services the educational psychologist had to offer:

'They define areas of failure and formulate programmes.'

'We need Mr X to continually assess children and act as
a check on our subjective impressions.'

There was an underlying conflict in the views the heads
had of the psychologist.   They felt he had a more 'scientific' objective view of the children and their problems
and possibilities than teachers could have, but at the
same time distrusted tests and programmes, particularly if
suggested by psychologists who had not themselves been
teachers.

The heads were less ambiguous when asked how they saw
the role of the medical officer in checking children
referred for special education, although again, they
tended to interpret this question in terms of the help
they got from medical officers once children had been
placed in their school:

'They diagnose the physical problems of children and
liaise with other specialists before the child gets to
school.'

'I've always been fortunate in my MOs.   We have a
special relationship with Dr Y.   He does a regular
clinic for us and prescribes drugs.' (An integrated
SSN/ESN school.)

One head said that he thought the job of the MO was to
'lower parental expectations' about their children's
educational possibilities.   He thought the status of
medical doctor was necessary for this: 'MOs are very
necessary - parents often have false expectations of their
children and it takes a doctor to indicate to them that
their children will not get far.'   On the other hand,
another head was positive in his condemnation of the
medical involvement in decision-making: 'I think it's
ludicrous that a doctor should recommend for special
schools - there is a danger that the MO could take over
the role of psychologist.'   Another head said that
although MOs usually 'knew about' special schools: 'a
doctor should not make educational decisions about children'.

Overall, though, the heads appeared to concede a more
positive role, connected to their status, to the medical
officers, than to the educational psychologists.

The heads were asked how they saw the role of the
special services in the referral and placement process.
Five heads answered this in terms of administration:

'I have contact with the casework clerk.'

'They send me all the papers on children;   I can make a
decision on whether to take a child the same day.'

'We've got to have administration.   They send me the
forms.   I can ring them up about anything concerned
with my school.'
One head saw the role of special services as: 'filtering
prospective students to the correct school placement'.
Four heads were critical of the administration:
'They are a bureaucracy designed to perpetuate themselves.'

'As long as they have all the children placed they
don't care where they go - it's not satisfactory.'

'We don't see enough of the inspectors - we need them
to take more of an interest in us.'
One head took advantage of this question to complain
that ESN schools will be used more as 'dumping grounds':
'I think the function of the ESN-M school will go - the
average ESN kid can be dealt with in remedial departments.   These schools will end up as dumping grounds -
it will be like in the past: poor teachers in ordinary
schools will be threatened with the sack or being sent
to teach in ESN schools.'
He saw the administration as being primarily responsible for the changing function (as he saw it) of the
ESN-M school.
To understand further how heads viewed the administrative procedures that have developed and which encapsulate
the decisions made about the children who arrive in their
schools, heads were asked about the use of the old HP and
new SE forms, and the extent of informal contacts they had
with other personnel.   Heads were unanimous in their
condemnation of forms, generally and specifically.   The
SE forms were not considered to be any improvement on the
HP forms:
'They [SE] are a waste of bloody time - they have only
to be ticked.   Few comments are required.   They are
worse than the HP forms.'

'I find them more complicated than the HPs to read.
They have a lot of ticks - what are we to assume from
that?   I find them incredibly complicated and there
are too many of them.'

'I get pages of photo-statted forms with nothing on
them - but it all depends on who fills the forms out.'
Heads felt that some information was unnecessary while
other information was not included on the forms, particularly concerning social background:
'There are too many of these forms, too many boxes on

them, a lot of the doctor's report is unnecessary.
There is not enough on the social background or family
and no list of who is directly concerned with the
child.'

'They are too unwieldy and there is nowhere for a
social worker's report.'

The head teachers' response over the use of the forms
indicated that the forms are probably more important for
the head at this final stage of decision-making than for
the other personnel.   Ideally, copies of all forms and
reports from people who have made decisions on, or had
contact with, a child and his family should eventually
arrive on file in the special school.   In fact, this
process, as several heads admitted, is far from perfect as
records are mislaid, forms not properly filled out, and
copies of forms not 'sent on' by the office.   Although
one head said that he was 'not interested in forms - only
in the child, the heads did, in fact, rely on the information passed on by the forms to provide as detailed a
picture as possible of the child they were about to take
into the school.   None of the heads were satisfied that
the SE forms gave sufficient information or the right kind
of information.   All the heads said that they depended on
informal contacts, usually by telephone, with the other
personnel involved for providing additional information on
the children, and all but one head were worried about the
records of children attending special schools.   As one
head said: 'I'm worried about records.   The children
sometimes move around and we often don't get the records
from other schools.   I think special school records are
in a mess and need revising.

In one school where some of the children's records were
read, they did appear relatively incomplete.   Neither, at
this particular school, were teachers particularly well
informed with past information about the children they
were teaching.   Information on children was mainly passed
by word of mouth between staff rather than by reading
detailed records.

Since the process of transferring to special schools is
an educational process, it was expected that the two major
educational decision-makers, the head of the ordinary
school and the head of the special school, would have contact over particular cases.   In the referring school
chapter, however, it was noted that 46 per cent of ordinary school heads said they had no contact with special
schools.   Eight of the ten special school heads said they
had contact with the schools who referred their children:

'I always ring the referring school and discuss the
child with the head.'

'I, or one of my staff, always try to visit the referring school and especially to talk with the class
teacher.'

'It's becoming more common now to have contact; we are
not so isolated.'

Two heads mentioned that their main contact was in
placing children back in normal school if they felt this
arrangement was justified, and hinted at 'unofficial'
arrangements:

'We have two boys here from X school; they haven't yet
been formally ascertained. They are doing very well
and may go back. We do send children back to ordinary
school and of course there is no formal de-ascertain-
ment nowadays.'

Head teachers were asked about the type and degree of
contact they had with parents before they admitted a child
to their school. This question produced some ambiva-
lence. While the heads all considered that they 'ought'
to have seen all parents, they were honest enough to admit
that the system was not perfect and that this was not in
fact the case. Several heads thought that parents felt
the stigma of special schooling before the child was
admitted, and were reluctant to come for an initial interview:

'I see parents if they will come, but often they are
reluctant; they still see a stigma to special schooling. It's the same when the child is attending - I
had a parents' evening last week and only 23 parents
turned up to represent 155 children.'

'I see parents before the child comes, with the child,
but if they refuse - and this has happened twice in the
last six months - I get the EWO to visit.'

One head said he personally visited parents in their homes
and kept an 'open door' policy: 'I think my school is
successful because of the verbal communication I have with
parents.'

Heads stressed that they needed the parents' co-operation if a child was to be successfully integrated into the
special school, but this was not an automatically easy
process, and 'public relations' might be needed. As one
head put it: 'I need parents' co-operation and for them
to see what the school is all about I have a social worker
I can send to see parents, as part of a public relations
thing.'

In general, heads were aware that there was a need to
involve parents of children admitted to special schools,
but were unsure how to go about this. They felt that the

reactions of parents to special schooling were likely to
be reluctant or hostile: 'Some parents get annoyed that
they don't have more say in what happens to their
children.'

But they felt that if parental involvement in ordinary
education was difficult, it was doubly difficult to
achieve in special education.

One head had given the matter some thought and elaborated on his plans: 'I'm starting a scheme where parents
are invited to school to discuss how they can help their
children. I already have a parents' evening once a month
where we do everything from discussing careers to playing
bingo.'

THE FUNCTION OF ESN SCHOOLS

One of the pragmatic ways in which the question 'What is
an ESN child?' has been resolved has been by assuming that
an ESN child is one who can be more suitably educated in
an ESN school than an ordinary school.   This begs the
question as to the function of an ESN school.   As noted,
the two most common assumptions about ESN schools are that
they have specially trained staff to teach smaller groups
of children, and in this study these two points were most
frequently mentioned by the referring schools.   It was
considered to be important therefore to discover what the
heads of special schools considered the function of their
schools to be, as this presumably has some bearing on a
head's decision to admit a particular child to his school.

The heads gave an interesting variety of answers to the
question about the function of their schools.

TABLE 6.2 Head teachers' views on the function of ESN
schools

Smaller classes/individual attention	4
Sheltered environment/acceptance of deviance	2
Social adjustment	3
Preparation for work	2
Provision of a therapeutic community	2
Basic literacy	1
Slower pace	1
Social work with family	2
Behaviour modification/treat disturbed children	3
Total	20

(More than one answer given.)

Some of the comments indicated that heads felt quite strongly that the smaller classes and individual attention were a major justification for placing children in their school rather than ordinary schools, but they did not necessarily feel that ordinary schools could not offer the same thing:

'We can give individual attention and special care, but I don't want to decry teachers in ordinary schools.'

'We have a more intimate relationship with smaller groups, but some of our colleagues in ordinary schools are trained to deal with slow learners.'

'We have smaller classes, a slower pace and fewer children in the school.'

Only one head mentioned basic literacy as a specific function: 'Urban children must be able to read and write; most of the children I get have enough between the ears to realise this.   Social adjustment is all very well but they must be able to read and write.'

It is likely that the other heads had basic literacy in mind when they noted smaller classes and individual attention, but one head was more specifically anti-literacy. He said: 'We are not after academic attainment; we see too many examples of the folly of developing specific skills out of context of the child's general level of awareness.'

This head, and one other, used the notion of a 'therapeutic community' to describe the function of their schools.   A third head noted a social work function: 'We notice bruising or neglected children - we have a number of kids from problem families and try to give them special care and attention.'

Two heads said that they aimed to make their children socially competent to hold down a job after leaving school, and one head specifically mentioned behaviour modification as a function of his school.   Two heads referred to the facilities of special schools in coping with violent or disturbed children.

The comments made by the head teachers concerning the function of their schools seem to be in line with Gulliford's statement that educational progress may not be the major aim of special education.   Only six comments referred to educational provision; fourteen comments referred to non-academic functions of the school.   There does seem to be some discrepancy in this study between parental expectations as to the educational progress of their children in special schools, and the heads' views as to the function of their school.   The special autonomy of

special school heads is perhaps illustrated by their
relative freedom to create a school which reflects their
views. One head, for example, said that she liked 'a
family atmosphere for the children', but later mentioned
that she rejected 'violent pupils'. Her model 'family'
presumably did not include conflict. One of the major
characteristics about ESN schools may, in fact, be the way
in which the views of the head teacher about the function
of an ESN school can fashion the whole style of the
school, and gives these schools their undoubted distinc-
tiveness within the education system.

THE PROBLEMS OF 'IMMIGRANT' CHILDREN

Finally, heads were asked whether West Indian, Asian and
Irish children had any special problems that made them
more likely to be referred as needing special education.
  Seven heads referred to the behaviour, language and
family problems of West Indian children:
  'Fifty per cent of my pupils are black; it is sufficient to say that the behaviour exhibited by some of
  the children made them uncontrollable in ordinary
  schools, irrespective of their IQ.'

  'They are more noisy and hyper-active than English
  children.'

  'Creole language means we can't understand them and
  they can't understand us, although this is changing
  now.'

  'West Indians have more language problems than
  Asians; they don't speak our English so thought and
  communication is different.'

  'A lot of West Indians come from one-parent families.
  It is the norm for them.'
  Three heads did not think West Indian children had any
particular problems that made them more likely to be
referred for special education. One head noted that he
seemed to be getting more West Indian children at his
(suburban) school and considered that 'immigration should
be stopped'. However, he felt he could cope with the
generation of West Indian children born in Britain better
than with immigrant pupils.
  Six head teachers thought that Asian children had difficulties with language and family communication that
could make them candidates for referral. Four noted an

organic handicap or under-nourishment, and two commented
on the difficulties of assessing Asian children.
> 'They have more speech problems, and often a handicap,
> like a spastic arm or a hearing defect.'

> 'They have to be bilingual and of course the mothers
> usually want to go back home.   Asian mothers are out
> of their depth in England.'

> 'Asian children are often under-nourished and have an
> organic handicap.'

One head commented that: 'Asian families are no trouble.
They respect their elders and the home is orderly.   I
find that very interesting.'
Four heads held very strong views about Irish children;
six did not think they had any special problems.
> 'I've got into trouble for saying that Irish children
> are some of the dirtiest, smelliest I've got.'

> 'They can be difficult and volatile;   a third of my
> school is Irish at the moment.   If they threaten me
> I send for the police;   they need studying to see if
> it's in-breeding.'

THE STUDY POPULATION CHILDREN

Given that head teachers felt that their schools had a
variety of functions apart from educational progress, a
check was made on the comments made by the heads about
the study population children.   What was the opinion of
the heads about the major problems that had brought these
children to the special school?

TABLE 6.3 Opinions of special school heads as to the
major problems of the study population children, expressed
as a percentage

Poor educational progress	28.6	(35)
Behaviour/educational problems	21.4	(32.5)
Organic/medical problems	10.7	(7.5)
Family problems	21.4	(10)
Truancy from normal school	7.2	(15)
Other/'not ESN'	10.7	–
Totals	100.0	100.0

(Figures in brackets adapted from Table 2.6 to compare the
reasons given by the referring agency for the initial
referral.)

Over a quarter of the children were considered to have
been admitted to the school mainly because of an educational problem:
'P. is an amiable child; he's properly placed in an
ESN-M school.'

'O. was a low-functioning child; he needed to come to
us.'

'R. seems to have done very little since he came, but
he's doing better than his IQ says.'
But twelve of the children were considered to have
mainly behaviour, emotional and/or family problems:
'This lad is forever in trouble - gets into fights.
He's not used to discipline, and his parents weren't
too happy about him coming here at first.'

'C. is a little angel now, but he came to us with a bad
family background and had temper tantrums and called
the teachers bastards.'

'D. is a nervous little lad; he is very apprehensive
and was picked on by other children.'

'All the children in this family are deeply disturbed.
The mother has an evangelical passion ... but goes
round to Social Services to complain about her husband.
... They are all sickle-cell anaemic.'
Three children, two of them Asians, were considered to
be in the school mainly because of an organic handicap:
'He's a dull child but above ESN; he has a lisp and poor
co-ordination.' Two children were also considered to be
'not ESN' but it was felt that their parents connived at
their truancy from ordinary school and special school:
'She's not an ESN child - she's got an IQ of 80. If
she'd come to school she could be reviewed and go back to
normal school.'
    Two other children were also considered to be 'not
ESN', but to be in need of remedial action in normal
school, but other problems had meant they were in the
special school: 'She's got an average attainment and
would be better off in the remedial stream of a comprehensive, but she's obese and nervous and I suppose is as well
here as anywhere.' One boy was considered to be maladjusted and was being considered for transfer to a residential maladjusted school. The head said: 'He highlights
the fact that we are a school for problems, not just an
ESN school.'
    The willingness of the heads of ESN schools to describe

some of their pupil intakes as 'not ESN' illustrates the
problematic nature of the output of an ESN school.   A
child may enter the school 'not ESN', yet the very fact of
his attendance at the school turns him into an 'ESN
child'.

The opinions of the special school heads as to the
major problem of the study population are interesting when
compared to the views of the referring agent.   Heads
considered organic problems and family problems to be
higher, but behaviour problems and truancy to be less
important problems than the referring agent.

Several heads referred specifically to the IQ of the
children when discussing the nature of their major problem.   One head noted that: 'C.'s IQ has gone up five
points whilst he's been here, but of course all IQ tests
have a five-point variant.'

CASE STUDIES

The following case study illustrates the way in which a
head saw the function of his school as providing an answer
to a child's home problems and truancy.
1 Alison P. had been referred to the Child Guidance
Clinic by a social worker who had been working for some
time with the family.   She was living in a small
cluttered home with an invalid mother - thin and
arthritic - her 'step-father', a young man who had himself
attended an ESN school, a grandmother and a younger
brother.   The step-father had been in prison for
grievous bodily harm, and had several times been to the
secondary school Alison attended, threatening the staff as
he said the girl was 'picked on'.   The head of the school
said Alsion, at thirteen years, was a truant and thought
the girl had 'awful home problems'.   The psychologist had
interviewed and tested Alison very promptly and had sent a
copy of his very full report to the head, with a request
that she fill out an SE 1.   He gave Alison's IQ as 73 and
recommended her for day ESN school.   He said that:
    'Alison is a culturally disadvantaged girl, who in
    addition has social and emotional problems causing it
    to be difficult for her to win friends.   She has a
    poor self-image and this is partly reinforced by her
    scholastic failure.'
He had interviewed Alison's parents and discussed special
education for Alison before the SE 1 had been filled in.
She had been given an appointment for a medical examination two months after psychological testing, and
presumably had kept this appointment, although the MO who

examined her could not remember her and could not 'find'
Alison's medical file.   The psychologist had suggested a
particular ESN school for Alison and had actually tele-
phoned the head of this school;   however, the administration sent Alison's papers to another ESN school.   The
school received Alison's papers and the head decided to
accept the girl immediately.   (In the interview, this
was the head who said he generally only took behaviour
problems at secondary school age.)   He said that from the
papers it appeared that Alison had been kept at home a lot
and her secondary school attendance had been 'pretty
rough'.   He thought she had become backward in her
school work because of this.   'She may not have needed
special education if it hadn't been for this.'   However,
he thought that Alison had come on very well at his
school.   'She mixes well, which goes against what her
last school said....   She's coming into her own and is
popular with the girls and the boys - she's a good-looking
girl.'   He thought that special school was the place for
her.

2   The case of Tania S. illustrates the way in which a
head accepted a child who in his opinion was 'not ESN'
although he was considering reviewing her case with a view
to returning her to normal school.   This had not been
done when the study finished.
     Tania S. had been taken by a teacher to the local
school clinic because she had been truanting, was backward
in her work, and the school was 'anxious about her'.   The
school clinic had passed her on to the Child Guidance
Clinic.   The school had also contacted the SCMO asking
for help with the girl.   The psychologist saw the girl
promptly, gave her IQ as 80 and recommended special
school.   He rang up what he considered to be the most
suitable ESN school and the head agreed to take the girl.
The SCMO saw the girl and concurred with the psychologist.
Her mother received a letter from the administration
telling her to take Tania to the special school the next
term, but she had written an anxious letter to the psychologist saying that the girl had gone to Shropshire to her
grandparents as a horse she looked after was ill!
Eventually the girl started at the special school.   The
head said she thought Tania was 'pushed in quick' and
intended to have her case reviewed and arrange for her to
be sent back to the ordinary school.   The head said,
'She's not an ESN child - she has an IQ of 80 and if she'd
actually come to the school she'd do well enough in the
ordinary school.'   The head blamed the parents who con-
doned Tania's absence and said they had almost been taken
to court by the EWO.

3 The case of Albert W. also illustrates a 'not ESN' boy
who nevertheless had become ESN by having to attend an ESN
school, much against his own and his parents' inclina-
tions. The head of the school who accepted this boy,
without going through the required medical procedure, was
a head who was concerned at the falling referral and
admission to special schools.

Albert W. was another child who was moved quickly from
ordinary secondary school to special school. He was the
fifth child in a family well known to the Social Services
to be sent to ESN school. He had been referred by his
secondary school remedial department with five other boys,
and when tested by the psychologist was described as 'the
worst of the referrals - can't cope in any aspect of
behaviour, get him into Y school as soon as possible'.
The psychologist contacted the special school that the
boy's brother attended (not the nearest) and the head
agreed to take the boy immediately. The psychologist and
head both thought that this boy's case showed that
remedial departments in secondary schools were not the
answer for all dull and difficult children. 'It proves
that in these large schools you need more than a simple
remedial teacher and special equipment - a whole special
environment is needed.' The MO arranged to see the boy
at the psychologist's request, but said that she too had
contacted Y school who would 'let the boy in without the
usual procedure'. The head said he knew this family as
they used to live in his area, and he now had three of the
boys in his school. He did not have a very high opinion
of Albert.

'He's one of Lady Wootton's band of delinquents with
IQs over 80. He's wrongly placed - he should be in a
remedial situation but he's got gaps in his learning.
He's got an inflated opinion of himself and a low
tolerance of frustration so he's unlikely to learn.
He's a petty pilferer and generally this is corrupt-
ing.'

There are three major conclusions to this chapter. They
concern how heads perceive themselves as part of the
decision-making process, how heads perceive the role of
the other professionals and parents involved, and what
heads perceive the function of their school to be,
particularly in terms of the sort of children they do
accept as 'ESN'.

Heads do see themselves as a definite part of the
decision-making process particularly in that they are able
to take or refuse a child for their school. They also
have their own personal styles on what type of child they

refuse (the 'cabbage', the 'violent child').   Thus, it
would appear that heads can to some extent shape the composition of their school and thus influence the image of
an 'ESN child' (given that ESN children are those in ESN
schools).

However, heads regard their major role in the decision-
making process as the administrative task of gathering
together all the documents and forms which record the
decisions made by other professionals - since this information will ideally be used as the school's basis for the
treatment of the particular child.   They are not happy
about the current efficiency of this process as they think
that records often end up incomplete.   They are particularly critical of the new SE procedure, which they do not
think records information about the children adequately.

As regards the other personnel, the heads of special
schools are somewhat ambivalent in their attitudes to
psychologists.   They are not too complimentary about
them personally, and they tend to distrust some of the
psychologists' suggestions, particularly if the psychologists have not had teaching experience.   At the same time
they regard the psychologists as more scientific and
objective in their testing of children and suggestions for
educational programmes.   The heads regard the IQ as a
valuable piece of information about children, which is
supplied by the psychologists.   The heads are less ambivalent about the medical officer.   They regard the MO as
providing a valuable service, both during and after
referral, which extends in some cases beyond a medical
function.   On the other hand, several heads were worried
that medical personnel should influence educational decisions made about the children.

Several heads felt that the administration was more
concerned with running an efficient bureaucracy than with
the children involved, and that the power to change the
function of ESN schools lay perhaps with the impersonal
administration.

The heads felt that contact with the referring schools
was vital, and attached more importance to contact than
the referring heads did reciprocally.   The heads felt
some strain in their relationship with parents.   This may
come about because of the aggressive or hostile reaction
of a few parents, since in this research once parents had
seen the special school they were, by and large, in favour
of their children attending.   Heads are aware that
parents may see attendance at special school as a stigma,
and are not sure how to improve parent-school relationships, a problem they share - in a more acute form - with
ordinary schools.

The heads of special schools do regard their schools as having diverse functions, not solely connected to the educational progress of children, although from an educational point of view they do think they can offer a more individualistic learning environment.   They do not see this function as too different from that offered in remedial departments of ordinary schools.

The heads are aware of the current debate on changing functions of special schools and they are giving some thought to the possible changing nature of their schools. On the whole they do not support the integration of severely subnormal children with the ESN-M children.   The heads seem to have more freedom to create a school which reflects their own views and 'style' than heads of ordinary schools.   This may be one result of the feeling that ESN education is 'outside' ordinary education.

While the heads do seem to have a model ESN child in mind, a 'dull' child with an IQ falling within certain limits, they do not feel that the majority of the children in their school correspond to this ideal type.   The ideal 'dull' child is implicitly considered to be genetically dull, corresponding to the 1946 'limited ability on a genetic basis'.   More particularly, they think the children they take in their schools as ESN have a variety of other problems, particularly connected to behavioural, emotional or family problems.   They are quite specific that certain children are 'not ESN' but they are willing to take these children until certain limits are reached, when they may try to move a child.   They also distinguish children who could function in the remedial departments of ordinary schools.   By and large, they do regard their schools as valuable places for children with a variety of problems.

The heads do not hold such stereotyped views of the problems presented by immigrant children as the heads of ordinary schools do, but they do mention the same problems - behaviour, family problems and language.   Since they tend, in smaller schools, to regard the children on a more individual basis, children are perhaps considered more in terms of their individual problems rather than their immigrant or colour status.

Heads' views on 'what is an ESN child?' relate quite closely to the 1946 guidelines issued by the Ministry of Education.   They distinguish a 'true ESN' child, a dull child of innate limited ability who exhibits few other problems, and who has an IQ falling within certain limits. Other children are in the schools for 'other conditions', particularly behavioural and emotional problems and family problems.

Although the empirical documentation concerning the perceptions of heads about the function of special schools is novel and interesting, it is important to briefly consider the function of the schools in a wider social and historical context.

The major function of special schooling from the 1890s would seem to have been to remove children from the normal schools who were troublesome in the sense of interfering with the smooth development of 'normal education' - either by exhibiting learning difficulties or behaviour which the teacher could not control.   Special schools appeared in countries with similar selective, competitive, occupationally oriented education systems at more or less the same time (UNESCO, 1973) and it can be suggested that normal education in industrial societies could not have developed as it has done without the 'safety-valve' of special education to remove children who demonstrably would not, or could not, conform to the system.

The absolute necessity for the creation of a system that was 'outside' the education system has allowed the relatively smooth development of normal education, unimpeded by certain kinds of undesirable children.   While Pritchard (1963), for example, would argue that special schools cater for more children who cannot cope with an increasingly high educational standard, it can also be suggested that it is the normal schools which are defining more children as troublesome in learning and behavioural terms, and seeking ways of ridding themselves of the children into some form of 'special education'.   The ingenious suggestions of the Warnock Report on extending the category 'ESN' would seem to legitimate this process.

7   The parents of the study population children

The purpose of this chapter is to describe and assess the
extent of the involvement of the parents of the forty
study population children, in the processes of referral
and assessment of their children.   The basic question
this part of the research attempts to answer is how far
and at what point are the parents consulted and involved
in the decisions that professional people make about their
children, as the children pass through the often lengthy
process of assessment that on some occasions results in
the child being placed in a special school.   As a pre-
amble, the chapter briefly examines previous research on
the parents of children in special education, and notes
the extent of statutory and non-statutory advice and
comment as to how far parents 'ought' to be involved in
the process.   The chapter then goes on to describe some
of the characteristics of the study population parents,
before considering their actual involvement and consultation by means of an analysis of the schedule used in the
research to interview the parents.

Post-war liberal concern with equality and fairness in
the distribution of education has tended to place parents
as a whole, and manual working-class parents in particular, in an invidious position.   The influence of the
'good home' on educational success has been extensively
documented in sociological literature (for example,
Musgrove, 1966; Floud, Halsey and Martin, 1956; Douglas,
1964; Craft, 1970; DES, 1967).   The supposed linguistic
deficiencies of working-class children has attained folk-
lore status (Bernstein, 1971) and popular explanations
have stressed the supposed failure of manual working-class
parents to equip their children with appropriate skills,
to participate in an individualistic, competitive educational system.   Post-Plowden research on home-school
relations has tended to concentrate on how parents can be

'improved' to enhance their child's chances of success within the system (Craft, 1970).   No democratic ideology has emerged so far within the English educational system which considers parents as equal participants in the educative process, with a right to be involved in educational decisions made about their children.   If a 'continuum of competence' is envisaged, along which professional people place the parents of the children with whom they deal, the parents of subnormal children would probably be placed towards the end of the continuum.   There is little rigorous research on the parents of handicapped children as a whole, and of ESN parents in particular, but there is a good deal of opinion and comment.   This tends to stress the probable incompetence of the parents and their need for help and advice, rather than equal consultation and involvement.   'Parental instinct, however strong and generous, is not infallible ... expert guidance ... can only be given by workers who possess a thorough knowledge of the growth and development of normal children' (Sheridan, 1965).

The Court Committee, reporting in 1976, also stressed that it was the responsibility of professionals to advise parents as to how to bring up their children.   The Committee noted that: 'We have found no better way to raise a child than to reinforce the ability of his parents, whether natural or substitute, to do so' ('Fit for the Future ...', 1976).

The attitudes of professionals towards parents have undoubtedly been influenced by the whole history of the concept of mental defect, and particularly by the early twentieth century notion that such 'defect' was an inherited characteristic within families, and was linked with a variety of social evils (see Tredgold, 1947; Burt, 1935).   Despite the point made by the 1908 Royal Commission on the Care of the Feeble-minded - that the higher social classes did produce defective children, but were able to provide for them privately - the belief has persisted that there is a 'natural' relationship between mental defect and membership of the lower social classes. Post-war, along with the variety of pressure groups that emerged to further the interests of all the categories of 'handicap' (Segal, 1974), there has been increasing recognition that severely handicapped or subnormal children can be produced by parents in all social classes, and accordingly, there is more dialogue between parents of the severely subnormal and professionals.   The journal of the National Society for Mentally Handicapped Children, 'Parents' Voice', provides a forum for discussion between parents and professionals.   Parents write to the journal

announcing that they have produced 'profoundly handicapp
ped' children and complain about the assistance and
services provided.

In contrast, no parents write announcing that they have
produced mildly subnormal children.   It is the parents of
the ESN-M who now bear the brunt of the stigmatisation
once reserved for the parents of all 'defective' children.
This is related to the fact that the parents of ESN-M
children are almost entirely manual working-class people,
and predominantly semi- and unskilled workers, and this in
turn is related to the 'social selection' by the professionals.   Teachers, doctors and other professionals do
not 'select' children from the higher social classes to be
ascertained as ESN-M.   Indeed 'children from the upper
social classes would appear to avoid ascertainment
altogether' (Stein and Susser, 1960).

Stein and Susser, both medical doctors, pointed to this
'social selection' in 1960, and were able to predict that
their defective patients from higher social classes would
suffer from brain damage or severe handicap - their mildly
subnormal patients would be entirely from the lower social
class (1960, pt. III   p. 1304).   It was noted in chapter 1
that the high incidence of children from the lower social
classes referred and ascertained as ESN-M began to be
openly recognised during the 1960s, when the explanation
of 'cultural disadvantage' had become popular in explaining poor educational achievement generally in school.
Williams and Gruber, in 1967, used the terms 'environmen-
tally damaged' to refer to the children attending ESN
school who were not 'organically damaged'.   This group of
children came predominantly from families in social
classes four and five.

Research on the poorer maternal nutrition and pre-natal
care, prevalent in the lower social classes, has sometimes
been used to justify the ascertainment decisions made
about children in lower social classes (Osler and Cooke,
1965).   Research into the 'psychological environment' of
subnormal children has tended to stress the deficiencies
of lower socio-economic groups in their child-rearing
patterns (Hess and Shipman, 1965), and Davies (1961) went
so far as to advance a 'disorder' theory of mental retardation in which he attributes poor learning capacity to
disturbed parent-child relationships.   Saunders (1973)
found in his research with ESN families that: 'In no case
can the home be regarded as entirely satisfactory in
facilitating the optimum educational progress of their
children.'   A study by Hunt (1973) of ninety-four parents
of ESN children produced a picture of economic and
cultural disadvantage.   Sixty per cent of the families

had over four children, 54 per cent of the fathers were
unskilled workers, 15 per cent of the families had no one
in work and almost all the parents had left school at the
minimum leaving age. Hunt concluded that: 'it can be
seen that the children in our sample are suffering
multiple disadvantage associated with the circumstances
of their parents', and that the parents were unable to
provide a 'warm and encouraging environment' for their
children. However, one additional disadvantage suffered
by the parents was their treatment by the professionals.
Fifty per cent of the parents reported being surprised or
shocked when their child was sent to a special school, and
60 per cent said the special school had not contacted them
at all. The juxtaposition of the large amount of
research on manual working-class children who are considered to be disadvantaged in various measures by their home
circumstances, plus the smaller literature on families
with subnormal children, incorporating historical links
with genetic inferiority, social inadequacy and environmental handicap, has resulted in a stringent focus on the
deficiencies or deviance of families whose children are
referred and ascertained as ESN-M. It is logical, given
existing power structures, that professional people will
not deem it necessary to consult or involve those whom
they consider deficient, and it is problematic, given a
paucity of research, how far the parents of ESN children
are involved in the decision-making processes about their
children. There is, however, some measure of official
comment on how far parents 'ought' to be involved in the
process.

INVOLVEMENT AND CONSULTATION

The statutory involvement and consultation of the parents
of children who may require special education has always
been cursory and occasionally punitive. The 1944 Education Act laid upon all parents the duty of causing their
children to receive 'efficient full-time education suitable to (their) age, ability and aptitude.' Under
Section 34(1) of the Act parents who failed to submit
their children for medical examination to ascertain
whether they were suffering from any 'disability of body
or mind', were liable to a five-pound fine. If an
authority decided a child needed special educational
treatment the only statutory requirement was that 'they
shall give to the parent notice of their decision'
(Section 34(4)). Under Section 34(2) the parents could
request the local authority to examine their child, which

would be done unless the request was 'unreasonable'.
Section 34(5) - the 'certification clause' notes that a
certificate stating the nature of a child's 'disability'
may be issued if necessary by parental or local authority
request, although in practice this clause has generally
been used, or threatened, if parents disagreed with their
child's attendance at special school.

The Handicapped Pupils (HP) forms, although non-
statutory, were used between 1946 and 1975 by most local
authorities as part of the formal procedures by which
children were referred and ascertained as in need of
special education.   The sections on the HP forms referring to parents indicates a minimum of parental involvement with little suggestion that parents may be caring and
responsible people, or that their citizenship rights in a
statutory situation should be explained to them.
Parents appear to be regarded as objects of possible
hindrance in the operation of smooth bureaucratic
procedures.

HP 2, Parts 1 and 3, which were intended for completion
by 'an officer of the L.E.A. or the medical officer signing Part 3', asks the 'examiner' of the child to record
important factors of the child's social history, home
conditions and any relevant family history.   There is no
instruction that the person signing the form should
actually have visited the home.   Similarly, Part 3 of
HP 2 asks for a personal history of the child and the
'examiner's impressions of parent(s)', followed by 'if not
present, state reasons'.   It is difficult to understand
how the preceding sections could have been completed
without parental co-operation.

HP 3, the form to be completed by the child's head
teacher, concludes with Section F (2) under a heading
'Additional information": 'Here make any observations
about the child which appear relevant (his home, his
family, co-operation of parents with school ... etc.)'.
There is no instruction to head teachers, usually the main
referring agent, to discuss the child and the referral
with the parents and there is no place on the form for
parents' views and opinions to be recorded.

Circular 2/75, intended by central government as a
landmark in the discovery of children requiring special
education, made a series of statements about parents
under the heading 'recent developments'.   The Circular
noted that the use of formal procedures, that is certification, to secure children's attendance in special schools
against their parents' wishes, was diminishing, and
parents were themselves more commonly bringing concern
about their children to the attention of specialists.

For the first time in central government recommendations,
a statement was made that parents should be involved in
the decision-making processes.   '(Parents) should be
involved at all stages of the assessment process, their
opinions should be sought and their legal rights explained
to them.   In these ways, their morale will be raised and
their child should benefit' (DES, 1975a).   There was,
however, no indication as to how the involvement should
take place, or who should seek parents' opinions and
inform them of their legal rights.   The Circular also
specifically mentioned problems that can occur with
immigrant children 'who speak English in a dialect that is
far removed from the standard form'.   In this case
recommendation is made that special arrangements be made
to involve 'somebody with knowledge of the language and
cultural background of the children concerned'.   The
local education authority from which the study population
children were drawn had made a practice, prior to
Circular 2/75, of automatically serving a formal notice on
parents, requiring them to submit their child for a
medical examination in connection with admission to
special school (see Appendix 1, chapter 5).   After the
extensive debate on new procedures to be followed, the
decision was taken that the notice will only be used
'where all other reasonable steps to obtain parental co-
operation have failed' (City of Birmingham, 1976, p. 5).
The authority's declared policy had previously been not to
enforce a child's admission to special school against the
parents' wishes, although the 1976 guidelines specifically
note that 'it remains within the Committee's power to
require admission to a special school, and they would
remain ready to use their powers in extreme cases'.   The
guidelines state that parents must be involved at an early
stage where a child is referred for a psychological or
medical examination.   'It is especially important in all
cases in which a child is being considered for special
education that the Head Teacher or other referring agency
should ensure that the parents have had full opportunity
to discuss the matter.'   However, there does not appear
to be any improvement, at either national or local level,
regarding the ways in which professionals record their
judgment on the parents of children referred, or in
recording parental views about the referral, assessment
and possible placement of their children.
    The SE forms, which replaced the HP forms after 1975,
still contain little suggestion of genuine parental
involvement on the basis that the parents are caring and
responsible people, or recognition that they may become
involved in a legal situation, on the basis of refusing to

allow their child to attend special school.   Neither is
there any provision for recording parents' views about the
referral and assessment of their children, except at
second-hand through a professional person's judgment of
the parents.   Thus, on SE 1 the head teacher is required,
under a heading 'Parental attitudes', to 'describe the
parents' reactions when the child's difficulties were
discussed and indicate their likely attitude to any forms
of special education that may be called for'.   The
medical officer, in completing form SE 2, is only required
to tick Section 9, 'Family, social and personal history',
if it is 'normal as far as is known'.   The educational
psychologist may complete Section 9 of SE 3, 'Any relevant
information about the child's family background', and
Section 11, 'Parental attitudes', indicating under a
suggested (a), (b) and (c) his opinion of the attitudes of
the parents.   The SE 4 (summary) form, which may be
filled out by an officer of the local authority who has
not even seen the child or parents, probably negates the
idea of genuine parental involvement by its actual wording.   This includes a simple four-fold classification
whereby the officer is required to list the parents as
either 'supportive, neutral, over-protective or rejecting', and indicate attitudes to special education under a
second four-fold category 'in favour, indifferent, unknown, opposed'.   It is difficult to equate the declared
genuine involvement with a necessity for stigmatic
characterisation of parents in this manner.   The Warnock
Committee has recommended that a new form - SE 6 - be
created, to be filled in by parents, but this recommendation has not yet been taken up.

CHARACTERISTICS OF THE STUDY POPULATION PARENTS

The forty parents in this study were visited and interviewed between April and December 1976 to ascertain the
extent and nature of their involvement in the referral and
assessment process of their children.   On twenty-five
occasions both parents were interviewed together;   twelve
mothers were seen separately, as were three fathers.
Before being asked specifically about 'involvement' an
attempt was made to gauge the kind of understandings the
parents held about 'normal' and about 'special' education.
Data was also collected, through observation, questioning
and discussion, on the social background, including occupation, of the parents, the type of housing, age, care and
condition of all the children in the family, the birth and
developmental history of the sample child, and 'deviance'

in the family that might indicate a measure of 'social incompetence', and other relevant factors, including a subjective interviewer checklist as to where the families could be rated on a scale of 'interested - apathetic - deferential' towards the education system. Information was also collected on attitudes to multi-racial education if the child was at or had attended a multi-racial school.

The data collected allows for a description of parental characteristics in terms of family size, social class and occupation, working mothers, housing type and 'standards', and extent and type of any family 'deviance'. This information is intended to provide a straight description of these families with an ascertained or potential ESN child, in order to add to the limited amount of descriptive material available on ESN families.

The forty families in this study comprise twenty-two 'indigenous' English families (four of these had one parent born in the Republic of Ireland) and eighteen 'immigrant' families, with one or both parents born overseas. The immigrant families comprise nine West Indian families, five Asian, one Turkish, one half-Ukrainian, one Italian-Indian and one half-Pakistani family, where the family surname is Asian, but the child in question is fair-skinned and blond. Fifteen of the immigrant sets of parents had arrived in Britain between 1960-and 1970, not necessarily both parents together; the remaining three families had one parent immigrant between 1950-60.

The forty families have produced between them a total of one hundred and eighty-five children. Only one mother was in her twenties with a single child, and the assumption has been made here that the families are by and large completed families. This gives a mean of 4.5 children per family, which is considerably larger than the average family size for England and Wales as a whole (Central Statistical Office, 1976). Although 'immigrant' families have tended to produce larger families on the whole (reflected in the 1966 and 1971 Census figures), the mean number of indigenous children per family in this study population exceeds the mean number for 'immigrant families. The twenty-two indigenous families produced a total of one hundred and four children, a mean of 4.7 children per family; the eighteen immigrant families produced a total of eighty-one children, a mean of 4.5 children per family.

The five Asian families (two Indian and three Pakistani) had produced a total of twenty-six children, a mean of 5.2 per family; the indigenous families had a mean number of 4.7 children per family; the West Indians, with forty children between them, had a mean of 4.4 and the 'mixed' marriages had produced the smallest mean

number of children, 3.75 per family.   Three families had
'only' children - the child referred;   nine of the
families in the study population were considered to be
'problem families', using Rutter and Madge's (1976)
definition. (1)   Of these, six were indigenous and three
were immigrant families.   The problem families tended to
be larger than average.

TABLE 7.1   Mean number of children per family by ethnic
parentage

WI (40)	Asian (26)	Other immigrant (15)	Indigenous (104)	Total-mean (185)
4.4	5.2	3.75	4.7	4.6

(Numbers in brackets indicate the number of children.)

Mrs T., a small disabled woman with a withered arm,
had produced nine children now aged between twenty-five
and two years, three of whom are currently in special
education.   The family is described as 'well known'
to the Social Services Department.

Mrs O'D., a small, plump, friendly lady, with ginger
curls, had had seven children, five of whom have been
taken into care.   She is separated from her husband
and lives with an unemployed man.   Several professionals are helping her to handle the children still
with her - otherwise she says she follows her mam's
advice - 'Don't hit him so it will show;   they'll see
him bruised when he has a bath at school'.

Mrs D., who came from a family of nineteen children in
Jamaica, has so far had seven children.   Her husband
is currently in prison and she had a breakdown during
which time the children were taken into care.   She
has two children currently in special education.
The larger Asian families tend to be 'respectable' and not
in contact with other social agencies.   One Indian family
with eight children has both parents working, a neat well-
kept home, and two daughters taking shorthand-typing
courses.
    Fifty per cent of the parents in the study fell into
the Registrar-General's occupational classification of
semi- and unskilled workers;   slightly more immigrant
heads of households, 52 per cent, fall into this category.
The types of occupation in the semi-skilled category
include GPO workers, car assemblers and a boatman on a

TABLE 7.2 Social class of parents

Professional/managerial	-
Intermediate	2
Skilled non-manual	2
Skilled manual	13
Semi-skilled	10
Unskilled	10
Residual	3
Total	40

local park lake.   Three West Indian female heads of
household were included in this category: a sack-maker,
a machine driller and a battery assembler.   The skilled
non-manual category included heads of households working
as bus, lorry and crane drivers, builders, pipe-fitters
and glass workers.   One indigenous family, had a head of
household in the 'intermediate' category, a school teacher
- the only 'middle-class' family in the study - and one
West Indian head of household was a qualified nurse.   The
two skilled non-manual heads of household were working as
a clerk and a self-employed grocer.   Only three heads of
household were unemployed, and of these one - a former
soldier - was actively seeking work.   Of the remaining
unemployed, one was a former ESN school pupil himself, and
one was a disabled settled Irish 'tinker'.   Thus,
although the families conformed to other studies of subnormal families in that they were predominantly manual
working class, 92 per cent had heads of households in work
at a variety of socially useful jobs.   Fourteen of the
forty families had a working mother; four of them West
Indian female heads of households, six mothers cleaning
schools and old people's homes, two working at a local
chocolate factory and two serving in shops.   The immigrant mothers tend to work in manufacturing rather than
service occupations.   The demographic spread of the
families around the city reflects the areas which the city
Child Guidance Clinics serve; since the children were
selected by psychologists working in three clinics.

   Child Guidance Clinic A serves the north and north-west
of the city, including a sizeable area of high 'immigrant' settlement, predominantly West Indian and Indian
people living in older housing in declared urban renewal
or improvement areas.   Although city boundary reorganisation has affected this clinic, it also serves inter-war
council estates and suburban private housing.

   Clinic B serves the south and south-east of the city,
with housing varying from older 'renewed' terraced

housing with a large Pakistani settlement, to large drab
inter-war council estates and suburban private and council
estates.

Clinic C serves an area to the south and south-west of
the city, an area of post-war council estates and private
housing, including a garden suburb.

The families of the study population were, therefore,
spread widely around the city, twenty families living in
the north/north-west area, ten to the south-east and ten
to the south-west of the city.

The indigenous families live predominantly in council
property, five families being housed in 'patched' property
due for demolition.   Only four of the immigrant families
live in council housing, fourteen of the eighteen families
living in private older housing.   Only two families in
the study population live in private suburban housing.
There seemed no necessary connection between housekeeping
standards and 'quality' of family life (as estimated
subjectively by the interviewer).   For example, one of
the estimated 'poor' housekeepers was Mrs S.:

> The S.'s house is actually two houses due for demoli-
> tion by the council, knocked together.   The rest of
> the road consists of demolished or boarded-up houses.
> The house was structurally falling apart and was dirty
> and untidy, but was warm and cheerful with an enormous
> coal fire.   A large Alsation and a terrier inspect all
> visitors.   Mrs S. was asleep in a chair with a crash
> helmet under one arm and a toilet roll under the other,
> at the time of the visit.

This family, 'deviant' on most social standards, appears
to have close, caring relations.   On the other hand:

> The C.'s smart, clean, modern council house had fitted
> carpets, good furniture and a telephone.   There was
> also a 'swear box' for the family to put money into if
> they didn't 'mind their language'.   Mr C. is decidedly
> boss in the house and both Mrs C. and the boy are quiet
> and nervous.

Another poor housekeeper with a cheerful family was Mrs
W.:

> The house was warm, dirty and rather smelly.   The
> walls and doors were papered with green paper with
> purple circles and hung with pictures of the children.
> Six crucifixes hung on chains down the walls and there
> was a glass cabinet with a hundred-odd ornaments - pot
> animals, etc. - in it.

The families were considered in terms of possible
'deviance' from such accepted social norms as 'law-abiding
citizens' and adequate mental and physical health.
Research has indicated a tendency for delinquent and

criminal people to have IQs slightly below average (West
and Farringdon, 1973) and has also pointed to inter-
generational continuities in respect to delinquency
(Rutter and Madge, 1976).   Bagley (1972), in reviewing
studies of deviance in minority group children noted that
there was a greater incidence of behavioural pathology in
migrant groups.   Nine of the indigenous families and six
of the immigrant families were subjectively estimated to
be 'deviant' in terms of 'delinquent' behaviour.   In two
families the father was, or had been, in prison - one for
rape, one for grievous bodily harm.   One father was a
transvestite and dressed in women's clothes at home.   In
one family the mother was living comfortably with two
men, and in another family the reverse was true, the
father living with two women.   One mother had attempted
suicide;   one had had a breakdown severe enough for her
children to be taken into care while she recovered;   one
mother had been deserted by her husband.   In three cases
the parents were violent towards the children.   One was
an Irish mother who frequently 'went berserk', but the
children had learned to run away fast.   In another case
the father, thought to batter the child, had been affected
by a tour of duty in the infantry in Belfast, where he had
seen his friends killed, and another mother had had four
children taken into care for their own safety.   In five
families the parents said they were physically violent
towards each other (one an apparently 'respectable' family
where the wife is battered if she objects to her husband's
girl friends).   Only nine of these fifteen families were
regarded as 'problem families' by the authorities and,
even in the three violent families, the parents were not
necessarily less caring or interested in their children
than the other parents in the study.
    Other 'deviance' included nine families who had more
than one handicapped child, seven families with other
children who appeared to truant from school or be 'minor
delinquents', eight families had mother in poor health,
and nine families had either illiterate or semi-literate
parents.   The five Asian families had either one or both
parents non-English speaking.   Some families rate more
than one aspect of 'deviance'.   For example, four of the
Asian parents, who are either both non-English speaking or
only one parent speaks English, are also illiterate or
semi-literate, and two indigenous families with other
handicapped children are also illiterate.   Seven of the
families have other children who are known to be truant or
delinquent in some way.   These are all boys, on probation
or in community homes.   One is a sixteen-year-old boy
living at home with his baby.   His mother said: 'D. had a

baby with his girl.   She didn't want it so she gave it to
him.   Well, I took it in to be company for my youngest
[aged one].'   One boy had been on trial for the group
murder of another youth, but had been acquitted.   Of the
mothers in poor physical health, four suffer from forms of
arthritis and have a hard time coping with housework.
    Before assessing the degree of involvement of the
parents in the actual referral and ascertainment process,
an attempt was made to assess the extent and type of
parental understanding about both 'normal' education and
special education.   Since there is so little research on
parents' views about the education system as a whole, or
aspects of it, there are few guidelines for the present
research.   Parental interest, for example, tends to be
measured in frequency of home-school contact (see, for
example, the Plowden Report, 1967); parents who contra-
vene particular norms held by educationalists are likely
to be labelled uninterested or apathetic. (2)   Parents
were asked specific questions about 'normal' education:
had they been to the school that referred their child, or
that their child was attending at the time of the
referral?   What did they like and dislike about this
school and what did they think of the teachers at this
school?   They were then asked about special education:
what did they think special ESN-M schools could do for
children, especially their own child?   Had they been to
the special school their child attended and what were the
teachers like at the special school?   The questions were
formulated in this manner after pilot interviews established that questioning about 'education' in general
produced little results.   The parents saw 'education'
specifically in terms of the schools their child attended,
and what they thought went on in the school.   It is
likely that parents who have had a child referred into
special education are not typical of parents as a whole in
measures of school contact, as the referral process itself
usually means that there is direct contact between the
homes and the school.   From a general discussion of
schools, arising out of the specific questions, the
parents' comments on schools were as in Table 7.3
    The parents were classified as interested/knowledgeable
if they were aware of the school's curriculum, teaching
methods, organisation, and teachers' responsibilities, and
saw a positive connection between the school and their
child's educational progress.   For example:
    Mrs P. talked about the curriculum in S.'s primary
    school and the differences in the special school
    curriculum.   She was particularly enthusiastic about
    the value of Art and Craft for S.

TABLE 7.3 Parental knowledge about normal schools

Interested/knowledgeable	9
Interested/ignorant	7
Deferential	12
School seen as irrelevant	5
Hostile to schooling	6
Apathetic	1
Total	40

Mrs V. knew about the teaching methods in primary schools and had strong views on play, literacy and homework. She visited the school often and had studied some psychology herself in an 'A' level course.

Parents were classified as interested/ignorant if they were favourably disposed to the school system and mentioned its value for their child, but had little idea of what actually went on in school.   Several Asian parents fell into this category:

The A.s did not understand the school organisation, methods or goals and did not visit the school.   Mrs A. could not speak English, and Mr A. worked shifts as a crane driver.   However, they had strong views on the value of the education their child was receiving - in this case they thought the special school was not good for their child, but they were not sure how to make their views heard.

Mrs S. was very happy that one of her sons had finally learned to read and write.   She did not seem to mind that he had to be sent to a community home before this happened.

Parents were classed as deferential - and nearly a third fell into this category - if they demonstrated unqualified praise for the education system without knowing much about it.   Several parents in this category blamed themselves for their children's backwardness.

'Mr L. said he had never had any schooling in Jamaica and that was why his children were backward.   He thought schooling was very good in Britain and was himself attending an adult   literacy class.'   Some parents saw school as irrelevant to their child's educational progress or future occupation.

Mrs S. didn't think school very important for T. and didn't mind if she stayed away.   She thought it more important that T. could run a home and look after children.   She said T. was very good with horses and could get a job as a stable girl.

Six parents were openly hostile to schools and school
personnel.

    Mrs C., an Irish mother, was adamant that reading had
    done her no good.   Her own brothers couldn't read and
    they earned good money in the building trade.

    Mr P., who had 'been inside' for grievous bodily harm,
    was of the opinion that the 'school was a dump' and
    he'd like to 'wrap the head round a lamp post'.

    The T.s, who tended to blame a lot of their troubles on
    black people, said that 'schools didn't do their job
    and there should be separate schools for coloureds!
Only one parent in this study could be fairly classified
as 'apathetic'.   'Mrs B., whose husband had left her, was
interested more in survival than education.   The daily
effort to find food and clothes for the children was
sufficient for her.'   It seems reasonable to assume from
the way the parents talked about their children, and
behaved to the children during the interview, that definitions of uninterested or apathetic parents need some re-
thinking.   Where parents do not see schools as particularly relevant or helpful places, parental interest in
'education' might be no guide to parental interest in the
child himself.   All the study population parents appeared
concerned and interested in their children even if this
interest was not manifest in the ways school thought it
'ought' to be.

UNDERSTANDINGS ABOUT NORMAL EDUCATION

Parents were asked if they had been to the 'referring
school' recently and who they saw.   Table 7.4 indicates
that parents tended to think in terms of 'being sent for'.

TABLE 7.4 Parents' contact with the referring school

Sent for/saw head	16
Sent for/saw head/teachers	2
Went to see head/teachers	8
Sent for frequently for child's behaviour/ learning	7
Parents' Night	1
Haven't been	6
Total	40

Eighteen parents (49 per cent of the study population)
said they had been 'sent for' by the head or the teachers,
and seven said they had been 'sent for' on more than one
occasion in connection with their child's learning or
behaviour problems.   Eight parents had been to see the
head or teachers of their own accord in connection with
their child's learning difficulties and six parents said
they had not been to the school.   The parents who were
hostile to the school and felt they had a grievance were
the most forthcoming when answering this question.

'My husband went up to the school - there was a row.
The head and my husband shouted at each other.   We
took P. away and he was at home for six months.'

'I've been up a lot about these girls.   I shouted at
the head.   She said J. was not fit to clean Mr
Powell's shoes, so I shouted at her that these kids
were not pigs because of their colour.'

Parents were asked what the teachers 'were like' at this
school, allowing scope for comments.   Answers to this
question tended to take the form of an adjective -
lovely, good, helpful - followed by a qualifying comment.
Twenty-one parents thought the teachers at the normal
school were good or helpful.

'They're lovely but they've got a terrible job there.'

'They are good.   They worked hard for her but she
didn't progress.'

'The teachers were helpful and worked out a programme
to help her read.'

Nine of the parents thought the teachers were 'no good'
and said so quite forceably.

'No good;   they put him in a corner and taught the
others.'

'No good;   they just pushed him around.'

'They were awful;   it's a bloody dump.'

The Asian parents who had not been to the school, or
talked to the teachers, had least comment to make.   The
Turkish family made a joke that although their son had
been caned by the teachers, 'he called it opportunity
knocks because he learned from it.'   Parents were asked
what things they specifically liked or disliked about the
school.   Eighteen parents made favourable comments about
the school, usually expressed by their perceptions of
what the school did for their child.

'He was in a small class and getting extra help.'

'The school seems all right but they tell me he forgets everything he's taught.'

Only one mother mentioned a specific aspect of the curriculum; she liked the cooking and woodwork offered. Nine parents were grateful for the special help their child was receiving at the ordinary school; twelve parents said they didn't like anything much.

Parents were asked what they disliked about the school and parents seemed to find it easier to say what they disliked although seven did not dislike anything very much. Ten parents mentioned that their child did not like the school or was teased.

'The teachers never stopped the other girls teasing her.'

'They let the child be teased. The others called him Pinnochio. I'd had enough and went to tell them.'

Six of the parents were upset that the school wanted the child moved out.

'They want her out and at a special school - never mind what we think.'

'It was a snob school - they turned my kid out.'

'If the child did anything she was blamed. They kicked her out.'

Five parents felt strongly that the referring school had not told them enough about their child's problems and progress.

'They don't tell us enough. We feel pushed around and don't know who to ask for advice.'

'The infant school should have told us he was backward and not let it go on until juniors.'

PARENTAL INVOLVEMENT IN THE REFERRAL PROCESS

The parents had been theoretically involved with the special education process for varying lengths of time, ranging from under three months to four years - counting the time it took from the referral of the study population children, to the time they were given a place in special school. Those whose children have not been placed have been involved for between nine months and three years (counted up to March 1977). Table 7.5 shows the length of time cases took if the child was placed. The 'length of time' was calculated from the time a child was referred, or re-referred, to the Child Guidance Clinic to the time he/she started at the special school.

TABLE 7.5   Time in ascertainment process (child placed)

	Indigenous children	Immigrant children	Total
1-3 months	1	-	1
4-6 months	3	3	6
7-9 months	-	3	3
10 months-1 year	-	3	3
1 year-1½ years	2	-	2
1½ years-2 years	5	-	5
2 years-2½ years	4	1	5
2½ years-3 years	-	-	-
3 years-3½ years	3	-	3
Total	18	10	28

The eighteen indigenous parents had been involved for a total of thirty-six years between the referral and placement of the child in question; a mean of two years per child.   The ten immigrant parents had been involved for a total of 9.5 years between referral and placement; a mean of 11.4 months, or just under one year. This highlights an interesting point.   Decisions were made more speedily on the immigrant children in this study population than decisions were made on the indigenous children.   This study is not a statistically valid one, therefore no inference can be drawn from the numbers, but it raises an interesting question in regard to numbers of immigrant children in special schools.   That is, are decisions made more speedily concerning immigrant children than concerning indigenous children?   All the parents together had waited a total of 49.25 years between referral and placement - a mean of 1.75 years.

This is not a guide to the length of time the parents have been involved with special education if they have other children in special schools, or if the child in question had been re-referred, after an original referral had not resulted in special school placement.   If total time of involvement is taken into consideration the indigenous families had been involved for a total of fifty-nine years, the immigrant families for a total of sixteen and a half years.   Families involved longest in the process tend to be the officially labelled 'problem' families.   For example,

The T.s, with three boys who had spent time at an assessment centre under Court Orders had been involved for eight years with special education.

The P.'s child had been transferred back to the normal
school, and then referred back again to special school
when she couldn't cope - a total of four and a half
years from first referral.
The parents whose children were still 'cases pending' or
who were objecting to special schooling have also been
involved for varying lengths of time in the process.

TABLE 7.6   Time in ascertainment process - child not
placed

	Indigenous children	Immigrant children	Total
1-9 months	-	-	-
10 months-1 year	1	1	2
1 year-1½ years	-	4	4
1½ years-2 years	1	3	4
2 years-2½ years	1	-	1
2½ years-3 years	1	-	1
Total	4	8	]2

The four indigenous families have so far been involved
for eight years, a mean of two years between referral and
March 1977.   Two of these cases were referred as early as
1974 but in three cases there are parental objections and
in one case the normal school is keeping the child.   The
eight immigrant families have been involved a total of
twelve years so far - a mean of 1.2 years between referral
and March 1977.

UNDERSTANDING ABOUT SPECIAL EDUCATION

The parents were all asked if they knew what special ESN-M
schools were supposed to do for children and whether they
had been to the school their child might attend.   Twenty-
eight of their children were actually at special school.
Of the remaining twelve 'pending' cases, four were
'indigenous' children and eight were immigrant.   The way
in which the cases were selected - reliance on the educational psychologists to provide cases referred or re-
referred over the past two years, 1974-6 - meant that some
children have been pending longer than others or were more
recently referred.   What was actually happening to the
twelve cases was as follows.   Two of the indigenous
parents were adamant that their children were not going
into special education.   One mother had just recently

been persuaded to allow her child to attend and one child
had been accepted by the local secondary school in the
remedial department.   One of the immigrant parents was
currently refusing special education for their child, one
child was waiting for psychological testing and two cases
had been passed to the Remedial Teaching Service.   One
boy was being kept at his primary school despite a recommendation by the psychologist for special education, and
another boy was being kept at his secondary school as a
new head had taken over who was willing to keep the boy.
Of the remaining two cases one was waiting to transfer
and one was still at his primary school, who wanted him
transferred, but the psychologist had not recommended him
for special education.

TABLE 7.7 Parents' perceptions of the functions of ESN-M
schools

Schools help reading/writing	11
Schools teach backward/handicapped children	12
Schools have small classes	5
Schools have sports facilities	2
Don't know	10
Total	40

Thirty parents gave positive replies indicating that
they knew something about the facilities that special
schools have to offer, although the replies were varied,
and not always complimentary.   Of those who replied that
the schools teach backward or handicapped children, some
were sceptical of the results.

'They are supposed to teach the backward children who
can't learn at the other school, but they are no good
either.'

'Children at special schools are backward.   They look
funny and are daft.'

'They teach backward children who've got sense.'

'They are awful.   They are for handicapped children.'

'They help children who have nerves or are a bit slow.'
Eleven parents commented specifically on literacy and were
disappointed that the schools had not helped their children more in this area.
'They are for kids with reading and writing problems.'

'We were told the school would help but he still can't
read or write.'
Five parents stressed the advantages of smaller classes.
'They are not there because they are silly.   The classes
are small and they feel safe with the teachers.'   Those
parents who reported that they did not know what special
schools were supposed to do were not necessarily those who
did not yet have a child there.   Twenty-six of the
twenty-eight parents who had a child at special school
said they had visited the school, either before the child
began attending or since that time.   The situation of
parents visiting actually reflects the decisions made so
far in cases rather than lack of interest on the parents'
part.   Three immigrant children who might 'qualify' for
special school on the basis of IQ were not in fact going,
and the parents had not been asked to visit.

Parents with children at special school were asked
their opinions of the school.   Some replies indicated
that parents had been against or reluctant about special
education until they visited the school.
'I dreaded going but after I'd been I was really
pleased.'

'It's a lovely school, with grass and tennis courts,
different from what I'd thought.'
Some parents were enthusiastic but with reservations:
'It's better than his ordinary school but he still gets
bullied.'

'We were told this school could help him but he still
can't read or write.'

'His school work is better but his behaviour is worse.'
One West Indian mother liked the special school because it
was 'less racialist' than the one her child had previously attended.   The parents were also enthusiastic
over the activities available for the children:
'Let's face it, these schools have got facilities;
only ten in a class, a holiday camp farm, swimming and
jumble sales.'

'She does painting, sewing and pottery now.'
Five parents specifically objected to the integration of
ESN with SSN.   One mother is objecting to her child
attending on this basis.
'We went to see the school.   It was such a shock to
see all the badly handicapped children.   She's not
like that.   She's not going there.'

'They've got mongoloid children with slanting eyes -
they get all the attention.   She needs a school
between this one and her ordinary one.   I was dis-
tressed when I first went there.'

'He has taken on some of the habits of the mongols.
We aren't satisfied with the school.'

The parents were asked what the teachers were like at the
special school.   Twenty out of the twenty-eight parents
thought that the teachers and/or head of the special
school were good, helpful or sympathetic.   Only four
parents volunteered that the teachers were 'not much
good'.   The majority of the parents with children at
special school were enthusiastic about the teachers or
specifically about the head teacher.

'They've got real patience.   They do a wonderful job.'

'She likes the head who is a very kind man.'

'The staff are sympathetic.   They've made an extrovert
out of him.'

Four parents felt the teachers were not much good:

'They don't tell us enough about the children.   We
feel pushed around by them.'

'They are funny, no good, and they always want the
last word.'

A crucial question was whether parents felt that their
child was 'getting on better' at his special school than
in his normal school.   Thirteen parents thought this was
the case, and they stressed the literacy aspect.   The
expectations that these parents had of the special school
were not radically different from their expectations of
normal schooling.

'He likes it a lot and his reading is better.   His
cousins tell him to learn to read quickly or he'll end
up a labourer.'

'He's making progress and I pray he'll be transferred
back to ordinary school.   It's never happened before
in our family - backwardness.'

Those parents who thought their child was not getting on
better tended to stress lack of progress towards literacy
and 'injustice' in the child's placement.

'She's bored already.   They only learn her to read one
word at a time.'

'I don't see much progress.   He's eleven and still on
baby books.'

'He's been done an injustice.   He shouldn't be there.'
A Pakistani mother who had been marked by the school as
'uninterested' had definite opinions about the school.
'It's a nutty school.   He's not making progress.   I
don't want him to stay there.'

PARENTAL CONSULTATION

With a background understanding of what parents thought
about the ordinary and 'special' education of their
children, they were then asked specifically about their
involvement and consultation from the time they first
realised or were told that their child needed special
help.   The majority of parents, almost two-thirds, had
learned that their child needed some form of special help
through the ordinary school or the head.   They seemed to
see this as being 'sent for and told' rather than as a
consultation of equals.
   'The school sent for me and said she needed another
   school.'

   'The head sent for me but didn't tell me what was
   wrong with her.   No one tells us anything.'

   'No one told me until I went to the school to see about
   her brother, then they told me she was slow.'

   'They just told me he should go to another school to
   stop his temper tantrums.'
Some of these parents had realised before the school
'sent for' them that there was something wrong with their
child's development but were bewildered by the way they
were presented with a change to another school as being
the solution.   They wanted to know what was 'wrong' and
what the alternatives were.   The point made by Holt
(1966) that the parents of 'handicapped' children do not
have a stock of communal knowledge to call on about
children whose development does not appear 'normal'
seemed very relevant here.
   Five parents had referred their children themselves.
The most interesting of these was a mother who had felt
the whole process to be so traumatic she broke down while
re-telling the story:
   'I needed help.   I had these two handicapped children.
   I took the bus to town to find the mental health
   people.   What do you do?   Stand in the Bull Ring and
   shout "Where are you?"   Well, a postman sent me back
   to my own area office.   Everyone promised to help but

nothing happened.   So I put on their coats and took
them to Councillor S. - the following Wednesday the
head (of the special school) was round and he's been
there ever since.'

Another mother had found difficulty with another authority
before she moved to the present one.   'We asked our
Council if he could go to special school when he was ten.
No one would help.   It was like a brick wall; then we
moved and his new school helped him to go to special
school.'   Three West Indian mothers said they had
referred their children themselves after consultation with
the head teacher.   They were worried about their
children's behaviour.

'He was so badly behaved for me.   I went to the doctor
and he got in touch with the Social Services.   They
sent me to the Child Guidance.'

'I was worried about his behaviour [setting the house
on fire] so I'd referred him to the clinic.'

One mother was particularly worried that her son's
aggressive behaviour might persist into his teens and she
felt that the white society she lived in was harder on
black adolescents than on white adolescents.

Four parents said the psychologist had been the first
person to tell them their child needed help.   One father
who felt that too many people had confused him over his
child's difficulties said: 'The only person who helped us
was the social worker.   The rest can go to bloody hell.'
The parents were asked if their child had seen a psychologist.   Five parents said they did not know what a psychologist was, but five recalled the psychologist visiting
them at home.   Twenty-three parents either took their
child to the Child Guidance Clinic for an interview with
the psychologist or knew the child had been seen.   Those
parents who had other children in special schools had had
contact with other social agencies, or who had referred
the children themselves, knew most about the personnel in
Child Guidance Clinics, and what educational psychologists
were supposed to do.

'Yes, they gave her some tests there; reading and
writing like.'

'Yes, they tested W. and said he was a slow learner.
We knew that already.'

'Yes, I was in and out of the place.   I was the only
one there.   They don't get much trade.'

Twelve parents said they hadn't seen a psychologist or
didn't know what a psychologist was.   Other remarks
expressed irritation with the psychological service.

'I referred him and took him to the clinic, but they
said there was a long waiting list to see the psychologist. They should take more on if that's the case.'

'He [psychologist] was supposed to go to the school to
test her, but he never turned up.'

The Asian parents were most confused about whether their
child had been seen by a psychologist.   Two said their
child had not been seen when in fact they had been tested
at school.   Two did not know what a psychologist was and
one family whose child was at her second special school
said 'no', she hadn't been seen by a psychologist.   No
one had explained to the parents, through an interpreter,
about psychological testing.

The parents were asked whether the psychologist had
been helpful to their child.   Answers to this question
indicated that parents largely did not understand the job
of the educational psychologist and felt that no one had
told them about it, even when they felt the child had been
helped in some way.

'I don't know who he was, or what he did, but he helped
S.'

'I suppose he was helpful.   He just had G. putting
some square pegs in round holes.'

The parents who felt the psychologist had been most
helpful were those who had been able to have a full discussion about special schools with the psychologist.

'He told me all about special school and how P. would
be a behaviour problem if he didn't go there.'

'He was helpful.   He got her a place, even though
places were short.'

None of the parents mentioned IQ or were aware of the part
played by psychological testing in determining whether
their child went to special school or not.   The Asian
parents again did not know if the psychologist helped or
what he did.

The parents were clearer as to whether they had taken
the child to see a medical doctor.   They understood the
medical side more clearly and could often specifically
give the name of the doctor, children's hospital and so
on.   Those who said they had not seen a medical doctor
were those whose children had not progressed in the 'process' and been given a medical appointment, although
several children did not have a medical examination until
after they had started at special school.

'Yes, I took her to see the doctor and she's under Dr
G. at the local hospital.   She goes regularly for her
weight and her nerves.'

'The doctor knocked his knee and measured his head and
said there was nothing wrong with him but his brain.'

'Yes, and when I saw the doctor she said she wanted P.
to go to a special school.'
Parents did not feel they had enough information from the
medical personnel.
'We took her to the hospital in town.   No one told us
anything and this worried us.' (In this case the
parents did not want the child to go to a particular
special school and the psychologist had let the case
'rest'. The paediatrician at the children's hospital
had also assessed the child as ESN but there had been
no communication between him and the psychologist.)

'Yes, we took him but the doctor never told us
nothing.'
Those parents who had not yet seen a doctor thought that
they might get more information.   'No, but I want him to
see a doctor.   It might be his glands or something that
is making him backward.'   A few parents resented being
told to take their child for a medical examination.   'I
can look after my own child's health, thank you.'   The
parents were asked whether the doctor had asked or told
them anything about their child.   Thirteen parents
answered 'no' to this question.   Parents wanted more
medical information about their children, and were somewhat confused when the medical officer introduced educational questions.
'They told me he had a bad foot.   I knew that.'

'The doctor didn't tell me enough.   She did say she
had a urine infection.'

'They said her eyes and ears were okay and asked me
which [special] school I wanted for her.'

'She told me not to rough the boy up but to help him
with his reading.'
One doctor, who disagreed with the psychologist's assessment of the child, did communicate this to the mother.
'She said she couldn't find anything wrong, and wasn't
going to sign any papers about A.'   Another parent felt
hostile to the doctor: 'I've had a couple of up and
downers with that doctor over S.   Me and her don't get
on', and another parent felt they should have had information much earlier.   'We kept asking for a medical in
our last place and when he finally got seen they told us
he was brain damaged.   We felt so let down.   We should
have been told about it sooner.'

Parents understand the role of medical personnel more clearly than that of psychologists, but still feel they are not adequately informed or consulted.   None of them realised the legal implications of a medical officer seeing their child, or were aware that it was the doctor who had authority to 'certify' children.   The parents of the children at special school were asked how they learned their child had a place in a special school - was it through an LEA letter?   Seventeen of the parents remembered receiving a letter from the local authority;   four parents said they had learned about their child's placement from the psychologist or the education welfare officer.   The others could not remember.   In the main letters were seen as annoying or irrelevant:

'I've had all sorts of letters and I've written them. They can go to hell.'

'I suppose we did.   We got all sorts of letters about the children.'

One West Indian mother, who objected to her child going to a particular school, said: 'No, the schoold told me the Education Committee couldn't force me to send him to X school.   His friends would have taken the Mickey out of him, so it was really me told them which school I wanted.' By the time the 'official' letter of placement arrived the majority of parents had been long enough in the process to have a reasonable idea which special school their child would attend, and to accustom themselves to the idea of their child moving to a special school.   The major factor which worried them was transport.   Over half the parents mentioned their initial worry that the child would have difficulty getting to the school or that it would take up a lot of the day taking or bringing the child.   However, the system of guides meeting the children, special taxis, or a minibus usually allayed this fear once the child had started school.   Also, since the city is well provided with special schools no child was travelling an inordinate distance unless the parents wished it. There was little evidence that the parents regarded special school as a stigma, once the child was attending. Only one parent, the wife of a car worker in a new council house, felt that her neighbours might 'look down on her' for having a child at a special school.   Most parents had felt that the child might not be developing 'normally' and might be in need of some special kind of help.   This was usually done by comparison with 'normal' brothers and sisters and neighbours' children.   But, by and large, they did not know how to initiate any proceedings or ask for help until the process was initiated by a professional

person.   The following table illustrates parental perceptions of what was 'wrong' with their children.

TABLE 7.8 Parental perceptions of the study population
children

No progress/slow	15
Badd/odd behaviour	7
Medical condition	10
Normal school at fault	4
'Something wrong'	5
'Nothing wrong'	9
Total	50

(More than one answer given.)

    Nine parents were adamant that there was 'nothing
wrong' with their child.

CASE STUDIES

The following studies illustrate the way in which the
professionals contacted and involved parents in the
referral process and the parents' views on what was
happening to their children.
1 The case of Tom illustrates the way in which professions, who think they are helping a child, may be creating
an anxious situation for parents.
    The R.s have a family of seven children: one boy
working, two at secondary school, the study population
child at special school, and the others at primary school.
One boy is a persistent truant.   Mr R. works shifts at a
local glass factory and Mrs R. serves in a greengrocer's
shop.   The family live in a pleasant council house on a
post-war suburban housing estate.   Mr and Mrs R. have
been 'involved' in special education for seven years, six
years between their son's first referral and his placement in special school.   Tom had been referred and
assessed as in need of special education in 1970.   He
was described then as a 'small, doll-like boy'.   He was
assessed again in 1973 and it was considered that 'he
would benefit from attendance at a school for ESN pupils'.
In this year Mrs R. attempted suicide.   Several professional people became concerned.   The head of the school
referred Tom again as an urgent case and told the clinic
that he had written to the parents but got no reply.   He
apparently wrote a number of letters to the R.s but never

visited the home. The R.'s understanding for the first
few years of the process was that 'they were trying to get
the boy away'. No one explained about special education
until 1975, when the psychologist visited the home, discussed Tom and his problems with the family and explained
about special schools. The psychologist said that 'at no
time has anyone attempted to define a problem, no one has
explained why they are trying to get this boy away'. Mrs
R. was unaware that her son had been twice assessed by
psychologists. She had been sent seven letters giving
Tom appointments for a medical examination and when she
finally attended was surprised that the doctor told her
Tom should go to special school. The psychologist
decided that 'the case had been dragging on' and rang an
appropriate special school to ask the head for a place for
Tom. Mrs R. was willing that Tom should go to this
particular special school. She had been worried he would
be sent to a nearer school which had severely subnormal
children attending. Once she had been to visit the
school, she was even more enthusiastic and is now resigned
to the fact that Tom is 'backward'. The R.s are regarded
as 'problem parents' by the professional people, and correspondence between the professionals centred around the
extent of their incompetence as parents. The parents are
in fact semi-literate and letters from 'authority' tend to
be disregarded. They do not see much relevance in school
but 'they tell us which schools to send the children to
don't they.'
     It would appear that this family very much needed to be
visited and told face-to-face about the referral process
and special education. Their involvement consisted of
five years of worrying and incomprehensible letters which
generated their hostility rather than co-operation. Once
one professional had taken a personal interest they felt
more informed and less threatened and were happy to have
Tom attend special school.

2 The case of Jill G. illustrates the gap in communication that exists strongly between professional people and
West Indian parents. Referring heads, as noted in
chapter 3, tend to hold strong views about the behaviour
of West Indian children, and fears of disruptive behaviour, even before it happens, are enough to make a head
keen to refer. However, West Indian parents also have
strong views on what happens to their children. In the
G.'s case, a 'strong-minded' but semi-literate mother
actually approved of ESN-M school because it was 'less
racialist' than the normal school.
     The G.s are a large noisy Jamaican family living in a

well-kept Edwardian terraced house.   Mr and Mrs G. came
to England in 1962 with four children; two children were
left with their grandmother, including Jill; another
child was born in 1975.   Mrs G. says she has ten children, as she counts the three who died.   Mr G. works long
hours as an unskilled factory worker and Mrs G. works as
a cleaner at the local tech.   Both parents are semi-
literate: Mrs G. is an energetic plump woman, Mr G. a
quietly spoken, gentle man.   The family speaks patois to
each other.   The eldest brother in the family was
charged, with five other youths, after a knife fight in
which a youth was stabbed; he was found not guilty and
released from custody.   One of the older sisters was
suspended from school for bad behaviour.   Mrs G. said
that after three months she went to the Education Office
in town and made a fuss, so that the girl was found a
place in another school.   Jill, who came to England aged
eight, transferred to secondary school unable to read or
write much.   Her secondary school referred her in July
1974.   The psychologist suggested to the head that Jill
be put back in primary school for a year but the head disagreed.   The head regards the area she works in as a
'black power' area and thinks girls like Jill are suscep-
tible to the influence of 'black power people, who destroy
black kids, especially the less able'.   She said they
liked Jill at the school - she wasn't yet anti-white.
The head had sent for Jill's parents to discuss the
referral with them.   The G.'s opinion of the school was
that it was racialist and that black children were insul-
ted and devalued.   The Child Guidance Clinic gave Mrs G.
an appointment at the clinic with Jill but they failed to
turn up.   Six months later, in March 1975, the psychologist said he wrote to the head, explaining this and
suggesting that he and the clinic social worker come to
school to talk to Mrs G. and Jill.   Jill was seen and
tested in the summer of 1975 and an IQ of 67 was recorded.
The psychologist said that he did not see Jill as an ESN
child although her educational retardation was considerable, but he sympathised with the head that Jill might
become a severe behaviour problem if left at her normal
school.   Jill and Mrs G. were seen in October 1975 by a
SCMO, who noted that Jill had fluent speech in West Indian
dialect but that her standard English was incoherent.
The G.s were in favour of Jill transferring to a special
school.   Mrs G. had talked to people where she worked
about it, and thought Jill needed special help in reading.
She had a letter from the special school in March 1976,
inviting her to visit and was pleased with the small
classes and special facilities.   However, her main reason

for approving of the change of schools was that the
special school was 'less racialist' than the normal
school.

This family had been consulted to some extent by the
referring school, and Mrs G., an articulate, energetic
woman, had involved herself in the process, talking to
friends and visiting the special school.   However, she
was not aware of any legal side to the proceedings and
thought the doctor's role was unimportant.

3   The case of Doreen C. illustrates the way that parents
are literally 'at the mercy' of the opinions of professionals in the referral process, despite any strong
feelings they may have on the subject.

In this case, although the head of the normal school
disliked the mother, her own feelings about special education coincided, and the child stayed out of special
education.

Mr and Mrs C. are an Irish couple who met and married
in England sixteen years ago.   They have four children;
two teenage girls, Doreen - the eleven-year-old study
population child, and a boy of eight, recovering from a
traffic accident.   They live in a neat, terraced house
with a small garden and have Indian neighbours, whom Mrs
C. does not like.   She is a heavily made-up lady of
about forty, who likes to wear mini-skirts and wants to
stay 'young-looking' as she says.   She also says she has
a very bad temper and can 'go berserk' at times.   Mr C.
works night shifts at a factory and sleeps most of the
day.   Doreen, a friendly little blond girl, was referred
in October 1974 by the family GP as 'possibly dyslexic'.
Mrs C. knew Doreen had trouble reading and writing but she
is not worried about this.   She said she came from a
family of fifteen in Ireland, of whom only five can read
and write.   'I can read, but look where it got me.   The
nuns used to pinch our noses and whack us, so I ran away
to England when I was fifteen.'   The GP had not discussed
the referral with the parents and they did not know about
it until the school 'sent for' them.   Mrs C. said she was
furious.   'I felt I would like to kill that doctor.'
Doreen was seen by the psychologist at the Child Guidance
Clinic in November 1974 and again in February 1975.   The
psychologist talked to Mrs C. and questioned her about the
family history, but he did not communicate what his function was or what his recommendations on Doreen were.   Mrs
C. did not know what a psychologist 'did' but she said he
had raised the question of special schooling for Doreen
and she was adamant that Doreen was not going 'anywhere
like that: children at special schools all look funny and

are daft.   She'll go over my dead body.   I'll take her
back to Ireland first.'   The psychologist said he had
sent a comprehensive report to the headmistress of
Doreen's school, a Catholic school with mainly white
children in an immigrant area.   The head, Miss L., had
quite strong views on special schools.   She thought they
were for 'strange types' and was all for keeping children
at their normal school if possible.   Consequently,
although she did not like Mrs C. - 'She is a spiteful and
unbalanced character, very ill-mannered and impudent in
her attacks on our school' - she was willing to keep
Doreen at her school.   The psychologist had recorded an
IQ of 64 for Doreen and said that 'her general intellectual skills place her in the upper ESN-M range according
to traditional interpretations'.   He had recommended a
transfer to ESN-M school but noted the parental objections
to special school.   The headmistress had been upset by
the wording of the psychologist's report, which she took
as criticism of her teachers, and this had strengthened
her resolve to keep Doreen in her school.   She had even
refused help for Doreen from the remedial teaching
service.   She had 'sent' for Mrs C. again and told her
she would keep Doreen and transfer her into the Remedial
Department of the Catholic secondary school.   'Special
school couldn't teach her: she might as well stay with
her friends, get married at seventeen and have a row of
little Doreens.'   Mrs C., who is not aware that the head
teacher dislikes her and thinks the school a 'lovely
school' feels very grateful that special school has not
been mentioned again.   She was not aware that Doreen had
been 're-assessed' at her primary school in 1976, nor that
the secondary school could re-refer Doreen as in need of
special education.   No one had attempted to discuss or
explain to the C.s about special education.

This chapter has attempted to describe some of the characteristics of the forty parents in the study population and
their understandings about normal and special education.
This was regarded as a necessary preliminary to asking
parents about their involvement and consultation during
the referral and assessment of their children.
  The families in this study are similar in several res-
pects to other ESN-M families' studies.   The social
class distribution supports other research evidence that
there is an over-representation of the lower social
classes in ESN-M schools.   The only middle-class
indigenous family in this study reacted strongly against
the suggestion that their child should attend an ESN-M
school.   The families were larger than average, again

similar to other research findings, and over a third of
the families were deviant in terms of currently accepted
norms of 'family life', although only two parents had
actually broken the law.   The families were also characterised by poor health of mother, other handicapped or
delinquent children and semi-literate parents.   Immigrant
parents tended to have other handicapped children and, if
Asian, to be semi-literate, but the parents were in good
health.   Indigenous parents tended to have other delinquent children and mothers in poor health.   The involvement of the parents in the decisions taken about their
children is likely to be closely connected with the social
class and status of the parents.   It was suggested at the
beginning of the chapter that professional people
generally tend to regard parents of handicapped children
as less competent and more in need of guidance than equal
consultation.

The first conclusion emerging from the parental interviews is that the stated official policy of involving and
consulting parents does not seem to work in an entirely
satisfactory manner.   On the whole the parents feel that
they are not sufficiently informed about decisions that
are made by the professionals about their children;   their
chlld's disabilities are not discussed with them in a
manner that they can understand and they feel 'pushed
around' by a complex system.   Even parents who actually
sought help were sometimes frustrated by what they saw as
the indifference of the professional personnel and by
their own lack of knowledge about how to get help.   The
exception seemed to be the West Indian mothers who were
more knowledgeable about some aspects of the system.   The
parents' initial involvement was usually with the referring school, but the parents saw this more as 'being sent
for and told' rather than the 'full opportunity to discuss
the matter' that the LEA guidelines mention.   The parents
had intuitively felt an element of compulsion in the
suggestion that their child might need special education,
although no one had explained to them any legal aspects of
the proceedings or that they had any legal rights.   The
Asian parents were particularly uninformed about the proceedings and the official suggestion that an interpreter
be used had not been taken up.   Only nine of the parents
were classified as knowledgeable about the school and they
saw the normal school largely in terms of the help given
to their own child, concerning the child's educational or
other difficulties.   There was some resentment that the
normal school 'wanted the child out' or allowed the child
to be teased, but some appreciation of the help their
child was receiving was expressed.   The referring school

is the first and most familiar agency that can involve and
consult the parents, but parents do not feel on the whole
that they are informed and involved to any extent at this
stage.

Parents did not, on the whole, understand the role of
the educational psychologist nor his importance in the
decision-making process.   Only two parents knew about
intelligence testing and the significance of IQ: one a
teacher, one a West Indian mother with an 'A' level in
psychology.   The parents who were most enthusiastic about
the psychological service were those where the particular
psychologist had discussed the meaning of special education and the procedures in some detail.   They understood
the medical side of the referral process more closely and
were largely enthusiastic for their children to be
medically examined as they, again intuitively, felt that
specific medical problems might be connected with their
children's difficulties.   However, they felt inadequately
informed and consulted, and in some cases were afraid to
question, the 'medical mystique'.   The difficulty of
travelling into the city centre for a medical examination
(before the procedure changed and medicals were given
locally) was also probably not appreciated by the medical
personnel.   The effort of physically travelling around
during the referral process, by people who do not normally
go far out of their own locality, and are dependent on
public transport, is much more of a problem for the
families than the professional personnel realised.

On the whole, the parents did not object to their
children being transferred for possible special help;   in
some cases they positively welcomed it.   Parental understandings about special schools were generally favourable,
usually after a visit had been made to the special school,
although parents tended to stress the literacy aspect -
the school could 'help' their child by making him
literate - which suggests that the parents do not regard
the task of special ESN-M schools as being radically
different from that of normal schools.   Several parents
felt that their own 'backward' children might suffer
educationally in schools which had severely subnormal
children attending.   Parents seem to be most involved and
feel freer to discuss their children's problems, when they
are actually placed in a special school.   Parents are not
generally aware that there is a special Department in the
Education Offices that is responsible for co-ordinating
the referral process and finding a school place, although
several parents were aware that they had some choice of
special school.

The second conclusion to this chapter is that there is

no machinery for parental consultation built into the
referral and assessment process.   The number of professional people concerned with the child should mean that
parents have several people with whom to discuss their
children's problems.   In practice, no professional seems
to do an adequate job of explaining their own role and
discretionary powers, discussing the child's handicap in
terms that the parents can understand and generally
treating the parents as equal and caring people with
'rights' in a complex process that still ultimately
carries a legal sanction.   The connection, noted in
research and in policy documents, between educational
retardation, low socio-economic status (and/or membership
of ethnic minority groups) has probably contributed to
the inadequate involvement and consultation of parents,
and the failure to establish formal links to involve
parents.   As a crude generalisation, middle-class professional people do not generally involve and consult as
equals lower-class people whom they associate with
'incompetency'.   This may be one of the crucial difficulties in developing adequate involvement and consultation with parents of ESN-M children.

8 The children of immigrant parentage

This study has so far suggested that there is no normative
agreement about what constitutes the category ESN.   At
some point in their school career a series of decisions
made over a span of time by professional people moves
children into this stigmatisèd category.   The category is
initially administrative and is supposedly demonstrating
to administrators, practitioners and parents innate
qualities of 'ESN-ness' within the child.   The condition
is not medical, although it may exist alongside demon-
strable medical pathologies.   A sociological analysis can
demonstrate the problematic qualities of the category,
which unlike the other categories of handicap, would
appear to have come into existence more to remove from the
normal school classroom, children who interrupt smooth
organisation and control.   Also unlike other categories
of handicap, the ESN category does not draw children from
all social classes;   the children are predominantly lower
social class children.

Since the settlement of coloured immigrants and their
children from former colonial countries, a further dimension has been added to the control and social class
dimensions of the ESN category.   This is a racial dimension.   Children of West Indian parentage are, as documented in chapter 1, over-represented in ESN schools in proportion to their numbers in the total school population.
Asian children are under-represented in this type of
education.   Of the study population children, eighteen
were the children of immigrant parents, nine West Indian,
five Asians and four 'others'.   The study children are
not a statistical sample and there is no claim made here
that these children are representative of the children of
immigrant parents referred and placed in ESN-M schools.

However, using the data presented by the case histories
of these children, this chapter explores particularly the

position of West Indian children in British schools in
terms of their achievement, and characteristics, that
might lead them to be referred as ESN-M.   The chapter
also uses the data collected from the professionals to
indicate that their beliefs about West Indian children
might lead to decisions to refer and classify these
children as ESN-M, in terms of the referral and assessment
criteria that are used.   Finally, the chapter briefly
examines the decisions made on the Asian and other immigrant children.

SOME ISSUES AFFECTING THE POSITION OF WEST INDIAN AND
ASIAN CHILDREN IN BRITISH SCHOOLS

The over-representation of the children of West Indian
parentage in ESN schools, far from being a minor relatively unimportant aspect of the education of West Indian
children in Britain, (1) does in fact have major implications for the education of all children of West Indian
origin, and further, has implications for the future
relationship of the children of West Indian parentage to
British society as a whole.
    The 'ESN issue' has taken on a profound symbolic signi-
ficance for the West Indian community.   The ESN classification has come to symbolise the general under-achievement
of West Indian children in the school system, and has
raised anxieties that through educational failure, West
Indian children will be destined for inferior employment
and status, and will fail to attain and keep equal
citizenship rights with their white peers.
    The children of immigrants from the West Indies and the
Asian sub-continent were entering the English education
system at a period when a variety of changes were in the
process of implementation and at a time of conflicting
ideologies over the aims and methods of education.   Chief
amongst these changes was the rejection of the tripartite
system in favour of a partial comprehensive reorganisation, an ending of overt selective procedures, and a
resulting confusion in primary schools, as the major goal
of preparing children for the eleven plus examination came
to an end.   These changes were confusing enough for
indigenous parents, doubly so for immigrant parents, who,
faced with handicaps of language and communication, had
difficulty finding their way around the school system
(Bagley, 1975).   For example, in the early 1960s it was
asserted (although there is no research on this point)
that some immigrant parents did not understand the meaning
of 'special' education and were under the impression it

was a superior type of education.   Comprehensive reorganisation meant that it was difficult to monitor the performance of West Indian children or their achievement in
terms of public examinations, but it would appear that a
large number of West Indian children were placed in the
remedial streams and departments that became a feature of
the newly organised comprehensive schools of the 1960s.
The close relationship between the remedial performance of
many West Indian children and the numbers referred for ESN
schooling was encapsulated, as noted in chapter 1, by the
evidence from the Brent West Indian Standing Committee.
'We are concerned more with the point that the majority of
youngsters who have been to so-called normal schools come
out having achieved as little on the academic side as the
children who went to ESN schools' (Select Committee on
Race Relations and Immigration, 1976-7, vol. 3).

The early 1960s period of New Commonwealth immigration
was also a period when the new poor and disadvantaged of
inner-city areas were being discovered.   Basically this
was a recognition that not only are there differences of
life chances, life styles and values, between white collar
and manual workers, there are also divisions between
manual workers, particularly those who have job security
and political and trade union protection of their social
rights and those who do not have such rights.   It was
unfortunate, in some ways, that the period of immigration
coincided with the discovery of the disadvantaged, since
it became politically expedient to subsume the problems of
immigrant groups with the problems of the disadvantaged.
Since housing policies (2) had given immigrants little
choice but to live in inner-city areas, they were also
geographically placed amongst the disadvantaged.

The research which led to interpretations of disadvantaged people as being in 'cultures of poverty' and 'cycles
of deprivation' (Lewis, 1968;   Rutter and Madge, 1976)
affected the ideological understandings of policy-makers
and practitioners in the field of special education. (3)
Just as the presence of low social class children in ESN-M
schools could now be explained by their social and
cultural disadvantage, so too could the presence of black
immigrant children who came from disadvantaged areas.

Immigrant parents however do not want their children to
be treated as though they were white disadvantaged low-
achieving children (Rex and Tomlinson, 1979, ch. 6).
Despite their colonial educational backgrounds, they do
expect from the English educational system more or less
what indigenous parents expect - that is: they expect
their children to be offered equality of opportunity for
social mobility through public examinations, or they

expect them to be offered skills and qualifications which will enable them to take respectable working-class jobs, and not slip into unemployment and the disadvantaged sections of the working class, and most emphatically, they do not want their children to receive a kind of education that carries a stigma of low intelligence and unemployability unless they are certain that a child can be helped by this type of education.

The geographical distribution of West Indian and Asian immigrants has meant that their children are heavily concentrated in urban schools, and their problems are the problems of the school.   There is very little information on the attitudes and professional characteristics of the urban teachers of black children, particularly the extent of their knowledge about, or opinions about, the colonial origin of the children they teach, and given the degree of autonomy and decentralisation that exists within the English education system there is no way of knowing what sort of education is offered to black children, particularly in terms of equality of opportunity and outcome. The position of West Indian children in urban schools is particularly problematic.   West Indian children come from a culture which has been systematically downgraded, and their current attempts to create a cultural identity are regarded as defiance and even as revolt (Rex and Tomlinson, 1979, ch. 7).   There are a variety of forms of black consciousness developing among the young, the cult of Rastafarianism being one of the most important, since Rastafari in its British growth and development is based on a culture of self-respect.   The overt political overtones of young West Indian assertiveness is currently creating much anxiety in urban schools.   The disruption of normal classroom activity by West Indian children is regarded as a serious control problem by teachers, (4) but the disruption may actually be regarded as political activity by some of the children and young people. (5)

The position of West Indian children as low achievers and as potential 'ESN children' also has profound significance for the development of nationalist and racist politics in Britain.   Coloured immigrants and their children have never been welcome in the metropolitan society, and they have increasingly been presented as 'non-legitimate' citizens.   Over the past twenty years a racist consciousness, incorporating the cultural beliefs of 300 years of Empire and colonialism, has been developing in Britain to exclude people who are increasingly being presented as colonial intruders (Rex and Tomlinson, 1979, ch. 2).   National Front propaganda uses the ESN issue to support their 'scientific racism' which purports to demonstrate the inferior intelligence of black people.

The position of Asian children vis-à-vis the education
system would seem to be less problematic. Asian children
have distinct language problems to surmount, but these
have always been recognised and help given (Tomlinson,
1977). The children also have a cultural security in
terms of having a home culture based on distinctive systems of language, religion and morality, set within a kinship structure, which is recognised by the majority society, and Asian parents usually have an instrumental
attitude to education which is a product of Indian
colonial education and accords well with the value system
within English education.

UNDER-ACHIEVEMENT

There is little comprehensive information on the comparative educational performance of black and white children
in schools, and the evidence comes from a limited series
of studies.   However, the issue has become politically
sensitive because the consensus of the research implies
that immigrant and black children under-achieve and under-
perform in comparison with their white peers, even when
born in Britain and receiving their whole education in the
English system.   The necessity for explanation of this
under-performance has placed educationalists in a dilemma.
The liberal ethos has made it difficult to resurrect
theories of scientific racism and suggestions of cultural
and genetic inferiority, although as noted, political
events have overtaken the liberals and the National Front
does overtly use this argument.   The conservative impulse
to defend the system has prevented explanations for lower
achievement being sought in schools and teachers, although
as the next section of this chapter shows, explanations
are now being sought in this area, and are being resisted.
    Ferron (1965) evaluated thirty years of literature on
racial differences in intelligence and performance in
1965, and concluded that 'when circumstances are such as
to ensure that white and coloured groups share a common
way of life and have equal educational opportunities,
differences are small or non-existent'.   Nevertheless,
research into possible differences in performance and
attainment levels, between 'races' has persisted.   For
example, Saint (1963) reported improvements in the IQ of
Punjabi-speaking children the longer their residence in
Britain, and Ashby, Morrison and Butcher (1970) found that
Asian children born in Scotland did not score lower than
their Scottish peers.   A study by Renhard (1971), reported by Stones (1979), indicated that when children from

different ethnic groups were given the opportunity of
learning complex concepts in similar conditions, the
groups performed similarly. On the other hand, McFie and
Thompson (1970) found immigrant (especially West Indian)
children poorer on verbal, mechanical and constructional
tasks, and Goldman and Taylor pointed out in 1966 that
West Indian use of dialect 'seems to be a major barrier to
educational achievement and motivation'. The major
project indicating poorer performance by West Indian
children has been the ILEA study (Little, 1975; 1978),
which concluded that at the end of primary schooling there
is a one-year gap between national reading age norms and
New Commonwealth immigrants, and that West Indian children
function at a level below socially disadvantaged white
children. The ILEA literary survey concluded that: 'it
is the child from the West Indian background whose needs
in terms of basic skill performance should be given
highest priority.' Similar conclusions about West Indian
children were drawn by the EPA project surveys (Halsey,
1972; Payne, 1974). West Indian children in London also
showed UK born West Indian children performing below the
average scores of indigenous children. The result of
Rutter's intensive study of West Indian children in London
(Yule, Berger and Rutter, 1975) also showed UK born West
Indian children performing below the average scores of
indigenous children. Rutter noted the anxiety and
resentment expressed by West Indian parents over the
apparently low level of educational attainment of West
Indian children, their low proportion in selective
academic schools, and the over-placement of West Indian
children in ESN schools. A study by Bagley, Burt and
Wong (1979) attempted to refine the concept of scholastic
under-achievement in West Indian children by asking
whether particular black children were considered to be
low achievers in the eyes of their teachers. Their
study indicated that in the teachers' opinion 'low potential' black children tended to be Jamaican and creole-
speaking, having absent fathers and coming from homes in
poor material circumstances. Ghuman's (1975) study also
indicated that the cultural and socio-economic background
of children from different ethnic groups was a crucial
factor in achievement at different levels of learning.
    A variety of explanations have been put forward to
explain the under-performance of West Indian children.
Overt genetic explanations are not currently popular,
apart from Eysenck's persistent support (1971), but as
Brittan (1976) and the Redbridge Study ('Cause for Concern', 1978) found, there are more subtle indications that
practitioners do in fact regard West Indian learning and

behaviour problems as more 'natural' and thus possibly
innate.   More popular explanations have tended to be
cultural: 'migration stress' and 'family disorganisation'
being quite well documented in the literature.   Bagley
noted in 1973 that 'Caribbean immigrants to Britain are
faced with a variety of stresses which tend to disorganise
family life and depress the possibilities of adequate
child rearing.'   The childminding of West Indian children
has particularly been singled out for comment (Jackson,
1973).   Research on the disruptive activities of West
Indian children has also tended to use 'culture-shock' and
'family strain' as explanations.   Nicol (1971) associated
the anti-social behaviour of West Indian boys with separation from their parents; Kitzinger (1972) connected
behaviour problems to the migration process and different
norms of behaviour in the West Indies.   Rutter, however,
linked educational failure with maladjusted behaviour in
schools.   He considered that 'when the two conditions
(reading retardation and behaviour disorder) are found
together, there is a better chance that reading retardation preceded behaviour difficulties, than the other way
round' (Yule, Berger and Rutter, 1975).   However, it
should be noted that Rutter and his colleagues considered,
on the basis of their research, that 'Much of the concern
about high rates of problem behaviour in West Indian
parents and children is unjustified.'

Although the black media have continued to assert that
the conditions black children face both in and out of
school affect their performance and behaviour, there are
few research studies; Milner's (1975) book on children's
racial attitudes includes a chapter on the educational
experiences of minority group children and there is a
growing literature on ethnic identity and assertion
(Verma and Bagley, 1979).   The links between educational
failure and black maladjusted or disruptive behaviour in
schools are very complex and cannot be equated with the
educational failure and disruptive activities of white
disadvantaged children.   Bagley is of the opinion that
the 'disobedience' or response to alienation (as he
prefers to call it), of black children in the classroom is
as likely as poor scholastic performance to lead to
removal to an ESN school (Verma and Bagley, 1979).   It is
just such an opinion as this that this part of the study
hopes to be able to substantiate somewhat.   An enquiry
into the whole issue of the performance of ethnic minority
children, with particular emphasis on the 'weaknesses in
the education system affecting the achievement of West
Indian children' was promised by the government in 1978
(The Rampton Committee on the educational achievement of
ethnic minority children began work at Easter, 1979.)

TEACHERS' PROBLEMS

When West Indian and Asian children did begin to arrive in
British schools after 1958 there was an automatic consensus that racial equality would exist and race would not,
per se, be regarded as a source of inequality in school.
There was no suggestion of segregation, or of a different
kind of education for black children.   The logic of this
liberal stance meant that no co-ordinated plans or policies were developed for immigrant children and the DES did
not take a lead in supplying advice, direction or central
resources.   The liberal ideology and the notion that
English culture was superior, and education was therefore
a vehicle for 'assimilation' (Commonwealth Immigrants
Advisory Council, 1964) resulted partly from the structural self-image which educational administrators and
teachers held.   This self-image incorporated an over-
whelming belief in the liberal traditions of British
education but included conservative and socialist beliefs.
Those educationalists who subscribed to a conservative-
imperialist ideology could believe in the inferiority of
certain races but not regard them as problematic - they
could be incorporated into the education system at the
appropriate level.   Similarly, the socialist ideal of the
brotherhood of man made it inadmissible to regard black
children as different.
    This approach has created one of the major current
problems for the education system - that of persuading
teachers, who regard their professional skills as being
equally available to all children, that they need to
positively recognise racial and cultural differences.
This 'persuasion' also includes asking teachers to accept
that many of their beliefs about black children may now be
inappropriate and ill-informed.   The recent Schools
Council research on multi-racial education pointed out
that the current hostile state of race relations in
Britain means that 'children are almost literally living
with our history and all its consequences, in a way which
few teachers can have experienced at that age', and an
ILEA document noted that 'teachers considering their own
personal response to this changed situation may well
realise that their own experience, education and training
has not helped them much', and a 'painful process of un-
learning attitudes ill-suited to a multi-racial society'
('New Society', 16 February 1978) is going on.   The
report on the project undertaken for the Schools Council
was not sanctioned by the Programme Committee until 'substantial editing has been undertaken' (Jarvis, 1978),
as the first part of the report was critical of teacher

attitudes and teacher competence to make assumptions about children from ethnic minorities.

Nevertheless, there is now a small amount of research which indicates that teachers do make assumptions, particularly about West Indian children, which may be inappropriate or ill-informed. Brittan's (1976) research on teachers' opinions on white, Asian and West Indian pupils, found that teachers were willing to make generalisations about West Indian children that led to large-scale stereotyping. West Indian children were perceived as of low ability and as creating disciplinary problems. They were less willing to make generalisations that led to stereotyping of Asian children, and unwilling to stereotype white children.

Edwards's (1978) research on language and under-performance concluded that: 'It would appear that teachers differ little from the rest of society in the stereotypes they hold of minority groups. They discriminate between working-class and West Indian speech and evaluate the latter negatively'. Edwards points out that the West Indian child's ability to learn is affected by his motivation and his motivation is affected by the feed-back he receives from teachers - if this is negative, then the child's educational performance will be affected.

Giles's (1977) study of the 'West Indian experience' in twenty-three London schools found that teachers had 'no policy or training ... and their own personal background and experience had been woefully limited in terms of exposure to culturally diverse peoples', and he considered that it was 'essential to stress the issue of teachers' racial attitudes which include stereotyping and discrimination in British schools.' He considered that teacher stereotypes and expectations do influence the way they behave to West Indian pupils and influence the interaction between teacher and pupil.

A small study group in Redbridge ('Cause for Concern', 1978) examining West Indian school performance, agreed that teacher expectations could affect pupils' performance, but there was a tendency for black members of the study group to stress teacher attitude and for white members to consider them unimportant. West Indian children were labelled as 'boisterous and noisy', 'bone lazy', 'aggressive' and 'colour conscious', and 'what was especially disturbing was the apparent assumption behind these general comments that such behaviour was a natural facet of West Indian behaviour'.

The school problems faced by black and mixed-race child children in a 'white racist society' is a theme of Verma and Bagley's recent collection of essays (1979) and they

are of the opinion that 'too often ... schools are
vehicles for oppression and alienation' (p. 9).

STUDY PERCEPTIONS OF WEST INDIAN CHILDREN

In this study the cultural perceptions of the head
teachers of referring schools about West Indian children
did appear to conform to the findings of previous
research.   The heads felt that the learning process was
slower for West Indian children, that they lacked ability
to concentrate for any length of time and that they tend
to under-achieve in school.   They were thought to be
'less keen' on education and creole dialects were thought
to impede learning.   West Indian children were extrovert,
which could lead to disruptive and even aggressive behaviour.   Family problems and different (family) cultural
standards were offered as the major explanations for this
behaviour.   The beliefs the heads held about West Indian
children did conform to the kind of belief described as
'stereotyped' in previous research. (6)   However, these
beliefs do not represent simple prejudice on the part of
heads and teachers.   The beliefs must be set within a
context, in which they do become logical - that is, an
historical context of 300 years of colonial domination,
culminating in late nineteenth-century imperialism, and
twentieth-century decolonisation.   The complex belief
structures which developed in Britain during the period of
empire and colonialism have hardly been studied (Rex,
1970; Fanon, 1961).   Beliefs about colonial people
varied with class position in England.   At the crudest
level, working-class people were encouraged to regard
colonial natives as inferior and met them largely in
situations of war.   However, the encounters of people who
participated in other capacities in colonial societies -
as administrators, officials, missionaries, settlers,
developed other sets of beliefs within the metropolitan
country, which often had parallels in the colonial
encounter.   For example, the head who said: 'I'd do anything for these boys - but I wouldn't want to live next
door to a black family - you may think that sounds bad but
I'm being honest....   People don't want integration but
we should be able to live together', was expressing a
complex set of beliefs about black people, compounded of
administrative benevolence and the need for social distance, which could be paralleled in many colonial situations.   On the other hand, the head who regarded her own
school as 'a black sink' and the area as 'a dangerous
black power area' was expressing beliefs about intellec-

tual inferiority and fear of black violence which was a
powerful set of beliefs during the period of decolonisation.   Heads in this study tended not to differentiate
between the background of West Indian parents, although as
noted previously, immigrants to Britain come from a
variety of social positions in their original countries.
One head described Mrs P. as 'an articulate arrogant woman
who thinks she's a cut above the rest'.   Mrs P. is from a
semi-professional family in the Bahamas; she has 'A'
levels in Sociology and Psychology and speaks standard
English.   On several criteria she was indeed 'a cut
above' the majority of Jamaican-born semi-skilled migrants
to Britain.   However, the beliefs about immigrants to
Britain seldom differentiate between the original social
positions of the migrants, and the head was expressing
this in her comment.

The heads of the 'high immigrant' areas were also aware
of one particularly active young black man who conducted a
self-appointed crusade against 'racism in schools'.   The
activities of this man have been documented in Rex and
Tomlinson (1979) - he is regarded by many as 'a figure
part menacing and part absurd'; but on several occasions
he has tried to persuade black children at the local ESN
school that they are wrongly placed, and the head has
called in the police.

However, the heads are by no means crude racists in
their beliefs or actions.   They have given a great deal
of thought to the problems West Indian children present in
their schools.   They were unanimous that West Indian
parents wanted their children to benefit from education
and do well at school.   They supported the local Society
for the Advancement of Multi-Cultural Education, and the
local National Association for Multi-Racial Education held
meetings at an educational guidance centre.   However,
this may not be sufficient to guarantee equality of educational opportunity or outcome with white suburban schools
if teachers do regard their pupils in the light previously
described.

Heads were also trying hard to understand the varieties
of defiance which were a feature of B's inner-city
schools, but lacking information, knowledge and direction,
often missed the point.   The guidance centre head who
published on this point wrote:

It is essential that teachers who teach in a multi-
racial environment take the trouble to find out as much
as possible about the different races.   When one of my
boys boasted that he was a Rastafarian and he was going
to kill all whites, it gave me great satisfaction to
inform him that a real Rastafarian had been invited to

talk to teachers, and to explain that Rastafarians were
devoted to the spreading of peace. (Dain, 1977)

Since the ways in which the Rastafarian movement is
used in B are in reality very complex, the cultural (and
defiance) gap between this head and the pupil probably
remained the same.

The relationship between the beliefs which heads and
teachers hold about West Indian children and their rate of
referral is also by no means simple.   Given the ways in
which they 'recognise' a potentially ESN child, there is
sufficient evidence, from previous research and in this
present study, to suggest that of all groups of children
in school West Indian children would be most likely to
meet the educational/behavioural criteria of referral.
It is probably reasonable to assume that the referral of a
disproportionate number of West Indian children during the
1960s and early 1970s was a result of the beliefs which
heads and teachers held about the children and the fact
that these beliefs accorded closely to referral criteria.
In the conclusions to this study there is quite striking
confirmation that this is so.

But other sets of beliefs can cross-cut cultural
beliefs about black children which have the effect of
circumventing referral and assessment.   Heads with
sufficient staff and remedial facilities who thought that
children should remain in normal school would only use ESN
referrals as a last resort.   Of particular importance
were the beliefs of some inner-city heads that they had a
'low' standard of achievement in their school which made
it possible to keep slow-learning children.   These
schools were likely to have large numbers of West Indian
children attending.   One head said that he seldom
referred children as the 'whole procedure is too cumbersome'.   He claimed that 40 per cent of the children in
his school were 'remedial'.   One-third of the intake are
West Indian and Asian children and a large proportion of
West Indian children go into the 'lower band'.   'Those
with the problems have IQs between 70 and 85 and can't
learn, yet are expected to keep up....   I don't know what
the answer to this problem is.'

There is no previous research to draw upon in considering the beliefs of educational psychologists and medical
officers about West Indian children and whether there is a
relationship between their beliefs and recommendations for
ESN schooling.   Overall, psychologists did not seem to
hold such stereotyped views of West Indian children in the
sense that they did not attribute characteristics of the
children without searching for a cause.   But this may be
a function of their selection, education and training.

However, although some of them saw the problems of West Indian children in a wider context of racial politics, they were not always able to relate this to their own work.   For example, testing and assessing children from other racial and cultural backgrounds was only mentioned as an overt problem by three psychologists and all the study population children tested had been administered the Stanford-Binet (revised) IQ test or the WISC.   Only one psychologist demonstrated that he put his reservations about testing children from other cultures into practice. But, as noted previously, there is not necessarily a connection between a given low IQ score and whether or not a child stays in his normal school.   The professional autonomy, permitted idiosyncracy and lack of any central direction make it possible for psychologists to make individual decisions which have wide-reaching consequences, but do not necessarily place a child in an ESN school.   The most dramatic instance of this was to be found in the case of the psychologist whose personal beliefs led him to decide not to test a West Indian boy: 'I'm bothered less and less to test West Indians because the instruments aren't valid.'   Because this boy did not go through the ESN procedures his possible deafness was not noted and he was treated solely as a behaviour problem.   In terms of the situation of unemployed, semi-literate West Indian boys in the city, the psychologists' decisions - based on 'non-racial' beliefs - in fact did nothing to help the boy or the wider 'racial problems'. In Merton's terms (1967, ch. 3) this was a latent function of the decision, since the psychologist himself was sensitive to West Indian problems, as he said, 'West Indian problems are also a political problem; what happens nationally affects what happens to children here.'

Although the psychologists regard IQ as only one factor in the assessment process, it is still seen as an important factor and the dubious history of the application of IQ testing, documented in chapter 1, does not seem to worry psychologists unduly.   However, this may be relatively unimportant if the psychologists' personal views about the assessment process do take precedence over IQ scores and racial beliefs.   A psychologist who held general stereotyped beliefs about West Indians said:

'The trouble with them is that they get into groups - sometimes black power groups - I'm not a racialist but we've got to stop any more coming in - we've got to give them jobs so they can get some self-respect.... I don't like the gangs of black youths.'

Nevertheless, he was holding up the assessment of a West Indian and an Asian child and would not recommend them for

ESN schooling, because he thought ESN schools were unnecessary if normal schools 'did their job' properly.

The psychologists also believed that 'rejection' by normal schools was a problem for West Indian children: 'The kids go to an ESN school because they are trouble, either backward or behaviour.'

The psychologists do regard the family environment of West Indians as a problem, in terms of the way the families socialise their children, and question whether developmental norms can be cross-cultural.

Connections between psychologists' beliefs and the high proportion of West Indian children assessed and placed in ESN schools can only be speculative.   (Older) psychologists, who believe in more static conceptions of intelligence, relied on IQ test results and believed that West Indian children did have particular family and developmental problems, might be more likely to recommend ESN-M schooling.   Psychologists who held a dynamic model of intelligence, did not rely overmuch on IQ test results, and did not think that ESN schools could necessarily help children, might be more likely not to recommend ESN-M schooling.   However, psychologists could also be influenced by school pressures to 'get rid' of troublesome children.

The doctors were, as might be expected, more medically oriented in their beliefs about the children of immigrant parentage.   They regarded sickle-cell anaemia as a particular problem for West Indian children and thus could see the migration process in a wider context than other professions.   In some cases they seemed to have taken over the school's definition of West Indian children as behaviour problems and were willing to stereotype them: 'they have ebullient natures', 'the little West Indians go berserk at school because of repression at home', and one doctor went so far as to describe disruptive behaviour as 'the West Indian syndrome'.   But some doctors saw West Indian behaviour in the context of the current racial situation - they were the only professionals to directly mention racial antagonism and conflict in their own dealings with West Indians.   One doctor raised the issue of too many West Indian children in ESN schools but dismissed the claim as 'unproven'.   Neither psychologists nor medical officers had full knowledge about this issue or regarded it as important.   As a speculation it might appear that doctors would be more willing to concur with schools' referral of children and with psychologists' recommendations for ESN schooling if the child was of West Indian origin.

Once West Indian children were placed in ESN school,

the heads of special schools did not have such stereotyped beliefs about the problems these children presented,
although behaviour, family problems and language problems
were mentioned.   This may be a function of the ideology
of the ESN school, which tends to regard children more on
an individual basis, rather than in terms of racial or
ethnic characteristics, and expects to have to cope with
children who are educational and behaviour problems.   It
may also be a function of the fact that some heads
regarded their schools as 'havens' where the outside
society should not intrude.   The heads who said that when
a Community Relations Commission official came to ask him
how many coloured children he had, he replied 'What colour
- I haven't an idea how many coloured children I have' was
presumably expressing his belief.

THE WEST INDIAN STUDY POPULATION CHILDREN

Eight of the West Indian children in this study had been
referred for actual or potential disruptive behaviour in
school as well as for educational problems:
Bertram was referred as an educational problem, but also
as 'a completely disruptive' West Indian boy who needs
constant attention.
Daren O. was referred as an educational problem but also
for 'aggressive and violent behaviour'.
Alan P. was referred for 'living in a world of his own'
and for 'being disruptive in class'.
David D. was referred as 'a nuisance to other children,
disruptive in class ... and below average school performance'.
Matthew B. was referred as 'not too bright ... a withdrawn
boy' who had tried to set his bedroom on fire.
Joy S. was referred for educational problems and 'un-
manageable behaviour'.
Jill G. was referred for educational problems and because
'behavioural problems are likely to develop'.
Winston C. was referred for disruptive and aggressive
behaviour.
    Only one boy, Warwick C., was referred only for educa-
tional backwardness, resulting from defective vision and a
'poor family background', as he had been sent back to the
West Indies for a period in his childhood.
    The study population West Indian children would thus
appear to support the proposition that West Indian children tend to be referred on behavioural as well as educational criteria, with the behavioural criterion taking
precedence.   This study did not pursue in detail which

kinds of aggressive behaviour were more likely to lead to
referral.   The teachers' comments indicate that being a
nuisance to other children, demanding too much of the
teacher's time and attention, not being manageable, i.e.
out of the teacher's control, are more likely to lead to
referral.

Eight of the children had been born in Britain, two
having returned to the West Indies to stay with grandparents for 1-2 years in their childhood.   The boy who
went to the guidance centre had arrived, aged nine, in
England and had received no special help at his primary
school.   Eight of the children had two 'parents', either
married or in stable unions;   one mother lived alone with
her child.   The mother with a husband in prison 'kept
herslef to herself' on an inter-war council estate, and
her neighbours spoke approvingly of the way she 'kept the
children'.

The parents of these children had arrived in the early
1960s with the purpose of finding work in Britain and in
eight families one or both parents were stably employed.
Seven mothers were working, two as nursing auxiliaries,
two factory assemblers, one sack-maker, one machine
driller, one cleaner.   One family was on social security
and the single-parent mother had difficulty in looking
after the child and doing her factory job.   Contrary to
the suggestion that they did not know about special
schooling, they were more knowledgeable than the white
parents, although in common with the white parents, they
were not fully informed about the decision-making process,
and the role of the personnel involved, nor about their
'rights'.

In three cases social workers in contact with the
families had explained the 'help' the Child Guidance
Clinic could give, and the parents of the four children
placed had visited the ESN school and spoken to the head.
There was no violent opposition to the referral and
placement of the children - more a resignation to the
inevitable.   They were aware that special education was a
stigmatised type of education and were dubious about the
children's employment prospects.   One mother thought her
child was better off in special school 'to get away from
the racism in her ordinary school', and another mother had
visited America to see if she could move the family there.
Three mothers had agreed with the head of the referring
school and had initially referred the child themselves to
the clinic.   Conversations with the mothers indicated
that this was for fear of the future prospects for their
children in white society if their children were aggressive.

Mrs P., who had been told by the school that her seven-year-old son was disruptive, said: 'It has to be broken. What will happen when he's about fourteen?   He might get in a rage and kill someone.   He gets on all right with white children now, but what about later?'

The mother of Matthew B., a nurse, said she was very pleased with the help she got from the Child Guidance Clinic when her son started playing with fire and bed-wetting.   She said she liked the English education system and would stay until all her children were educated, then take them 'home' as she was worried about their future in England.

David D.'s mother also sought help from the clinic on the advice of a social worker, and was grateful to the clinic staff although she didn't know what they had done. (The psychiatrist had advised residential school, but had been ignored.)   Mrs D. was grateful to the head of David's school for keeping him in check as she thought black children easily got into trouble.

What were the behaviour and characteristics of the study population children and their families which might have helped to lead to their referral?   The case of Winston C., who could have benefited from the complex assessment procedures, but whose unruly behaviour led him to a guidance centre, has been documented.   The case of Jill G. is appended to the parents' chapter, and the case of Bertram has been used to illustrate the referring schools' chapter and the section on the remedial teaching personnel.

The following three case studies can be used to initiate further discussion.

Joy S. is the second child in a family of five child-ren, all born in Britain.   The parents came to find work in 1960;   Mr S. is a metal polisher, Mrs S. an auxiliary nurse.   The family carries the sickle-cell anaemia gene and one child died, but as yet the others show no ill-effects.   Joy has two brothers, both admitted to ESN-M schools when aged seven;   she was placed in 1972 at age nine.   Her mother, who is very worried about racial hostility in Britain, went to the States that year to see whether America might be a more suitable place for the children.   She was very depressed by the slums of New York and decided not to move the family.   On her return in 1974 she objected to Joy's placement and the girl was moved to a local comprehensive school.   The school re-referred her in 1975 as she was anti-social and 'couldn't fit in with our system having been at [ESN] school'.   The head of the lower school said he 'put pressure on the parents as they objected to Joy going back to ESN-M

school'.   He said they beat the child at home and felt
the ESN school could provide a more 'stable environment'.
Joy was moved back to ESN school in 1976.   Neither she
nor the parents wanted this.   Joy said in interview that
she wanted to learn to read and write but the ESN school
just 'took her on trips' and didn't do much work.   Mr S.
was described by a social worker as 'an easy-going
gentleman, very fond of his children but not a dominant
force in the home'.   He attends adult literacy classes
locally.   Mrs S. was described as

> a more intelligent person and it is she who plays the
> more dominant role....   She is depressed and reli-
> gious, and gives a vivid account of the squalor and
> degredation she saw in the slums of New York, and
> expresses a fatalistic view of the plight of contem-
> porary black youth in England.

In the study interview Mr S. said that he blamed himself
for his children's backwardness: 'I never had no schooling in Jamaica.'   Mrs S. blames the schools and racial
hostility.

The psychologist who tested Joy in 1976 gave her IQ as
81 'but it may be as high as 89'.   He saw the parents
and said that:

> the mother had a measure of confidence and yet was
> modest in that pleasant way Africans often display.
> I asked her why she had gone to the USA....   She said
> she had gone to see what America was like.   How they
> are able to do this financially or politically I do not
> know.

After her return to ESN school Joy was noted as having
a marked deterioration in behaviour, being depressed and
throwing stones.   She was seen by the psychiatrist who
prescribed drugs for her depression.   The SCMO said, 'I
thought she was schizo but the psychiatrist did not think
so.'   She thought the 'parents were a bit dim' and suspected a non-accidental scalding injury.   The head of the
special school said of Joy: 'The tragedy is she's very
ugly - and the cosmetic side is important.   She has a
deep resentment, is it her colour or her image of herself?
She's chosen another sick West Indian child as her
friend.'   He has arranged for her to go to the clinic for
sessions with a psychologist and wanted her checked again
by a psychiatrist.

Warwick C. was first referred in 1972 at the age of
eight, by his primary school.   The psychologist who saw
him did not recommend ESN-M school.   Warwick was born in
England, a premature baby weighing 4lbs.   At one year old
he was in hospital for several months with pneumonia.   At
six he was sent back to the West Indies for a year as his

mother, a factory assembler, had had to find childminders
for him.   He returned with his elder brother, who had
been left in the West Indies, and is now doing well at
secondary school.   In 1975 Warwick was re-referred by his
secondary school; his IQ was given as 75 and the psychologist said that 'his ability is above that usual for
ESN....   While he is not the kind of boy who would
normally be placed in ESN school it is felt that such a
placement for a period of approximately one year could be
of benefit to this boy.'   The SCMO found that the boy had
perceptual problems 'cross lateral with dominant right
hand but left eye'.   When she explained this to his
mother, the mother 'thought his brain was twisted'.   The
doctor said the boy had had a 'terrible childhood, left
with minders and sent back to the West Indies', but she
thought he was 'a nice lad who may only need special
education for a few years'.   The head of the referring
school said he needed special education as he was 'writing
gibberish' and was amazed that the process of assessment
took so long (it only took six months).   The head of the
local ESN school visited the mother to 'persuade' her to
send the boy to his school.   In the study interview she
said Warwick 'liked the school a lot and his reading is
better', but she only wanted it to be a temporary placement.   'I tell him to hurry up and learn or he'll end up
as a labourer.'

Daren O. was referred in 1975 at age eight for educational and disruptive reasons.   He came from the
infants' school as a non-reader, and the head said he 'had
time off to look after the babies at home'.   Also 'he is
often aggressive ... in PE he is often removed from these
lessons until he has calmed down'.   The psychologist gave
his IQ as 67 and said that 'his attainments place him
firmly in the ESN range'.   The psychologist also noted
white pigmentation on the boy's lips.   'He looks like a
minstrel - poor lad!'   The SCMO also recommended ESN
schooling and noted that 'he was an odd-looking boy with
puffy eyes and leucoderma skin on lips'.   His mother is
bringing up six children while her husband is serving a
prison sentence for rape.   She came from Jamaica to work
in a factory in 1962, married and had her childreniin
England.   She had a nervous breakdown and the children
were temporarily in care and she said she missed Daren
the most.   She has a younger boy at deaf school, and had
been 'persuaded' by the psychologist to let Daren go to
ESN school on condition that he did not go to the local
ESN school as 'his friends would call him names'.   The
head of the school to which he did go said 'mother didn't
want him to go to the barmy school on her patch'.   After

visiting the school Mrs O. thought Daren got good special
help but she wanted him to go back to normal school at
eleven.   'They told me that if he makes enough progress
to satisfy the education committee he can go back....   I
don't want him at that ESN-M school until he's sixteen.'
    The major characteristic of the West Indian study
population children was undoubtedly their 'behaviour'.
But it is interesting that although the 'disruption' was
initially offered as a reason for referral it was seldom
discussed again.   It was a taken-for-granted characteristic, in much the same way that the Redbridge study found
'aggressive behaviour' was regarded as a natural facet of
West Indian behaviour.   The fear of future aggressive
behaviour was mentioned.   In one case the head of the
referring school overtly said that the girl in question
might be 'influenced by black power people'.   The activities of the local black holiday schools, run by a group of
black community workers, were the 'black power' she had in
mind.
    The major characteristics of the children which were
discussed by the professionals in making decisions, were
family organisation and structure, the child's socialisation and migration, and miscellaneous attributes of the
child.   These characteristics were discussed using
majority society cultural 'norms' and, not surprisingly,
the children and families were regarded as deficient.
Again, this cannot be explained in terms of crude racism -
it illustrated how deeply the colonial belief system
influenced the judgment of even sensitive and educated
professionals. // The head who described a child as 'ugly'
was using Western standards of beauty.   In the Sudan the
child would have been regarded as beautiful.   The psychologist who described the boy as looking 'like a minstrel'
was sharing a cultural heritage (with the interviewer)
which included 'nigger-minstrel shows'.   The migration
process was usually thought of in negative terms.   A
feature of colonisation was to send white children back to
the metropolitan country for periods - this was seldom
considered to have a bad effect on the children.   The
reverse process, sending back black children to the West
Indies, is believed to be bad for the children.   Disorganised family structure was most discussed in the
decision-making process.   Working mothers, single-parent
families, common-law unions, mothers as the dominant
marriage partner, childminding of children, were all
regarded as deviating from an idealised family structure
within which, presumably, children did not become categorised as ESN.
    There was no discussion of innate factors leading to

educational failures, apart from categorisations of
parents being 'a bit dim' and IQ was a variable factor in
whether the child was actually placed.   A girl whose IQ
'might be 89' was placed;   a boy with an IQ of 72 remained
in his normal school;   and one boy described as 'not
normally the kind placed in ESN school' was placed.
Creole dialect and language problems were rarely
mentioned. (7)   Neither, in the case of the West Indian
families, was the concept 'disadvantaged' used, although
in several of the white families this was used as an
explanation of the difficulties.

In conclusion, if these case studies add anything to
our knowledge about the reasons for the rate of referral
and placement of West Indian children in ESN schooling, it
is first that educational and behavioural criteria for
referral (always an important criteria) are regarded as
'natural' in West Indian children.   Also their educational retardation is explained in terms of family
environment and socialisation - an explanation which has
always loomed large in ESN assessment but in these cases
the family environment has racial rather than simply low
social class characteristics.

Second, a major impression is that the children are
handicapped in the referral process by being treated the
same as white children and, paradoxically, this may have
led to their over-placement in the past.   There is an
assumption that all children start out 'equal' in the
process.   If race was taken into consideration, and the
process took account of the position of the black child
in a hostile white society, and the belief systems of the
professionals, black children might start out into the
assessment procedures 'equal' to white children.

WEST INDIANS AND THE WARNOCK REPORT

Some local authorities now claim that they do not place
West Indian children in ESN schools unless the parents are
in agreement (although this study has shown how parents
can be 'persuaded') and the DES have pointed to the drop
in referrals generally, which includes a drop in West
Indian referrals.

However, the whole of special education has recently
been reviewed and a series of recommendations made by the
Warnock Committee.   If implemented, some of these recommendations would have far-reaching consequences for a
large number of children of West Indian origin in schools.
The Warnock Committee began by specifying that the content
and recommendations of their Report are of a general

nature and references to particular kinds of disability
are merely illustrative.   Education is defined as 'a
good ... to which all human beings are entitled' ('Special
Educational Needs', 1978) and special education 'embraces
the notion of any form of additional help ... to overcome
educational difficulty'.   Thus the terminology of the
Report - 'good', 'help', 'handicapped', 'special needs',
places it in the nineteenth-century humanistic tradition
that claims to be 'doing good' to a section of the population.   The Report's claim that a civilised society does
indeed care for its differently disabled children and
seeks ways of helping these children towards the 'good' of
education, and that in previous periods many of these
children may not have survived, is laudable.   It is particularly laudable when applied to blind, deaf, epileptic,
physically handicapped, severely subnormal children and so
on.   However, the claim becomes more problematic when it
is applied to mildly educationally subnormal children and
these are half the children the Report is talking about:
in 1975 49.8 per cent of all 'handicapped' children in
maintained schools were ESN-M.   The compilers of the
Report cannot have been unaware of the relationship
between social class and the ESN-M category, but preclude
any discussion of this by stating at the outset that 'we
are fully aware that many children with educational difficulties suffer from familial or wider social
deficiencies'.

The Report makes both ideological and commonsense
assumptions about genetic endowment, family capabilities
and the stratification system, which are similar to those
made by Cyril Burt throughout his writings, by the Wood
Committee of 1929, the Court Committee of 1976, and which
find reinforcement in the 'cultural disadvantage' model
of the 1960s - that is, the tautological assumption that
mental or educational retardation is a characteristic of
'deficient families' of the lower social classes, therefore the lower social classes exhibit mild retardation -
this 'fact' is taken as so self-evident in the Report that
it is not even discussed.

Similarly the Report touches on the issue of the disproportionate number of West Indian children in ESN-M
schools in one paragraph out of 416 pages.   It 'recognises that the incidence of learning difficulties which
arise from living in a new cultural and ethnic setting is
a matter of sensitive concern' (p. 64), and does not raise
the matter again, apparently unaware of the significance
of the ESN issue for the West Indian community or the
relationship just noted between educational subnormality
and race.

The reluctance of certain social classes and racial
groups to be 'done good to' which necessitated Warnock's
recommendations that the threat of certification should
still be retained, does make the Report more problematic
and less laudable, when applied to half of the children
whom it is discussing.

The Report extends the notion of special education
beyond the education provided in special schools.   It
notes that in the 1960s a variety of forms of remedial
education were developed to cater for children in comprehensive schools who had not been ascertained as ESN-M.
It concludes that 'a meaningful distinction between
remedial and special education can no longer be maintained' (p. 47) and thus remedial children now become
'special'.

Special education is also, if the recommendations are
taken up, to embrace 'educational help for children with
emotional or behavioural disorders who have previously
been regarded as disruptive' (p. 47).

Thus the term 'children with learning difficulties'
would constitute a vast and further extension of the
educationally subnormal category, embracing remedial and
disruptive children.

The whole framework, the Report notes, is intended to
establish special education as additional and supplemen-
tary, rather than separate or alternative.   However, the
provision suggested for children with learning difficulties would certainly separate them from children receiving normal education, in separate classrooms, units or
buildings.

What is the significance of the Warnock recommendations
for West Indian children?

There would appear to be considerable significance
numerically.   Warnock considered that one child in five
would need some form of special educational provision at
some time during their school career.   If West Indian
children continued to be over-represented in this special
education, as they now are in ESN-M schooling, one in two
West Indian children would require some form of special
educational provision.   However, more realistic calcula-
tions could probably be made by examining the proportion
of children of West Indian origin currently classe as
'remedial' in urban schools, and those placed in disruptive centres or units.   An estimate from these might
probably be that one-third of all children of West Indian
origin in schools might in the future be considered in
need of some form of special educational provision. (8)

The Warnock recommendations would make the symbolic
significance of 'ESN schooling' redundant.   For the West

Indian community the 'special educational provision' for
their children would become their major educational
problem.

The basis for calculation of these numerical possibilities must lie, of course, in the examination of the
current referral and assessment criteria for special education, in the current under-achievement of West Indian
children in schools generally, and in the schools' perception of disruptive behaviour.

To recapitulate on these: the stereotyped beliefs
which professional people hold about West Indian children's ability, behaviour and attitudes to education,
together with an acceptance that these are somehow
'natural' racial attributes, have in the past made it
likely that West Indian children met the criteria for
referral for special education. The way the educational
retardation of West Indian children is explained in terms
of (racial) family environment and organisation and
socialisation, contributed to the commonsense understandings that this over-referral did not really merit discussion. The assumption that black children started equal
in the referral and assessment processes, with no account
being taken of the hostile white society, or the
colonially influenced beliefs of professionals have further 'disadvantaged' West Indian children in the processes leading to ESN-M schooling.

There is no reason to suppose that under the new
Warnock suggested procedures, beliefs and assumptions
about black children will be changed. Indeed the
teachers, who hold the most stereotyped beliefs, are to be
the very people who will initiate the stages of decision-
making as to whether a child has 'special educational
needs'.

Similarly, while discussion of general under-achievement cannot be undertaken here, it seems likely that
similar belief systems and assumptions that influenced the
ESN over-referrals have also influenced the categorisation
of large numbers of West Indian children as 'remedial'.
As long as heads continue to assert that 'they don't know
what the answer to this problem is' there is no reason to
suppose the numbers of 'remedial' West Indian children
will diminish.

The inclusion of disruptive units and centres as
special educational provision makes for administrative
convenience and recognises what is already happening -
that is, the units are locked on as a form of special
education to which a child can speedily be removed. Two
suggested types of special education might very well provide for numbers of West Indian children who are currently

considered disruptive. These are the third category providing education in normal schools: 'iii) Education in a
special class or unit with periods of attendance in an
ordinary class'.

This type of arrangement has apparently been operating
well for children with emotional and behavioural disorders
'as well as moderate learning difficulties' at some
schools ('Special Educational Needs', 1978, p. 105).

Also, for those sent to special school, category ii:
'Children with severe emotional or behavioural disorders
... whose behaviour is so extreme or unpredictable that it
causes severe disruption in an ordinary school' (p. 123),
might well contain numbers of West Indian children.

It was pointed out in chapter 5 that there can legitimately be conflict and lack of consensus over what is
appropriate 'behaviour', and it was also noted earlier in
this chapter that the disruption caused by black children
cannot be equated with the disruptive activities of white
children.   There is an emergence of a culture of defiance
and revolt amongst young black people in Britain which is
increasingly finding an expression in schools, the more so
now the activities of the National Front have encouraged
overt racial hostility in the schools.   It is to be
expected that this 'disruption' will increase, not
decrease, and it may not be too fanciful to suggest that
West Indian pupils, if isolated from normal education for
their disruptive activities, may begin to regard themselves as something like 'political prisoners'.

For the schools, the education of West Indian children
is far more complex than the education of white children,
and Warnock's recommendations, when applied to West Indian
children, would appear either naive or politically
motivated.

ASIAN AND OTHER IMMIGRANT CHILDREN

Asian children and the decisions made about them will be
discussed here in terms of the low rate of referral,
assessment and placement of Asian children in ESN schools.
In 1972 only 284 Indian children and 169 Pakistani children were attending ESN-M schools.

The position of Asian children in the education system
is, as previously noted, qualitatively different from that
of West Indian children, just as the position of Asians
as a minority group is different from that of West
Indians.   The major difference, so far as the response of
the majority society is concerned, is that Asians are
recognised to have distinct cultural identities in terms

of kinship networks, religion, morals, language and
customs, which are accorded some measure of respect.
Amongst young Asians, in particular, this gives not only a
sense of cultural belonging but also acts as some protection against racial hostility (Brah Atvah, 1977).   Comparisons between West Indian and Asian children are often
detrimental to the former.   One psychologist in this
study remarked: 'This Indian boy is well looked after.
Indian families are cut higher than West Indians - they
have fewer behaviour problems - they have a family
tradition which doesn't depend on belting the kids.'

Asian children arriving as immigrants in the early
1960s benefited from the policy situation whereby English
language teaching was perceived to be the problem for
immigrant children.   Initially language classes for non-
English-speaking pupils were presented as a vehicle for
'assimilation', but in the 1970s the language issue became
reversed as Asian minorities demanded the right to retain
their own language.   These demands have been largely
respected and provision made (EEC, 1975), unlike the
situation with regard to West Indian creole dialects.
Major research efforts were devoted to producing materials
to assist teachers of English as a second language in the
1960s.   The Scope materials resulting from the Leeds
project are extensively used (Schools Council, 1969).   By
contrast, the material produced by Wight for teaching West
Indian children (Wight, 1970) is little used.

The City of B set up a department for teaching English
as a second language in 1960 and eventually three immigrant reception centres were set up to initiate non-
English-speaking children into the education system.   Few
West Indian children found their way to these centres.

The beliefs of the professionals in this study were
that Asian children did not have as many problems as West
Indian children.   The problem mentioned most frequently
was language, but this was regarded as a temporary
phenomenon, which could be overcome: 'Once they get over
our stupid language they do well.'   The professionals
had given considerable thought to specific aspects of the
language problem.   Difficulties of mastering idiom,
grasping concepts, and comprehension and reading for en-
joyment were mentioned by the psychologists.   Language is
regarded as an educational problem which falls within the
competence of schools and teachers.

Family and cultural problems were mentioned with respect to Asian children, but usually with different assumptions than those made about West Indian children.   Children were seen to 'get good family support' even to the
extent of being 'over-protected'.   Families are seen to

be 'keen on education' and sometimes to push the children
too hard.   Some families are held to be 'real peasant
families' and non-English-speaking parents may be regarded
as a problem, but overall the professionals' beliefs support the generalisation that Asian family and cultural
attributes are respected more than West Indians'.

Assessment problems were mentioned as a problem if
Asian children were referred for special education.   But
the problem of testing was not regarded as crucial since
the children were seldom referred.   One head said 'There
are real problems of assessment', and added 'but I haven't
referred any Asians'.   The psychologists also mentioned
assessment problems, but noted that they seldom tested
Asian children or recommended any for ESN-M schools.

The Asian children in this study had been tested, but
with a variety of reservations.   In two cases only a
'performance' IQ score was given, the verbal test being
omitted, and the Goodenough draw-a-man test was also used.
One girl's IQ score was given as 43, but the psychologist
said: 'These results suggest she is of inferior intelligence.   However, I would not take them at face value as
she only came to England last June and does not speak much
English.'   The head who had referred this girl had noted
the 'great language barrier' and that she 'could not read
in Punjabi'.

The professionals who perceived Asian children to have
most problems were the doctors, but the problems were
primarily medical - TB, rickets, poor nutrition and the
difficulty of getting adequate medical histories from
Asian mothers were believed to be problems, but no relationship between these problems and mental or educational
retardation was noted except in the case of lead poisoning, which one doctor suggested as a cause of retardation.
Asian children were not behaviour problems and did not
generally conform to the doctors' understandings of 'dull'
children.   The families were even perceived to have
'positive' racial qualities in terms of 'these people know
how to get their own rights'.   The senior specialist
speculated that Asian immigrants came to obtain medical
care for their children.

Although there is no previous research on this point,
it is tempting to generalise from the beliefs about Asian
children expressed by the professionals in this study,
that the major reason for the low referral rate of Asian
children for special schooling is that they simply do not
meet the referral criteria, either in terms of behaviour,
educational retardation, or negative family characteristics or socialisation of children.   There is certainly
evidence to support this in the conclusions to this study.

There was no mention of any innate qualities which might lead to under-performance in education, apart from medical conditions, and Asian cultural and family attributes were, overall, seen in favourable terms.   The language problems of Asian children were regarded as problems falling within the competence of the school, with some assistance from the provisions already made for ESN, and it may be possible that educational retardation which would be noted in West Indian or English children, may be defined as a language problem for Asian children.   The corollary of this would be that if extra help is then given the educational retardation might be overcome.   Asian children were not, on the whole, perceived to have any intrinsic or 'natural' qualities which would accord with the referral criteria for ESN schooling.

The most noticeable characteristic of the Asian children in this study is that four of the five children were referred for educational retardation associated with a medical handicap.   One Indian girl was referred for educational retardation, but described as 'weird', 'makes strange noises ... suspected brain damage ... scar on neck'.   A Pakistani boy was under treatment for febrile convulsions at the time of his referral.   He was noted as having marginal microcephaly and being grossly retarded in attainment.   Another Pakistani boy had a club foot and suspected rickets;   although he was described as 'dull-ESN ... performance IQ 77', he was sent to a delicate school.   Another Indian girl had suspected brain damage, had been knocked down by a lorry, and had language problems.   The only boy referred purely for lack of progress and 'low intelligence' was considered by the psychologist to have an IQ 'up to the 90s' and he would not recommend him for ESN schooling.   Four of the children had been born in England;   the parents had arrived in the middle or late 1960s, were working at unskilled or semi-skilled jobs and were semi- or illiterate both in English and their own language.   Three sets of parents had difficulty with English.

The following case studies illustrate how the professionals dealt with Asian children.

Rashan was referred by her head teacher in 1975 at the age of eight for 'educational retardation', although he also suspected brain damage.   He thought the child might be autistic as she 'was weird, made strange noises, and hid in cupboards'.   He had seen the child's father and thought she came from a good Sikh family, but she must be a 'one off job in the family' as she had normal brothers and sisters.   The psychologist considered that she was 'definitely handicapped', mainly by her medical condition

and she was placed in the local ESN school almost at once.
However, after a week the family moved to a neighbouring
authority and she was transferred to a second ESN school.
Neither the psychologist, nor the MO who had seen her,
were aware that she had left the authority when interviewed.   The MO could not remember had and could not
'find the file', although presumably it had been transferred to the new authority.   However, Rashan had been
noted by the psychologist as having a history of bronchi-
tis, orthopaedic trouble and a tracheostomy scar on her
neck.   Her mother said she had had difficulty in breath-
ing after birth and had to stay in hospital for over two
years.   The family was pleased that special education was
provided for children like Rashan.

Mohammed was referred in 1975 at the age of seven, by
his junior school head for backwardness.   'He does
nothing; he can't even play.'   The head said he had been
told Mohammed had had a brain operation but didn't know if
that was true, as he had not seen the boy's parents - only
an elder brother.   He did not know that the boy was being
treated at the District Hospital for convulsions.   The
psychologist said the mental age of the boy was $4\frac{1}{2}$ years
and had some correspondence with the SCMO about the boy's
medical history.   The doctor, herself Indian, confused
this child with another Pakistani boy with a similar name.
The boy's parents were aware that he was different.   His
mother said she had been told that 'there was something
wrong with his blood' and she was aware that he was 'different' as he did not play like her other children.   She
was in favour of special education as she thought it would
help the boy.   She herself could not go to visit any of
the schools as she lived in strict purdah, but she had
sent her male relatives to the schools.

The Asian cases perhaps illuminate the professionals'
beliefs that they find communication with Asian families
difficult.   Although they are aware of, and respect,
cultural differences, they are often not aware of the pre-
cise nature of the cultural differences and how they will
affect communication.   Thus, the head of Mohammed's
school did not understand the nature of purdah; he found
difficulty in recording family relationships, and even
the Indian SCMO found similar Pakistani names confusing.

The 'other immigrant' children within the study population were respectively - a half-Indian child, a half-
Pakistani child, a half-Ukranian child and a wholly
Turkish child.   As with the West Indian and Asian children, the time between referral and placement or other
decisions on these children tended to be shorter than for
the white children.   The 'abnormal' backgrounds of these

children made for a situation similar to the cultural-
communication difficulties noted for the Asian children.
The professionals found some difficulty in recording
accurate information on the children.   The referring
head thought the Turkish boy's family was 'Greek or
Polish, or one of the middle European countries' initially
- the SCMO who first saw the half-Indian child said she
thought the mother was half-Chinese.   A second doctor who
saw this child and her parents thought the mother 'looked
coloured - she had probably found it difficult to get
married so she married this man'.   The half-Pakistani
child was thought to be 'pure white - like her mother,
despite the Asian surname'.

Apart from this, the cases of the 'other immigrant'
children tended to be treated in the same manner as the
indigenous cases - the professionals did not hold any
particularly strong beliefs about the half-immigrant
status of these children that appeared to affect their
decisions.

In conclusion, it is the West Indian children who provide a problematic racial dimension in the referral,
assessment and placement process.   Given the ways the
professionals 'recognise' a potential ESN child, West
Indian children meet the referral criteria;   Asian children do not, and 'other immigrant' children tend to be
treated much as indigenous children.

9   Conclusions

This study has been concerned to question the epistemological status of the concept of mild educational subnormality, by an empirical examination of the way in which professional people make decisions which place children within the category, and by examining the accounts and explanations they give about the process.   It was suggested in the Introduction that the decisions and judgments professionals made are constituted by their own beliefs about 'what is' an ESN child, rather than on any agreed objective criteria, and there is thus no normative agreement about what constitutes the category ESN-M.   In the literature and in interviews with professionals, the criteria upon which they based their decisions about ESN children appeared to be complex, sometimes unformulated and unclarified, based upon qualities within the child and his family other than upon educational qualities, and being closely connected to the vested interests of the professionals although overlain by an ideology of humanitarianism.   The professionals regard ESN-M children as a social problem, and complex procedures have developed during the twentieth century to deal with this problem. A sociological account of ESN-M children can go beyond professional explanations to examine the way in which professionals socially construct a category of people who have been denied a 'normal' education, and have received instead a stigmatised 'special' or non-education but who are subsequently used as part of the lowest strata of a productive work-force.   The professionals can be regarded as legitimating the continuation or reproduction of a part of the lower social class, and the category ESN can be regarded as a form of social control for a potentially troublesome section of the population.   Indeed, a major social function of the category of mild educational subnormality, and the 'special' education for those in this

category - may be to allow the relatively smooth development of the 'normal' education system. The conclusions
to this study must, first of all, draw together the conclusions from each chapter, attempting to clarify the
following:
1 What, in terms of the professionals interviewed for
this study, is an ESN-M child and what sort of accounts
and explanations are used to justify decisions made about
children who are considered to be ESN-M?
2 How do professionals regard the other professionals
involved in the assessment processes, considering that
during the twentieth century there has been an historical
conflict of competing vested interests over the definitions of ESN-M (and thus over the power to allot children
to this category and determine their future lifestyles)?
3 What is the involvement of the parents of potentially
ESN children in the assessment processes?
4 Can any conclusions be drawn about the involvement of
the 'other personnel'?
5 How is the category ESN-M socially constructed in terms
of the use of procedures?
6 What kinds of cultural beliefs about the problems of
the children of immigrant parents do professionals hold,
and is there any connection between these and the over-
referral and placement of West Indian children?
    The conclusions must then attempt to assess the find-
ings within the wider implications of the functions of the
category for industrial society. During the twentieth
century, particularly since 1944, increasing numbers of
children have been selected for exclusion from normal
education. The process has been legitimated both by an
ideology of humanitarianism 'for the good of the child'
and the meritocratic ideology that 'lack of intelligence'
justifies selection out of the education system, just as
'high intelligence' justifies selection for success within
the system. From a structural point of view the special
education system can be regarded as institutionalising the
exclusion of a section of the population from chances of
social mobility, from the acquisition of cultural and
economic capital, and as a mechanism for ensuring their
placement in the lowest social class. In addition, the
historical development of the concept, particularly link-
ing moral depravity and degeneracy with subnormality has
meant that there is a lingering stigma and inferiority
attached to those categorised as educationally subnormal.
Finally, the 'racial' dimensions of the category must be
considered in terms of the problem metropolitan British
society currently faces over the incorporation of the
children of black immigrant workers into the class

structure.   If a 'special' education can legitimate the
relegation of a group of people to semi- and unskilled
employment or unemployment, it may be in the interests of
some groups thus to legitimate the exclusion of as many
black children as possible from skilled work and social
mobility.

The introduction to this study suggested that there
were ten possible accounts which professionals might
offer to describe and explain what they considered an
'ESN-M' child to be.   The accounts were envisaged as
broad generalisations incorporating a variety of meanings
to those who used them, and it was not envisaged that the
accounts would be mutually exclusive.   In fact, professional groups and parents offered a variety of accounts
about ESN-M children in general, and each group stressed
a different account as being more important in describing
and explaining ESN-M children.

A major conclusion to this study is that professionals
do differ in their beliefs about 'what is' an ESN-M
child.   The following section draws together the accounts
and explanations used by the professionals and the way
they regard the involvement of other professionals in the
referral process.

THE REFERRING HEADS

The referring heads are the people who actually make the
initial decisions to institute the complex and lengthy
process of ascertainment, although to them it is a small
and relatively unimportant aspect of the role of the head
teacher.   Primary school heads tended, in this research,
to adopt a more paternalistic style, involving themselves
to a quite considerable and personal extent, in what they
saw to be the problems of particular children.   Secondary
school heads tended to adopt a more managerial style,
being less personally involved, and delegating their part
in the referral to deputies or heads of remedial departments.   In terms of accounting for ESN children, heads
overwhelmingly used functional and behaviour criteria.
This is illustrated by Figure 9.1 in which out of the
variety of replies the thirty heads gave accounting for
ESN-M children, the percentage of replies has been calculated out of the total replies and shown on a histogram.
In this way it is possible to see at a glance the different kinds of accounts offered by the heads, and compare
them in further tables to the other groups.

Referring heads make a pragmatic response to their
'professional' understanding that some children are beyond

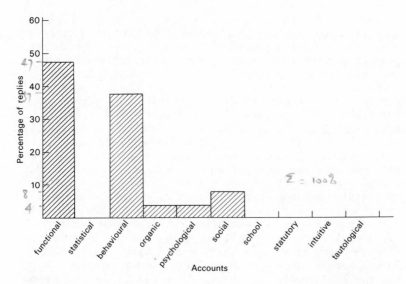

FIGURE 9.1 Referring heads' accounts of ESN-M children
(This figure was constructed from Table 3.3.)

the capacity of the school to deal with them in both
functional and behavioural terms.   The heads think they
can distinguish remedial children from those potentially
ESN-M.   The functional understandings are given by the
heads in terms of 'slow learning', 'poor learning'
'inability to progress' and speech and reading problems.
The level at which the problem was regarded as beyond the
capacity of the school was measured in terms of available
school resources, particularly whether teachers were
willing and able to cope, and 'slow learning' was usually
measured in comparison with a child's class-mates.   Thus,
heads who felt their schools had a low standard of
achievement generally were more willing to keep slow
learners.   This applied particularly to inner-city
schools. (1)   Almost 40 per cent of the replies given by
the heads indicated that they used behavioural criteria
to refer children: 'vicious', 'unsocial behaviour',
'aggressive', 'maladjusted', 'disruptive', 'disturbed'
were some of the terms used to describe troublesome children.   The head who said that 'if children can't be controlled in the normal school the ESN school should take
them' was expressing a general feeling that ESN schools
were as much concerned with the control of children who
could not be controlled in normal schools as with education.   Heads, unlike other professional groups, were not
particularly concerned to offer explanations for their

descriptive accounts of learning and behaviour problems.
Identification, rather than explanation, appeared to be
their most pressing practical problem.   Less than 10 per
cent of general replies concerned social explanations.
One head linked low intelligence with socially disadvantaged families and unemployment, in the tradition of Cyril
Burt's 'The Subnormal Mind' and several spoke of problem,
and one-parent, families.   In contrast, when referring
specifically to the study population children (Figure 9.2)
the heads did offer more social accounts, e.g. 'low
quality families' and 'home problems causing truancy'.
Although only one head offered an organic explanation, 'it
may be genetics' at a general level.   More heads referred
to organic problems when referring specifically to the
study population children.   The referring heads' accounts
specific to the study population children were largely
functional and behavioural, and it did appear that the
tipping-point at which a child should remain as 'remedial'
in the normal school, or be referred as potentially ESN,
was the behaviour exhibited by the child in the classroom.

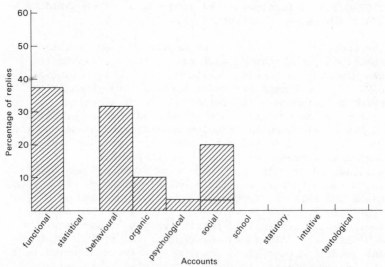

FIGURE 9.2   Referring heads' accounts of the study
population children
(The figure was constructed from the referring heads'
data.)

The heads' accounts of ESN children were the kinds of
accounts that were offered by heads and teachers of normal
schools in the 1890s, when candidates for the first
special schools were being selected.   Heads' understand-

ings of their job are that children shall be 'educated' in
a controlled, orderly environment.   Children who do not
meet the requirements for learning and order are possible
candidates for a 'special' education.

Historically, heads of referring schools were excluded
from actual involvement in the decision-making process.
Their role was simply to put forward possible candidates.
As psychologists became more powerful in the decision-
making processes the heads looked to them to endorse the
children the heads had 'selected' as potentially ESN.   In
this study the heads sometimes viewed psychologists with
antipathy, regarding them as people with considerable
power, including the power to frustrate the initial referral.   The heads had considerable expectations of the
Child Guidance Clinics and of the educational psychologists, which were often not fulfilled.   They considered
that the psychologists possessed special skills for
assessing children and for providing special learning
programmes, but felt the psychologists were 'too slow' or
'too busy' or such a scarce resource that 'it's no bloody
good referring children - it takes too long'.   Some heads
felt the psychologists' skills amounted to a mystique of
'IQ and long words' which could baffle and frustrate the
referring school.   A major reason for disagreement
between heads and psychologists could lie in their differing perceptions of potential ESN-M children.   As Figure
9.3 indicates, psychologists barely use behavioural
accounts, which are an extremely important criterion for
heads, in accounting for ESN children.   Psychologists
also use school accounts - schools have 'rejected' or
'failed' children - an explanation not likely to be
popular with head teachers.

Although the medical officers' accounts, shown in
Figure 9.4, conform even less to the heads' accounts,
there does not seem to be antipathy to the doctor.   This
may be because the heads saw the MO's role as purely
medical, had little contact with them and considered them
less important than the psychologists in the decision-
making processes.   They thought that the doctors were
important in eliminating any possible organic cause of
backwardness, which may be why their general accounts of
ESN-M children barely mentioned organic causes.

The heads had little contact with special school heads,
particularly the secondary heads, although a few schools
hinted that they operated informal 'swap' arrangements
with special schools.   In the busy life of the head of a
normal school, special education did not appear to be
something they gave a great deal of thought to - special
schools were 'outside' normal education and were places

where children who had been referred should go as speedily
as possible.   According to the referring heads they were
places which could take over children 'who we have reached
the limit in our ability to educate' but their enthusiasm
for special school facilities was tempered by the acknowledgment that it was still 'the barmy school' to which
they were referring children.

Heads whose schools had participated in training for
the SET programme were enthusiastic about screening for
educational risk, in agreement with the staff inspector's
report (2) that feedback from teachers was enthusiastic.
Some heads felt that it might make a difference to their
referrals on 'learning' grounds, particularly if they were
offered extra staff and resources, but indicated that they
would continue to refer on behavioural grounds.   The
significance of programmes to identify more remedial and
backward children, before (as Bernstein might argue) they
have been offered more than one year of actual education,
will be taken up later.

THE EDUCATIONAL PSYCHOLOGISTS

In this study the educational psychologists emerged as
crucial figures in the decision-making machinery by which
children move from normal to special school.   It is the
psychologists, working within a 'scientific' model and
possessing skills which the schools do not possess, who
may legitimate the schools' judgment that a child 'is
ESN'.

To be able to conclude this from a study in the mid-
1970s indicates that in the historical struggle for domination over definitions of educational subnormality
between the medical and the psychological professions, the
educational psychologists have emerged as the dominant
definers - a situation that, as this study also indicates,
the medical officers do resent, as any professional group
who has 'lost' an area of competence might resent.   It
must be emphasised, however, that although the psychologists would claim that the decisions have thus become more
'educational', the referring schools, whose business is
education, do not feel that they themselves play any large
part in those supposedly educational decisions.   They are
more inclined to feel tension between the psychologists'
decisions and their own judgments.   One of the reasons
for these tensions may be that there is a discrepancy in
the accounts of 'what is' an ESN child, offered by the
schools and the educational psychologists.   Figure 9.3
shows that the educational psychologists account for ESN

children predominantly in functional terms, which they
describe as 'low attainment', and 'low intellectual
functioning', and they partially account for this by 'low
IQ', 'organic' problems and social and psychological
accounts.   Social accounts are usually in terms of
'culturally disadvantaged families', and psychological
accounts in terms of 'the child suffering emotionally'.
The psychologists also use school accounts, 'the school
couldn't cope', 'is the school adaptable?', 'schools refer
children they want to be rid of'.

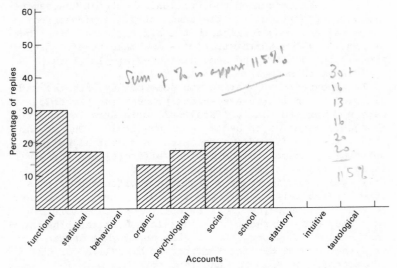

FIGURE 9.3 Educational psychologists' accounts of ESN-M
children
(This figure was constructed from Table 4.1.)

There appears to be a strong potentiality for conflict
between the schools who, traditionally, use behavioural
criteria to judge who is potentially ESN-M, and psychologists, who reject this as a criterion.   The psychologists
also use school accounts, and are able to act upon their
beliefs that a school should cope with a child, by choos-
ing not to visit the school or not to recommend the child
for ESN schooling.   Schools, again traditionally, would
like to see children with whom they feel they could cope,
removed.
    The power of the psychologist appears to stem partly
from the permitted idiosyncratic nature of the job.
There are no statutorily defined functions and although
the psychologists do resent the medical officers'
statutory role in the assessment process, the personality

and beliefs of the psychologist can affect the way they
work and the kinds of decisions they make about children.
With no standard criteria to inform their practices, the
psychologists do have considerable freedom to make decisions on the basis of their own beliefs, for which, given
their professional autonomy, they need not account.   This
makes their decisions about children difficult to question
and puts them in a powerful position in the assessment
process.

Of all the personnel interviewed, the psychologists
were the most concerned and critical about the assessment
procedures, particularly the administrative procedures.
There was a strong feeling that their decisions might be
overruled by the administration - 'we make careful decisions about a child and some sixteen-year-old clerk
decides which school to send the kid to'.

It appeared that, having won some parity with the medical profession in the assessment process the psychologists
were now worried that a 'faceless' administration might
develop strategies to become more powerful.   One psychologist saw the assessment decision as a 'mutual balance
between psychologists and medical officers' and the administration as a 'great obstacle' to this.

It was noted in chapter 2 that a shortcoming of this
study is its failure to study the administration and thus
to understand how the local authority officers actually
work and perceive their role in relation to the other professionals.   However, it was also noted that in the City
of B the head of Special Services is himself a former
educational psychologist and thus possibly more in
sympathy with psychological decisions. (3)

The psychologists did feel they now had parity of
esteem with the medical profession in the assessment process, and regarded medical officers as fellow-profes-
sionals, although there was a lingering suspicion that 'at
the smell of a medical decision we will all be working
under the old terms'.   The 'old terms' as they saw it,
were medical personnel making educational decisions and
using a medical model of diagnosis.   The psychologists
were well aware that the doctors still had a statutory
involvement in the process, which they lacked.   In
summary, the psychologists have been developing and consolidating their influence in the assessment processes
since the 1920s.   By the mid-1970s they had considerable
power, tempered by the fear that administrative decisions
might overrule their decisions, and the knowledge that
they still had no statutory powers.

THE MEDICAL OFFICERS

Medical involvement in the assessment processes for
special education has a history as long as the provision
of special schooling and has a statutory base in the 1944
Education Act.   Doctors in this study took their role in
the process very much for granted.   Their job was to make
a physical examination of children and then to recommend a
particular type of schooling.   Only one doctor in the
study expressed a worry that 'people who aren't concerned
with education' should make decisions about schooling.
The doctors in this study did not administer IQ tests to
the children.   But, on the basis of short, or part-time,
courses all were qualified to do so.   Figure 9.4 shows
the kind of accounts that medical officers gave about
ESN-M children.   They were interesting in that, of all
the professionals, they tended to use social accounts the
most.   ESN-M children were likely to be of low social
origin, and to be 'rough' children.   The doctor who
developed a neurological screening test had concentrated
upon the Registrar-General's social classes 4 and 5 as she
felt these were the children most at risk.   The doctors
operate upon the tautological assumption, also expressed
in the Court Report, that an ESN-M child is essentially
a lower social class child, and that mild mental retardation is characteristic of lower social class children.

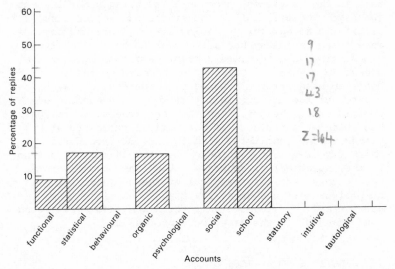

FIGURE 9.4 Doctors accounts of ESN-M children
(This figure was constructed from Table 5.1.)

The doctors also tend to use the terminology 'mental' and 'educational' retardation as synonymous, as in pre-war terminology.   Their image of the ESN-M child does conform closely to Cyril Burt's description of the 'dull' child. They consider that this type of child can be distinguished from severely retarded children, who should be educated in separate schools.   The doctors, like the psychologists, do not account for ESN-M children in behavioural terms. They do use statistical accounts of 'low IQ', organic accounts of 'defects in make-up' and school accounts, 'failure of the normal school to help the child'.   The doctors also consider that a true ESN-M child should be distinguished from the 'low normal' remedial child, although they worry about the difficulty of differentiat- ing the children.   They do not think ESN-M children suffer from particular medical pathologies although two doctors offered genetic accounts in terms of the child's 'innate dimness' and one doctor mentioned lead poisoning. In general the doctors' views of an ESN child seems very much a pre-war view, mild mental retardation being pri- marily a lower social class characteristic and the admin- istrative category ESN-M being regarded almost as a type of pathology in itself.

The doctors in this study were very much aware of the increased powers of the educational psychologists as com- pared to the 'old days'.   The youngest doctor saw her role in the assessment procedures as being subordinate to the psychologists, but the other doctors seemed less willing to accept the psychologists.   There was some resentment that they had lost power to another profes- sional group and this was evident particularly over the use of IQ testing.   This was considered by the referring heads to be a particular area of competence of psycholo- gists, but the doctors felt that they were capable of administering the tests, as they had done so in the past. The autonomy and status of the medical professional probably also conflicted with the new SE procedures which stressed that the doctor was simply part of a team in the assessment procedures.   Like the psychologists, the doctors were also critical of the administration, and suspicious that the authority might manipulate them, particularly by withholding information, and thus become more powerful in the assessment processes.

THE SPECIAL SCHOOL HEADS

It was noted in the special schools chapter that there has been little research on how ESN schools function nor on the staff of ESN-M schools, and this study was not able to devote much time to these questions. However, the head teachers of the schools emerged, in this research, as a most interesting professional group, within, yet distanced from, the normal teaching profession with strong charismatic personalities. Earlier in the twentieth century comments from teachers indicated that special education rapidly became regarded as 'outside' education as it was generally understood, and in this research ESN-M education was still regarded by the heads and teachers of normal schools in this way.

It seemed that normal schools regarded special schools as having control and custodial functions, as much as educational functions, and this was rationalised by jokes that the schools were, after all, still for 'daft' children. Implicit in the comments that special schools provided 'smaller classes' and helped 'social adjustment' was the acknowledgment that the business of special schools was control.

One effect of this distancing from the education profession as a whole seems to have been that the heads of ESN schools have more freedom to create a school which reflects their own views and 'style', and to impose their - often strong - personalities upon their schools in terms of function, goals and curriculum. This is partly because there is no external pressure on the schools to prepare children for examinations or, despite lip-service paid to the idea, to re-examine numbers of children for transfer back to normal schools. It is perhaps too much to expect that any professional group would voluntarily do themselves out of business by letting their clients go, and some heads in this study expressed worries that the number of possible candidates for their schools was dropping, or that they were having to take the 'wrong' sort of child.

The heads of special schools, post-1944, have not played any direct role in the assessment of potentially ESN children, but their major influence on the process lies in the fact that, acting with the autonomy that all head teachers enjoy within the English education system, the final decision to admit a child to their school does rest with the head. Thus, the schools can shape the composition of their school and can influence the image of 'what is' an ESN-M child to a considerable extent. Indeed, if ESN children are products of ESN schools, the public image of educational subnormality can largely be shaped by the judgments heads make on the kind of children they admit and what happens to the children in their schools.

Thus in a suburban ESN-M school where the head rejected 'violent' children, the local image of an ESN child was that of a dull, slow child. In an inner-city integrated ESN-SSN school, where the head felt he had an ability to deal with difficult children, the local image of ESN children was that of 'crazy', disturbed children.

Figure 9.5 illustrates the special school heads' accounts of ESN children, referring particularly to the study population children.

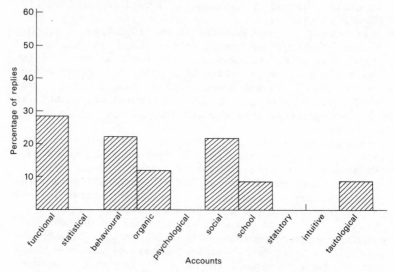

FIGURE 9.5 Special school heads' accounts of ESN-M children
(This figure constructed from Table 6.3)

There is a close correspondence with the views of the referring schools concerning the study population children. Functional accounts, a 'low functioning child', 'an educational failure' are the most popular accounts, with behavioural accounts coming a close second. The behavioural accounts offered by the heads of special schools are much milder than the accounts offered by referring heads - children are 'deeply disturbed' rather than 'vicious'. It seeems that the heads of the special schools expect to cope with behaviour that the normal schools consider uncontrollable, and they are very much aware that the children in their schools are there for 'other conditions' than educational conditions.

Some resentment was expressed by heads that their schools were 'dumping grounds' for problem children, and several offered school accounts of ESN children as 'throw-

outs' from other schools.   A tautological account was
offered about several of the study population children who
were described as 'not ESN', despite having been accepted
into the ESN school.   However, heads do think they are
able to distinguish children who could stay in the remedial departments of the normal school and they account for
the presence of such children in their schools in behavioural and social terms - 'culturally disadvantaged
families' and 'problem families' were some of the social
explanations offered about several of the children.
Apart from two heads who had 'integrated' severely subnormal children, the heads were not enthusiastic about
mixing the children.   It appeared that these heads had a
view of their school which was sufficiently 'educational',
to reject the more medical or overtly custodial models
which they associated with severely subnormal schooling.
Like the doctors, the heads of special ESN-M schools did
seem to have in mind the ideal-type ESN child of the 1946
pamphlet - a dull conforming child with a fixed IQ, who
may be innately retarded.   But they do not feel that the
majority of children in their schools correspond to this
ideal-type.   They think the children are also in ESN
schools for behaviour and family problems, occasionally,
'dumped' by the normal schools.

The opinions of the heads about the functions of their
schools does seem quite strongly to support the notion
that ESN schools are outside normal education.   Only one
head mentioned basic literacy as a specific function of
his school, and one head was specifically against
'developing skills out of context'.

The comments of the heads seemed to be in line with
Gulliford's comment that educational progress may not be
the major aim of ESN education.   The heads certainly
expect control - expressed in the form of social adjustment - to be a major goal.   It is in this area that the
expectations of parents about special schools differs most
sharply from professional judgments.   Thus, despite talk
of removing the 'stigma' of special education, the major
stigma of this type of education may be that it is really
a non-education, and to have no education in industrial
society is itself a stigma and a major handicap.   To say
this is not to deny the validity of the heads' views that
their schools can offer children an individualistic
learning environment and freedom from outside pressures,
but it would seem that assignment to ESN-M education is
partly a legitimating act to contain 'problems' that are
not necessarily educational.

In common with the psychologists and the doctors, the
special school heads voiced a mistrust of the administra-

tion, whom they occasionally felt were more concerned with running an efficient bureaucracy than with anything else. The heads were not happy with the current efficiency of administrative arrangements, and were (in 1976) beginning to be worried by the prospect that the functions of ESN schools might be altered without full consultation and comment.   Like the other professional groups, the heads of special schools have a strong vested interest in retaining their autonomy and control over their own particular area of competence.   The heads regarded the psychologists as possessing valuable skills, but were ambivalent over psychologists' claims to educational expertise, particularly if they had not been teachers. They were less ambivalent about the medical officers, regarding them as valuable colleagues before, during and after, the ascertainment process.   However, like the psychologists, they too were suspicious that medical officers might make educational decisions and impose a medical model as their schools.

PARENTS

Although the new procedures for assessment put forward by the Warnock Committee include the suggestions that a form (SE 6) could be filled out by parents, there has been no formal machinery within the assessment process for involving parents, and no democratic ideology has so far emerged, that would consider parents as equal participants in the process, with a 'right' to be involved in decisions about their children.   Stemming from the late nineteenth- and early twentieth-century view that lower working-class life was disorganised, impulsive and morally degenerate, with unco-operative parents who lacked a work ethic and self-control, the lower working-class parents of subnormal children were always regarded with some apprehension.   It was by no means clear that they would co-operate in the admissions of their children to special schools.   Thus a 'certification' procedure developed, retained in a different form by the 1944 Act, and no change in 'enforceable procedures' is recommended for the future.   Sociological research and teacher ideology in the later twentieth century tended to place manual working-class parents in general in an invidious position. The ideology of the 'good home' with its correlates for educational success, and the supposed failure of the manual working class to equip their children to participate in a competitive educational system has been taken to its furthest extreme in dealing with the parents of

educationally subnormal children.   Despite professing a
caring humanitarianism, professionals generally act in
such a way that the parents of the ESN receive peremptory
treatment, and it is the social origins of the parents
which guarantee this treatment.   The few middle-class
parents who inadvertently find themselves as potential ESN
parents are treated differently from working-class
parents.   Literature on the parents of handicapped children in general has tended to stress their probable incompetence and need for professional help and advice, but
what little evidence is available would suggest that the
parents of severely subnormal children, spanning all
social classes, are treated differently fron ESN-M
parents, who are predominantly of the manual working
class.   As regards the ESN-M, the old HP forms simply
asked for 'examiners' impressions of parents'.   The new
SE summary forms also ask for a four-fold classification
as to whether parents are 'supportive, neutral, over-
protective or rejecting', and the Warnock Report suggests
a secret file to be kept by referring heads regarding
'sensitive information ... about a child's social background or family relationship'.

Booth's study (1978) noted the way in which professionals had to suggest and reinforce to parents the
notion that they had severely subnormal children.   This
study suggests that professionals see their major task as
'persuading' parents that they have educationally subnormal children, and they have developed a variety of quite
successful strategies of persuasion.   The persuasion
could be a disguise for the more brutal truth, which no
professional in this study actually explained to the
parents, that enforceable procedures were available if
persuasion failed. (4)

The heads of referring schools ideally thought parents
should be consulted before their children were referred,
and by and large carried this out.   Their major pre-
occupation was to persuade the parents to agree to a type
of schooling which carried a 'social slur' as one head
put it.   They had a number of successful strategies for
this - 'We suggest that the child needs help and guidance
and that way we get a hundred per cent co-operation.'
The heads appealed 'tactfully' to a general parental concern to do the best for a child;   further strategies
included 'sowing the seed', and 'wearing out' parents by
reiteration that a child needed 'help', presenting the
special school as a privilege, visiting the parents (an
uncommon occurence within English education), or, at
worst, threatening to suspend or expel a child.   'Persuading' parents did not include presenting parents with

full information about special schooling, and while this
could represent a failure to deal honestly with the
parents, it is explicable on two counts. First, heads of
referring schools do not have a great deal of contact with
special schools, and do not understand too much about
them.   Second, their task is to present the special
schools as an alternative type of 'education', with the
knowledge that it is really a non-education, stigmatising
the child.   This dichotomy put both heads of referring
schools and heads of special schools into an ambivalent
position regarding parents.

The special school heads are in a particularly
ambiguous position, as this study suggests that parents
overestimate the 'educational' functions of special
schools.   This is shown by their enthusiasm for the
schools after visits, which generally appear to be very
much like ordinary schools.   The parents of the children
attending the integrated ESN-SSN schools were noticeably
less enthusiastic, as educational functions appeared to be
subordinate to control and medical functions.   However,
once the parents realise that their children are 'not
getting on' at special schools their enthusiasm wanes,
and, as one head found 'only 23 parents turned up to
represent 155 children'.   It is not surprising that heads
felt parental involvement in special education was more
difficult to achieve than in ordinary education.   Psychologists too were ambivalent in their attitudes to
parents, expressing concern at the current lack of
involvement of parents in the assessment process and at
the same time viewing parents as potential threats if they
raised objections to special schooling.   The solution, as
one psychologist put it, was for 'decisions to be made and
then the parents get consulted'.   However, psychologists
also saw 'persuasion' as their major mode of dealing with
parents.   Their strategies included interviewing parents
at the clinic with the child, visiting the home - often
several times, or arranging for a social worker to visit.
The psychologists were able to express the dichotomy that
heads of referring schools were aware of - that they were
presenting parents with an idea of 'education' while being
aware that special schools were 'not just concentrating on
attainment', and were not educational establishments in
the sense that the parents understood.   Thus, while they
regarded some special schools as caring havens, they
expressed a preference for remedial classes in normal
schools.   The psychologists seemed uneasily aware that
they were dealing with a 'certain socio-economic group' of
parents who had few strategies of defence in the face of
professional powers.

The medical officers, on the other hand, are more
definite about the kind of parents they are dealing with.
They regard their job as 'viewing the whole child', that
is, interviewing the parents at the time of the medical
examination.   Since the parents they saw were almost
entirely manual working class, they operated on the
assumption that potential ESN-M children were of low
social class.   It was as recently as 1974 that the
authority ceased to send out the peremptory letter telling
parents to attend for a medical examination with the
child.   However, the brisk treatment sometimes offered
parents by the medical officers is probably no different
from the treatment that working-class people receive
generally from the medical profession.   The medical
officers are also willing to use strategies of persuasion
if they see that parents are reluctant about special
education.   Their persuasion takes the form of a 'good
long chat', or holding up procedures until the psychologist has persuaded the parents to agree.   The parents
themselves accounted for their children as shown in
Figure 9.6.

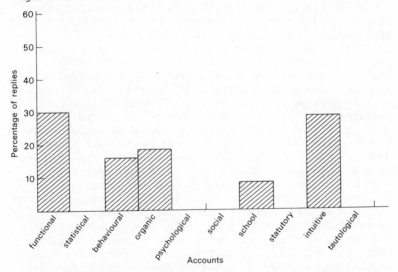

FIGURE 9.6 Parental accounts of their (potentially) ESN-M
children
(This figure was constructed from Table 7.8.)

The most popular account of their children was a functional account, closely followed by intuitive accounts.
The functional accounts were in terms of 'he's a bit
slow', 'he doesn't make progress', and had often been

formulated after the referring school had 'sent for' them
and presented their children as problems.   Two-thirds of
the parents said they had learned that their child needed
special help from the ordinary school.   The parents were
very dependent on the referring head's presentation of
'what was wrong with the child' and how a special school
would 'help', and this dependency probably eased the
head's self-appointed task of persuasion.   Parents by and
large were either deferential or displayed an angry
impotence at the idea of their child being 'kicked out' of
normal school.   Over half the parents with a child at
special school thought the child was not getting on better
or wanted him back at normal school.

The next most popular parental account was intuitive,
but while five parents presented this as 'we knew something was wrong with him' - usually in comparison with a
sibling - nine parents were adamant that 'there's nothing
wrong with him'.   Some of the parents were bewildered by
the way a change of school was presented as the answer to
their child's learning problems;   one mother was angry
that her child 'had been done an injustice' but added
'what can I do?'.   Intuitive accounts do emphasise the
feeling of impotence that parents feel in not understanding or being fully informed about the processes.

Despite the referring school's pre-occupation with
behavioural accounts, only 14 per cent of the parental
replies accounted for their children in behavioural terms,
and then usually in acceptance of the school's definition
- 'they told me another school would stop his temper
tantrums'.   Two mothers specifically saw special education in control terms - one mother hoped it would prevent
her son from starting on a criminal career, and a West
Indian mother hoped it would prevent her son from causing
'racial' trouble.   The third most popular parental
account of their children's problems was organic.   In the
parental interviews, thirty-two cases of illness or injury
in early childhood were mentioned by the mothers.   It
appeared that the parents were more at ease with the
medical side of the referral than with the psychological
side, and they looked intuitively, and with hindsight, for
medical explanations of their children's problems.   However, they rarely had their organic accounts confirmed by
the doctors, did not feel adequately informed, and were
afraid to question what to them was a 'medical mystique'.

Four of the parents accounted for their children's
problems in terms of 'schools that didn't do their job
properly' but again felt powerless to do anything about
this.   The parents in this study had been involved in the
special education process, from time of referral to place-

ment in special school (of the twenty-eight placed), for
an average of 1.75 years.   Since immigrant children were
placed more speedily, indigenous parents had been involved
for an average of two years, three parents for nearly
three and a half years.   The lengthy process is usually
officially represented as a scarcity of professionals, or
overworked professionals, but in fact partially represents
the length of time needed to 'persuade' parents that their
children needed special education, as well as psychologists' deliberate decisions not to pursue referrals,
medical officers' difficulties with their administration,
and the special services' 'adjustments' with placements.
It is difficult to imagine selection procedures in any
other area of education taking this length of time, or
being tolerated by parents.   The possible explanations
for this tolerance must lie in the individualistic nature
of the assessment process, wherein parents are isolated
from other parents, are dependent on professionals and
are either deferential or impotent.   It is also difficult
to imagine articulate middle-class parents accepting this
kind of process, and reinforces the image of the ESN-M
parent as the 'disadvantaged unfortunate' that the literature has tended to describe.

The connection between the inadequate involvement and
consultation with parents, and the failure to establish
formal links with parents, is connected to the low socio-
economic status of the parents.   Crudely, middle-class
professional people do not involve and consult as equals
lower-class people whom they regard as 'less competent'
and 'disadvantaged'.

THE OTHER PERSONNEL

Conclusions concerning the other personnel in this study
must be especially tentative.   They were not asked to
'account' for ESN children, but were studied to examine
whether their involvement did affect or reinforce the
accounts offered by others.   There is no previous
research regarding the involvement of other professionals
in the assessment process for special education and, since
the relationship of the seven 'other' types of professionals to the children was qualitatively different, they
cannot be considered together in any way.   For example,
the educational guidance centres and the remedial teaching
services are alternative directions in which a child can
be moved rather than towards ESN schools.   Psychiatrists,
speech therapists and education welfare officers, are
catering for specific aspects of a child's behaviour -

'maladjustment', speech defects and truancy in these
cases, which may or may not affect the assessment process
for ESN school.   The Probation Service is a separate
process in which a child may be involved as well as ESN
assessment.   Clinic social workers, however, do appear to
play a part in the assessment process in that their work
can involve reinforcement of the decisions of other professionals.   In particular, social workers appeared to
assist psychologists in their persuasion of parents
reluctant to agree to special education.   The assessment
centres also can act as reinforcement to formulated or
semi-formulated decisions about the kind of schooling a
child should receive.

This research did not set out to study withdrawal,
educational guidance or suspension centres and units.
The rapid expansion of these places in the 1970s and the
examination of the causes of disruptive behaviour in
schools is a separate study.   However, the strong connection between the growth of these units and the assessment
process for ESN-M schooling is that the relative speed and
ease with which the children can be transferred to the
units compared to the lengthy ESN assessment process has
meant that some children formerly referred as ESN-M are
now referred to the centres.   The criteria for referral
to either place are similar - disruptive behaviour and
learning problems, and heads are understandably pleased
that children who disrupt the orderly process of 'education' in schools can now be removed more speedily.   The
rapid growth of these centres and units without any
central DES direction appears to have induced some anxiety
at central levels, and the Warnock Report recommended a
neat rationalisation for procedures which are already in
existence.   Disruptive children are officially seen
to require special education, and the units and
centres may officially become part of special education.   Again, this is understandable in terms of the
problems of control which troublesome children pose for
schools but it has no 'educational' justification.   The
Warnock Report's rhetoric concerning the 'special needs'
of the child, becomes, in this context, almost totally
irrelevant.   The major 'needs' for which centres and
units cater are the 'needs' of normal schools for an
orderly environment.

The case of Winston illustrates the way in which the
current procedures can work against the 'needs' of the
child.   The major need of this boy was medical, but his
needs were subsumed under a generalised stereotyped fear
on the part of schools and centres of 'West Indian disruption'.   The case also illustrates the problematic

functions of the centres.   While ESN-M schools do ostensibly have an educational justification, the major justification for these centres is control.   And while there
can be some normative agreement over the functions of
ESN-M schools (although this study showed little agreement) there can legitimately be a lack of consensus over
causes, treatment and 'needs' of disruptive children.
This issue particularly affects West Indian children.
Chapter 8 noted that part of the increasing disruption on
the part of West Indian children is partly a political
response to racism and could be regarded as legitimate.
The disruptive behaviour and the control of West Indian
children is different and more complex than the disruptive
behaviour of white children, but there is little overt
discussion of this issue;   instead attempts are made to
subsume some West Indian children's legitimate problems
with their schools under disruptive behaviour generally.

The remedial teaching service provides an alternative
process into which children referred to the Child Guidance
Clinic could be directed.   However, this direction is a
decision made by the senior psychologist - a further
illustration of the power of the psychologists to affect
the referral.   Psychologists who disapprove of ESN
schooling could use the remedial service as a means of
keeping a child at his ordinary school.   However, the
case of the young boy referred by his school, partly for
disruptive behaviour and initially put under the remedial
service, illustrates the conflict that can arise between
the school and the psychologist's decision.   The school
wanted the boy removed and was pressuring the psychologist
to alter his original decision.   The remedial teaching
service would appear to be considered helpful to schools
when a child is posing learning problems but not for disruptive behaviour.

The objective of the assessment centre is to consider
the child and all reports made on him by professionals,
with a view to a suitable placement in a residential
school, or day school if he is allowed home under supervision.   Children can arrive at the centre already
attending ESN-M school, in which case the centre would not
be involved in any decisions concerning ESN assessment.
However, the case of Karl W. illustrates that the head of
the centre can affect the assessment process for ESN-M
education if he receives a child already in the process.
Like other professionals, the head appeared to be
influenced in his decision to recommend the boy for ESN-M
schooling by the boy having two brothers in ESN schools,
despite a class teacher's report that 'his actions are not
those of an unintelligent boy'.   Throughout this study it

was obvious that a child's chances of being placed in an
ESN school increased if he had siblings there already and
can be seen more as the function of a stereotype that the
family is a 'problem' family than intrinsic qualities
within the child.

The psychiatrists appear to have a more realistic view
of the assessment process than the ideology of 'team-work'
which permeates official documents. As one psychiatrist
put it, 'Amongst people who make decisions on children
there are bound to be resentments and jealousies'. However, from the cases studied where a psychiatrist was
involved it appeared that the influence of psychiatrists
on the decision-making process was minimal: their reports
often appeared irrelevant or their decisions were ignored.
The use of psychiatric models and theories did not seem
appropriate to the practical administrative process and
the poor communication with other professionals meant that
the psychiatrists were forced to alter their recommendations as a case progressed and new information came to
light.

The involvement of social workers in the assessment
process needs more attention than this study was able to
give. From the small amount of information gathered it
did appear that the clinic social worker was particularly
important in reinforcing psychological and medical decisions to the families, in helping persuade reluctant
parents and even in directly influencing the type of
school the child subsequently attended. In the case of
Anthony the social worker saw herself as an equal col-
league of the psychologist - doing a 'joint intervention'.
She decided to press for a day rather than a residential
ESN school and the result of this decision was both a dis-
satisfied mother and head of the day ESN-M school.
Social workers do appear to have some power to affect the
decision-making process for ESN-M education.

As a general conclusion, the more professionals there
are involved in a case, the longer the process takes, the
more problems of communication arise, and the more
pressure is put on families through interviews with, or
visits from a variety of people.

THE SOCIAL CONSTRUCTION OF THE CATEGORY ESN-M

The result of professional 'accounts' of ESN-M children
are, from a phenomenological stand-point, 'the way reality
is perceived as an artifact'. The professionals see
themselves as doing a job, but they are also constructing
a 'reality'. An ESN-M child is a social construct who

comes into existence through the judgments and decisions
of professional people.   This study suggests that the
construction of the category is influenced by the perceived interests of professionals who, objectively, have
vested career interests in defining ESN children.   The
professionals offer a variety of accounts, and, as has
been documented, the accounts conflict, particularly those
of referring heads and psychologists, medical officers and
other professionals.   The dominant accounts appear to be
those of the professional group who currently have most
power, expressed by an ability to impose their accounts
on others.   Thus, psychologists have power to define
children as 'not ESN' when the school asserts that they
'are ESN'.   A special school head has taken children whom
he asserts are 'not ESN', and a medical officer says that
she should not make educational decisions and concurs with
a psychologist's decision that a child 'is ESN'.   All the
professionals assert their status over parents and impose
their accounts of the children on to the parents largely
through the mechanism of persuasion.   Although this may
be resented, it is in the end accepted as and becomes a
reality to the parents.   To the parents of the ESN-M, the
realities of professional power have to be accepted as the
'way it is'.   It is worth noting that no professionals
account for ESN-M children in statutory terms.   Neither
the psychologists nor the medical officers nor heads
offered accounts of ESN-M children as those who could, if
necessary, be compulsorily designated as such.   Yet it is
partly the threat of enforceable procedures that provide
the professionals with the basis for their power.   This
point will be taken up later in a discussion of the
symbolic nature of professional power and autonomy.
     The official picture of the procedures by which the
category ESN-M is 'socially constructed' is that of smooth
team-work operating through a series of formal processes,
documented in writing, which produces a consensus on the
special needs of certain children and the way in which
these special needs can be met.   It has already been
noted that this official picture represents an ideal
rather than reality.   How, in this study, did the formal
processes actually work to 'construct' and document the
ESN-M child?
     The head teachers begin to construct possible ESN-M
children from those whom teachers had brought to their
notice;   and as Sharp and Green (1975) have noted the way
in which teachers begin to distinguish their problem
children is itself problematic - the children usually
taking on a reified identity as abnormal.   The research
did not investigate this area, but it is at this point in

the referral process that teachers can press for the
removal from their classrooms of children who are troublesome.   The head who asked for reports on problem children
'down to the backward and smelly' was typifying the kind
of child who might be potentailly ESN-M.

Head teachers' formal referral of children, using the
official forms, was undergoing a change in 1976, as the
new SE procedures began to be used in B.   Few heads at
this time were aware of the DES Circular 2/75 and the
suggested new procedures.   Those who were aware of the
changed procedures were somewhat resentful that they had
not been consulted over the initiation of the new procedures.   Heads were familiar with the old HP forms but
vague about the new.   Although heads were clear that they
were obliged to fill out the forms, over two-thirds
reported other methods of contacting other professionals.
The telephone was the favourite method of informal contact
- 'a short cut to get things done' or 'a way to harass
them'.

The head who actually tore forms up in front of the
telephone was expressing a general feeling that as a
method of communication no form was considered adequate.
Heads also complained of long delays in the assessment
process after form-filling before they were contacted
again, delays which, although not explained to the heads,
were due to deliberate decisions on the part of the psychologists, or to the time it took to persuade parents.
One feature that emerged in this study was the acquies-
cence of the head teacher in the length of the process.
They, like the parents, felt that once the referral had
been made, events had gone beyond their control and they
were relatively powerless to do anything but wait for the
next decision.   It is only when a child is really
troublesome that a head will 'harass' a psychologist by
phone or letter, or re-refer via a medical officer.
Heads can begin the 'construction' of the ESN child, but
after this are relatively powerless in the process.

The psychologists thus emerged as the professional
group with the power to carry on the formal construction
of the ESN child through procedures of interview, testing
and form-filling.   However, they were critical of the
use of forms and used 'other procedures' to contact other
professionals.   These included telephoning, informal
letters, visiting the school and home and using social
workers' help.   The psychologists worried that the forms
might record subjective impressions rather than objective
information, and did not regard the forms as helpful communication.   Forms were a necessary evil, a 'key to
unlock a place in special education', as one psychologist

put it.   However, the psychologists seemed to be the professional group who have gained most from the introduction of the new forms;   they feel the forms represent the change from medical to educational decision-making, and were the group most closely consulted by the administration in developing the new local form.

The medical officers, far from feeling themselves in a position to effect smooth team-work, were embroiled in administrative problems, partly stemming from the 1974 re-organisation of the Health Service.   The Warnock comment that 're-organisation made co-operation at the local level more, rather than less, difficult' appeared to be an understatement as far as the doctors were concerned. They considered communication with other professionals to be an important problem, either forms did not arrive or arrived incomplete, and even informal methods of communication could not be relied on - 'We'd keep ringing Mrs A. to ask what was going on.'   They felt they were not kept fully informed of decisions made by other professionals and there was some suspicion that the authority might manipulate their decisions.   The doctors were also keenly aware of the illogical situations that arise from poor communications between professionals - as in the case of the child referred around to five doctors.   The doctors showed little enthusiasm for the SE forms, particularly their own SE 2 form - described as 'daft' by one doctor.   The doctor who worried that 'SE 2 sets out the problems for a teacher, not a doctor' was encapsulating anxiety that the doctor's power to define categories of children primarily in their, medical terms, was being withdrawn.   The SE forms do emphasise that the doctor is now part of a 'team' in the assessment process - something which they perhaps find more difficult than other professionals to accept, given the status and autonomy of medical qualifications.   The doctors had developed strategies to overcome their problems.   'I ignore the headings and write what I want', as one doctor put it.   The doctors also used the telephone extensively to inform themselves, and used other departments than special services in the local education authority to help in specific problems.

The special school heads, who ultimately 'construct' the ESN child by accepting him into their school, were the most critical of the written procedures which supposedly supply information upon which they can make their decisions and cater for the 'special needs' of the child once he is in their school.   The set of forms (or duplicates) recording all known information about a child and the decisions of the other professionals, supposedly end up with the head.   In practice, the forms are often incom-

plete, fail to arrive, or arrive late.   The heads were
unanimous in their condemnation of all forms, particularly
the SE forms, described by one head as 'a bloody waste of
time'.   The special school heads feel a particular need
to gather social information on a child's family and feel
that the forms do not supply much social information.
They too rely heavily on informal contact by telephone.

The actual way in which formal procedures operate to
'construct' the ESN child are, in fact, at variance with
the official picture.   Rather than a matter of smooth
team-work between professionals, there are conflicts
between professional interests and anxieties over power
and status.   There is considerable antipathy to the
official forms, which are thought to be intrinsically
inadequate and used inefficiently.   There is a heavy
reliance on informal means of communication, particularly
the telephone, during which unrecorded information can
pass between professionals.   This information can be
subjective and not available for verification, and since
much of it concerns the family background, the persuasion
of parents and the schools' difficulties with a child,
the whole process becomes more questionable in terms of
the 'needs' of the child.

BELIEFS ABOUT THE CHILDREN OF IMMIGRANT PARENTAGE

Part of the initial impetus for undertaking this study
came from the observation of the situation developing in
the late 1960s when 'too many' West Indian children were
being referred, assessed and sent to ESN schools.   A
variety of suggestions were put forward in the 1970s to
'explain' this situation.   Coard (1971) suggested that
normal schools made West Indian children ESN, particularly
by denying their identity in the classroom.   The Secretary of State for Education (Select Committee on Race
Relations and Immigration, 1973) suggested that assessment
processes were at fault, and the DES (1973a) suggested
language problems and teachers unable to cope with the
children.   Despite suggestions for examining and monitoring numbers of West Indian children in special schools
(Select Committee on Race Relations and Immigration,
1976-7), no move towards this has as yet been forthcoming
and the Warnock Committee did not mention this issue.

This study attempted to collect some empirical evidence
on the issue by asking professionals what they considered
the problems of West Indian and Asian children to be,
related to school.   The question was designed to elicit a
'cultural' response from the professionals in that their

perceptions of the problem were held to be dependent on
their cultural beliefs about black immigrants and their
children.   The replies could then be set against the
referral and assessment 'accounts' already documented to
see whether there was any connection.   The referring
heads' perceptions of the problems of West Indian children
are documented in Figure 9.7.

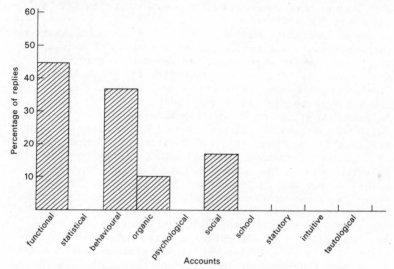

FIGURE 9.7 Referring heads' perceptions of the problems
of West Indian children
(This figure was constructed from Table 3.6)

If this figure is compared with Figure 9.1 it can be
seen at once that the criteria the heads use to account
for ESN children corresponds almost exactly to the heads'
perceptions of the problems of West Indian children.   ESN
children are accounted for by functional and behavioural
criteria - the problems of West Indian children are primarily functional and behavioural.

A noteworthy aspect of the head teachers' views of
West Indian pupils' problems is that, as the Redbridge
Study ('Cause for Concern', 1978) found, West Indians as a
(racial) group are considered to possess 'natural' functional handicaps, although suggested reasons for this are
as likely to be environmental as innate.   The children
were 'bound to be slower, it's their personalities' or
they were 'a representative bunch ... slow, docile and
low-functioning', and they were also 'less keen on education'.

Similarly the behavioural problems of the West Indian

children are taken as a 'natural' characteristic - 'the
usual problems, hyper-activity and anti-authority', 'if I
referred every West Indian with temper tantrums, I'd refer
them all'.   The close correspondence between the heads'
referral criteria for ESN-M school and their cultural
perceptions of the 'natural' problems of West Indian
children make it highly probable that as a group, more
West Indian children would be regarded as potential candidates for ESN-M schools.

As an important conclusion to this particular aspect of
the research, it is suggested, on the basis of this specific aspect of the work, that the general over-referral
during the past fifteen years of West Indian children for
ESN-M education has been closely connected to their meeting the referral criteria used by the head.   A further
inference that can be drawn from this is that if the
learning and behavioural problems of West Indian children
are regarded as 'natural', and therefore as intransigent,
it is less likely that the head would attempt to find
solutions within the school, and more likely that he would
refer to have the child removed from school.   The evidence for these conclusions does seem to support a further
conclusion noted in chapter 8 - that West Indian children
are likely to be handicapped in the referral process by
the assumption that all children start out 'equal' in the
process.   If West Indian children's problems are thought
to be more intransigent than whites, they do have a
greater chance of being placed in special school.   Asian
children, on the other hand, do not meet the referral
criteria for ESN-M schooling.

Figure 9.8 shows that heads' perceptions of the problems of Asian children are totally different from those of
West Indian children.   Asian children are thought to have
functional problems, particularly related to language and
communication, but the problems are not considered
natural or intransigent.   They are regarded as understandable features of immigration and cultural pluralism,
that can be overcome with additional help within the
school.

Once Asian children have 'mastered the language' even
if 'keeping their own culture slows them down', Asian
children are regarded as 'keen on education' and their
parents are seen as valuing the education process.
Accounts of the problems of Asian children no not mention
behaviour - the other important referral criteria.   The
heads do stress the social aspects of Asian children's
problems - family, culture and language - but these do not
constitute referral criteria for the heads.   Similarly
any assessment problems are seen as a fault of the educa-

tion system, and both heads and psychologists note that while assessment might be a problem for Asian children, they seldom refer or test any.

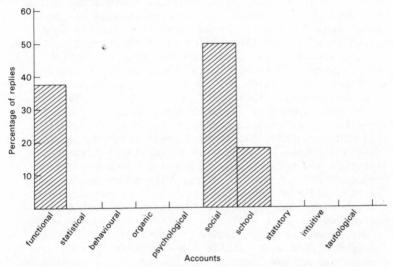

FIGURE 9.8   Heads' perceptions of the problems of Asian children
(This Figure was constructed from Table 3.7.)

As a conclusion to this part of the study, one of the reasons for the small number of Asian children at ESN-M school as a proportion to their numbers in the school population, would seem to be that they do not meet the referral criteria of the head teachers.

ESN-M AND SOCIAL STRUCTURE

Finally, the findings of this study must be placed within a wider structural context. The micro-problem of the accounts of a group of professionals as to why and how they come to construct the category ESN-M as they do, must be related to the macroscopic problem of the functions of the category for industrial society.   It was noted in the Introduction that the study constitutes a critique of phenomenologically based analyses, since it is almost impossible to generate any general propositions about education within complex social structures, from phenomenological assumptions.
While one ideology claims that ESN-M education is a special education catering for the special needs of

certain children, and while empirical research can demonstrate that this form of special education is also a
mechanism for control to assist the orderly working of
normal education, and to re-socialise troublesome children, the 'real' functions may be more related to the
social demands of established dominant interests at a
macro-level, rather than the needs of individual children.
The activities of the professionals could be regarded as:
'the unintended consequences of co-operative activity
which makes a hierarchical structure of differential
power and control' (Sharp and Green, 1975, p. 219).

The development of education systems in industrial
societies is related to transformations in the socio-
economic structure, and to the way in which the society
perpetuates its own conditions of existence through the
selection and transmission of varying amounts and kinds of
education and schooling.   It is this function, as
Bourdieu and Passeron would support, that reproduces class
relationships and propagates ideologies to legitimate the
status quo.

The expansion of education in the twentieth century has
provided higher level skills and expertise for the
society but at the lower levels has created a problem of
absorbing individuals into low-status jobs or legitimating
unemployment.   While Pritchard (1963) traces the expansion of special education to more people being unable to
cope with higher educational and technological demands
made upon them, this study suggests that the expansion of
the category ESN-M has two major functions.   The first
function is that of ensuring that an orderly normal education system runs smoothly without the presence of children
who might create problems.   The second function is that
it is a mechanism for legitimating the 'transmission of
ignorance'.   If disruptive, disaffected groups can
legitimately be classified into special education, a major
threat to established interests will be partially contained, as these groups can legitimately be dismissed as
'daft'.   It was suggested in the Introduction to this
study that there is a relationship between professional
decisions made from a dominant power position and the
placement of children in special education, which reproduces them within the lower positions in the class structure.   This relationship is expressed through the cultural beliefs of the professionals.   As part of a dominant
social group they impose the 'cultural arbitrary' of their
group and their decisions are related to the interests of
this group.   Part of the value system of dominant groups
in industrial society is that as many people as possible
should be productive and self-sufficient.   Yet the

education system cannot be effective if troublesome or potentially non-productive people disrupt its smooth working.   Professionals, working as representatives of the dominant interest groups, have throughout the twentieth century, faced the dilemma that while special education could 'cool out' (Clarke, 1960) potential competition for even low-status jobs, the alternative would be a group of people who were dependent on the state for subsistence.   The dilemma as to whether subnormal individuals should be encouraged towards maximum economic usefulness or merely controlled so that social order could be better maintained was so clearly articulated in the 1908 Report of the Royal Commission, and in 1978 the same dilemma is still in evidence.   The Warnock Report noted that the economic self-sufficiency of the 'handicapped' was in the interest of society, and expressed the same fear that, ESN-M school leavers in particular might become a charge upon the state, in much the same way that the 1908 Report feared for dependence on Poor Law Relief. (5)   Nevertheless, there is a growing tendency within the normal education system to remove or identify on an individual level, children who are troublesome in both learning and behavioural terms.   The increasing use of educational 'at risk' programmes, typified by B's use of the SET programme, points to an increase in the use of 'deficit models'. (6)   Basil Bernstein was arguing, in 1971, that rather than focus on the supposed deficiencies of children, the context of the educational environment could be changed (Bernstein, 1971, vol. 1, ch. 10).   He pointed out that research which proceeds by assessing criteria of attainment that schools hold, then measuring the competence of different social groups in reaching these criteria, is bound to produce results showing that some groups lack the attributes of success.   We should instead be asking how the conditions and context of the educational environment could be changed to accommodate all children.   The fact that the system has not changed, apart from concentrating upon the identification of increasing numbers of children who are categorised as in need of a special education, either within the normal school or outside it, must lead to a questioning of the social purposes of this identification.   Again, this study would suggest that the special education is not so much for 'the good of the child', but is a mechanism by which social order can be maintained both within and outside the education system and a low socio-economic group can legitimately be reproduced.

By transferring or removing children who upset the smooth running of the normal education system, an orderly

controlled system is better ensured.   Indeed, the development of special education for the mildly subnormal
appears to have been a necessity for the smooth development of 'normal' education systems in all industrial
societies during the twentieth century.   It is the
'safety-valve' of the normal system.   The recognition
that in the later twentieth century more and more children
are troublesome to the system, has produced the transfer
of more and more children out of the system.   At the same
time the fact of selection legitimates the preparation of
these children for low socio-economic, but hopefully self-
sufficient, status.   Although the overt control functions
implicit in early twentieth-century care for 'defectives'
have altered, special education can be regarded as a
powerful form of social control.   This study demonstrated
that a major goal of special education is 'social adjustment' and although illegitimacy and crime are now not so
strongly linked to subnormality, at least one boy in this
study was put in ESN-M school to control his criminal
tendencies, and one girl to prevent a possible pregnancy.
Similarly, although eugenic fears of the 'degeneracy of
the British race' have diminished, the stigma of 'idiocy'
and 'degeneracy' have become part of the cultural beliefs
of all social groups.   There is a stigma attached to
those classed as in need of special education, and this in
itself is a powerful form of control.   The behaviour of
those so classified is under close subsequent scrutiny
(Omar, 1971) and the process of attending special schools
or classes further legitimates the exclusion from any
other than low-status occupation.

    This legitimation of low social status by exclusion
from normal education, turns back to front the literature
on ESN-M children which attempts to trace causal explanations for educational subnormality in socio-economic
status or cultural disadvantage.   Dominant social groups
need to control inferior groups.   Cyril Burt saw the need
for this clearly when he spoke of the problems 'civilised'
society faced in coping with the dull, backward, unemployed and habitually delinquent.   The development of
special ESN-M education is a mechanism to solve the
problem and control these troublesome groups.   Thus,
there is little possibility that children other than those
of low socio-economic status or with 'cultural disadvantage' would find their way to ESN-M schools.   The
'middle class' are part of the dominant social groups, and
their dull children do not need to be controlled or legitimated as of low status.

    The procedures by which children come to be classified
as ESN-M are extremely complex, and are usually explained

by an ideology of 'making sure the child is correctly
assessed'.   In reality, complex social procedures serve
social functions.   It is suggested that the procedures
have developed in their present complex form partly to
legitimate the concealment of the 'objective truth'
(Bourdieu and Passeron, 1977) of classification as ESN-M,
and partly because of the historical development of the
struggle for domination of the procedures by professional
groups.

Early selection procedures for special education gave
primacy to medical 'diagnosis'.   Despite a medical
mystique parents were reluctant to allow their children to
be sent to special schools.   The problem for the (dominant) professional group was to exercise the 'symbolic
violence' described by Bourdieu and Passeron, and established a 'legitimate right' to impose 'special' education
on a group that did not want it.   While the 1921 Education Act established the legal basis for coercion of unwilling parents, the more professionals that were seen to
be participating in the assessment process, the more
legitimate this process would appear.   This is partly the
basis for the increasing involvement of more professional
groups in the assessment process.   However, the involvement of different professional groups added a further
complexity.   The power relationship between professionals
involved in the ascertainment process has been in a permanently dynamic state for most of the twentieth century.
Blau's (1964) concept of power differentials as emerging
from the inter-dependence of groups may be relevant here.
Once procedures involved medical, educational and later
psychological personnel, there was no question of any
group being ignored in the decision-making machinery.   A
recognition of mutual interdependence, together with a
desire for status-assertiveness, has led the professional
groups to jockey for the major power position in the
assessment process.   Indeed, a strong reason for the complexity of the process, and the increased complexity
suggested by Warnock, is the recognition of the inter-
dependence of those involved in making the decisions.   If
all parties concerned have their own form, demonstrating
their area of competence, power appears to be shared.   In
fact, the struggle continues in terms of forms not being
'satisfactory', that is (usually) an area of competence
being passed to another group, any smooth team-work that
ensues is more a result of suspension of hostilities, or a
recognition that shared power is better than no power.
Thus, in the early part of the century, powerful medical
officers still had to consider teachers, who were powerful
enough to help prevent the Board of Control taking over

'educable defectives', and in the 1970s while psychologists and heads of special schools have power to influence
the shape of ESN schools, normal school heads were recognised as having initial powers of referral.   No end is
yet envisaged to this historical struggle and it is likely
that procedures will become more complex both to accommodate this and to legitimate the processing of the larger
numbers of children who are to be drawn into 'special'
education.

The area where the cultural beliefs of professionals
are most strongly related to the 'reproduction' of a particular social group, is the area of the over-referral and
classification of the children of West Indian immigrants
as ESN-M.   This is regarded as a particular problem by
the West Indian community in Britain, to whom the issue
has come to have a profound symbolic significance, and
who tend to view the regulations of West Indian children
to ESN-M schooling as a relegation to non-education and
low status rather than for the 'good' of the children.
West Indian immigrants generally are clustered in semi-
and unskilled jobs and most are eager for their children
to have better opportunities than themselves (Rex and
Tomlinson, 1979).   The relegation of their children to
remedial classes or special education is currently a
matter of desperate urgency to them.   However, the educational administration has tended to ignore the problem -
suggestions that the numbers of West Indian children in
ESN-M schools be monitored have to date met with little
response, (7) and a major report on special education (the
Warnock Report) managed to ignore the issue.   This suggests that categorising West Indian children as ESN-M
does have a social function which dominant social groups
would prefer to deny.

The cultural beliefs of head teachers, the initial
referring agents, about the 'natural' learning capacities
and behaviour problems of West Indian children, accord
with the beliefs on which heads base their referral for
ESN-M.   Psychologists and medical officers, although more
cautious, do hold beliefs about the children which would
make them likely to proceed with the assessment.   Psychologists - on the basis of beliefs about family and cultural differences rather than behaviour, doctors - on the
basis of beliefs about behavioural characteristics.
Doctors were the only professionals to directly mention
racial hostility in their own dealings with West Indians,
but denied the validity of West Indian claims about an
over-placement of the children in ESN-M schools.   The
professionals appeared to be attempting to rationalise
their practices in terms of their cultural beliefs about

black children, and by a denial of the pragmatic racialism
which is increasing (Rex and Tomlinson, 1979, ch. 2) in
Britain.   Heads who are directly in the line of black
militancy in the face of this racialism, are reacting in
terms of fear of the disorder and conflict offered by this
social group.   Despite their beliefs and rationalisation
the professionals did not generally question the assumption that black and white children start out 'equal' in
the assessment process.   Paradoxically, it is this
assumption and the failure to examine seriously the whole
referral and assessment process as it affects black
children in a hostile white society, that may have led to
the continuing issue of West Indian children in ESN-M
schools.   The normal schools may, as Coard asserts,
'make' West Indian children ESN, but the way in which the
beliefs of heads about West Indian children accord so
neatly with their referral criteria, and the way in which
the other professionals act in the assessment would
certainly work towards an over-referral and placement of
these children in ESN-M schools.   Asian children, in
contrast, do not fit the referral criteria and the cultural beliefs and subsequent decisions of the professionals
about these children are different to those of West Indian
children, and they tend not to be sent to ESN-M schools.
The suggestion made by the Warnock Committee - that former
remedial and disruptive children become classified as in
need of special education - has serious implications for
the schooling of West Indian children in Britain.   For the
West Indian community 'special educational provision'
might become the major form of educational provision for
their children.   From the point of view of dominant
groups in white society, this would serve a quite positive
social function.   Schools in 'multi-racial' areas in
Britain literally do not know what to do with the children
of West Indian immigrants.   Within the society generally,
beliefs about West Indian children systematically down-
grade the children and their culture, and liberal pedagog-
ical ideologies are being stretched to their utmost in
assuming that West Indian children are 'equal' to white.
The legitimation of as many West Indian children as possible as ineducable and as candidates for special education, reduces the total number of children the schools
will have to deal with, and particularly reduces the
number of troublesome children.   Thus, again, the use of
special education as a mechanism for maintaining order in
schools is operating, this time with the additional
function of solving a 'racial' problem.   At the same
time, the more West Indian children who can legitimately
be shown to have only received a special education and

thus be qualified only for low-status occupations or unemployment, the less competition will be posed by blacks
for superior jobs or status and the more the position of
West Indians in their current relationship to the British
class structure will be legitimated.

Finally, Archer has recently noted (1979, p. 3) - to
understand the nature of education at any time we need to
know not only who won the struggle for control but also
'who lost and how badly they lost'.   The ESN-M would
appear to be losers in the education system.   They comprise half the children currently designated as 'handicapped' and in need of special education, yet they are not
handicapped in the sense of the other designated categories.   They comprise a group of 'less intelligent'
citizens, produced by parents of low socio-economic
status, who are themselves lacking in cultural competence
and devoid of any power vis-à-vis professional decisions.
The children can be compulsorarily placed in a stigmatised
type of 'special' education, which for future occupational
purposes is a non-education, yet their labour will be used
when necessary, and put aside in time of recession - when
they will be further stigmatised as a charge upon the
state.   They are the nearest group to a Greek Helot class
that twentieth-century British society has developed.

This study concludes with a plea to the professionals
to recognise that their undoubted human concern for, and
moral commitment to, individual children must be seen
within a wider structural and political context.   The
decisions which categorise children as ESN-M or CWLDs, and
the schools themselves, are not insulated from wider
social processes.   The question must be asked: in whose
interests are these children being sent to special schools
or classes, or categorised out of 'normal' education in
any way?   It is not enough to assert that the children
are 'handicapped', 'have special needs' and so on.   A
naive liberalism works less in the interest of the child
than an awareness of the political conditions needed for
moral concerns to be truly realised.

Notes

INTRODUCTION

1 The term 'educational subnormality' is used in this
introduction to refer to children who were categorised
as ESN under the 'Handicapped Pupils and School Health
Service Regulations, Statutory Rules and Orders', no.
1076, HMSO, 1945 and who, after the 1971 Education
(Handicapped Childrens) Act became referred to as
ESN-M (mild or medium).

2 See also Baller and Charles's study reported in L.T.
Hilliard and B.H. Kirman (eds) (1965), 'Mental
Deficiency', Churchill, London. Their study of pre-
war 'defective' children, followed up post-war, found
that 66 per cent (of the subjects) required no other
assistance than their own wage.

3 In this study 'professionals' refers to all those
practitioners who make decisions on ESN children, i.e.
head teachers, educational psychologists, medical
officers, psychiatrists, social workers and others.

4 Mental deficiency has been described as 'a condition
of subnormal mental development present at birth or in
early childhood and characterised mainly by limited
intelligence'. See W. Mayer-Gross, E. Slater and
M. Roth (1954). For a discussion of the historical
development of the concept, see chapter 1.

5 In 1929 the report presented by Dr E.O. Lewis to the
Wood Committee on Mental Deficiency estimated 105,000
'feeble-minded' children aged 7-16 years in England
and Wales. In 1946 the Ministry of Education
pamphlet no. 5 'Special Educational Treatment' suggested that 1-2 per cent of the school population would
need to be educated in special (ESN) schools. 8-9
per cent of the dull school population could be provided for in ordinary school. An ILEA estimate in

September 1974 suggested that 'between 12-20% of children of primary and secondary school age ... needed special attention for varying periods of time'. The Warnock Report, in April 1978, suggested that 20 per cent, one child in five, is likely to require special educational provision at some time in their school career.

6   'Race' is used here to refer to a social categorisation of people on the basis of distinctive physical characteristics.   See L. Kuper (ed.) (1975).

1   AN OVERVIEW OF THE CONCEPT ESN-M, THE POLITICS OF IQ AND THE WEST INDIAN 'GRIEVANCE'

1   This section of the study is indebted to D.G. Pritchard (1963), chapter 5.

2   Klemm documents the German 'hilfs-schule', partially adopted as a model for the first English special school, particularly in terms of the curriculum, which had a manual orientation.

3   The teacher, Mrs Burgwin, was the first teacher of special classes in London.   She eventually became superintendent of London special schools.

4   In 1907, the Medical Branch of the Board of Education had been given the task of inspecting special schools, and by 1920 it inspected and reported to the Board on all special schools.

5   The 1908 Royal Commission on the Care and Control of the Feeble-Minded noted in chapter 14 that the 'higher social class' did not take advantage of state provision for defective children - they provided privately for their defective children.

6   Chapter 15 in S. Segal (1974).   He describes the teacher pressure and central government pressure to co-ordinate Social Services which moved towards bringing the severely mentally handicapped into the school system.   Voluntary organisations and parents also campaigned for the integration of severely mentally handicapped children into the education system.   See the Journal of the National Society for Mentally Handicapped Children, 'Parents' Voice'.   As noted in the Introduction, the parents of ESN-S children tend to cross-cut all social classes.

7   See, for example, A.H. Halsey (1972), p. 3.   'To find a strategy for educational roads to equality!   That has been a central theme of educational discussion from the beginning of the twentieth century.'

8   The 1908 Royal Commission first noted the difficulty

of separating 'defective' children from the 'dull and backward'.

9 In this study, six out of eight educational psychologists interviewed were sceptical about the use of IQ testing.

10 Burt (1935, pp. 32-3) describes the way in which he used Binet's work to arrive at a concept of Mental Ratio, or IQ. He attributes the first use of the phrase 'intelligence quotient' (IQ) to an American - W. Stern.

11 Burt's explanation of a backward child as working at lower than the required school 'standard', as prescribed in the 1862 Codes of Education can be found in Burt, 1935, p. 118. It is here that Burt also describes an 'educationally sub-normal child' as one with an IQ below 85.

12 The Department of Education and Science definition of an 'immigrant child' for the purpose of collecting statistics between 1967 and 1972 referred to a child born overseas, or one born in Britain whose parents had lived in the country for less than ten years.

13 See 'Race Today', 1973. Oct./Nov./Dec. Article by M. Duncan, and reply by D. Jarratt-Yashy and M. Phillips.

14 This comment was interesting considering that little priority was being given to developing 'culture-fair' tests.

2 METHODOLOGY, LOCAL AUTHORITY AND CHILDREN

1 Chapter 1 documented the way in which mildly subnormal people tend to be used as replacement labour. Evidence for this is provided by City of Birmingham (1977):

> The majority of ... leavers from special schools in 1974 found employment with comparative ease. The largest group of leavers were those from the schools for slow learners and most of these had jobs as soon as term ended. They entered a variety of occupations such as polishing, assembling, machine work, warehouse work, building, packing, canteen and occasionally office work.... By 1975, however, the situation was difficult. Many special school leavers were affected by the recession and those requiring routine or semi-skilled work found it most difficult. (p. 15)

2 See, for example, a discussion on population in G.V. Glass and J.C. Stanley (1970, p. 240).

3   The tests were developed by a teacher, Mrs Rawsthorne, under the supervision of R.K. Gulliford.   See D. Gray and J. Reeve,   Ordinary schools – some special help, 'Special Education - Forward Trends', vol. 5, no. 1, 1978.
4   Letter from an educational psychologist to chief educational psychologist, 1976.
5   'Organic: of the bodily organs: affecting the structure of an organ: constitutional, inherent, fundamental, structural', 'Concise Oxford Dictionary', 1956.

3   THE REFERRING SCHOOLS

1   Teachers' decision-making is the subject of a recent study edited by S.J. Eggleston (1979).   A study of teachers' decisions concerning the referral of potentially ESN children would have to be set within a context of teachers' beliefs about the 'intellectual' capacities of all their pupils.

4   THE EDUCATIONAL PSYCHOLOGISTS

1   Functions of the educational psychologist in Scotland are defined by the Education (Scotland) Act 1969.
2   This 'resentment' is not publicly documented, since it largely takes the form of private anxieties revealed in interviews.   At a conference of Midlands educational psychologists - 16 October 1976 - at the University of Birmingham, the point was encapsulated by an educational psychologist in discussing Circular 2/75:

> The crux is that procedures have formally been medically dominated, but now we are moving away from this - but to where? - To administrative decisions?   The SCMO is still the only person legally entitled to 'certify' a child with SE 5 - there is no mandatory legal employment of psychologists in LEA's.

3   Private communication, September 1978.

5   THE MEDICAL OFFICERS AND OTHER PERSONNEL

1   Dr Jaffa reported that 'screening thus identified 76.6% of the educational "failures" and 87% of the "successes"'.
2   Lead poisoning is currently being advanced as a cause

of vulnerability.   See D. Bryce-Smith and M.A. Waldron (1974);   D.G. Beevers et al. (1976).

3   For example: Liverpool Teachers Advisory Committee,
1974.   'The Suspended Child'.   The decline of classroom behaviour is blamed on TV, lurid paperbacks,
parents, society, and the 1969 Children and Young
Persons Act.

6   THE SPECIAL SCHOOLS

1   Although one delicate school is subsumed under the
term 'ESN schools', the term used in this chapter
refers to ESN-M schools, and ESN-S where indicated.

2   During 1976, when the schools were visited, there was
much speculation concerning possible recommendations
of the then forthcoming Warnock Report.   Post-1978,
Warnock's recommendations on 'integration' have pro-
voked a vigorous debate about the future of special
schools.   'The principle of educating handicapped and
non-handicapped children together, which is described
as "integration" in this country, "mainstreaming" in
the U.S.A. ... and "normalisation" in Scandinavia and
Canada ... is not new to education' (Warnock Report,
p. 99).   See also E. Britton, (1978).

3   The early development of special institutions encouraged the transfer of children back to normal school,
but this practice did not become general.   As Omar
wrote in 1971, to be ESN was to be 'labelled for
life'.

4   The 'Special Schools Journal' was the Journal of the
Special Schools Association, which became the Associa-
tion ofr Special Education in 1962.   In 1974 the
Association for Special Education, the College of
Special Education and the Guild of Teachers for Back-
ward Children merged to form the National Council for
Special Education and published the first issue of a
new Journal - 'Special Education   (incorporating
Forward Trends)' in March 1974.

5   This accords with Durojaiye's (1970) research in which
heads of special schools considered that they had a
more adequate staff (and better discipline) than
normal schools.

7   THE PARENTS OF THE STUDY POPULATION CHILDREN

1   '"Problem" families are those selected on the basis of
contact with "multiple social agencies".'

2 An article in the 'Birmingham Mail', 13 May 1977,
   noted that: 'problem pupils whose parents take no
   interest in their education should leave school at 15,
   instead of 16'.

8 THE CHILDREN OF IMMIGRANT PARENTAGE

1 (The Warnock Report) - 'Special Educational Needs.
   Report of the Committee of Enquiry into the Education
   of Handicapped Children and Young People' (1978).
   The Report dismissed this issue in one paragraph on
   p. 64 out of a Report of 416 pages long.
2 For a comprehensive account of demographic patterns of
   settlement and housing see 'New Community', vol. 6,
   nos 1 and 2.   Winter 1977-8.
3 This assertion is made after many conversations and
   interviews with policy-makers and practitioners who
   take it for granted that there is a relationship
   between the disadvantaged and 'ESN-ness'.
4 Conversations with teachers of black children in B.
5 Conversations with black children and leaders of black
   militant groups in B.
6 Stereotyping has received considerable attention in
   social psychology and the literature on inter-group
   relations.   Here it is used in Milton Gordon's sense:
   'stereotyping ... stems from what would appear to be
   widespread cognitive inadequacies, reinforced by
   affective tendencies and lack of equal status primary
   contact between groups' (1978, p. 79).
7 Viv Edwards's (1979) study of the part played by
   language in West Indian under-achievement, suggests
   that teachers may take 'poor' West Indian speech for
   granted so much that they do not feel it worth
   mentioning.
8 Conversations with heads in schools with a high proportion of West Indian children indicated that heads
   in general considered a third of their West Indian
   pupils to be 'remedial'.   Half the pupils at one
   Educational Guidance Centre in the City of B in 1976
   were of West Indian origin.   Apart from this kind of
   'indication', there is no way in which numbers of West
   Indian children who may be classed as 'children with
   learning difficulties' can be compiled.

9   CONCLUSIONS

1   This raises the important question as to whether
    inner-city schools are able to offer children an
    'equal' education, if teachers really believe stan-
    dards are different in inner-city schools.
2   Report on the Birmingham Special Education Treatment
    Programme by Mr E.J. Griffiths, Staff Inspector
    (1977).
3   In discussion with educational psychologists working
    with other LEAs, more anxiety has been expressed that
    the administration might overrule psychological
    decisions.
4   The 'persuasion' has been noted as an irritation in a
    smooth process.   In 1978 a confidential report on the
    ILEA Special Education Service noted that 'a strict
    limit should be placed on the time devoted to persua-
    sion and there should be more positive steps for
    statutory enforcement of special school admission'
    ('Times Educational Supplement', 20 October 1978).
5   'Report of the Royal Commission on the Care and Con-
    trol of the Feeble-Minded', 1908, p. 85.   See also
    Warnock Report, 1978, p. 163.
        Extra help for school leavers with moderate learn-
        ing difficulties or emotional or behavioural dis-
        orders might enable them to hold down a job and
        reduce the chances of them entering a cycle of
        frequent changes of job, leading to long-term unem-
        ployment and dependence on social and psychiatric
        services.
6   Views of the child as *deficient* have been discussed by
    (for example) F. Reismann (1962) and M. Rutter and
    N. Madge (1976).
7   The reply by the government to the demand from the
    Select Committee on Race Relations and Immigration on
    the collecting and monitoring of statistics is con-
    tained in: 'The West Indian Community', Observations
    on the report of the Select Committee, HMSO, April
    1978.

Bibliography

Ainscow, M., Bond, J., Gardner, J., and Tweddle, D.
(1978), A new role for the special school, 'Special Educa-
tion - Forward Trends', vol. 5, no. 1.
'A Language for Life' (1975), Report of the Committee of
Enquiry under the chairmanship of Sir Alan Bullock, HMSO,
London.
Anastasi, A., and Foley, J.P. (1949), 'Differential
Psychology', Macmillan, London.
Archer, M.S. (1979), 'Social Origins of Education
Systems', Sage, London.
Ascher, M.A. (1970), The attainments of children in ESN
school and remedial departments, 'Educational Research',
vol. 12.
Bagley, C. (1972), Deviant behaviour in English and West
Indian children, 'Research in Education', 8.
Bagley, C. (1973), The education of immigrant children - a
review of Policy and Problems, 'British Journal of Social
Policy', vol. 2.
Bagley, C. (1975), The background of deviance in Black
children in London, in Verma, G.K. and Bagley, C. (eds),
'Race and Education Across Cultures', Heinemann, London.
Bagley, C., Bart, M., and Wong, J. (1979), Antecedents of
scholastic success in West Indian ten year olds in
London, in Verma, G.K., and Bagley, C. (eds), 'Race,
Education and Identity', Macmillan, London.
Baldamus, W. (1977), 'The Structure of Social Inference',
Martin Robertson, London.
Beevers, D.G., et al. (1976), Blood levels and hyperten-
sion, 'Lancet' (ii), London.
Bell, P. (1970), 'Basic Teaching for Slow Learners',
Muller Educational, London.
Berger, A., and Mitchels, G. (1978), Multitude of sin
bins, 'Times Educational Supplement', 7 July.
Berger, P. and Luckmann, T. (1966), 'The Social Construc-
tion of Reality', Penguin, Harmondsworth.
356

Bernbaum, G. (1973), Headmasters and schools - some preliminary findings, 'Sociological Review', August.
Bernbaum, G. (1976), The role of the head, in Peters, R.S. (ed.), 'The Role of the Head', Routledge & Kegan Paul, London.
Bernstein, B. (1971), 'Class Codes and Control', vol. 1, Paladin Books, St Albans.
Bhattacharyya, A.C. (1974), Present roles and practices of L.E.A. educational psychologists and psychiatrists in child guidance clinics, unpublished MEd dissertation, University of Birmingham.
Binet, A. (1909), 'Les Idées Modernes sur les enfants', Flammarion, Paris.
Binet, A., and Simon, T. (1914), 'Mentally Defective Children', trans. W.R. Drummond', E.J. Arnold, London.
Birley, D. (1970), 'The Education Officer and his World', Routledge & Kegan Paul, London.
Blau, P. (1964), 'Exchange and Power in Social Life', Wiley, New York.
Block, N., and Dworkin, G. (1977), 'The I.Q. Controversy', Quartet, New York.
Bloor, M. (1976), Bishop Berkeley and the adenotonsillectomy enigma: An exploration of variation in the social construction of medical disposals, 'Sociology', vol. 10, no. 1.
Blumer, H. (1962), Society as symbolic interaction, in A. Rose (ed.), 'Human Behaviour and Social Processes', Routledge & Kegan Paul, London.
Board of Education (1926), 'Report of the Consultative Committee on the Education of the Adolescent' (Hadow Report), HMSO, London.
Board of Education and Board of Control (1929), 'Report of the Joint Departmental Committee on Mental Deficiency' (The Wood Committee), HMSO, London.
Board of Education (1937), 'The Education of backward children', Education Pamphlet 112, HMSO, London.
Booth, T. (1978), From normal baby to handicapped child, 'Sociology', vol. 12, no. 2.
Bourdieu, P., and Passeron, J.C. (1977), 'Reproduction in Education, Society and Culture', Sage, London.
Brah Atvah (1977), Age, Race and Power relations - the case of South Asian youth in Britain, paper to British Sociological Association Annual Conference, Sheffield.
Brennan, W.K. (1974), 'Shaping the Education of Slow Learners', Routledge & Kegan Paul, London.
Brennan, W.K. (1979), 'Curricular Needs of Slow Learners', Evans/Methuen, London.
Brigham, C.C. (1923), 'A study of American Intelligence', Princeton University Press.

Brindle, P. (1973), The Ascertainment of mild subnormality in Education, unpublished MEd dissertation, University of Birmingham.

Brittan, E. (1976), Teacher opinion on aspects of school life - pupils and teachers, 'Educational Research', vol. 18, no. 3.

Britton, Edward (1978), Warnock and integration, 'Educational Research', vol. 21, no. 1.

Bryce-Smith, D., and Waldron, M.A. (1974), Review of pre-1974 evidence relating to lead-induced disturbance of intellect, behaviour and personality, 'Ecologist', no. 4.

Burden, R.L. (1976), Training educational psychologists to work in schools - the Exeter approach, 'Remedial Education', vol. 11, no. 2.

Burt, C.L. (1917), 'The Distribution and relations of Educational Abilities', London County Council report.

Burt, C.L. (1920), 'Report of an Investigation of Backward Children in Birmingham', City of Birmingham Stationery Department.

Burt, C.L. (1921), 'Mental and Scholastic Tests', King, London (2nd edn 1947, Staples).

Burt, Cyril (1935), 'The Subnormal Mind', Oxford University Press.

Burt, Cyril (1937), 'The Backward Child', London University Press.

Cameron, A.C. (1931), 'Reorganization and the Retarded Child', Local Authority Conference, Great Yarmouth, NUT, London.

Carroll, H. (1974), The changing role of the educational psychologist, 'Collegiate Faculty of Education Journal', University of Swansea.

Case, C. (1924), What is a social problem?, 'Journal of Applied Sociology', 8.

'Cause for Concern - West Indian Pupils in Redbridge' (1978), Black People's Progressive Association and Redbridge Community Relations Council.

Cave, C., and Maddison, P. (1978), 'A survey of recent research in special education', NFER, Slough.

Central Statistics Office (1976), 'Social Trends', no. 7, HMSO, London.

Charity Organisation Society (1893), 'The Feeble-Minded Child and Adult', London.

Chazan, M. (1964), The incidence and nature of maladjustment among children in schools for the educationally subnormal, 'British Journal of Educational Psychology', vol. 34, no. 3.

'Children and Their Primary Schools' (1967), Report of the Central Advisory Council (England) for Education (The Plowden Report), HMSO, London.

'Children and Young Persons (Scotland)' (1969), Report by the Committee appointed by the Secretary of State for Scotland, Cmnd 2306, HMSO, London.

Cicourel, A., and Kitsuse, J. (1963), 'The Educational Decision-Makers', Bobbs Merrill, Indianapolis.

Cicourel, A. (1973), 'Cognitive Sociology', Penguin, Harmondsworth.

City of Birmingham (1972), Working Party on Suspension Units, Report, Education Department.

City of Birmingham (1976), Notes for professional staff of the Education and Health Service, Special Services Guidelines, September.

City of Birmingham (1977), 'Triennial Report', Education [careers sub-] committee, March.

City of Liverpool (1974), 'The Suspended child', report by Liverpool Teachers Advisory Committee.

City of Liverpool College of Higher Education (1977), 'Syllabus' for a degree in Mental Handicap.

Clarke, A.M., and Clarke, A.D.B. (1958), 'Mental Deficiency', Methuen, London.

Clarke, A.M. and Clarke, A.D.B. (1965), 'Mental Deficiency - The Changing Outlook' (2nd edn) Methuen, London.

Clarke, B. (1960), The cooling out function in Higher Education, 'American Journal of Sociology', IXV, May.

Cleugh, M.F. (1961), 'Teaching the Slow Learner in the Special School', Methuen, London.

Coard, B. (1971), 'How the West Indian Child is made Educationally Sub-normal in the British School System', New Beacon Books, London.

Cohen, L. (1970), School size and headteacher bureaucratic role conceptions, 'Educational Review', no. 23.

Colgate, H.A. (1976), The role of the secondary head, in Peters, R.S. (ed.), 'The Role of the Head', Routledge & Kegan Paul, London.

Collman, R.D. (1956), Employment success of ESN pupils in England, 'The Slow-Learning Child', vol. 3, also in 'American Journal of Mental Deficiency', vol. 60.

Commonwealth Immigrants Advisory Council (1964), '2nd Report', Cmnd 2458, HMSO, London.

Conference proceedings (1976), one-day conference of educational psychologists in the Midlands, University of Birmingham, 16 October.

Cook, A., and Mack, H. (1972), The headteacher's role, 'British Primary Schools Today', vol. 2, Macmillan.

Cookson, Clive (1978), Courts will decide whether tests are culturally biased, 'Times Educational Supplement', 20 October.

Cope, C., and Anderson, E. (1977), Special units in ordinary schools, unpublished paper, Institute of Education, University of London.

Coulson, A.A. (1976), The role of the primary head, in
R.S. Peters (ed.), 'The Role of the Head', Routledge &
Kegan Paul, London.
Court Report, see 'Fit for the Future ...' (1976).
Craft, M. (1970), 'Family, Class and Education - a
Reader', Longman, London.
Cronbach, L.J. (1969), 'Essentials of Psychological
Testing', Harper & Row, New York.
Crowley, R.H. (1936), 'The problem of the Backward
Child', NUT Conference, Southport.
Curr, W. (1969), Critical notice, 'British Journal of
Educational Psychology', 39.
Dain, P. (1977), Disruptive children and the Key Centre,
'Remedial Education', vol. 12, no. 4.
Data Analysis Block 4, 'Methods of Educational Enquiry,
341, Open University, Milton Keynes.
Davies, D.R. (1961), A disorder theory of mental retarda-
tion, 'Journal of Mental Subnormality', 7.
Davis, A.G., and Strong, P.M. (1976), Aren't children
wonderful - a study in the allocations of identity in
developmental assessment, in Stacey, M. (ed.), 'The
Sociology of the NHS', Sociological Review monograph, 22.
Denzin, N.K. (ed.) (1970), 'Sociological Method - a
Source-Book', Aldine, Chicago.
Department of Education and Science (1964), 'Slow Learners
at School', Education Pamphlet no. 46, HMSO, London.
Department of Education and Science (1965), 'Special
Education Today', Report on Education, no. 23, HMSO,
London.
Department of Education and Science (1969), 'The Health of
the School Child 1966-68', Report of the chief medical
officer to the DES, HMSO, London.
Department of Education and Science (1971a), 'The Educa-
tion of Immigrants', Education Survey, 13, HMSO, London.
Department of Education and Science (1971b), 'The Last to
Come In', Report on Education, no. 69, HMSO, London.
Department of Education and Science (1972), 'The Health of
the School Child 1969-70', Report of the chief medical
officer to the DES, HMSO, London.
Department of Education and Science (1973a), Educational
arrangements for children who may need special education,
letter to chief education officers, November.
Department of Education and Science (1973b), 'Special
Education - a Fresh Look', Report on Education, no. 77,
HMSO, London.
Department of Education and Science (1973c), 'Staffing in
Special Schools and Classes', Circular 4/73, HMSO, London.
Department of Education and Science (1974a), 'Educational
Disadvantage and the Needs of Immigrants', Cmnd 5720,
HMSO, London.

Department of Education and Science and Department of Health and Social Security (1974b), 'Child Guidance', Circular 3/74 and H SC.(ls) 9, HMSO, London.

Department of Education and Science (1974-6), 'Statistics in Education', vol. 1, 'Schools', HMSO, London.

Department of Education and Science (1975a), 'The Discovery of Children Requiring Special Education and the Assessment of Their Needs', Circular 2/75, HMSO, London.

Department of Education and Science (1975b), 'Handicapped pupils (certificate) (amendment) regulations 1975', S.I. no. 328, HMSO, London.

Department of Education and Science (1977), Circular 2/75 - review of Forms SE 1 - SE 6, letter to chief education officers.

Descoeudres, Alice (1928), 'The Education of Mentally Defective Children', Harrop, London.

Devlin, T. (1977), Stringent rules likely to delay integration of handicapped pupils, 'Guardian', 1 June.

Dhondy, F. (1974), The Black explosion in schools, 'Race Today', February.

Douglas, J.W.B. (1964), 'The Home and the School', McGibbon & Kee, London.

Douglas, Jack (1971), 'Understanding Everyday Life', Routledge & Kegan Paul, London.

Dugdale, D. (1910), 'The Jukes - A Study in Crime, Pauperism and Disease', Putman, New York.

Durojaia, M.O.A. (1969), Occupational choice and special education of ESN children, 'British Journal of Educational Psychology', vol. 39.

Education Department (1898), Report of the Royal Commission on Defective and Epileptic Children, 2 vols, HMSO, London.

Edwards, V.K. (1978), Language attitudes and under-performance in West Indian Children, 'Educational Review', vol. 30, no. 1.

Edwards, V.K. (1979), 'The West Indian Language Issue in British Schools', Routledge & Kegan Paul, London.

EEC (1975), Draft directive to member states on The education of migrant workers.

Eggleston, S.J. (1974), 'Contemporary Research in the Sociology of Education', Methuen, London.

Eggleston, S.J. (1980), 'Teachers' Decision-Making in the Classroom', Routledge & Kegan Paul, London.

Eysenck, H. (1971), 'Race, Intelligence and Education', Temple-Smith, London.

Fanon, F. (1961), 'The Wretched of the Earth', Penguin, Harmondsworth.

Ferron, O. (1965), The test performance of Coloured Children, 'Educational Research', vol. 8, no. 1.

Fethney, V. (1972), ESN children - what the teachers say,

'Race Today', no. 4.

'Fit for the Future'.   The Report of the Committee on Child Health Services',(1976) (The Court Report), Cmnd 6684, HMSO, London.

Floud, J., Halsey, A.H., and Martin, F.M. (1956), 'Social Class and Educational Opportunity', Heinemann, London.

Foucault, M. (1967), 'Madness and Civilisation', Tavistock, London.

Fowler, G. et al. (eds) (1973), 'Decision-Making in British Education', Open University Books, Milton Keynes.

Frith, S., and Corrigan, P. (1977), The politics of education, in Young, M. and Whitty, G. (eds), 'Society State and Schooling', Falmer Press, Brighton.

Fuller, R., and Myers, R. (1941), Some aspects of a theory of social problems, 'American Sociological Review', 6.

Furneaux, B. (1969), 'The Special Child', Penguin, Harmondsworth.

Fyvel, T.R. (1978), The insecure offender in retrospect, 'New Society', 20 July.

Galton, F. (1869), 'Hereditary Genius - an Inquiry into its Laws and Consequences', Macmillan, London.

Galton, F. (1889), 'Natural Inheritance', Macmillan, London.

Galton, F., and others (1909), 'The Problem of the Feeble-Minded', King, London.

Gellner, R. (1968), Holism versus individualism, in M. Brodbeck, (ed.), 'Readings in the Philosophy of Science', Collier-Macmillan, New York.

Ghuman, A.S. (1975), 'The Cultural Context of Thinking - a Comparative Study of Punjabi and English Boys', NFER, Slough.

Giles, R. (1977), 'The West Indian Experience in British Schools', Heinemann, London.

Gillie, O. (1976), 'Who do you think you are - man or superman, the Genetic Controversy', Hart-David MacGibbon, London.

Glaser, B.G., and Strauss, A. (1967), 'The Discovery of Grounded Theory', Aldine, Chicago.

Glaser, B.G., and Strauss, A. (1971), 'Status Passage', Routledge & Kegan Paul, London.

Glass, G.V., and Stanley, C.J. (1970), 'Statistical Methods in Education and Psychology', Prentice-Hall, Englewood, Cliffs, N.J.

Goddard, H.H. (1912), 'The Kallikak Family', Macmillan, New York.

Goffman, E. (1970), 'Stigma: Notes on the Management of Spoiled Identity', Penguin, Harmondsworth.

Goldman, R., and Taylor, F. (1966), Coloured immigrant children - a survey of research studies and literature on their educational problems and potential in Britain, 'Educational Research', vol. 8, no. 3.

Gordon, Milton (1978), 'Human Nature, Class and Ethnicity', Oxford University Press.

Green, L. (1976), Development in special education - implications for children in ordinary schools, 'Remedial Education', vol. 11, no. 3.

Griffiths, E.J. (1977), Report on the Birmingham Special Education Treatment programme, Conference proceedings, 'The Identification of Children with Special Education Needs', Southport.

Gulliford, R. (1966), Special Education for the ESN, 'Conference proceedings: What is Special Education?', NASE, July, London.

Gulliford, R.K. (1969), 'Backwardness and Educational Failure', NFER, Slough.

Gulliford, R.K. (1971), 'Special Educational Needs', Routledge & Kegan Paul, London.

Gunzberg, H.C. (1968), 'Social Competence and Mental Handicap', Balliere Tindall and Cassell, London.

Hadow Report, see Board of Education (1926).

Halsey, A.H. (1972), 'Educational Priority E.P.A. Problems and Policies', vol. 1, HMSO, London.

Hegarty, S., and Lucas, D. (1979), 'Able to Learn - the Pursuit of Culture-Fair Assessment', NFER, Slough.

Herbert, G.W. (1973), Educational Psychology in Practice, 'Bulletin of the British Psychological Society', 26.

Herrnstein, R.J. (1973), 'I.Q. in the Meritocracy', Allen Lane, London.

Hess, R.D., and Shipman, V.C. (1965), Early experience and the socialisation of cognitive modes in children, 'Child Development', vol. 36.

Hewett, S. (1970), 'The Family and the Handicapped Child', Allen & Unwin, London.

Hiller, Peter (1973), Social reality and social stratification, 'The Sociological Review', 21.

Hilliard, L.T., and Kirman, B.H. (1965), 'Mental Deficiency', Churchill, London.

Holt, K.S. (1966), Individuals and family problems, Conference proceedings, 'Community Care for the Mentally Handicapped', National Society for Mentally Handicapped Children.

Hughes, Everett (1971), 'The Sociological Eye', Aldine, Chicago.

Hunt, Sonya (1973), 'Parents of the ESN', National Elfrida Rathbone Society, Liverpool.

Inner London Education Authority (1966), 'The Education of Immigrant Pupils in Primary Schools', Report of a Working Party of members of the Inspectorate and School Psychological Service, report 959.

Inner London Education Authority (1967), 'The Education of Immigrant Pupils in Special Schools for ESN Children', report 657.

Isaac-Henry, K. (1970), The politics of comprehensive education in Birmingham, unpublished MEd dissertation, University of Birmingham.

Itard, J.M.G. (1894), 'De l'Education d'un sauvage', Paris ('The Wild Boy of Aveyron', trans. Humphrey, G. and M., New York, 1932).

Jackson, Brian (1973), The child-minders, 'New Society', 29 November.

Jackson, Robin (1978), Are we being unrealistic about jobs?, 'Special Education - Foreward Trends', vol. 5, no. 1.

Jackson, S. (1969), 'Special Education in England and Wales', Oxford University Press.

Jackson, S. (1970), The education of the slow learner 1870-1970, Conference of College of Special Education.

Jaffa, E. (1977), Learning disorders in young school-children - is neuro developmental screening of value?, 'Public Health', vol. 19, London.

Jarvis, F. (1978), letter to the 'Times Educational Supplement', 24 February.

Jensen, A.R. (1969), How much can we boost I.Q. and scholastic achievement, 'Harvard Educational Review', 39.

Jensen, A.R. (1973), 'Educability and Group Differences', Methuen, London.

Jerrold, M.A., and Fox, R. (1968), Pre-jobs for the boys, 'Special Education', vol. 57, no. 2.

Kamin, L.J. (1977), 'The Science and Politics of I.Q.', Penguin, Harmondsworth.

Kanner, L.A. (1964), 'History of the Care and Study of the Mentally Retarded', Springfield, Mass.

Karabel, J., and Halsey, A.H. (1977), 'Power and Ideology in Education', Oxford University Press.

Kershaw, J.D. (1966), 'Handicapped Children', Heinemann, London.

Kirman, B.H. (1965), The educationally subnormal child, in Hilliard, L.T. and Kirman, B.H. (eds), 'Mental Deficiency', Churchill, London.

Kirman, B.H. (1972), 'The Mentally Handicapped Child', Nelson, London.

Kitzinger, S. (1972), West Indian Children with problems, 'Therapeutic Education', Spring.

Klemm, L.R. (1891), 'European Schools', Appleton, New York.

Knight, D.J., and Walker, M.A. (1965), The factory day at school, 'Special Education', vol. 54, no. 3.

Knowle, J., and Scott, H. (1970), Staff management and Special Schools, 'Special Education', vol. 59, September.

Kogan, M. (1971), 'The Politics of Education', Penguin,
Harmondsworth.
Kogan, M. and Van der Eyken, W. (1973), 'County Hall',
Penguin, Harmondsworth.
Kuhn, S. (1962), The structure of scientific revolutions,
'International Encyclopaedia of Unified Science', vol. 2,
no. 2.
Kuper, L. (ed.) (1975), 'Race, Science and Society',
Allen & Unwin, London.
Larson, Magali S. (1978), 'The Rise of Professionalism - a
Sociological Analysis', University of California Press.
Lazarsfeld, P.F., and Rosenberg, M. (1955), 'The Language
of Social Research', Free Press of Glencoe, Chicago.
Lee, J.M. (1963), 'Social Leaders and Public Persons',
Oxford University Press.
Lewis, E.O. (1931), Types of mental deficiency and their
social significance, 'Journal of Mental Science', 79.
Lewis, O. (1968), The culture of poverty, in Moynihan,
D.P. (ed.), 'On Understanding Poverty', Basic Books, New
York.
Lindsay, G.A. (1975), Birmingham screening instruments,
unpublished paper, University of Birmingham School of
Education.
Lindsay, M.M. (1957), Special schools now and in the
future, 'Special Schools Journal', vol. 46, no. 1.
Little, A. (1975), The educational achievement of ethnic
minority children in London schools, in Verma, G.K., and
Bagley, C. (eds), 'Race and Education Across Cultures',
Heinemann, London.
Little, A. (1978), Educational policies for multi-racial
areas, inaugural lecture, Goldsmiths College, London.
Lorenz, K. (1973), 'Civilised Man's Eight Deadly Sins',
Methuen, London.
Lovell, K. (1968), Backwardness and retardation, in
Butcher, H.J. (ed.), 'Educational Research in Britain',
University of London Press.
Lumsden, J. (1935), 'The Special School and the Elementary
School', NUT Scarborough Conference.
McFie, J. and Thompson, J. (1970), Intellectual abilities
of immigrant children, 'British Journal of Educational
Psychology', vol. 40.
Mack, J. (1978), Warnock in retrospect, 'New Society',
25 May.
Marland, M. (1975), 'The Craft of the Classroom - a
Survival Guide to Classroom Management', Heinemann,
London.
Mauss, A.L. (1975), 'Social Problems as Social Movements',
Lippencott, Philadelphia.
Mayer-Gross, W., Slater, E., and Roth, M. (1954), 'Clini-
cal Psychology', Cassell, London.

Mays, J.R. (1962), 'Education and the Urban Child', Liverpool University Press.
Mead, G.H. (1934), 'Mind, Self and Society', University of Chicago Press.
Medlicott, P. (1974), Special teaching for special children, 'New Society', 21 March.
Mercer, J. (1965), Social system perspective and clinical perspective - frames of reference for understanding career patterns of persons labelled as mentally retarded, 'Social Problems', 13.
Merton, R. (1967), 'On Theoretical Sociology', Free Press, New York.
Milner, D. (1975), 'Children and Race', Penguin, Harmondsworth.
Ministry of Education (1945), Handicapped Pupils and School Health Service Regulations, 'Statutory Rules and Orders', no. 1076, HMSO, London.
Ministry of Education (1946), 'Special Educational Treatment', Pamphlet no. 5, HMSO, London.
Ministry of Education (1956), 'Education of the Handicapped Pupil 1945-55', Pamphlet no. 30, HMSO, London.
Ministry of Education (1961a), 'The Use of Independent Schools for Handicapped Pupils', Circular 4/61, HMSO, London.
Ministry of Education (1961b), 'Special Educational Treatment for Educationally Sub-normal Pupils', Circular 11/61, HMSO, London.
Ministry of Education (1961c), Handicapped pupils (certificate) regulations. S.I. no. 476, HMSO, London.
Ministry of Education (1962), Handicapped pupils and Special School amending regulations. S.I. no. 2073, HMSO, London.
Mittler, P. (1970), 'The Psychological Assessment of Mental and Physical Handicap', Methuen, London.
Moore, R.B.W. (1969), The nature of educational psychology in school psychological and child guidance services, 'Bulletin of the British Psychological Society', 22.
Moser, C.A., and Kalton, G. (1971), 'Survey Methods in Social Investigation', Heinemann, London.
Mowat, C.L. (1916), 'The Charity Organisation Society 1869-1913', Methuen, London.
Musgrove, F. (1966), 'Family, Education and Society', Routledge & Kegan Paul, London.
National Children's Bureau (1970), 'Report of a Working Party on Children with Special Needs' (The Younghusband Report), London.
National Union of Teachers (1930), 'The Education of Mentally Defective Children reply to the Wood Committee Report', London.

National Union of Teachers (1961), 'The ascertainment of
ESN children', Pamphlet no. 232, London.
National Union of Teachers (1964), 'The special school -
aims, facilities and amenities', London.
National Union of Teachers (1979), 'Special Educational
Needs - the N.U.T. response to the Warnock Report',
London.
'New Society' (1978), Race and teachers, the Schools
Council study, 16 February.
Nicol, A. (1971), Psychiatric disorders in children of
Caribbean immigrants, 'Journal of Psychology and Psychia-
try', vol. 12.
O'Connor, N., and Tizard, J. (1956), 'The Social Problems
of Mental Deficiency', Pergamon Press.
Omar, R. (1971), ESN children - labelled for life, 'Race
Today', January.
Osler, S. and Cooke, R. (1965), 'The Biological Basis of
Mental Retardation', Johns Hopkins Press, Baltimore.
Patterson, S. (1963), 'Dark Strangers', Oxford University
Press.
Payne, J. (ed.) (1974), 'EPA Surveys and Statistics',
vol. 2, 'Educational Priority', HMSO, London.
Plowden Report, see 'Children and their Primary Schools'
(1967).
Presland, J. (1970), Who should go to ESN schools?,
'Special Education', vol. 59, no. 1.
Prince, S. (1967), Mental health problems in pre-school
West Indian children, 'Maternal and Child Care', 3.
Pritchard, D.G. (1963), 'Education and the Handicapped
1760-1960', Routledge & Kegan Paul, London.
Pritchard, D.G. (1972), The Development of Educational
Provision for mentally handicapped children, in Laing,
A.F. (ed.), 'Educating Mentally Handicapped Children',
University College of Swansea.
'Psychologists in the Education Service. The Report of a
Working Party appointed by the Secretary of State for
Education and Science' (1968) (The Summerfield Report),
HMSO, London.
Race and teachers - the Schools Council study, 'New
Society' (1978), 16 February.
Reismann, F. (1962), 'The Culturally Deprived Child',
Wiley, New York.
Renhard, D.M. (1971), An attempt to increase non-verbal
intelligence test scores by the programming of the
principles of inductive reasoning, unpublished MEd dis-
sertation, University of Birmingham.
'Report of the Committee on Maladjusted Children' (1955)
(The Underwood Report), HMSO, London.
'Report of the Royal Commission on the Blind, the Deaf,

the Dumb and others of the United Kingdom' (1889), 4 vols
(The Egerton Commission), HMSO, London.
'Report of the Royal Commission on the Care and Control of
the Feeble-Minded' (1908), 8 vols, HMSO, London.
Rex, J. (1970), 'Race Relations in Sociological Theory',
Weidenfield & Nicolson, London.
Rex, J. (1972), Nature versus nurture - the significance
of the revived debate, in Richardson, K., and Spear, D.
(eds), 'Race, Culture and Intelligence', Penguin, Har-
mondsworth.
Rex, J., and Tomlinson, S. (1979), 'Colonial Immigrants in
a British City - a Class Analysis', Routledge & Kegan
Paul, London.
Rose, S., Hambley, J., and Haywood, J. (1973), 'Science,
Racism and Ideology', Socialist Register re-print.
Rousseau, J.-J. (1961), 'Emile', Garnier, Paris.
Rutter, M., Tizard, J., and Whitmore, K. (eds) (1970),
'Education, Health and Behaviour', Longman, London.
Rutter, M., and Madge, N. (1976), 'Cycles of Disadvan-
tage', Heinemann, London.
Saint, K. (1963), Scholastic and sociological adjustment
of Punjabi-speaking children in Smethwick, unpublished MEd
dissertation, University of Birmingham.
Sampson, O.C. (1976), Treatment practices in British child
guidance clinics - a historical overview, 'Educational
Review', vol. 29, no. 1.
Saunders, M. (1973), Home influences affecting ESN child-
ren, unpublished MPhil. dissertation, University of
Nottingham.
Savage, R.D. (1968), 'Psychometric Assessment of the
Individual Child', Penguin, Harmondsworth.
Schools Council (1969), 'Scope 1 - an introductory course
for immigrant children', Longman, London.
Schonell, F. (1942), 'Backwardness in the Basic Subjects',
Oliver & Boyd, London.
Schutz, A. (1962), 'Collected Papers', vol. 1, Martinus
Nijhoff, The Hague.
Schutz, A. (1967), 'The Phenomenology of the Social
World', Northwestern University Press.
Scott, M.B., and Lyman, S.B. (1968), Accounts, 'American
Sociological Review', vol. 33, no. 1.
Seeley, J. (1966), The 'making' and 'taking' of problems,
'Social Problems', 14.
Segal, S. (1960), The ascertainment of ESN children,
'Forward Trends', vol. 5.
Segal, S. (1974), 'No Child is Ineducable', Pergamon
Press, Oxford.
Select Committee on Race Relations and Immigration (1973),
'Education', 3 vols, HMSO, London.

Select Committee on Race Relations and Immigration (1976-7), 'The West Indian Community', 3 vols, HMSO, London.

Sharpe, R. and Green, A. (1975), 'Education and Social Control', Routledge & Kegan Paul, London.

Shearer, E. (1975), Survey of ESN schools in Cheshire, 'Special Education - Forward Trends', vol. 4, no. 2.

Sheridan, M.D. (1965), The handicapped child and his home, National Convocation lecture.

Shockley, W. (1971), Models, mathematics and the moral obligation to diagnose the origin of Negro I.Q. defects, 'Review of Educational Research', 41.

Shuttleworth, G.E. (1888), The education of children of abnormally weak mental capacity, 'Journal of Mental Science', vol. 34, no. 145.

'Special Education - Forward Trends' (1977), vol. 4, no. 3. Interview with the Secretary of State for Education and Science.

'Special Educational Needs. Report of the Committee of Enquiry into the Education of Handicapped Children and Young People (1978) (The Warnock Report), Cmnd 7212, HMSO, London.

Spectre, M., and Kitsuse, J.I. (1978), 'Constructing Social Problems', Cummings, California.

Squibb, P. (1977), Some notes towards the analysis of the less-able or backward child, 'Journal of Further and Higher Education', vol. 1, no. 3.

Stein, Z., and Susser, M. (1960), The families of dull children - a classification for predicting careers, 'British Journal of Preventative Social Medicine', 14.

Stein, Z., and Susser, M. (1960), Families of dull children pt II - identifying family types and subcultures, 'Journal of Mental Science', vol. 106, no. 445.

Stein, Z., and Susser, M. (1960), Families of dull children pt III - social selection by family type, 'Journal of Mental Science', vol. 106, no. 445.

Stein, Z., and Susser, M. (1960), Families of dull children pt IV - increments in intelligence, 'Journal of Mental Science', vol. 106, no. 445.

Stones, E. (1979), The colour of conceptual learning, in Verma, G.K., and Bagley, C. (eds), 'Race, Education and Identity', Macmillan, London.

Stott, D.H. (1966), 'Studies of Troublesome Children', Tavistock, London.

Summerfield Report, see 'Psychologists in the Education Service ...' (1968).

Sutton, A. (1977), 'Retardation and Education pt one - The ESN(M) a problem of definition', Centre for Child Studies, University of Birmingham.

Sutton, A. (1977), 'Retardation and Education pt two -

towards a re-definition', Centre for Child Studies, University of Birmingham.

Tansley, A.E. (1967), 'Reading and Remedial Reading', Routledge & Kegan Paul, London.

Tansley, A.E. (1973), Special Education Treatment in schools, 'Review' (Journal of the Education Development Centre, Birmingham), no. 14.

Tansley, A.E., and Gulliford, R. (1960), 'The Education of Slow-Learning Children', Routledge & Kegan Paul, London.

Taylor, W. (1968), Training the head, in Allen, R. (ed.), 'Headship in the 70's', Blackwell, London.

Terman, L.M. (1916), 'The Measurement of Intelligence', Houghton Mifflin, Boston.

Terman, L.M., and Merrill, R. (1960), 'The Stamford-Binet Intelligence Scale Manual for the third revision of the L-M', Houghton Mifflin, Boston.

'The West Indian Community: Observations on the Report of the Select Committee on Race Relations and Immigration', Cmnd 7186, HMSO, London.

Tomlinson, S. (1977), Race and education in Britain 1960-77 - an overview of the literature, 'Race Relations Abstracts', vol. 2, no. 4.

Townsend, H.E.R., and Brittan, E. (1971), 'Immigrant Pupils in England', NFER, Slough.

Tredgold, A.F. (1947), 'A Text-Book of Mental Deficiency', 7th edn, Balliere, Tindal & Cox, London (first edn, 1914).

Underwood Report, see 'Report of the Committee on Maladjusted Children' (1955).

UNESCO (1951), 'The Race Concept', Paris.

UNESCO (1973), 'The Present Situation and Trends of Research in the Field of Special Education', Paris.

Vaizey, J. (1978), Special Schooling for all, 'Times Educational Supplement', 23 June.

Verma, G.K. and Bagley, C. (eds) (1979), 'Race, Education and Identity', Macmillan, London.

Vernon, P. (1969), 'Intelligence and Cultural Environment', Methuen, London.

Waller, W. (1932), 'The Sociology of Teaching', Wiley, New York.

Warner, F. (1888), A method of examining children as to their development and brain condition, 'British Medical Journal', September.

Warnock Report, see 'Special Educational Needs ...' 1978).

Weber, Max (1930), 'The Protestant Ethic and the Spirit of Capitalism', Unwin University Books. London.

Weber, Max (1964), 'The Theory of Social and Economic Organisations', Free Press, New York.

Wechsler, D. (1949), 'The Wechsler Intelligence Scale for Children', The Psychological Corporation, New York.

West, D.J., and Farringdon, D.P. (1973), 'Who Becomes Delinquent?', Heinemann Educational, London.
Who's educating who - the Black Education movement and the struggle for power (1975), 'Race Today', August.
Wight, J. (1970), Teaching English to West Indian children, Schools Council working paper 29, Evans-Methuen, London.
Williams, P. (1965), The ascertainment of ESN children, 'Educational Research', vol. 7, no. 2.
Williams, P. (1970), Slow learning children and educational problems, in Mittler, P. (ed.), 'The Psychological Assessment of Mental and Physical Handicap', Methuen, London.
Williams, P. (1974), Advances in training educational psychologists, in Pringle, N.K., and Verma, V.P. (eds), 'Advances in Educational Psychology', University of London Press.
Williams, P., and Gruber, E. (1967), 'Response to Special Schooling', Longman, London.
Winch, P. (1958), 'The Idea of a Social Science', Routledge & Kegan Paul, London.
World Health Organisation (1968), 'Organisation of Services for the Mentally Retarded', Report series 392, Geneva.
Yerkes, R.M., and Foster, J.C. (1923), 'A Point Scale for Measuring Mental Ability', Wariwck & York, Baltimore.
Yule, W., Berger, M., and Rutter, M. (1975), Children of West Indian immigrants, 2. Intellectual performance and reading attainment, 'Journal of Child Psychology and psychiatry', vol. 16.

ACTS OF PARLIAMENT

1867 Metropolitan Poor Act, Victoria c.6.
1870 Elementary Education Act, Victoria c.75.
1876 Elementary Education Act, Victoria, c.79.
1886 Idiots Act, Victoria c.25.
1891 Lunacy Act, Victoria c.65.
1893 Elementary Education (Blind and Deaf Children) Act, Victoria c.42.
1889 Elementary Education (Defective and Epileptic Children) Act, Victoria c.32.
1902 Education Act, Edward, c.42.
1903 Elementary Education (Defective and Epileptic Children) amendment act, Edward VII, c.13.
1913 Mental Deficiency Act, George V, c.28.
1914 Elementary Education (Defective and Epileptic Children) Act, George V, c.45.

1918   Education Act, George V, c.39.
1921   Education Act, George V, c.51.
1927   Mental Deficiency Act, George V, c.33.
1944   Education Act, George VI, c.31.
1946   National Health Services Act, George VI, c.81.
1948   Education (Miscellaneous Provisions) Act, George VI, c.40.
1959   Mental Health Act, Elizabeth II, c.72.
1970   Education (Handicapped Children) Act, Elizabeth II, c.52.
1976   Education Act, Elizabeth II.

Index

Routledge Social Science Series

Routledge & Kegan Paul   London, Henley and Boston

39 Store Street,
London WC1E 7DD
Broadway House,
Newtown Road,
Henley-on-Thames,
Oxon RG9 1EN
9 Park Street,
Boston, Mass. 02108

Contents

*Authors wishing to submit manuscripts for any series
in this catalogue should send them to the Social Science Editor,
Routledge & Kegan Paul Ltd, 39 Store Street,
London WC1E 7DD.*
● *Books so marked are available in paperback.*
○ *Books so marked are available in paperback only.*
*All books are in metric Demy 8vo format (216 × 138mm approx.)
unless otherwise stated.*

International Library of Sociology
General Editor John Rex

GENERAL SOCIOLOGY

Barnsley, J. H. The Social Reality of Ethics. *464 pp.*
Brown, Robert. Explanation in Social Science. *208 pp.*
● Rules and Laws in Sociology. *192 pp.*
Bruford, W. H. Chekhov and His Russia. *A Sociological Study. 244 pp.*
Burton, F. and **Carlen, P.** Official Discourse. *On Discourse Analysis, Government Publications, Ideology. About 140 pp.*
Cain, Maureen E. Society and the Policeman's Role. *326 pp.*
● **Fletcher, Colin.** Beneath the Surface. *An Account of Three Styles of Sociological Research. 221 pp.*
Gibson, Quentin. The Logic of Social Enquiry. *240 pp.*
Glassner, B. Essential Interactionism. *208 pp.*
Glucksmann, M. Structuralist Analysis in Contemporary Social Thought. *212 pp.*
Gurvitch, Georges. Sociology of Law. *Foreword by Roscoe Pound. 264 pp.*
Hinkle, R. Founding Theory of American Sociology 1881–1913. *About 350 pp.*
Homans, George C. Sentiments and Activities. *336 pp.*
Johnson, Harry M. Sociology: *A Systematic Introduction. Foreword by Robert K. Merton. 710 pp.*
● **Keat, Russell** and **Urry, John.** Social Theory as Science. *278 pp.*
Mannheim, Karl. Essays on Sociology and Social Psychology. *Edited by Paul Keckskemeti. With Editorial Note by Adolph Lowe. 344 pp.*
Martindale, Don. The Nature and Types of Sociological Theory. *292 pp.*
● **Maus, Heinz.** A Short History of Sociology. *234 pp.*
Myrdal, Gunnar. Value in Social Theory: *A Collection of Essays on Methodology. Edited by Paul Streeten. 332 pp.*
Ogburn, William F. and **Nimkoff, Meyer F.** A Handbook of Sociology. *Preface by Karl Mannheim. 656 pp. 46 figures. 35 tables.*
Parsons, Talcott and **Smelser, Neil J.** Economy and Society: *A Study in the Integration of Economic and Social Theory. 362 pp.*
Payne, G., Dingwall, R., Payne, J. and **Carter, M.** Sociology and Social Research. *About 250 pp.*
Podgórecki, A. Practical Social Sciences. *About 200 pp.*
Podgórecki, A. and **Łos, M.** Multidimensional Sociology. *268 pp.*
Raffel, S. Matters of Fact. *A Sociological Inquiry. 152 pp.*
● **Rex, John.** Key Problems of Sociological Theory. *220 pp.*
Sociology and the Demystification of the Modern World. *282 pp.*
● **Rex, John.** (Ed.) Approaches to Sociology. *Contributions by Peter Abell, Frank Bechhofer, Basil Bernstein, Ronald Fletcher, David Frisby, Miriam Glucksmann, Peter Lassman, Herminio Martins, John Rex, Roland Robertson, John Westergaard and Jock Young. 302 pp.*
Rigby, A. Alternative Realities. *352 pp.*
Roche, M. Phenomenology, Language and the Social Sciences. *374 pp.*
Sahay, A. Sociological Analysis. *220 pp.*
Strasser, Hermann. The Normative Structure of Sociology. *Conservative and Emancipatory Themes in Social Thought. About 340 pp.*
Strong, P. Ceremonial Order of the Clinic. *267 pp.*
Urry, John. Reference Groups and the Theory of Revolution. *244 pp.*
Weinberg, E. Development of Sociology in the Soviet Union. *173 pp.*

FOREIGN CLASSICS OF SOCIOLOGY

● **Gerth, H. H.** and **Mills, C. Wright.** From Max Weber: *Essays in Sociology. 502 pp.*

● **Tönnies, Ferdinand.** Community and Association *(Gemeinschaft und Gesell-schaft).\Translated and Supplemented by Charles P. Loomis. Foreword by Pitirim A. Sorokin. 334 pp.*

SOCIAL STRUCTURE

Andreski, Stanislav. Military Organization and Society. *Foreword by Professor A. R. Radcliffe-Brown. 226 pp. 1 folder.*

Broom, L., Lancaster Jones, F., McDonnell, P. and **Williams, T.** The Inheritance of Inequality. *About 180 pp.*

Carlton, Eric. Ideology and Social Order. *Foreword by Professor Philip Abrahams. About 320 pp.*

Clegg, S. and **Dunkerley, D.** Organization, Class and Control. *614 pp.*

Coontz, Sydney H. Population Theories and the Economic Interpretation. *202 pp.*

Coser, Lewis. The Functions of Social Conflict. *204 pp.*

Crook, I. and **D.** The First Years of the Yangyi Commune. *304 pp., illustrated.*

Dickie-Clark, H. F. Marginal Situation: *A Sociological Study of a Coloured Group. 240 pp. 11 tables.*

Giner, S. and **Archer, M. S.** (Eds) Contemporary Europe: *Social Structures and Cultural Patterns, 336 pp.*

● **Glaser, Barney** and **Strauss, Anselm L.** Status Passage: *A Formal Theory. 212 pp.*

Glass, D. V. (Ed.) Social Mobility in Britain. *Contributions by J. Berent, T. Bottomore, R. C. Chambers, J. Floud, D. V. Glass, J. R. Hall, H. T. Himmelweit, R. K. Kelsall, F. M. Martin, C. A. Moser, R. Mukherjee and W. Ziegel. 420 pp.*

Kelsall, R. K. Higher Civil Servants in Britain: *From 1870 to the Present Day. 268 pp. 31 tables.*

● **Lawton, Denis.** Social Class, Language and Education. *192 pp.*

McLeish, John. The Theory of Social Change: *Four Views Considered. 128 pp.*

● **Marsh, David C.** The Changing Social Structure of England and Wales, 1871–1961. *Revised edition. 288 pp.*

Menzies, Ken. Talcott Parsons and the Social Image of Man. *About 208 pp.*

● **Mouzelis, Nicos.** Organization and Bureaucracy. *An Analysis of Modern Theories. 240 pp.*

● **Ossowski, Stanislaw.** Class Structure in the Social Consciousness. *210 pp.*

● **Podgórecki, Adam.** Law and Society. *302 pp.*

Renner, Karl. Institutions of Private Law and Their Social Functions. *Edited, with an Introduction and Notes, by O. Kahn-Freud. Translated by Agnes Schwarzschild. 316 pp.*

Rex, J. and **Tomlinson, S.** Colonial Immigrants in a British City. *A Class Analysis. 368 pp.*

Smooha, S. Israel: Pluralism and Conflict. *472 pp.*

Wesolowski, W. Class, Strata and Power. *Trans. and with Introduction by G. Kolankiewicz. 160 pp.*

Zureik, E. Palestinians in Israel. *A Study in Internal Colonialism. 264 pp.*

SOCIOLOGY AND POLITICS

Acton, T. A. Gypsy Politics and Social Change. *316 pp.*

Burton, F. Politics of Legitimacy. *Struggles in a Belfast Community. 250 pp.*

Crook, I. and **D.** Revolution in a Chinese Village. *Ten Mile Inn. 216 pp., illustrated.*

Etzioni-Halevy, E. Political Manipulation and Administrative Power. *A Comparative Study. About 200 pp.*

Fielding, N. The National Front. *About 250 pp.*

● **Hechter, Michael.** Internal Colonialism. *The Celtic Fringe in British National Development, 1536–1966. 380 pp.*

Kornhauser, William. The Politics of Mass Society. *272 pp. 20 tables.*

Korpi, W. The Working Class in Welfare Capitalism. *Work, Unions and Politics in Sweden. 472 pp.*

Kroes, R. Soldiers and Students. *A Study of Right- and Left-wing Students. 174 pp.*

Martin, Roderick. Sociology of Power. *About 272 pp.*

Merquior, J. G. Rousseau and Weber. *A Study in the Theory of Legitimacy. About 288 pp.*

Myrdal, Gunnar. The Political Element in the Development of Economic Theory. *Translated from the German by Paul Streeten. 282 pp.*

Varma, B. N. The Sociology and Politics of Development. *A Theoretical Study. 236 pp.*

Wong, S.-L. Sociology and Socialism in Contemporary China. *160 pp.*

Wootton, Graham. Workers, Unions and the State. *188 pp.*

CRIMINOLOGY

Ancel, Marc. Social Defence: *A Modern Approach to Criminal Problems. Foreword by Leon Radzinowicz. 240 pp.*

Athens, L. Violent Criminal Acts and Actors. *104 pp.*

Cain, Maureen E. Society and the Policeman's Role. *326 pp.*

Cloward, Richard A. and **Ohlin, Lloyd E.** Delinquency and Opportunity: *A Theory of Delinquent Gangs. 248 pp.*

Downes, David M. The Delinquent Solution. *A Study in Subcultural Theory. 296 pp.*

Friedlander, Kate. The Psycho-Analytical Approach to Juvenile Delinquency: *Theory, Case Studies, Treatment. 320 pp.*

Gleuck, Sheldon and **Eleanor.** Family Environment and Delinquency. *With the statistical assistance of Rose W. Kneznek. 340 pp.*

Lopez-Rey, Manuel. Crime. *An Analytical Appraisal. 288 pp.*

Mannheim, Hermann. Comparative Criminology: *A Text Book. Two volumes. 442 pp. and 380 pp.*

Morris, Terence. The Criminal Area: *A Study in Social Ecology. Foreword by Hermann Mannheim. 232 pp. 25 tables. 4 maps.*

Rock, Paul. Making People Pay. *338 pp.*

● **Taylor, Ian, Walton, Paul** and **Young, Jock.** The New Criminology. *For a Social Theory of Deviance. 325 pp.*

● **Taylor, Ian, Walton, Paul** and **Young, Jock.** (Eds) Critical Criminology. *268 pp.*

SOCIAL PSYCHOLOGY

Bagley, Christopher. The Social Psychology of the Epileptic Child. *320 pp.*

Brittan, Arthur. Meanings and Situations. *224 pp.*

Carroll, J. Break-Out from the Crystal Palace. *200 pp.*

● **Fleming, C. M.** Adolescence: Its Social Psychology. *With an Introduction to recent findings from the fields of Anthropology, Physiology, Medicine, Psychometrics and Sociometry. 288 pp.*

● The Social Psychology of Education: *An Introduction and Guide to Its Study. 136 pp.*

Linton, Ralph. The Cultural Background of Personality. *132 pp.*

● **Mayo, Elton.** The Social Problems of an Industrial Civilization. *With an Appendix on the Political Problem. 180 pp.*

Ottaway, A. K. C. Learning Through Group Experience. *176 pp.*

Plummer, Ken. Sexual Stigma. *An Interactionist Account. 254 pp.*

● **Rose, Arnold M.** (Ed.) Human Behaviour and Social Processes: *an Interactionist Approach. Contributions by Arnold M. Rose, Ralph H. Turner, Anselm Strauss, Everett C. Hughes, E. Franklin Frazier, Howard S. Becker et al. 696 pp.*

Smelser, Neil J. Theory of Collective Behaviour. *448 pp.*

Stephenson, Geoffrey M. The Development of Conscience. *128 pp.*

Young, Kimball. Handbook of Social Psychology. *658 pp. 16 figures. 10 tables.*

SOCIOLOGY OF THE FAMILY

Bell, Colin R. Middle Class Families: *Social and Geographical Mobility. 224 pp.*
Burton, Lindy. Vulnerable Children. *272 pp.*
Gavron, Hannah. The Captive Wife: *Conflicts of Household Mothers. 190 pp.*
George, Victor and **Wilding, Paul.** Motherless Families. *248 pp.*
Klein, Josephine. Samples from English Cultures.
  1. Three Preliminary Studies and Aspects of Adult Life in England. *447 pp.*
  2. Child-Rearing Practices and Index. *247 pp.*
Klein, Viola. The Feminine Character. *History of an Ideology. 244 pp.*
McWhinnie, Alexina M. Adopted Children. *How They Grow Up. 304 pp.*
● **Morgan, D. H. J.** Social Theory and the Family. *About 320 pp.*
● **Myrdal, Alva** and **Klein, Viola.** Women's Two Roles: *Home and Work. 238 pp. 27 tables.*
Parsons, Talcott and **Bales, Robert F.** Family: Socialization and Interaction Process. *In collaboration with James Olds, Morris Zelditch and Philip E. Slater. 456 pp. 50 figures and tables.*

SOCIAL SERVICES

Bastide, Roger. The Sociology of Mental Disorder. *Translated from the French by Jean McNeil. 260 pp.*
Carlebach, Julius. Caring For Children in Trouble. *266 pp.*
George, Victor. Foster Care. *Theory and Practice. 234 pp.*
  Social Security: *Beveridge and After. 258 pp.*
George, V. and **Wilding, P.** Motherless Families. *248 pp.*
● **Goetschius, George W.** Working with Community Groups. *256 pp.*
Goetschius, George W. and **Tash, Joan.** Working with Unattached Youth. *416 pp.*
Heywood, Jean S. Children in Care. *The Development of the Service for the Deprived Child. Third revised edition. 284 pp.*
King, Roy D., Ranes, Norma V. and **Tizard, Jack.** Patterns of Residential Care. *356 pp.*
Leigh, John. Young People and Leisure. *256 pp.*
● **Mays, John.** (Ed.) Penelope Hall's Social Services of England and Wales. *368 pp.*
Morris, Mary. Voluntary Work and the Welfare State. *300 pp.*
Nokes, P. L. The Professional Task in Welfare Practice. *152 pp.*
Timms, Noel. Psychiatric Social Work in Great Britain (1939–1962). *280 pp.*
●   Social Casework: *Principles and Practice. 256 pp.*

SOCIOLOGY OF EDUCATION

Banks, Olive. Parity and Prestige in English Secondary Education: a Study in Educational Sociology. *272 pp.*
● **Blyth, W. A. L.** English Primary Education. *A Sociological Description.*
  2. Background. *168 pp.*
Collier, K. G. The Social Purposes of Education: *Personal and Social Values in Education. 268 pp.*
Evans, K. M. Sociometry and Education. *158 pp.*
● **Ford, Julienne.** Social Class and the Comprehensive School. *192 pp.*
Foster, P. J. Education and Social Change in Ghana. *336 pp. 3 maps.*
Fraser, W. R. Education and Society in Modern France. *150 pp.*
Grace, Gerald R. Role Conflict and the Teacher. *150 pp.*
Hans, Nicholas. New Trends in Education in the Eighteenth Century. *278 pp. 19 tables.*
●   Comparative Education: *A Study of Educational Factors and Traditions. 360 pp.*
● **Hargreaves, David.** Interpersonal Relations and Education. *432 pp.*
●   Social Relations in a Secondary School. *240 pp.*
  School Organization and Pupil Involvement. *A Study of Secondary Schools.*

● **Mannheim, Karl** and **Stewart, W. A. C.** An Introduction to the Sociology of Education. *206 pp.*
● **Musgrove, F.** Youth and the Social Order. *176 pp.*
● **Ottaway, A. K. C.** Education and Society: An Introduction to the Sociology of Education. *With an Introduction by W. O. Lester Smith. 212 pp.*
 Peers, Robert. Adult Education: *A Comparative Study. Revised edition. 398 pp.*
 Stratta, Erica. The Education of Borstal Boys. *A Study of their Educational Experiences prior to, and during, Borstal Training. 256 pp.*
● **Taylor, P. H., Reid, W. A.** and **Holley, B. J.** The English Sixth Form. *A Case Study in Curriculum Research. 198 pp.*

SOCIOLOGY OF CULTURE

 Eppel, E. M. and **M.** Adolescents and Morality: *A Study of some Moral Values and Dilemmas of Working Adolescents in the Context of a changing Climate of Opinion. Foreword by W. J. H. Sprott. 268 pp. 39 tables.*
● **Fromm, Erich.** The Fear of Freedom. *286 pp.*
● The Sane Society. *400 pp.*
 Johnson, L. The Cultural Critics. *From Matthew Arnold to Raymond Williams. 233 pp.*
 Mannheim, Karl. Essays on the Sociology of Culture. *Edited by Ernst Mannheim in co-operation with Paul Kecskemeti. Editorial Note by Adolph Lowe. 280 pp.*
 Merquior, J. G. The Veil and the Mask. *Essays on Culture and Ideology. Foreword by Ernest Gellner. 140 pp.*
 Zijderfeld, A. C. On Clichés. *The Supersedure of Meaning by Function in Modernity. 150 pp.*

SOCIOLOGY OF RELIGION

 Argyle, Michael and **Beit-Hallahmi, Benjamin.** The Social Psychology of Religion. *256 pp.*
 Glasner, Peter E. The Sociology of Secularisation. *A Critique of a Concept. 146 pp.*
 Hall, J. R. The Ways Out. *Utopian Communal Groups in an Age of Babylon. 280 pp.*
 Ranson, S., Hinings, B. and **Bryman, A.** Clergy, Ministers and Priests. *216 pp.*
 Stark, Werner. The Sociology of Religion. *A Study of Christendom.*
  Volume II. *Sectarian Religion. 368 pp.*
  Volume III. *The Universal Church. 464 pp.*
  Volume IV. *Types of Religious Man. 352 pp.*
  Volume V. *Types of Religious Culture. 464 pp.*
 Turner, B. S. Weber and Islam. *216 pp.*
 Watt, W. Montgomery. Islam and the Integration of Society. *320 pp.*

SOCIOLOGY OF ART AND LITERATURE

 Jarvie, Ian C. Towards a Sociology of the Cinema. *A Comparative Essay on the Structure and Functioning of a Major Entertainment Industry. 405 pp.*
 Rust, Frances S. Dance in Society. *An Analysis of the Relationships between the Social Dance and Society in England from the Middle Ages to the Present Day. 256 pp. 8 pp. of plates.*
 Schücking, L. L. The Sociology of Literary Taste. *112 pp.*
 Wolff, Janet. Hermeneutic Philosophy and the Sociology of Art. *150 pp.*

SOCIOLOGY OF KNOWLEDGE

 Diesing, P. Patterns of Discovery in the Social Sciences. *262 pp.*

● **Douglas, J. D.** (Ed.) Understanding Everyday Life. *370 pp.*
● **Hamilton, P.** Knowledge and Social Structure. *174 pp.*
  Jarvie, I. C. Concepts and Society. *232 pp.*
  Mannheim, Karl. Essays on the Sociology of Knowledge. *Edited by Paul Kecskemeti. Editorial Note by Adolph Lowe. 353 pp.*
  Remmling, Gunter W. The Sociology of Karl Mannheim. *With a Bibliographical Guide to the Sociology of Knowledge, Ideological Analysis, and Social Planning. 255 pp.*
  Remmling, Gunter W. (Ed.) Towards the Sociology of Knowledge. *Origin and Development of a Sociological Thought Style. 463 pp.*
  Scheler, M. Problems of a Sociology of Knowledge. *Trans. by M. S. Frings. Edited and with an Introduction by K. Stikkers. 232 pp.*

URBAN SOCIOLOGY

Aldridge, M. The British New Towns. *A Programme Without a Policy. 232 pp.*
Ashworth, William. The Genesis of Modern British Town Planning: *A Study in Economic and Social History of the Nineteenth and Twentieth Centuries. 288 pp.*
Brittan, A. The Privatised World. *196 pp.*
Cullingworth, J. B. Housing Needs and Planning Policy: *A Restatement of the Problems of Housing Need and 'Overspill' in England and Wales. 232 pp. 44 tables. 8 maps.*
Dickinson, Robert E. City and Region: *A Geographical Interpretation. 608 pp. 125 figures.*
  The West European City: *A Geographical Interpretation. 600 pp. 129 maps. 29 plates.*
Humphreys, Alexander J. New Dubliners: *Urbanization and the Irish Family. Foreword by George C. Homans. 304 pp.*
Jackson, Brian. Working Class Community: *Some General Notions raised by a Series of Studies in Northern England. 192 pp.*
● **Mann, P. H.** An Approach to Urban Sociology. *240 pp.*
  Mellor, J. R. Urban Sociology in an Urbanized Society. *326 pp.*
  Morris, R. N. and **Mogey, J.** The Sociology of Housing. *Studies at Berinsfield. 232 pp. 4 pp. plates.*
  Mullan, R. Stevenage Ltd. *About 250 pp.*
  Rex, J. and **Tomlinson, S.** Colonial Immigrants in a British City. *A Class Analysis. 368 pp.*
  Rosser, C. and **Harris, C.** The Family and Social Change. *A Study of Family and Kinship in a South Wales Town. 352 pp. 8 maps.*
● **Stacey, Margaret, Batsone, Eric, Bell, Colin** and **Thurcott, Anne.** Power, Persistence and Change. *A Second Study of Banbury. 196 pp.*

RURAL SOCIOLOGY

Mayer, Adrian C. Peasants in the Pacific. *A Study of Fiji Indian Rural Society. 248 pp. 20 plates.*
Williams, W. M. The Sociology of an English Village: *Gosforth. 272 pp. 12 figures. 13 tables.*

SOCIOLOGY OF INDUSTRY AND DISTRIBUTION

Dunkerley, David. The Foreman. *Aspects of Task and Structure. 192 pp.*
Eldridge, J. E. T. Industrial Disputes. *Essays in the Sociology of Industrial Relations. 288 pp.*
Hollowell, Peter G. The Lorry Driver. *272 pp.*
● **Oxaal, I., Barnett, T.** and **Booth, D.** (Eds) Beyond the Sociology of Development.

Economy and Society in Latin America and Africa. 295 pp.

Smelser, Neil J. Social Change in the Industrial Revolution: *An Application of Theory to the Lancashire Cotton Industry, 1770–1840. 468 pp. 12 figures. 14 tables.*

Watson, T. J. The Personnel Managers. *A Study in the Sociology of Work and Employment, 262 pp.*

ANTHROPOLOGY

Brandel-Syrier, Mia. Reeftown Elite. *A Study of Social Mobility in a Modern African Community on the Reef. 376 pp.*

Dickie-Clark, H. F. The Marginal Situation. *A Sociological Study of a Coloured Group. 236 pp.*

Dube, S. C. Indian Village. *Foreword by Morris Edward Opler. 276 pp. 4 plates.*
India's Changing Villages: *Human Factors in Community Development. 260 pp. 8 plates. 1 map.*

Fei, H.-T. Peasant Life in China. *A Field Study of Country Life in the Yangtze Valley. With a foreword by Bronislaw Malinowski. 328 pp. 16 pp. plates.*

Firth, Raymond. Malay Fishermen. *Their Peasant Economy. 420 pp. 17 pp. plates.*

Gulliver, P. H. Social Control in an African Society: a Study of the Arusha, Agricultural Masai of Northern Tanganyika. *320 pp. 8 plates. 10 figures.*
Family Herds. *288 pp.*

Jarvie, Ian C. The Revolution in Anthropology. *268 pp.*

Little, Kenneth L. Mende of Sierra Leone. *308 pp. and folder.*
Negroes in Britain. *With a New Introduction and Contemporary Study by Leonard Bloom. 320 pp.*

Tambs-Lyche, H. London Patidars. *About 180 pp.*

Madan, G. R. Western Sociologists on Indian Society. *Marx, Spencer, Weber, Durkheim, Pareto. 384 pp.*

Mayer, A. C. Peasants in the Pacific. *A Study of Fiji Indian Rural Society. 248 pp.*

Meer, Fatima. Race and Suicide in South Africa. *325 pp.*

Smith, Raymond T. The Negro Family in British Guiana: *Family Structure and Social Status in the Villages. With a Foreword by Meyer Fortes. 314 pp. 8 plates. 1 figure. 4 maps.*

SOCIOLOGY AND PHILOSOPHY

Adriaansens, H. Talcott Parsons and the Conceptual Dilemma. *About 224 pp.*

Barnsley, John H. The Social Reality of Ethics. *A Comparative Analysis of Moral Codes. 448 pp.*

Diesing, Paul. Patterns of Discovery in the Social Sciences. *362 pp.*

● **Douglas, Jack D.** (Ed.) Understanding Everyday Life. *Toward the Reconstruction of Sociological Knowledge. Contributions by Alan F. Blum, Aaron W. Cicourel, Norman K. Denzin, Jack D. Douglas, John Heeren, Peter McHugh, Peter K. Manning, Melvin Power, Matthew Speier, Roy Turner, D. Lawrence Wieder, Thomas P. Wilson and Don H. Zimmerman. 370 pp.*

Gorman, Robert A. The Dual Vision. *Alfred Schutz and the Myth of Phenomenological Social Science. 240 pp.*

Jarvie, Ian C. Concepts and Society. *216 pp.*

Kilminster, R. Praxis and Method. *A Sociological Dialogue with Lukács, Gramsci and the Early Frankfurt School. 334 pp.*

● **Pelz, Werner.** The Scope of Understanding in Sociology. *Towards a More Radical Reorientation in the Social Humanistic Sciences. 283 pp.*

Roche, Maurice. Phenomenology, Language and the Social Sciences. *371 pp.*

Sahay, Arun. Sociological Analysis. *212 pp.*

● **Slater, P.** Origin and Significance of the Frankfurt School. *A Marxist Perspective. 185 pp.*

Spurling, L. Phenomenology and the Social World. *The Philosophy of Merleau-Ponty and its Relation to the Social Sciences. 222 pp.*

Wilson, H. T. The American Ideology. *Science, Technology and Organization as Modes of Rationality. 368 pp.*

International Library of Anthropology
General Editor Adam Kuper

● **Ahmed, A. S.** Millennium and Charisma Among Pathans. *A Critical Essay in Social Anthropology. 192 pp.*
  Pukhtun Economy and Society. *Traditional Structure and Economic Development. About 360 pp.*

Barth, F. Selected Essays. *Volume I. About 250 pp.* Selected Essays. *Volume II. About 250 pp.*

Brown, Paula. The Chimbu. *A Study of Change in the New Guinea Highlands. 151 pp.*

Foner, N. Jamaica Farewell. *200 pp.*

Gudeman, Stephen. Relationships, Residence and the Individual. *A Rural Panamanian Community. 288 pp. 11 plates, 5 figures, 2 maps, 10 tables.*
  The Demise of a Rural Economy. *From Subsistence to Capitalism in a Latin American Village. 160 pp.*

Hamnett, Ian. Chieftainship and Legitimacy. *An Anthropological Study of Executive Law in Lesotho. 163 pp.*

Hanson, F. Allan. Meaning in Culture. *127 pp.*

Hazan, H. The Limbo People. *A Study of the Constitution of the Time Universe Among the Aged. About 192 pp.*

Humphreys, S. C. Anthropology and the Greeks. *288 pp.*

Karp, I. Fields of Change Among the Iteso of Kenya. *140 pp.*

Lloyd, P. C. Power and Independence. *Urban Africans' Perception of Social Inequality. 264 pp.*

Parry, J. P. Caste and Kinship in Kangra. *352 pp. Illustrated.*

Pettigrew, Joyce. Robber Noblemen. *A Study of the Political System of the Sikh Jats. 284 pp.*

Street, Brian V. The Savage in Literature. *Representations of 'Primitive' Society in English Fiction, 1858–1920. 207 pp.*

Van Den Berghe, Pierre L. Power and Privilege at an African University. *278 pp.*

International Library of Phenomenology and Moral Sciences
General Editor John O'Neill

Apel, K.-O. Towards a Transformation of Philosophy. *308 pp.*

Bologh, R. W. Dialectical Phenomenology. *Marx's Method. 287 pp.*

Fekete, J. The Critical Twilight. *Explorations in the Ideology of Anglo-American Literary Theory from Eliot to McLuhan. 300 pp.*

Medina, A. Reflection, Time and the Novel. *Towards a Communicative Theory of Literature. 143 pp.*

International Library of Social Policy
General Editor Kathleen Jones

Bayley, M. Mental Handicap and Community Care. *426 pp.*

Bottoms, A. E. and **McClean, J. D.** Defendants in the Criminal Process. *284 pp.*

Bradshaw, J. The Family Fund. *An Initiative in Social Policy. About 224 pp.*

Butler, J. R. Family Doctors and Public Policy. *208 pp.*
Davies, Martin. Prisoners of Society. *Attitudes and Aftercare. 204 pp.*
Gittus, Elizabeth. Flats, Families and the Under-Fives. *285 pp.*
Holman, Robert. Trading in Children. *A Study of Private Fostering. 355 pp.*
Jeffs, A. Young People and the Youth Service. *160 pp.*
Jones, Howard and Cornes, Paul. Open Prisons. *288 pp.*
Jones, Kathleen. History of the Mental Health Service. *428 pp.*
Jones, Kathleen with **Brown, John, Cunningham, W. J., Roberts, Julian** and **Williams, Peter.** Opening the Door. *A Study of New Policies for the Mentally Handicapped. 278 pp.*
Karn, Valerie. Retiring to the Seaside. *400 pp. 2 maps. Numerous tables.*
King, R. D. and **Elliot, K. W.** Albany: Birth of a Prison—End of an Era. *394 pp.*
Thomas, J. E. The English Prison Officer since 1850: *A Study in Conflict. 258 pp.*
Walton, R. G. Women in Social Work. *303 pp.*
● **Woodward, J.** To Do the Sick No Harm. *A Study of the British Voluntary Hospital System to 1875. 234 pp.*

International Library of Welfare and Philosophy
General Editors Noel Timms and David Watson

● **McDermott, F. E.** (Ed.) Self-Determination in Social Work. *A Collection of Essays on Self-determination and Related Concepts by Philosophers and Social Work Theorists. Contributors: F. P. Biestek, S. Bernstein, A. Keith-Lucas, D. Sayer, H. H. Perelman, C. Whittington, R. F. Stalley, F. E. McDermott, I. Berlin, H. J. McCloskey, H. L. A. Hart, J. Wilson, A. I. Melden, S. I. Benn. 254 pp.*
● **Plant, Raymond.** Community and Ideology. *104 pp.*
Ragg, Nicholas M. People Not Cases. *A Philosophical Approach to Social Work. 168 pp.*
● **Timms, Noel** and **Watson, David.** (Eds) Talking About Welfare. *Readings in Philosophy and Social Policy. Contributors: T. H. Marshall, R. B. Brandt, G. H. von Wright, K. Nielsen, M. Cranston, R. M. Titmuss, R. S. Downie, E. Telfer, D. Donnison, J. Benson, P. Leonard, A. Keith-Lucas, D. Walsh, I. T. Ramsey. 320 pp.*
● Philosophy in Social Work. *250 pp.*
● **Weale, A.** Equality and Social Policy. *164 pp.*

Library of Social Work
General Editor Noel Timms

● **Baldock, Peter.** Community Work and Social Work. *140 pp.*
○ **Beedell, Christopher.** Residential Life with Children. *210 pp. Crown 8vo.*
● **Berry, Juliet.** Daily Experience in Residential Life. *A Study of Children and their Care-givers. 202 pp.*
○ Social Work with Children. *190 pp. Crown 8vo.*
● **Brearley, C. Paul.** Residential Work with the Elderly. *116 pp.*
● Social Work, Ageing and Society. *126 pp.*
● **Cheetham, Juliet.** Social Work with Immigrants. *240 pp. Crown 8vo.*
● **Cross, Crispin P.** (Ed.) Interviewing and Communication in Social Work. *Contributions by C. P. Cross, D. Laurenson, B. Strutt, S. Raven. 192 pp. Crown 8vo.*

- **Curnock, Kathleen** and **Hardiker, Pauline.** Towards Practice Theory. *Skills and Methods in Social Assessments. 208 pp.*
- **Davies, Bernard.** The Use of Groups in Social Work Practice. *158 pp.*
- **Davies, Martin.** Support Systems in Social Work. *144 pp.*
- **Ellis, June.** (Ed.) West African Families in Britain. *A Meeting of Two Cultures. Contributions by Pat Stapleton, Vivien Biggs. 150 pp. 1 Map.*
- **Hart, John.** Social Work and Sexual Conduct. *230 pp.*
- **Hutten, Joan M.** Short-Term Contracts in Social Work. *Contributions by Stella M. Hall, Elsie Osborne, Mannie Sher, Eva Sternberg, Elizabeth Tuters. 134 pp.*
- **Jackson, Michael P.** and **Valencia, B. Michael.** Financial Aid Through Social Work. *140 pp.*
- **Jones, Howard.** The Residential Community. *A Setting for Social Work. 150 pp.*
- (Ed.) Towards a New Social Work. *Contributions by Howard Jones, D. A. Fowler, J. R. Cypher, R. G. Walton, Geoffrey Mungham, Philip Priestley, Ian Shaw, M. Bartley, R. Deacon, Irwin Epstein, Geoffrey Pearson. 184 pp.*
- **Jones, Ray** and **Pritchard, Colin.** (Eds) Social Work With Adolescents. *Contributions by Ray Jones, Colin Pritchard, Jack Dunham, Florence Rossetti, Andrew Kerslake, John Burns, William Gregory, Graham Templeman, Kenneth E. Reid, Audrey Taylor. About 170 pp.*
- ○ **Jordon, William.** The Social Worker in Family Situations. *160 pp. Crown 8vo.*
- **Laycock, A. L.** Adolescents and Social Work. *128 pp. Crown 8vo.*
- **Lees, Ray.** Politics and Social Work. *128 pp. Crown 8vo.*
- Research Strategies for Social Welfare. *112 pp. Tables.*
- ○ **McCullough, M. K.** and **Ely, Peter J.** Social Work with Groups. *127 pp. Crown 8vo.*
- **Moffett, Jonathan.** Concepts in Casework Treatment. *128 pp. Crown 8vo.*
- **Parsloe, Phyllida.** Juvenile Justice in Britain and the United States. *The Balance of Needs and Rights. 336 pp.*
- **Plant, Raymond.** Social and Moral Theory in Casework. *112 pp. Crown 8vo.*
- **Priestley, Philip, Fears, Denise** and **Fuller, Roger.** Justice for Juveniles. *The 1969 Children and Young Persons Act: A Case for Reform? 128 pp.*
- **Pritchard, Colin** and **Taylor, Richard.** Social Work: Reform or Revolution? *170 pp.*
- ○ **Pugh, Elisabeth.** Social Work in Child Care. *128 pp. Crown 8vo.*
- **Robinson, Margaret.** Schools and Social Work. *282 pp.*
- ○ **Ruddock, Ralph.** Roles and Relationships. *128 pp. Crown 8vo.*
- **Sainsbury, Eric.** Social Diagnosis in Casework. *118 pp. Crown 8vo.*
- Social Work with Families. *Perceptions of Social Casework among Clients of a Family Service. 188 pp.*
- **Seed, Philip.** The Expansion of Social Work in Britain. *128 pp. Crown 8vo.*
- **Shaw, John.** The Self in Social Work. *124 pp.*
- **Smale, Gerald G.** Prophecy, Behaviour and Change. *An Examination of Self-fulfilling Prophecies in Helping Relationships. 116 pp. Crown 8vo.*
- **Smith, Gilbert.** Social Need. *Policy, Practice and Research. 155 pp.*
- Social Work and the Sociology of Organisations. *124 pp. Revised edition.*
- **Sutton, Carole.** Psychology for Social Workers and Counsellors. *An Introduction. 248 pp.*
- **Timms, Noel.** Language of Social Casework. *122 pp. Crown 8vo.*
- Recording in Social Work. *124 pp. Crown 8vo.*
- **Todd, F. Joan.** Social Work with the Mentally Subnormal. *96 pp. Crown 8vo.*
- **Walrond-Skinner, Sue.** Family Therapy. *The Treatment of Natural Systems. 172 pp.*
- **Warham, Joyce.** An Introduction to Administration for Social Workers. *Revised edition. 112 pp.*
- An Open Case. *The Organisational Context of Social Work. 172 pp.*
- ○ **Wittenberg, Isca Salzberger.** Psycho-Analytic Insight and Relationships. *A Kleinian Approach. 196 pp. Crown 8vo.*

Primary Socialization, Language and Education
General Editor   Basil Bernstein

Adlam, Diana S., *with the assistance of Geoffrey Turner and Lesley Lineker.* Code in Context. *272 pp.*

Bernstein, Basil. Class, Codes and Control. *3 volumes.*
● 1. *Theoretical Studies Towards a Sociology of Language. 254 pp.*
   2. *Applied Studies Towards a Sociology of Language. 377 pp.*
● 3. *Towards a Theory of Educational Transmission. 167 pp.*

Brandis, W. and **Bernstein, B.** Selection and Control. *176 pp.*

Brandis, Walter and **Henderson, Dorothy.** Social Class, Language and Communication. *288 pp.*

Cook-Gumperz, Jenny. Social Control and Socialization. *A Study of Class Differences in the Language of Maternal Control. 290 pp.*

● **Gahagan, D. M.** and **G. A.** Talk Reform. *Exploration in Language for Infant School Children. 160 pp.*

Hawkins, P. R. Social Class, the Nominal Group and Verbal Strategies. *About 220 pp.*

Robinson, W. P. and **Rackstraw, Susan D. A.** A Question of Answers. *2 volumes. 192 pp. and 180 pp.*

Turner, Geoffrey J. and **Mohan, Bernard A.** A Linguistic Description and Computer Programme for Children's Speech. *208 pp.*

Reports of the Institute of Community Studies

Baker, J. The Neighbourhood Advice Centre. A Community Project in Camden. *320 pp.*

● **Cartwright, Ann.** Patients and their Doctors. *A Study of General Practice. 304 pp.*

Dench, Geoff. Maltese in London. *A Case-study in the Erosion of Ethnic Consciousness. 302 pp.*

Jackson, Brian and **Marsden, Dennis.** Education and the Working Class: *Some General Themes Raised by a Study of 88 Working-class Children in a Northern Industrial City. 268 pp. 2 folders.*

Marris, Peter. The Experience of Higher Education. *232 pp. 27 tables.*
●   Loss and Change. *192 pp.*

Marris, Peter and **Rein, Martin.** Dilemmas of Social Reform. *Poverty and Community Action in the United States. 256 pp.*

Marris, Peter and **Somerset, Anthony.** African Businessmen. *A Study of Entrepreneurship and Development in Kenya. 256 pp.*

Mills, Richard. Young Outsiders: *a Study in Alternative Communities. 216 pp.*

Runciman, W. G. Relative Deprivation and Social Justice. *A Study of Attitudes to Social Inequality in Twentieth-Century England. 352 pp.*

Willmott, Peter. Adolescent Boys in East London. *230 pp.*

Willmott, Peter and **Young, Michael.** Family and Class in a London Suburb. *202 pp. 47 tables.*

Young, Michael and **McGeeney, Patrick.** Learning Begins at Home. *A Study of a Junior School and its Parents. 128 pp.*

Young, Michael and **Willmott, Peter.** Family and Kinship in East London. *Foreword by Richard M. Titmuss. 252 pp. 39 tables.*
    The Symmetrical Family. *410 pp.*

Reports of the Institute for Social Studies in Medical Care

Cartwright, Ann, Hockey, Lisbeth and **Anderson, John J.** Life Before Death. *310 pp.*
Dunnell, Karen and **Cartwright, Ann.** Medicine Takers, Prescribers and Hoarders. *190 pp.*
Farrell, C. My Mother Said. . . *A Study of the Way Young People Learned About Sex and Birth Control. 288 pp.*

Medicine, Illness and Society
General Editor W. M. Williams

Hall, David J. Social Relations & Innovation. *Changing the State of Play in Hospitals. 232 pp.*
Hall, David J. and **Stacey, M.** (Eds) Beyond Separation. *234 pp.*
Robinson, David. The Process of Becoming Ill. *142 pp.*
Stacey, Margaret *et al.* Hospitals, Children and Their Families. *The Report of a Pilot Study. 202 pp.*
Stimson, G. V. and **Webb, B.** Going to See the Doctor. *The Consultation Process in General Practice. 155 pp.*

Monographs in Social Theory
General Editor Arthur Brittan

● **Barnes, B.** Scientific Knowledge and Sociological Theory. *192 pp.*
Bauman, Zygmunt. Culture as Praxis. *204 pp.*
● **Dixon, Keith.** Sociological Theory. *Pretence and Possibility. 142 pp.*
The Sociology of Belief. *Fallacy and Foundation. About 160 pp.*
Goff, T. W. Marx and Mead. *Contributions to a Sociology of Knowledge. 176 pp.*
Meltzer, B. N., Petras, J. W. and **Reynolds, L. T.** Symbolic Interactionism. *Genesis, Varieties and Criticisms. 144 pp.*
● **Smith, Anthony D.** The Concept of Social Change. *A Critique of the Functionalist Theory of Social Change. 208 pp.*

Routledge Social Science Journals

The British Journal of Sociology. *Editor – Angus Stewart; Associate Editor – Leslie Sklair. Vol. 1, No. 1 – March 1950 and Quarterly. Roy. 8vo. All back issues available. An international journal publishing original papers in the field of sociology and related areas.*
Community Work. *Edited by David Jones and Marjorie Mayo. 1973. Published annually.*
Economy and Society. *Vol. 1, No. 1. February 1972 and Quarterly. Metric Roy. 8vo. A journal for all social scientists covering sociology, philosophy, anthropology, economics and history. All back numbers available.*

Social and Psychological Aspects of Medical Practice
Editor   Trevor Silverstone

Printed and bound in Great Britain by
Redwood Burn Limited, Trowbridge & Esher